CURATED BY
JÉRÔME SANS

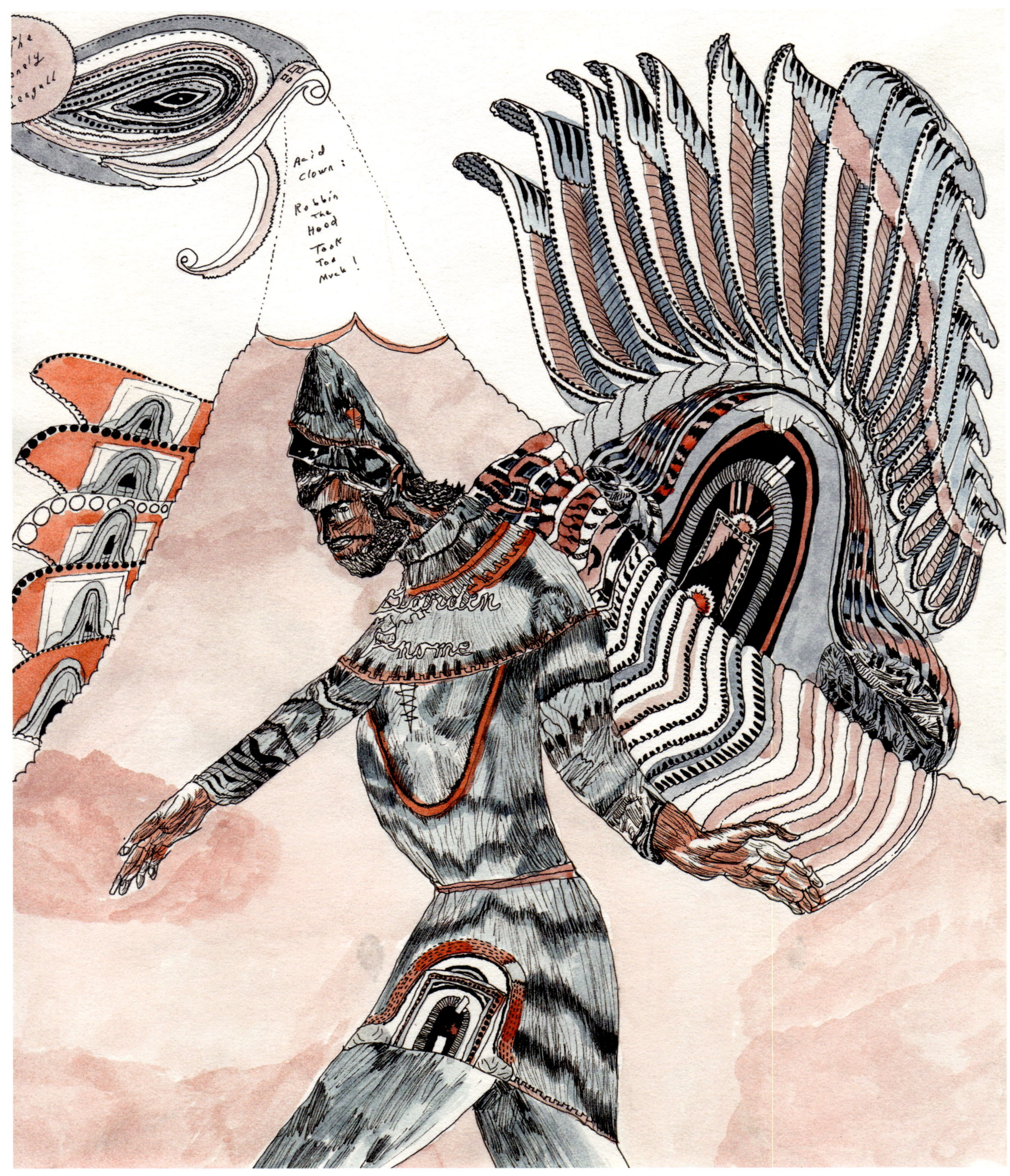

Kyle Field
Untitled
2004
Ink and watercolor on paper
20 x 24 cm
Collection of Yves Brochard, Paris
Courtesy of Cardenas Bellanger
© Kyle Field

FOREWORD

— **PATRICK DEWAEL,
INTERIOR MINISTER OF BELGIUM**

An exhibition on the theme of rock 'n' roll is certainly not a given at an institution such as the Centre for Fine Arts. In this modern temple to the arts, one wouldn't necessarily expect to come across a formal presentation of what was at one time the definitive symbol of counter-culture, even if nowadays it has been generally adopted and integrated into our collective experience and daily life.

But while the Centre for Fine Arts (Bozar) has for a long time displayed a natural excellence in presenting classical music, it has in more recent years widened its scope to include genres such as jazz, electronic, and rock. Music, albeit singular in form within the universes of the artists who produce it, is also plural in the variety of forms that take shape within the program at Bozar. The diversity of styles presented today is in itself a fantastic invitation to a voyage of discovery. As such, it is vital that such diversity be fostered by local authorities.

The interest surrounding a project such as IT'S NOT ONLY ROCK'N' ROLL, BABY! A STORY OF ART AND MUSIC is derived also from the unusual curatorial approach: displaying the visual work of popular idols who are more often to be seen strutting on stage or at summer festivals, guitar in hand. The exhibition presents the lesser-known talents of these artists, whose fans will make plenty of surprising discoveries here. It is also a tremendous encouragement for young people – who are accused, often incorrectly, of being disinterested in cultural issues – to cross the threshold of a major institution, where they will have the opportunity to discover other programs and artistic approaches with which they are perhaps less familiar.

Rock transcends and unites generations. It is a federative theme par excellence, stirring the same emotions in the young and the less-young – from today's teenagers to the 60-somethings who witnessed its birth in the 1950s. This vast expanse of time is reflected in the exhibition, in which the works, paintings, sculptures, videos, installations, and sketches of the artists give us insight into their personalities, and provide us with a snapshot of the eras of their creation. The exhibition also highlights the breadth of such an ambitious approach, which is at the heart of these Bozar exhibitions, and which is exemplified here from the outset in the work of these artists – the reflection of a natural process.

Let's dare to believe that this highly original approach by our arts centre will reinforce even further the multidisciplinary nature of the program of the Centre for Fine Arts and continue to spark the public's imagination.

— **BERT ANCIAUX,
FLEMISH MINISTER FOR CULTURE, YOUTH AND
SPORT IN BELGIUM'S FLEMISH REGION.**

The recognition and encouragement of cultural diversity are leitmotivs of the goals of the Flemish government. IT'S NOT ONLY ROCK'N' ROLL, BABY! A STORY OF ART AND MUSIC establishes an important partnership between the Flemish government and the Rock Werchter Festival, and stands as a perfect example of this. It demonstrates that culture can be a popular choice, without being reduced to the common denominator. A deliberately different choice also: to exhibit the visual art of musicians whose work is rarely seen in a contemporary art context, to prove that genuine artistic talent is multi-faceted and defies attempts to confine or label it. Affirming my support of an exhibition like this, in which music becomes the invisible framework for visual expression, is the opportunity to invite a wide audience perhaps unfamiliar with the corridors of the Centre for Fine Arts, to go beyond their preconceptions and discover a dynamic venue which seeks to strike the right tone, through a courageous vision that is anchored to the realities of today. If this approach can foster visitors' desires to return on another day, the mission will have been accomplished. Audience participation is an essential element and a sine qua non condition for the success of any cultural exhibition, the cornerstone on which the legitimacy of an institution heavily subsidized by the local authority can be based. This public participation – if driven essentially by the quality and the interest of the artistic program, as well as by the ability and hard work of the museum teams to raise as much public awareness as possible – can also be the result of deliberate policy such as reduced admission fees.

In this way, the choice that we are supporting – to propose an extremely reasonable admission fee – is a clear message to the public, from every background and community, and especially with youth in mind. This also reinforces the idea that culture is not a superfluous luxury but a fundamental right, and that this right has to be reaffirmed and supported politically. We often hear that art has no price. But the price of accessibility is something that the Flemish government is willing to pay, to guarantee that above and beyond artistic creation such work can be enjoyed by the widest possible audience, via quality exhibitions that are enjoyable and that foster an immediate rapport with the public.

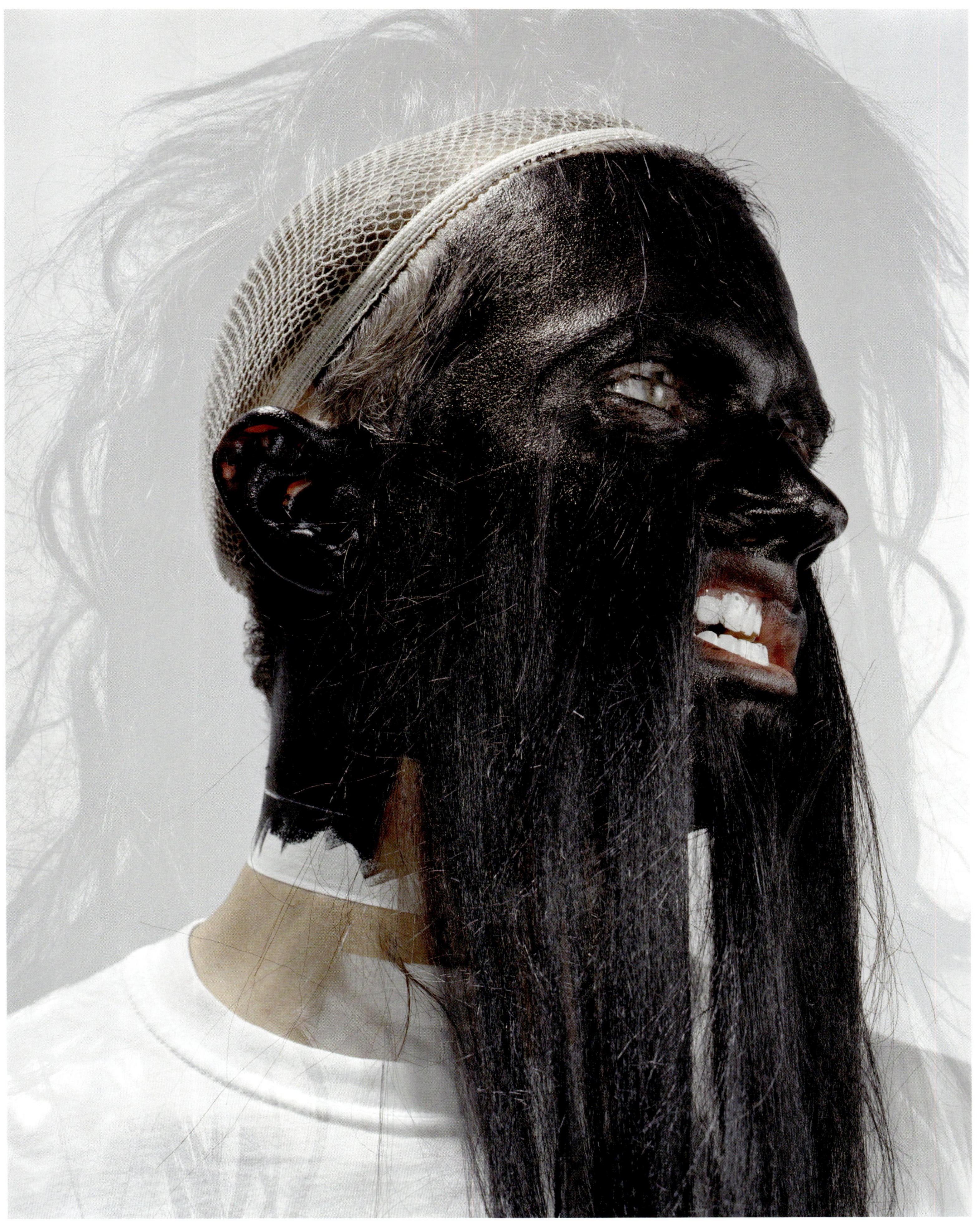

Fischerspooner
Monster
2003
Five images, C-print
Edition of 3
127 x 130,81 cm
Courtesy of Deitch Projects, New York
Photo Credit © Roe Ethridge

7

A FESTIVAL ON A MEADOW?

— HERMAN SCHUEREMANS,
FESTIVAL ORGANISER SINCE 1975

Rock Werchter. It's been 33 years now. A third of a century. Half of the artists on the 2008 programme weren't even born by the time of our first festival, in 1975. But we certainly are part of the most crucial generation.

In the middle of the '70s, rock in Belgium wasn't the top-class sport it is today. Concerts by foreign bands were a rarity. A sold-out Vorst (the Brussels concert venue) was a small miracle. Packaging various artists together on a larger program, however, greatly improved chances of attracting bigger crowds. It is no coincidence that today's largest European festivals are held in small countries: Roskilde (DK), Montreux (CH), Pinkpop (NL), and Werchter (B). Together with their contemporary, Glastonbury (GB), "the little ones" still rank among the absolute top in the world.

Over three decades Rock Werchter has grown to become the premier event in a strongly music-loving country. Over the past five years we have been recognized four times ('04, '05, '07, '08) as Best Festival in the World, by the International Live Music Conference. That this award for "top-quality organization and an impressive line-up" comes from 3,500 professionals of the music world only increases our pride; no one knows better than a baker how hard it is to bake a good cake.

You can also only be the best if you have the best on all fronts. That also means having the best audience, which you both have to spoil and surprise.

A MUSEUM IN A MEADOW?

Undoubtedly something like that does exist somewhere. But a museum in a meadow in the middle of a festival in full swing? Where 300,000 people mingle over the course of four days? That sounds like a logistical nightmare.

Not so at Werchter. We've been incorporating museums into our formula for three years now. The basic idea is as simple as it is innovative: What if the Rock Werchter bracelet doubled as a free pass to a number of museums? The young organization AmuséeVous, a dating agency between young people and museums, collaborates with us on this. The initiative was an instant success: During the summer of 2005, 8,000 bracelet-wearers visited 26 museums. Some 20,000 festival-goers also visited the festival museum. They saw work by rock-stars-

with-another-talent, and films in which big names – Arno,
Mauro, Tim Vanhamel – promoted museums. Ralf Hütter of
Kraftwerk came on a visit and now feels the itch to set up
something similar in Germany.
In 2007 art was integrated into the festival itself. Countless
attendees walked through the giant bikini girl by Dutch artist
Joep Van Lieshout. The grounds also featured a piece by
South African artist Kendell Geers – an army tank painted
in pink, and emblazoned with the word "FUCK". This is
Belgium. Land of daredevils and surrealists.

A FESTIVAL IN A MUSEUM?

IT'S NOT ONLY ROCK'N' ROLL, BABY! A STORY OF ART
AND MUSIC is a logical consequence. For the past few
years we at Werchter have been enticing more and more
young people to Bozar. Now that our audience has the hang
of it, we are encouraging them even further, with reduced
entrance fees to the museum. And with this partnership, a
whole new adventure begins.
As you will have already read between the lines, we like to
keep things neat and tidy, but thrilling. In this spirit, let us
paraphrase The Clash and say, "Rock the Bozar".

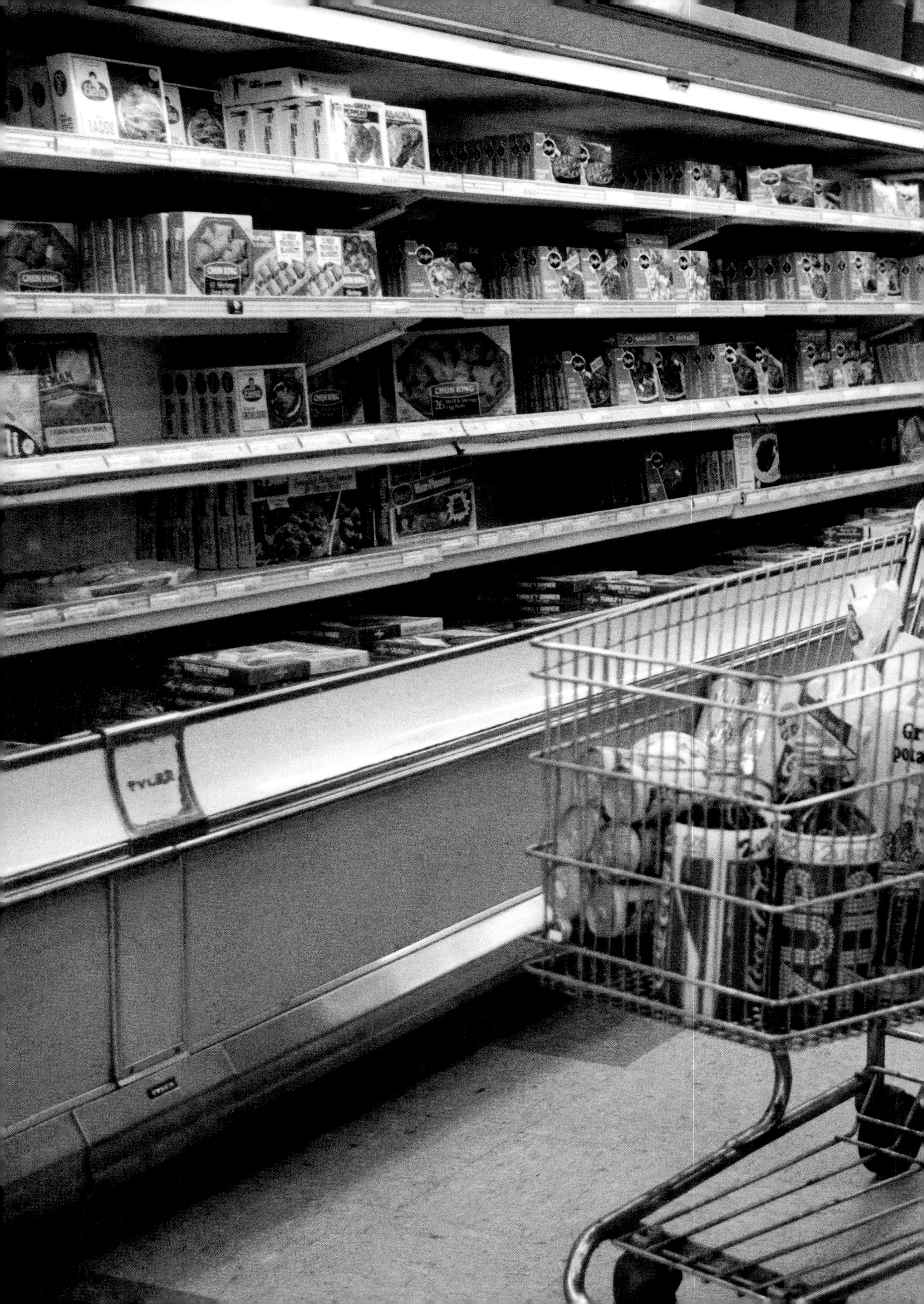

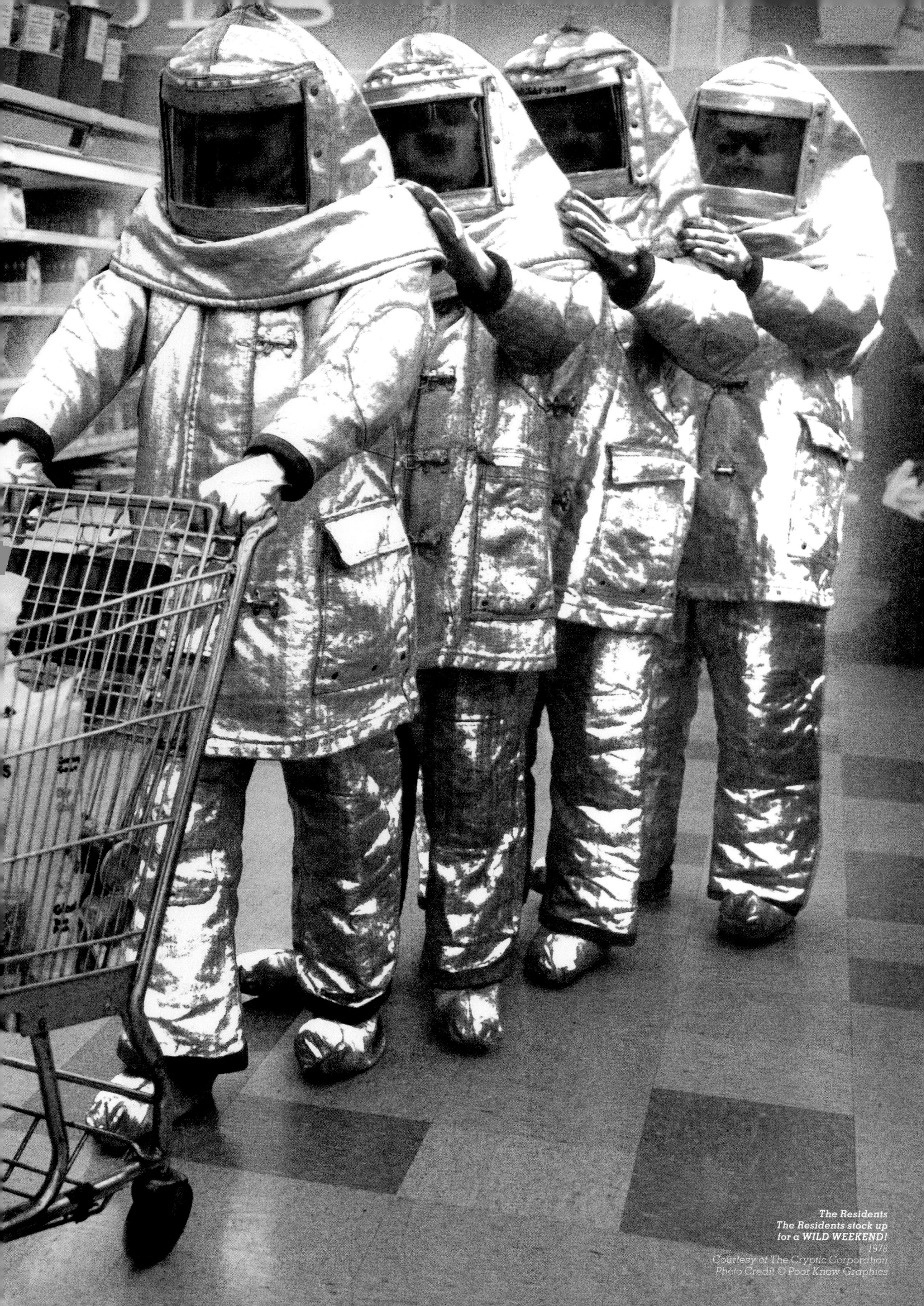

The Residents
The Residents stock up
for a *WILD WEEKEND!*
1978
Courtesy of The Cryptic Corporation
Photo Credit © Poor Know Graphics

IT'S NOT ONLY ROCK'N'ROLL, BABY! A STORY OF ART AND MUSIC

— ETIENNE DAVIGNON,
CHAIRMAN, CENTRE FOR FINE ARTS, BRUSSELS
— PAUL DUJARDIN,
GENERAL DIRECTOR, CENTRE FOR FINE ARTS,
BRUSSELS

From the outset of its tumultuous history, rock music has maintained strong ties with the world of art. The two forms have tread similar, passionate paths and have often criss-crossed in displays of intense creative energy. The most emblematic example is certainly that of the Factory, which, with the blessing of "the pope of pop", Andy Warhol, thrust onto a rapidly changing musical and artistic landscape the highly rock "UFO" sound of The Velvet Underground. This band has continued to impact deeply upon the perception of music as an audio terrain inviting exploration beyond harmony and art, a borderless zone as permeable to performances and concerts as to installations and pictorial expression. Beyond this decisive artistic fact – which fit the interdisciplinary approach of Warhol, who took as his subject matter the icons of the rock and pop culture of his day, from the Rolling Stones to Iggy Pop, from Elvis Presley to Blondie – the examples of rock being deeply rooted into the world of art are many and varied.

The emphasis of the exhibition IT'S NOT ONLY ROCK 'N' ROLL, BABY! A STORY OF ART AND MUSIC is remarkable in that it reconsiders the personalities of musicians and leading rock stars in the context of their work as visual artists. There are many among them who attended art school before picking up their guitars and embracing the stage. What's more, this creative flow never ceased to stimulate their musical production, and played a key role in the construction of a coherent image in which the visual object, whatever form it took, reflected the music and provided its finishing touches. Art schools have also often been the breeding grounds for generations of innovative groups as they adopt radical art practices in their musical approaches.

This exhibition thereby aims to demonstrate that certain musicians well-known to the general public, deliberately but with great sincerity draw from the history of art, and are nourished by its challenges and developments. Often the visual work of these artists enables them to give expression to visions which stand out from the limited framework and diktats of the record-industry, and reveals their ability to exist in different worlds or systems.

Via a selection which honors the vast range of musical styles that have dominated the rock landscape over the last 40 years, the exhibition bears witness to the explosion of existing systems which opens the way to stimuli, to fresh ideas, to influences derived from a rapidly changing environment. It highlights the original, authentic approaches of unique worlds, in which the visitor can stroll through the silent music of the objects and images on display.

Illustrating music via design, paintings, sculpture, or video art, allows it to be heard differently. This exhibition enables visitors to appreciate in a different way the recordings of groundbreaking artists such as Yoko Ono, Patti Smith, Brian Eno, Chicks on Speed, Fischerspooner, Devendra Banhart, CocoRosie, Alan Vega, and David Byrne. All of these artists and groups have fervent followings whose members are drawn by the intransigence, freedom, and unlimited creativity which these artists have all demonstrated. Our aim was therefore to offer the missing piece of a vibrant artistic jigsaw that will provide a fuller appreciation of these committed artists – for what they are really worth, and for the absolute sincerity of their commitment, and the integrity of their work.

IT'S NOT ONLY ROCK'N' ROLL, BABY! is also the result of an exceptional collaboration between the Brussels Centre for Fine Arts and Rock Werchter, one of the biggest music festivals in Europe. Rock Werchter is celebrating its 33rd anniversary this year, and has been crowned the World's Best Rock Festival for the fourth year by the International Live Music Conference in London. These two institutions have joined forces for this unique series of events and performances by exhibited artists.

We would like to warmly thank all those who have contributed to this project. First and foremost, Jérôme Sans – exhibition director, pioneering founder of the Palais de Tokyo in Paris, and recently appointed director of the Ullens Centre for Contemporary Art in Beijing – who was not afraid to stray from the familiar paths of contemporary art by taking alternative routes and select work by committed artists who don't always benefit from public recognition for their visual work. His approach takes a fresh look at the work of popular figures while refusing compromise, established rules and simple solutions. It also serves to shorten the distance that can exist between the world of art – often perceived as elitist – and the public, who will be more receptive to the work by artists with whom they already closely identify.

I would also like to thank the team from the exhibition department of the Centre for Fine Arts, led by Director of Exhibitions Johan Vansteenkiste with Anne Mommens as Senior Exhibitions Director, with a special mention for Laurence Leunen, General Project Coordinator. Our thanks also go of course to Herman Schueremans, director of Live Nation, for the excellent collaboration with the Werchter Rock Festival, and to BOM publishers, responsible for the publication of this fine catalogue.

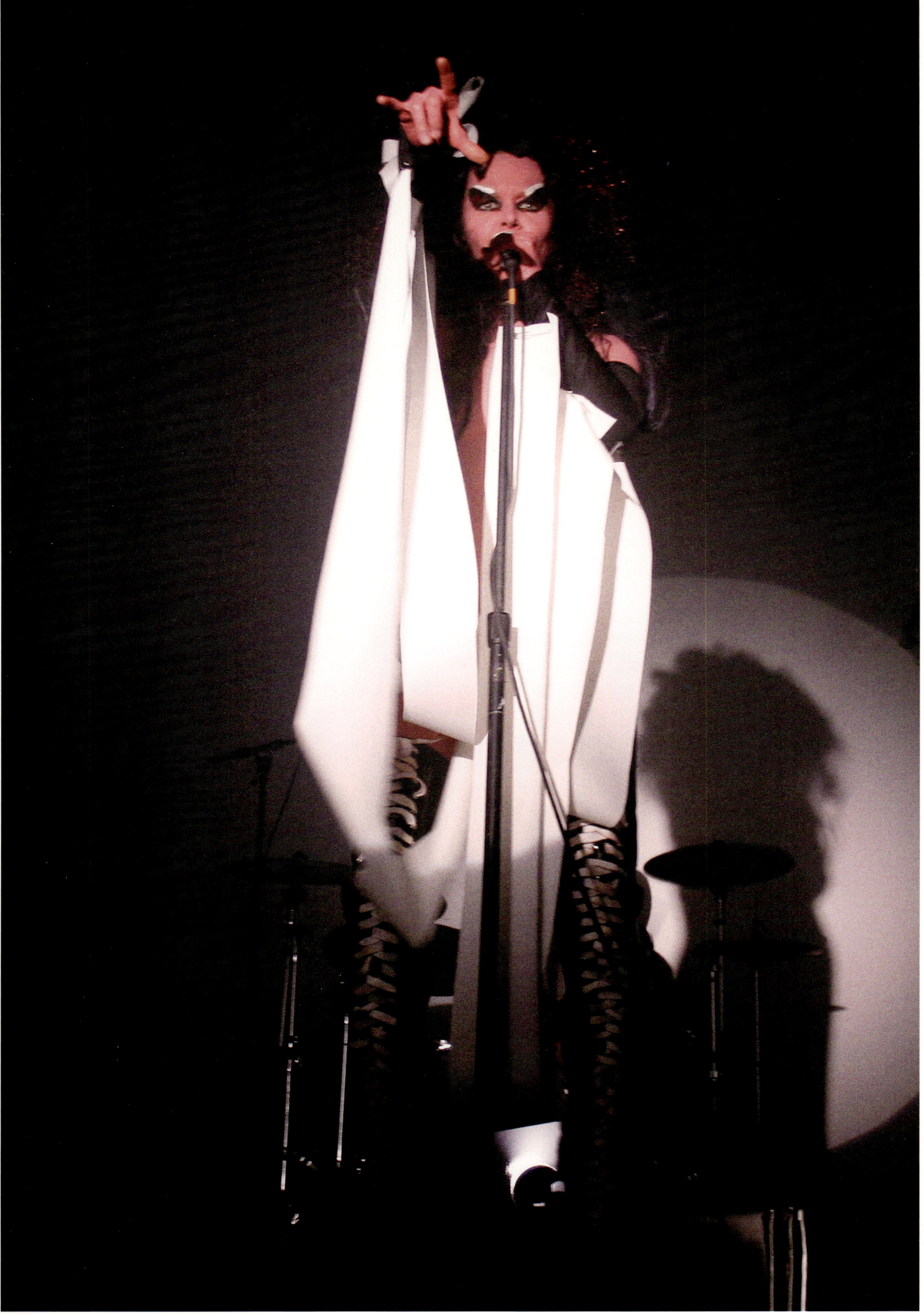

USE YOUR EYES TO KEEP YOUR EARS OPEN

— Jérôme Sans, curator

I have always been attracted by the idea of accompanying
an artist who is launching a unique project, or of presenting
to the Art world the visual side of an artist whose work is
recognized in quite different spheres. Music has always been
a part of my world and featured in most of my exhibitions.
I have often involved musicians in projects that I have
organized over the last two decades. With the 'Live' exhibition
at the Palais de Tokyo (Paris) I demonstrated how music
– not with an experimental approach, but resolutely Pop –
was the building block used by numerous visual artists,
and I organized monographic exhibitions for such artists as
Chicks on Speed or Brian Eno. I also created my own rock
band Liquid Architecture and am currently working on a
second album.

For years, music and art have fostered a mythical relationship,
often explored in the light of their theoretical and historical
links. IT'S NOT ONLY ROCK'N'ROLL BABY! is aiming to tell
the intimate and unusual story of around twenty artists for
whom art is the bedrock of a transversal artistic universe.
IT'S NOT ONLY ROCK'N'ROLL BABY! is the electric exhibition
of the summer which reveals for the first time an alternative
history of Rock, that of musicians, of artists born in the world
of art. Some twenty musical legends have come together for
the first time, not for a concert but to present their plastic art.
Organized with the urgency of a festival, in the space of 5
months, this exhibition does not represent a movement, but
gathers together artists who, in their individual ways, view
art and music as a common entity, as a shared thought; they
demonstrate how two forms of expression, though distinct,
are indistinguishable. If art and music do not reach the same
audience, nor the same number of people, if one evolves as
a solitary work of art whilst the other develops around the
phenomenon of audience participation, it is in fact these
contrasting strengths that produce such a close bond. IT'S
NOT ONLY ROCK'N'ROLL BABY! is a gathering of artists, most
of whom were visual artists before becoming musicians, and
whose visual roots at the heart of their artistic process are
often little-known and viewed as separate from their musical
fame. IT'S NOT ONLY ROCK'N'ROLL BABY! demonstrates that
the voice of Rock was also birthed by Art, and that music
has given Art a truly powerful expression.

This exhibition features a unique compilation of major works
by musicians from the 1970's to the present day (from Yoko Ono,
Patti Smith, and Brian Eno, to Chicks on Speed, Fischerspooner
and Devendra Banhart, CocoRosie or Pete Doherty, via Alan
Vega, David Byrne, etc) including some that have rarely or
never been exhibited, and some that have been produced
specifically for this occasion. As such, this is not an exhaustive,
scientific or historical exhibition. It is an initial overview of
a subject which is not seeking to establish a chronology or
hierarchy, but rather to open to the public a free passage into

the universe of each artist. It is a climate change, an immersion
into the environment of those whose voice we recognize, but
not their visual perspective.

The enthusiasm of these artists to take part in this exhibition
and to openly identify the central role of art throughout their
artistic journeys, demonstrates that this mental and physical,
cerebral and sonic combination of art and music continues
to be at the core of artistic expression in the widest sense,
which refuses to choose one medium over the other. It is
an association in which each is the instrument of the other
to enable the composition and diffusion of a multi-facetted
message. It's a combination in which the sound becomes
the image and vice-versa, in which the phase of solitary
and meditative artistic creation inevitably leads to a further
phase of joint participation with the audience.

IT'S NOT ONLY ROCK'N'ROLL BABY! is also a reference
book, halfway between Rock magazine and Art book, with
exclusive interviews by artists and a variety of photos of
their work; a preface by Michael Bracewell, art critic and
author, highly-acclaimed in England, whose books explore
art, fashion and music.

IT'S NOT ONLY ROCK'N'ROLL BABY! also represents an
exceptional collaboration between the Brussels Centre for
Fine Arts and the famous Rock Werchter festival, one of
the biggest music festivals in Europe which this year will
celebrate its 33rd anniversary. Two institutions united around
a series of events and performances by artists.

IT'S NOT ONLY ROCK'N'ROLL BABY! is like the opening pages
of a story, the springboard for other projects to be birthed with
these different artists.

Finally, none of this would have been possible without
the immediate enthusiasm that the Centre for Fine Arts
demonstrated for this project.

(To be continued...)

Jérôme Sans, Director of the Ullens Centre for Contemporary
Arts Beijing, China.

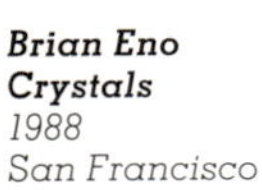

Brian Eno
Crystals
1988
San Francisco

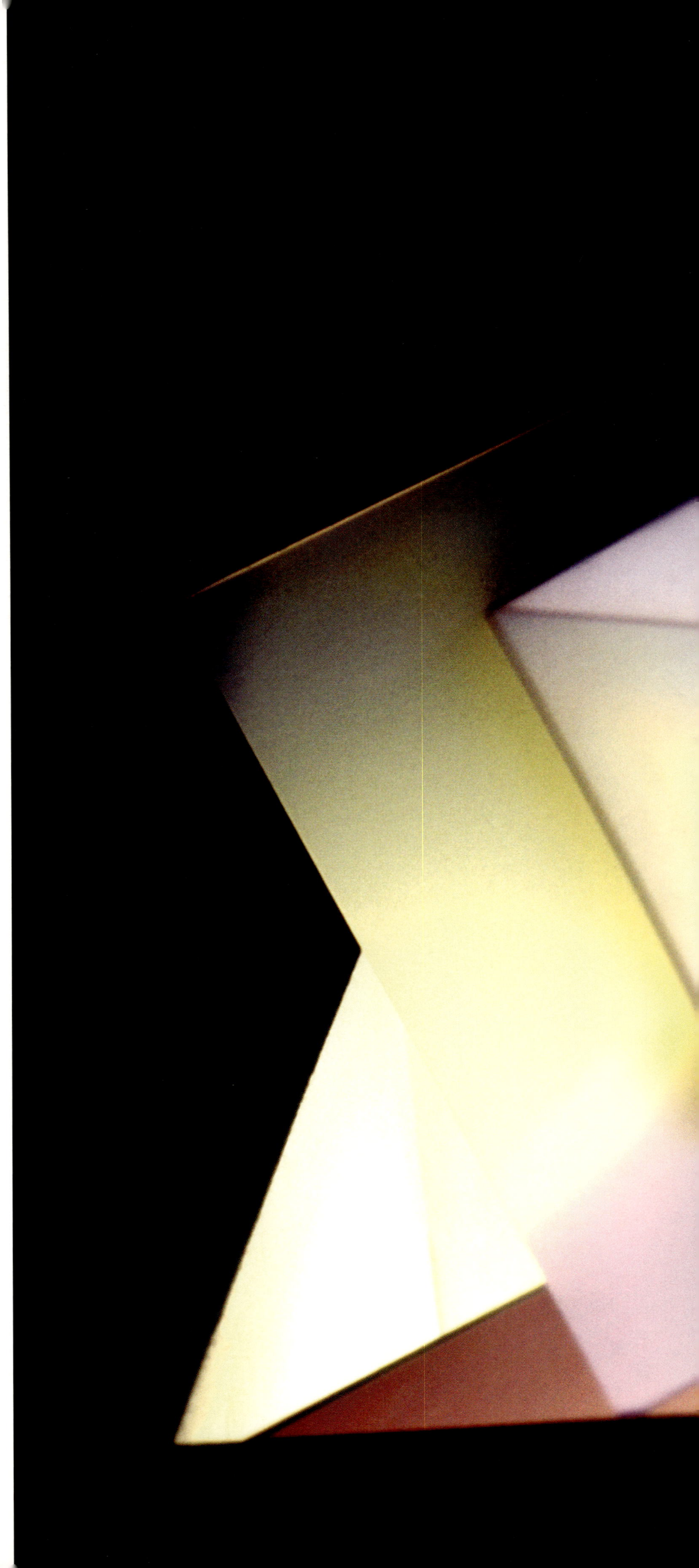

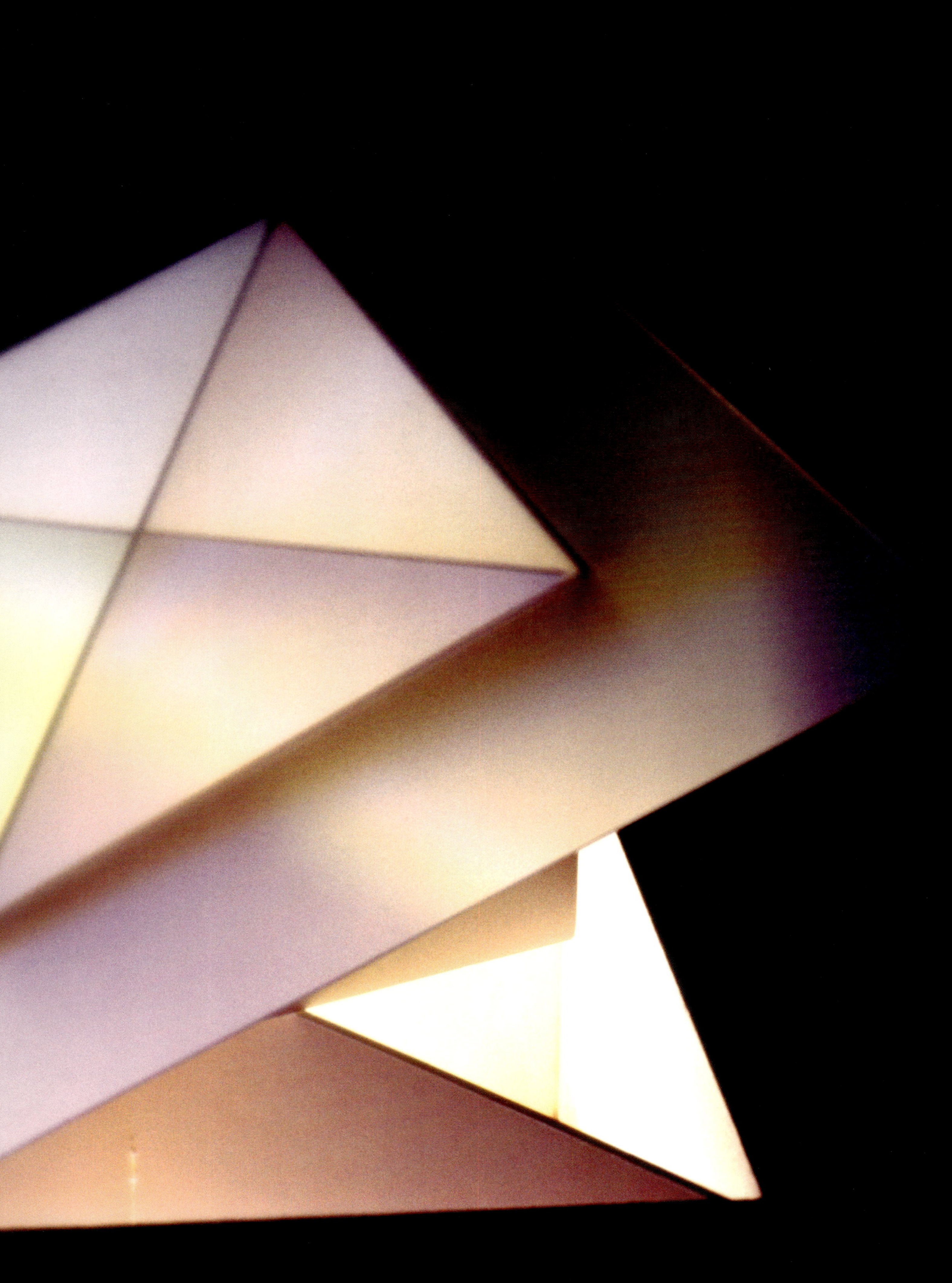

PORTRAIT OF A YOUNG MAN AS AN ART STUDENT

— Michael Bracewell

"and the Serpentine will look just the same
and the gulls be as neat on the pond
and the sunken garden unchanged
and God knows what else is left of our London
my London, your London"
— Ezra Pound, from Canto LXXX

The house was semi-detached, with three bedrooms, a
pleasant, cottage-style garden and a grey wooden fence
overhung at one end by a lilac tree. Built of Dorking brick
in 1922 – the year that T. S. Eliot's poem 'The Waste Land'
was published – it stood on a road of similar houses, deep
into London's furthest suburbia. Like many of its neighbors,
the house had received enemy fire during World War II, in
the form of incendiary bullets. Across the bay of the French
windows you could still see a neat, diagonal row of scorch-
marks in the parquet flooring; in time they had become as
much a feature of the room as the inherited piano stool, the
oval, gilt-framed mirror, and the crystal cockerel.
This was London's southern commuter belt, a landscape
created in the '20s around the rural gentility of Edwardian
estates, common fields, and Victorian cottages. A land, noted
by the novelist E. M. Forster, "of amenities, where success
was indistinguishable from failure". But that seems harsh.
By the time this essay opens in the middle of the '70s, the
house and its suburban road, mellowed by 50 years of soft
April evenings and amber autumn Sundays, still appeared
a place of unbroken respectability, of order and routine, held
fast by codes so rigid that they were barely spoken or referred
to. An outpost of Eliot's 'Waste Land'? Perhaps, but only in
those threadbare places where an old, underlying sadness
showed through the neatness and modest prosperity, more
of a desperate tiredness, in fact. Hugh Kenner writes of Eliot:
"… Mrs. Eliot reported to Pound that her husband had done
no work of the kind that augments vortices, not for weeks. He
returned daily from the bank and fell into a leaden slumber
until bedtime".
In the '30s, in a comfortable villa just 10 minutes' walk from
the Dorking brick semi, a young man called Dennis was
seen to preen himself. His parents had not known what to do
with him, and so they sent him to the local art school, which
he attended half-heartedly. He was aloof, contrary, and at
times obnoxious. He took to wearing makeup in the streets,
and when asked once what he intended to do with his life,
he answered, "Breathe". He made friends with a crippled girl

21

who would later become a nun. In damp suburban parks they took the air, one hobbling, the other mincing – in his own words – "as though his legs were bound at the knee".

In the late spring of 1977, in the bedroom at the front of the semi, another young male art student was reading a book called The Naked Civil Servant. This was the first volume of Denis's autobiography, written after he had "dyed" his name (as he said) and begun calling himself Quentin Crisp. And although Crisp described himself as "an effeminate and self-evident homosexual", the book was about being queer in a much broader sense. Punks like Crisp could lay claim to being what the latter termed (as a self-portrait), "an auto-fact – self created." On a small stereophonic record player in one corner, to a jagged little drum line, a football terrace voice leered out, "I wanna be a field day for the Sundays/ so they can fuck up my life".

The young art student's experience was that of not being in the right place at the right time. Intellectually, emotionally, and finally geographically, he spent his days on the edges. And it was on the edge of London that he became a witness to the shock waves of cultural anarchy: a twilit hinterland, as obscure and melancholy as the library carpark on a winter's afternoon. But he would be determined to make any journey, suffer any amount of abuse, in order to try and track down some glittering, elemental moment of punk's refined glamour. On the outside, but yearning for the center across nine miles of residential housing, dual carriageways, commuter lines, recreation grounds, and bitter, mean, parades of shops, he seemed to live the movement more intensely. His longing became the acid bath that stripped away apathy, and kept a keen edge on his consciousness of some extraordinary sense of newness. And on the edges of things was where strangeness and intensity seem to roam.

His bedroom and the art school, deep in the London suburbs, were both dressing room and theatre. When he got ready to go out, the 18-year-old was wearing a charity-shop suit, its lapels burned and ripped, safety-pinned up one side, and a faded T-shirt badly printed with the face of a serial killer. His hair looked as though it had been cut with the bread knife and then dyed with the dregs of school ink; his lower eyelids were crudely lined with black pencil. Crisp had written: "As my appearance progressed from the effeminate to the bizarre, the reaction of strangers passed from startled contempt to outraged hatred. They began to take action. If I was compelled to stand still in the street in order to wait for a bus, or on the platform of an Underground station, people would turn without a word and slap my face. If I was wearing sandals, passers-by took care to stamp on my toes; and once a crowd had started to follow me, it grew and grew until no traffic could pass down the road…".

The years immediately preceding the moment when, in a friend's bedroom, our boy had heard 'Roadrunner' by The Modern Lovers, now seemed far-off and somnambulant, curiously pastoral in tone, a time which was at once as soft as petals, yet flicked with little dry cat-licks of glamour. Then, slowly, drifting as though to the pull of some magnetic north in the zeitgeist, various influences had seemed to hint at the constellation of a new direction. The middle years of the '70s had seemed to the boy both lulling and anticipatory, a perfumed suburban doze. But he had become aware that he was joining in with a covert, intoxicating celebration of artifice, the ceremonies of which had seemed all the more intense for being experienced, not in the bohemian demimonde of Ladbroke Grove or Chelsea, where otherness was the fashion, but to the smell of damp asphalt, privet, and Sunday lunch, out in suburbia. Art school provided a safe haven from working in some office.

Now, it seemed to him that if punk – the recently agreed-upon label for this vivid new sense of aggressive modernity – was a coming together of disaffected outsiders, then he was even outside the outsiders, a man who fell to Earth, forever the alien. W. H. Auden wrote, in his 'Musée des Beaux Arts', "…must have seen something amazing, a boy falling out of the sky". (The line was repeated on the first page of Walter Tevis' novel – filmed starring Bowie – 'The Man Who Fell To Earth'). And that's how our boy liked to think of himself. Punk had been the ignition of a volatile mix of chemicals, the brewing of which, it turned out, had been in hand for some time. For instance: One Tuesday afternoon in the early winter of 1975, with the cold, fallen-leaf damp of the park on his pullover, the boy had carried home Joris-Karl Huysmans' novella 'Against the Grain' from the varnish-scented local library. It was the old Penguin paperback edition, with Boldini's dove-blue portrait of the etiolated, satanic-looking Compte de Montesquiou on the cover.

The aesthetic experiments of Huysmans's decadent count, Des Esseintes, had seemed to sit well with the boy's favourite records: David Bowie's 'Diamond Dogs' – "Just another future song, lonely little kitsch…" And in late afternoon, when the stretched oblong of amber streetlight had fallen on his carefully positioned poster depicting Henry Wallis' pre-Raphaelite painting, The Death of Chatterton, the haunting, mournful title track of Roxy Music's 'For Your Pleasure' would follow, with Bryan Ferry's oddly robotic and contorted vocal sounding like the pronouncements of a drugged matinee idol. Then the shimmering-surface sound of Fripp and Eno's mesmeric instrumental, 'Evening Star'. Words and music had all seemed to speak of the end of eras – the end of history? Modernity itself reaching critical mass? Meanwhile, at 430 Kings Rd., Chelsea, they'd been thinking of calling a shop 'Modernity Killed Every Night'.

23

But these strange soundtracks to a futuristic landscape had become – as Eno himself would later remark – "new, imaginary worlds", while outside, the silence of the crescents and cul-de-sacs, the warm smell of woodsmoke and rain, had seemed to heighten the potency of the music. It was all against nature; and Des Esseintes had chosen to live where? Out in the suburbs of Paris, away from the wearying sophistry of fashionable society.

But of course, the boy longed for London, the box of delights. And as father had commuted up to town, so suburban punks found their way to the station. On the more remote lines, this would be a risky business, even in the late '70s. Platforms and subways were the boy's first punk landscape – broken windows in the waiting room, the rich, dank smell of stale cigarette smoke, the humming of wires as the train approached. These journeys between the infantilist security of his semi-detached home and the volatile glamour of the city felt like commuting between Innocence and Experience.

In the months just prior to punk he had found his way to the Roundhouse, for example, to see the Lindsay Kemp troupe perform their mimed celebration of the life of Jean Genet, 'Flowers'. That had been an epic journey in more than one sense, from the southern suburbs to beyond Camden, to what seemed like the entrance to a catacomb – sweating walls, men wearing black lipstick. The old venue – used back in the Sixties for freak-outs like the 'Dialectics of Liberation' all-nighter, when they claimed the CIA spiked the sangria with LSD – had seemed like some profane church.

For 'Flowers' they were burning clumps of pachouli-scented incense. The performance was all mirrored coffin lids, glitter, blood, white bodies. In fact it was the church of David Bowie to most of the audience, a congregation it seemed of street aesthetes, absorbed in a style which came across as nostalgia for archaic visions of the future. The ambiguous conformity of Kraftwerk, for instance. Young men from London in the middle '70s, dressed like an idea of Berlin bank clerks from the '30s – 'die Mensch Maschine'. Peter York, in an essay written for Harpers & Queen in 1976, would identify these aesthetes as "Them".

Punk would expand the boy's discovery of London; the two phenomena would be entwined, would seem to invent one another, become infused with each other's countenance and energy. For years to come, his memory of London would seem like the bildungsroman of punk rock: that 19th-century school of naturalistic fiction in which the provincial outsider attempts to come to grips with the social geography and glamour of the big city. You felt your way through this landscape, learning its contours, partly as a consequence of taste and instinct, and partly by following the trail of a code.

It was a mutual recognition of the code which had formed the little gang our suburban boy sometimes went around with. Throughout punk's first brief springtime (in retrospect it felt like a decade; in reality it was barely a year), it seemed as though every suburb, town, and small city created its own version of Andy Warhol's "superstars" – a collection of hedonists, misfits, interested observers, and slaves to the notion of glamour who collectively seemed to illustrate John Waters's definition of camp: "the tragically ludicrous and the ludicrously tragic". Many were distinguished solely by the fact that they would suffer any amount of abuse – fatally, in some cases – in the pursuit of their idea of glamour.

And yet their very hopelessness was the essence of their undeniable style. In the boy's suburb for instance, the local punk tribe included Lorraine, a tall, willow-thin Irishwoman posing as a Belgian countess; Gasson, a speed-freak queen obsessed with Bowie; David, who had a pink triangle dyed in the back of his hair; Woods, who looked like one of T. S. Eliot's crowd on London Bridge; and Mark Black, who worked in a bed factory and formed a group called The Void. At one time or another they all worked shifts in the little pizza restaurant on the suburban High Street, a place of potted palms and painted mirrors, where off-duty firemen brought their girlfriends. This little gang blurred all the accepted notions of class; their attitude to the subject would have offended – quite intentionally – Marxist academics and right-wing politicians alike. When questioned on class, Lorrie most probably would simply have said, "Well, we hate everyone", and departed with a flickering wave of divinely decadent green nail polish. It was all "Kevin and camp Sheila" – strong women and fey boys, sitting up at night playing Patti Smith's Horses and 'I am a Cliché' by X-Ray Spex.

Within the punk tribe you always saw fellow travelers from the suburbs who seemed distinguished by their social awkwardness. At the Nashville or the Marquee or the 100 Club or the Lyceum, even at the Rock Garden, you could spot the loners: timid yet determined, orbital to the louder crowd, dressed up in outfits they'd been scared to wear on the train. Boys with thin faces wearing an old grey raincoat, a beret and a safety-pin through their left earlobe; chunky girls with antique National Health glasses and an old string shopping bag; a black boy wearing green wraparound dark glasses and a dog collar. There they all were, loitering between sets on the dark edges of the crowd – accepting one through a code.

At the old East Croydon station, back in 1977, the spring evening smelt of flowers and petrol. East Croydon, the celebrated Bavarian Anglophile architectural historian Nicklaus Pevsner had decreed, "resembled down-town Johannesburg from the air." Seen from the flyover at dusk, the modernist office blocks – built during the Space Race in the late '60s, and

named accordingly, 'Zodiac House', 'Apollo House', 'Lunar
House' – had a paradoxically Soviet air, their featureless
windows, concrete and glass, like punk itself, timelessly
modern – the modern as a worn out thoroughfare. "And then
we went to Croydon!" as Mott The Hoople once sang.
The Greyhound – where Siouxsie and The Banshees were
playing, darkly glittering – was separated from these towers
by an underpass. Evening traffic slid into the tunnel, its dark
entrance marked with dirty planks of cold white light. Brake
lights gleamed scarlet in the dusk. The boy walked with his
arms folded tightly across his chest, head lowered, hopelessly
self-conscious yet oddly defiant. Commuters gaped and
laughed; some were openly hostile. The audience for the
evening's performance had considered their appearance.
Traveling alone, they had each become Quentin Crisp,
attempting not to make eye contact with anyone; en masse
they seemed to move like pantomime dames, or walked
with their shoulders hunched as though trying to become
invisible. Lad types and punk skins spat mouthfuls of lager
at one another, while the art-school peculiars were graduates
from their twin obsessions with Roxy Music's dandified time-
travel – "we wanted to look like members of the intergalactic
parliament", Brian Eno would recall – and David Bowie's
glamorous alien on a dying planet, stuck on your eyes.
In amongst what Liz Naylor would memorably describe as
"the regular knob-heads wearing straight-leg Lee Coopers",
this scattering of suburban punk poseurs sourced their
look from Weimar Germany, science fiction, Andy Warhol,
pornography and the Sex Pistols: bondage trousers that
forced you to mince and hobble, skirts made of black PVC,
diamante, plastic macs, winkel-picker boots. This was the
last time that street fashion was actually dangerous for the
wearer: These clothes didn't just offend the passers by, they
inspired pure hatred. The early punk fashions, at a time
when most men wore brown suits and hair that just clipped
their ear-lobes, were beyond audacious; they were so wildly
exaggerated, so contemptuous of their social context, that
they provoked open hostility as much as incredulity. Today,
when all looks are just another look, it is almost impossible
to imagine the sheer violence which seemed to scream off
the rhetoric of early punk style.
Now punk and all its works have become like a new Bloomsbury
Group. The personnel and venues, artefacts and anecdotes,
are the stuff of university conferences, coffee-table survey
volumes, articles like this one, and museum collections. The
era is subject to the most proprietorial and jealously guarded
notions of witness and authorship. How ironic that Malcolm
McLaren, former Croydon art student, had announced, "History
is for pissing on"; punk was as historical as Agincourt. And
yet its articulation of modernity, its ability to mint "newness",
seems yet to be updated. Like the collages and typography

employed by Dada, the components of punk retain the blank, pristine modernity of machine parts. The names of first-wave punk groups expressed this modernity – sharp, functional, with an industrial sheen: Wire, Magazine, Adverts, Buzzcocks, Television.

Time passed like a speed blur. '76 flipped into '78 and it seemed as though everything had gone industrial and grey. Derek Jarman had announced, "It feels as though the bomb has gone off in our heads, already". Anxiety was the defining mood, a kind of nervous, insomniac energy which kept so many on so many drugs. This new, portentous sense of the modern, locked in the numerology of the year itself – 'Two Sevens Clash' – was apparent when the suburban reader of Quentin Crisp took the train into central London to see an exhibition by the artists Gilbert & George: their Dirty Words Pictures, 1977. The monochromatic, blood-red panels of these monolithic photographs showed a London he recognized as the theatre of his auto-faction, a place of timeless modernity – like the towers of East Croydon – yet concentrated, intense, never-ending (Crisp had said that style was to know what you were and to do it like mad).

Gilbert & George showed London in 1977 as a montage of office towers, railinged city streets, night buses, lowering skies, faces in the crowd, derelicts, broken glass, sun-bursts off the NatWest tower, the blank windows of the offices at London Wall. From the suburbs to the city, for the young art student, was the journey to – remembering that leering football terrace voice, again, speeded up – "an evening of fun in the metropolis of your dreams…" or Bowie's instrumental soundscapes on Low, that Jon Savage called "post-everything music."

Here was punk London shown in art: London at a time when rubbish was piled in the streets because of the strikes, and corrugated iron seemed to stretch from Chelsea to Covent Garden. He looked at the pictures, with their titles like those of pulp novellas: 'Are You Angry Or Are You Boring', 'Cunt Scum', 'Fucked Up'. They looked to him like maps of a secret geography, a London which he would always recognize, for years to come, as his London, as much a consciousness as a place, a territory deep inside himself.

This London had its own arcane topography. By 1978, in fact, too much of the network had been exposed to the light of day (One sunny afternoon along Ladbroke Grove an old, wizard-like hippy had sold him a second-hand copy of Nico's Marble Index. "Now this is the last time I want this record to see daylight", he had said, as his frail hands trembled in a dust-filled sunbeam). Having plucked up the courage to go into Sex, at World's End (even the location was suitably named), the suburban boy outsider went next to PX near Floral Street WC2 (gaining access through the low door set into the iron shutters), and then bought himself a silver earring off a blonde woman wearing tank goggles in Detail, on Endell Street.

When it opened, he felt that he'd been waiting for that changing
room from the 21st century which was Antony Price's shop
Plaza, at the top of the Kings Road, below 20th Century Box
and facing Beaufort Market. By now, sometime around 1978,
punk had fragmented into an eclectic array of sub-sections,
from earnest social realists to futurist aesthetes. Plaza was a
minimalistic quartermaster store for the youth modern(e) who
urged the moment to renew itself from the instant cliché of a
two-chord rant. Fabric samples and garment samples were
fastened to perpex sheets on the racks, and then the human
mannequin behind the mirrored counter handed you your
chosen items. The changing rooms were totally mirrored, like a
voyeur's dream or the nightmare of the insecure. They looked
like the room on the cover of Fripp and Eno's mesmeric post-
everything record, No Pussyfooting, and that was enough.
Price had been deeply involved with Roxy Music's styling,
and he later caught an early post-punk sub-strand by creating
clothes like fetishized sci-fi uniforms – girls in military shirts,
with purple lurex and black crepe epaulettes. Pop-art clothes
for post-pop people.
So soon, the cartoon anarchy of early punk was a wretched
fun-fair. The future lay in new audacities, authorized by
punk's pro-active approach to rule-breaking. Public Image
Ltd's Metal Box became a new soundtrack for suburban
London in the grip of mid-winter, the string synthesizer of the
closing track 'Radio Four' sounding like the music for punk
rock's final credits to roll. Odd new groups from provincial
northern cities had also picked up the challenge of newness.
On Sunday nights at the old Lyceum Ballroom on Wellington
Street, there would be quadruple bills of these newcomers:
Mekons, Gang of Four, The Human League, and Stiff Little
Fingers; Delta 5, Cabaret Voltaire, Ludus, This Heat. Each
brought with them to London's mix of brutalist concrete and
Dickensian side streets their own richly atmospheric sense of
place: ruined industrial cities in the north, where science and
technology were framed by blackened Gothic grandeur.
Covent Garden then was also mostly derelict. Violin menders
and esoteric bookshops kept their air of the '30s, undisturbed
by any sense of change. For years the ceremonial entrance to
the Empire mansion block opposite the Lyceum had rusted
railings drawn across its porch, a withered bouquet laced
through its chains. On the benighted, poorly lit streets of
Covent Garden in the late '70s, the theatrical melodrama
of New Romanticism – punk's major successor – was first
identified. Dusty and deserted districts of central London –
Holborn, Grays Inn Road, Fitzrovia – were co-opted as moodily
lit stage sets for young people dressed as though Lord Byron
had tutored with Radcliffe Hall.
It is maybe a common experience for every generation that
their defining period (an enlargement of what Virginia Woolf
describes as "a moment of being" – when one's consciousness

seems fully engaged in the present) makes a single sensation
of memory and geography. Walking through London, in
this sense, becomes like walking through the chapters of
your autobiography, with sites and routes doing the work
of written chapters.

The suburbs, meanwhile, seemed to remain largely unchanged.
True, London was expanding all the time, and what had
seemed in 1960 to be little more than county market towns
would seem by 1980 to be fully absorbed into the grey mass
of the greater city. But something more fundamental had
remained – that modest prosperity, rigid code, and ancient
tiredness, perhaps – which would only begin to fracture and
fall away across the following decade.

The punk experience of suburbia enabled one still to walk
– in post-everything clothes – through a residential and
civic landscape which Stevie Smith would have recognized
from the late '40s, and Betjeman might have celebrated as
the ruins of interwar gentility. In the suburbs in 1976, there
were still graveled drives to private tennis courts, and Tudor
tea rooms, and leaded windows in the style of Lutyens. It
was only towards the building boom of the early '80s, when
whole clusters of little postmodern artisan cottages – called
"Cheyne Cloisters" and other such aspirational names –
were built on what had once been some Edwardian villa's
back lawn, that it all began to change. In this much, you'd
find suburban punks who inhabited the last dusk of the old
domestic landscape of the post-war middle classes. Punk
never seemed to be the people's music for our boy, but more
what Howard Devoto – the man later dubbed "the Orson
Welles of punk" – would term: "trouble-shooting modern
forms of unhappiness".

For those who found their way on to the arcane geography
of punk in London, many of the movement's venues and
passes now seem possessed of a somewhat poeticized
obscurity – the old Electric Ballroom, where Wire taunted
an audience largely comprised of drunk skinheads, with a
three-hour piece of performance art; the furthest reaches
of the Portobello Road, where you could buy imported
bootlegs of records by The Residents, Devo, and Pere Ubu;
West Kensington Underground station by the old Nashville;
a room full of Polaroids in a tall house in Notting Hill Gate;
the Notre Dame Hall in Leicester Square…

The most indelibly etched of these sites were the ones which
you simply had to know how to find, drawn as though by a
need from the far-flung bedroom in the Dorking brick semi,
charmed by a 7-inch single in a weird sleeve which seemed to
promise that this would be the entrance to that secret London
of relevance and newness which you felt sure existed, and
which would change your life forever, but which you had first
to track down. And the boy, now late-middle-aged, thinks
how it can still all bring a tear to this old sheriff's eye.

29

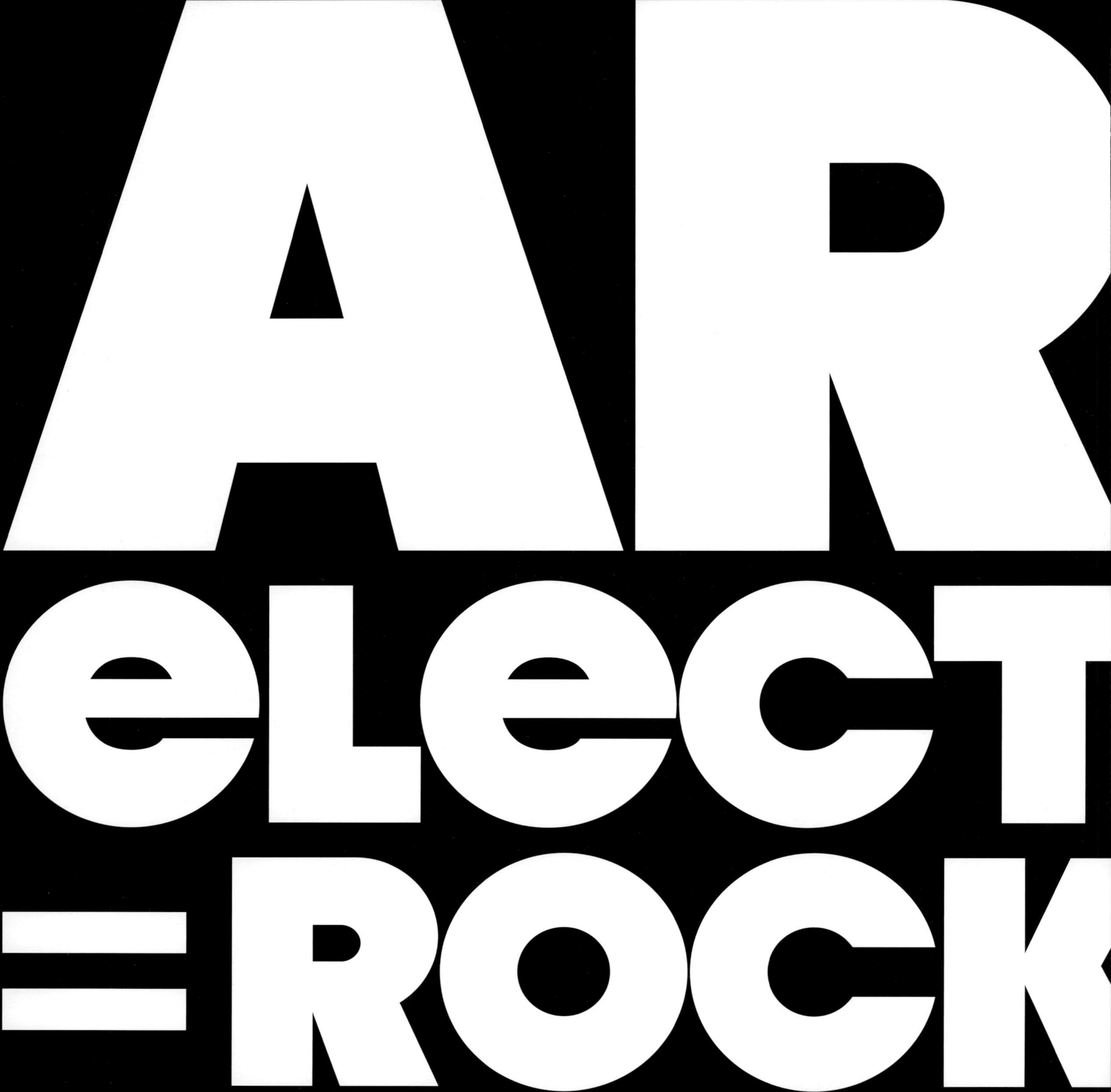
AR
ELECT
=ROCK

T✝RICITY 'N'ROLL

(PATTI SMITH)

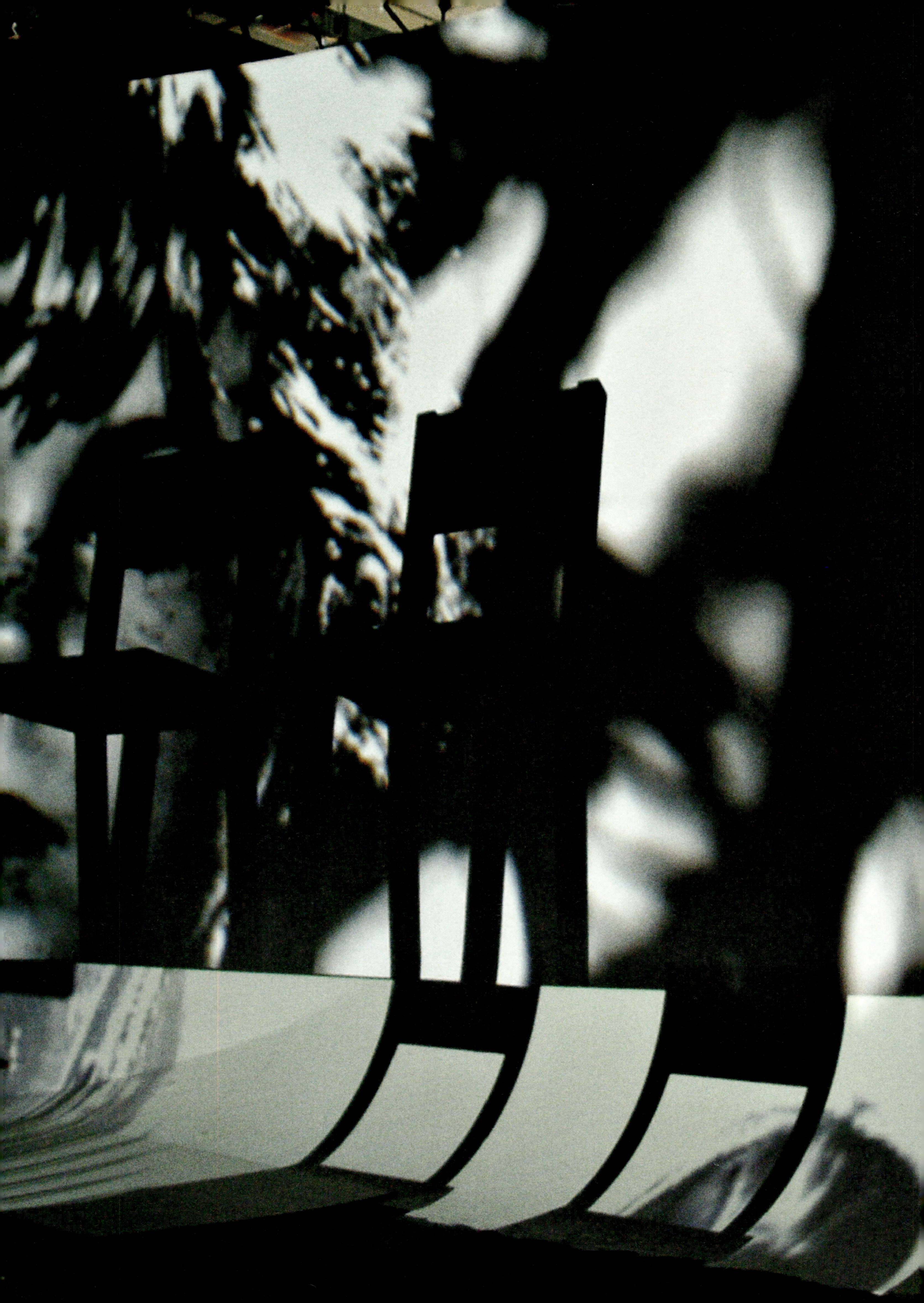

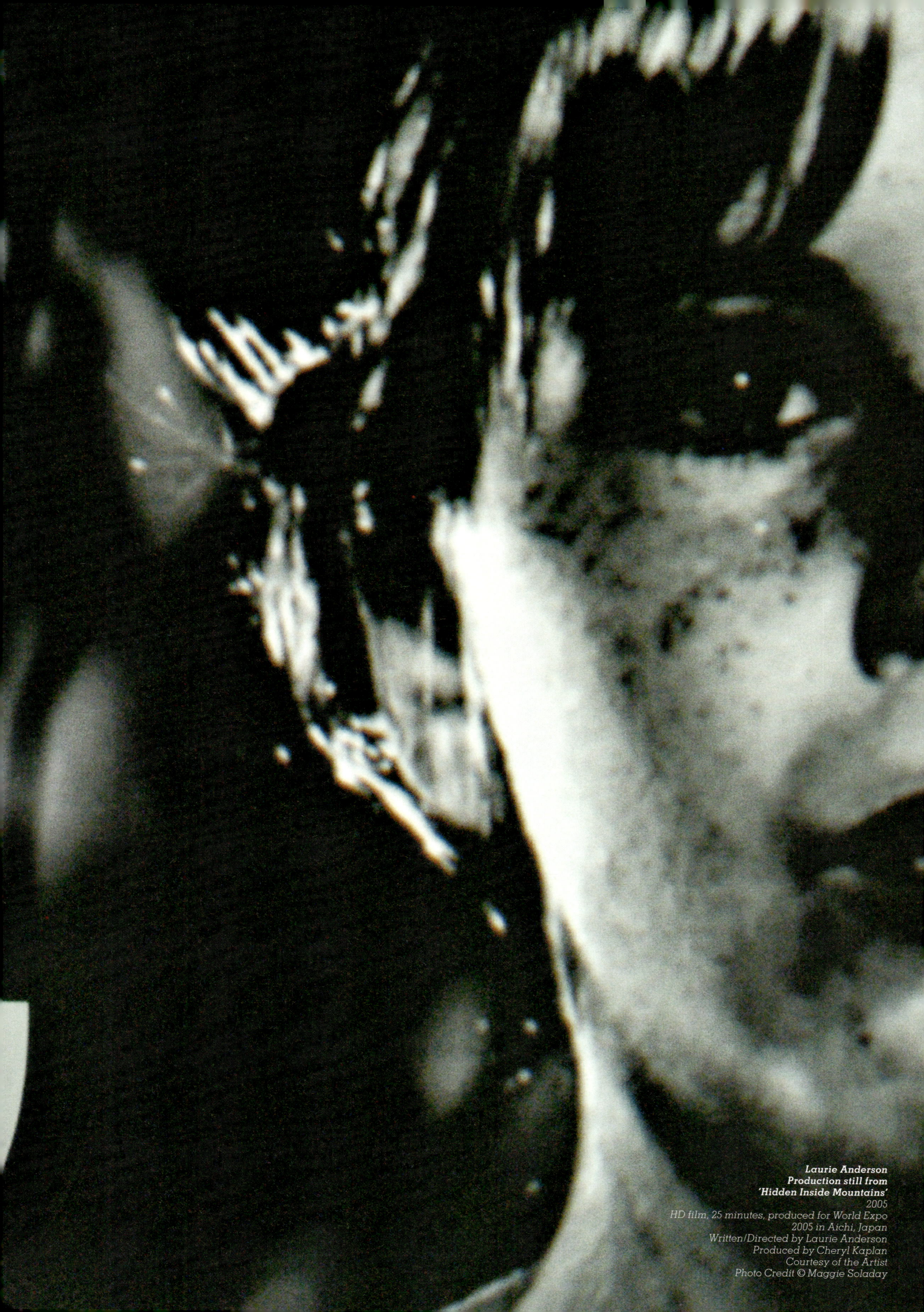

Laurie Anderson
Production still from
'Hidden Inside Mountains'
2005
HD film, 25 minutes, produced for World Expo
2005 in Aichi, Japan
Written/Directed by Laurie Anderson
Produced by Cheryl Kaplan
Courtesy of the Artist
Photo Credit © Maggie Soladay

LAURIe
ANDe

RSON

A graduate of Barnard College, with a degree in sculpture and art history, Laurie Anderson is an experimental artist known for her multimedia performances and musical productions. Her first single, "O Superman", in 1981, initially confidential, became a surprise hit and introduced her to the general public. Through a variety of media, and with collaborators ranging from William Burroughs to Lou Reed via Phillip Glass, she has continually explored the theme of technology and its link with humanity.

Her artistic creations took the form of minimalist sculptures in the early '70s, and have since evolved to take on more political themes, notably in large multimedia installations. Since 2000 she has been concentrating on her musical production, and in 2003 was hired as the first artist in residence at the NASA. A major retrospective of her work, Laurie Anderson: The Record of the Time, traveled in 2003–2005 to a number of institutions around the world. Her new album, Homeland, is due for release in 2008.

— Laurie Anderson was born in 1947 in Chicago, Illinois, and lives in New York City.

LAURIE ANDERSON INTERVIEWED BY JÉRÔME SANS

LIFE ON A STRING

YOU ORIGINALLY STUDIED SCULPTURE AND ART HISTORY. WHAT LED YOU TO MUSIC AND PERFORMANCE?

I made sculptures that talked and had music inside them, which led me to reinventing different kinds of violins. Also there was very little distinction at the time between art forms, so there were no barriers between art forms. Dance, painting, and music were all presented in the same loft spaces.

What led me to stories and music was, among other things, Vito Acconci. He had made a natural and exciting combination of performance, writing, and sculpture. He chose me in an artist-choose-artists series at Artists Space, and that was how I got my start in galleries. Also, I loved minimal music and wanted to make my own minimal music plus voice.

COULD YOU DESCRIBE YOUR SCULPTURAL WORKS FROM THE 1970S?

Eva Hesse. She was my idol. And some of my work in school looked exactly like hers, or as close as I could make it. Also, there were leaning sticks, and bricks made from The New York Times. I'd have to say conceptual/minimal would sum it up.

WHOSE WORK DID YOU FEEL CLOSE TO AT THE TIME, AND WHICH ARTISTS TO YOU FEEL CLOSE TO NOW?

Sol Lewitt, who was my teacher. I did a number of music pieces for him – string quartets mainly – using his number series. Also Phil Glass, Gordon Matta-Clark, Richard Nonas, and Trisha Brown.

HOW WOULD YOU DEFINE YOURSELF TODAY? DO YOU CONSIDER YOUR WORK NOW TO BE MORE ABOUT VISUAL ART THAN TECHNOLOGY?

I am and always have been a storyteller. Whether it's songs or films or images, there's always a story at the bottom. So I guess I'm mostly in love with words. Technology has always been a complicated love–hate scenario. Like most people, I love small, efficient, beautiful, and powerful tools. Also like most people, I resent being on the economic and marketing treadmill that leads you to updating your stuff every other weekend.

WHAT WAS YOUR RESIDENCY AT NASA?

This job really came out of the blue. They called and asked if I'd like to be the first artist in residence at NASA. And I said, "What does that mean with a space program?" And they said, "We don't know what it means. What do you think it means?" And I thought, "Who are these people?" I took the job, though, and for two years I went around to places like Mission Control in Houston, and the Jet Propulsion Lab in Pasadena, and The Hubble Space Telescope center in Baltimore, and it was amazing. I got to meet a lot of people I would never run into – nanotechnologists, robotics engineers, astronauts, and weapons designers.

YOU'VE COMPOSED ORIGINAL SCORES FOR MOVIES, PLAYS, AND BALLETS THROUGHOUT YOUR CAREER. ARE YOU STILL WORKING ON SUCH PROJECTS?

Yes, usually I'm working on something like that. The most recent have been some pieces for the Trisha Brown Dance Company and their collaborations with the Paris Opera.

> **I am and always have been a storyteller. Whether it's songs or films or images, there's always a story at the bottom.**

AS A LEADER IN THE USE OF TECHNOLOGY IN THE ARTS, YOU COLLABORATED WITH LABORATORIES IN THE EXPLORATION OF NEW CREATIVE TOOLS. ARE YOU RESEARCHING IN THE FIELD TODAY?

I'm working on some speech programs now with two different teams. Top secret! We'll see what happens; they may never even see the light of day.

WOULD YOU SAY THAT YOUR WORK ISN'T DEFINED BY INSTRUMENTS BUT INSTEAD THAT THE INSTRUMENTS ARE DEFINED BY YOUR MUSIC? WHAT ABOUT YOUR PRACTICE OF COMPOSING MUSIC FOR INSTRUMENTS THAT MAY NO LONGER EXIST?

I'm not really sure what you mean by that. The music and the instrument are so codependent. They're constantly changing each other. Recently I wrote some music for Chinese erhu – their two-stringed violins – and even though other musicians are playing those parts in my shows, you can still hear the hoarse sound of those small violins. The main thing I made that can no longer be played is a CD ROM called 'Puppet Motel', and there are no formats that can support it anymore. A lost work!

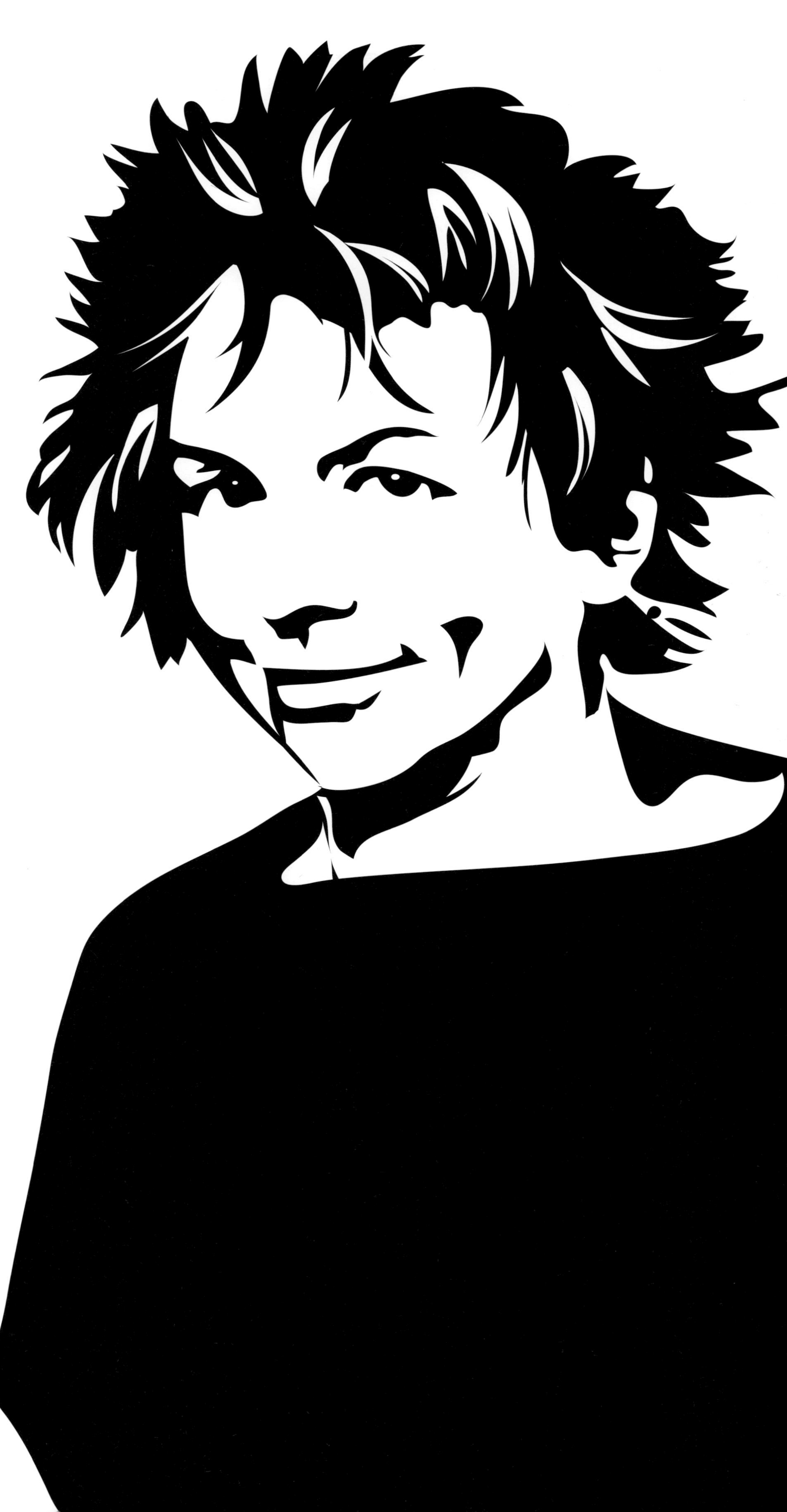

YOU SAID IN 1985: "THE SECOND THAT TECHNOLOGY BECOMES THE MOST SALIENT FEATURE OF MUSIC IS THE POINT I THINK THE MUSIC BEGINS TO FAIL. THEN YOU'RE AT A TRADE FAIR LISTENING TO THE LATEST IN MODERN TECHNOLOGY. NOW, THAT'S VERY INTERESTING BUT IT HAS NOTHING TO DO WITH ART. NOTHING". DO YOU STILL AGREE WITH THIS ASSERTION?

First of all, I can't imagine using the word "salient". That aside, I suppose it depends on the technology. Some technology can be so playful and inventive that it literally becomes the work. But in the end, the argument gets pretty silly. Like saying the pencil isn't contributing to the meaning of the drawing. Usually the role of technology is supportive, blank.

YOU HAVE A ROLE OF SOCIAL COMMENTATOR, BEING ACTIVE, FOR INSTANCE, IN THE BATTLE AGAINST THE WAR IN IRAQ. WHAT MAKES YOU WANT TO FIGHT IN TODAY'S SOCIETY?

The illusion that we're so plugged in and well-informed. When in fact we're all being distracted by cars and computers. We live in an information society where real information is actually hard to get.

WHAT KINDS OF PROJECTS DO YOU WANT TO DEVELOP IN THE FUTURE?

I'm writing some plays, finishing a record. I'd like to do an opera.

DO YOU STILL INTEND TO PERFORM SOLO AND WITHOUT BIG, MULTIMEDIA SETS?

Like I said, I'm always changing my mind. It seems like every time I say I'll never do another big, high-tech show, the next thing I find myself doing is another big, high-tech show. So much for intentions!

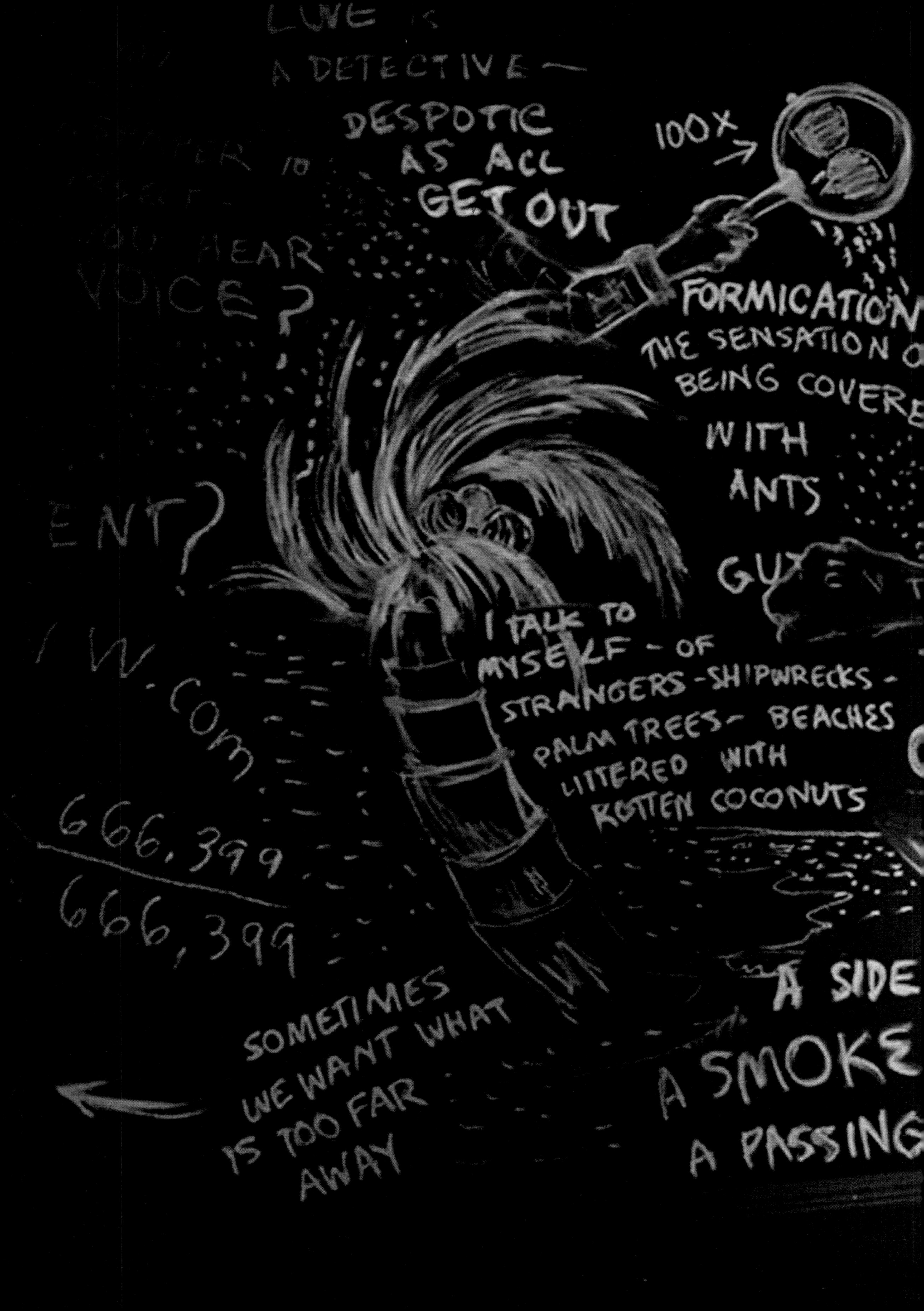

LOVE IS
A DETECTIVE —
DESPOTIC
AS ALL
GET OUT

100X →

FORMICATION
THE SENSATION OF
BEING COVERED
WITH
ANTS

YOU HEAR
VOICE?

ENT?

W.com

666,399
666,399

I TALK TO
MYSELF - OF
STRANGERS - SHIPWRECKS -
PALM TREES - BEACHES
LITTERED WITH
ROTTEN COCONUTS

SOMETIMES
WE WANT WHAT
IS TOO FAR
AWAY

A SIDE

A SMOKE

A PASSING

KNOW.
RE ARE
TS OF
NGS THAT
BY NATURE
POSSIBLE
LIKE TAKING
A WALK
WITH
A LIBRARY
LIBRARY
MEATBALL IN A WINE GLASS
"FAME IS THE SUNSHINE OF THE DEAD"
TOO MANY PEOPLE ARE TAKING PROZAC...
AND SOME TIMES EVEN HATRED CAN BE BEAUTIFUL...
WHEN
AS
AS
AS
DIAM
HONORE DE BALZAC
THE PURPOSE OF ART IS TO PROVIDE WHAT LIFE cannot
YES NO
OW-
CREEN-
NDSCAPE
here's my THEORY OF PUNCTU
instead of a period at the end of each sentence there should be a tiny CLOCK that tells you HOW LONG it took you to write that sentence
the FUTU
BELO
CRA
RO
OK!
ACTION

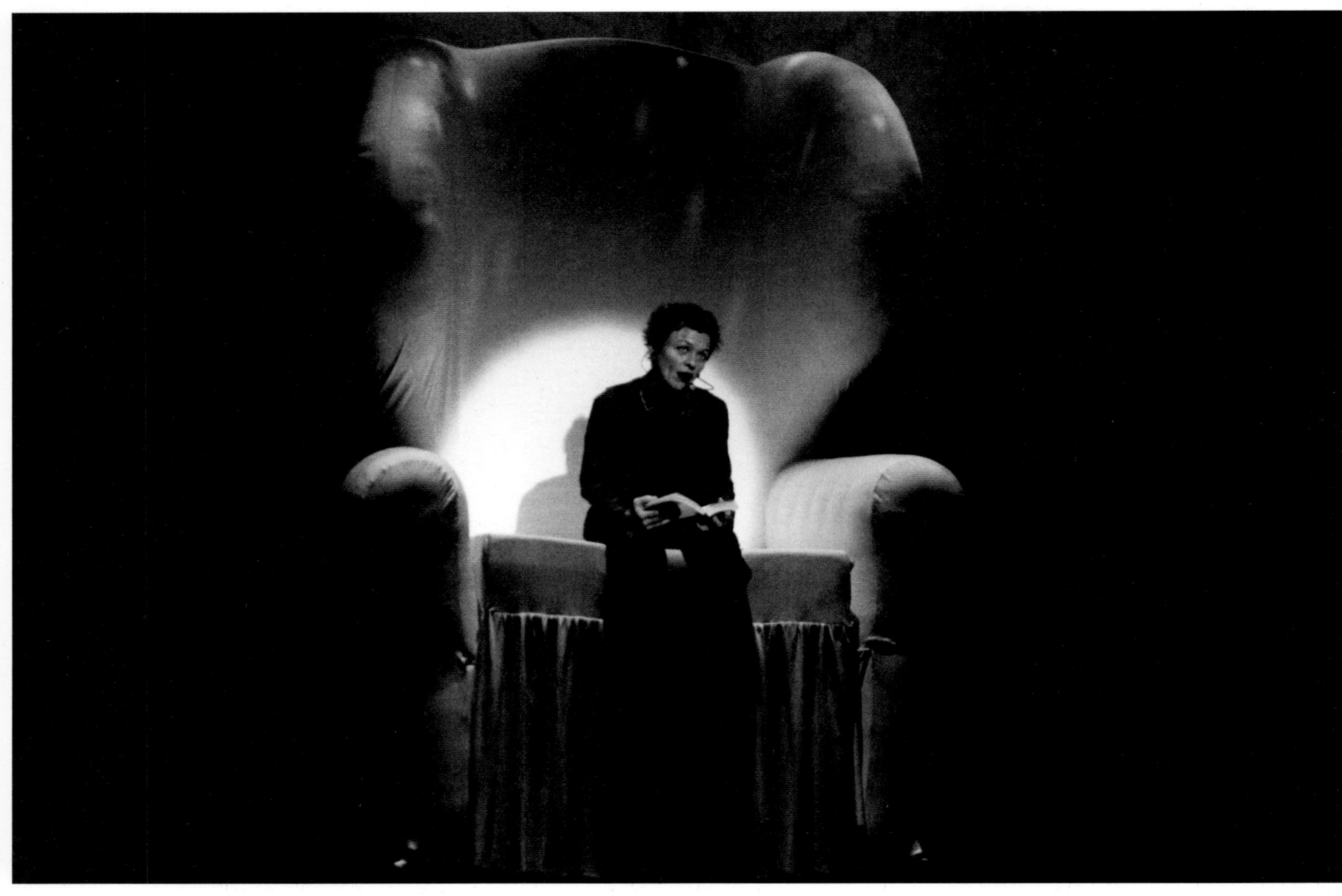

Page 38/39
Animatronic Parrot
2005
Installation view
Irish Museum of Modern Art, Dublin, Ireland
Courtesy of the Artist

Playing 'The Talking Stick' from
'Songs and Stories from Moby Dick'
1999
Brooklyn Academy of Music
Courtesy of the Artist
Photo Credit © Frank Micelotta

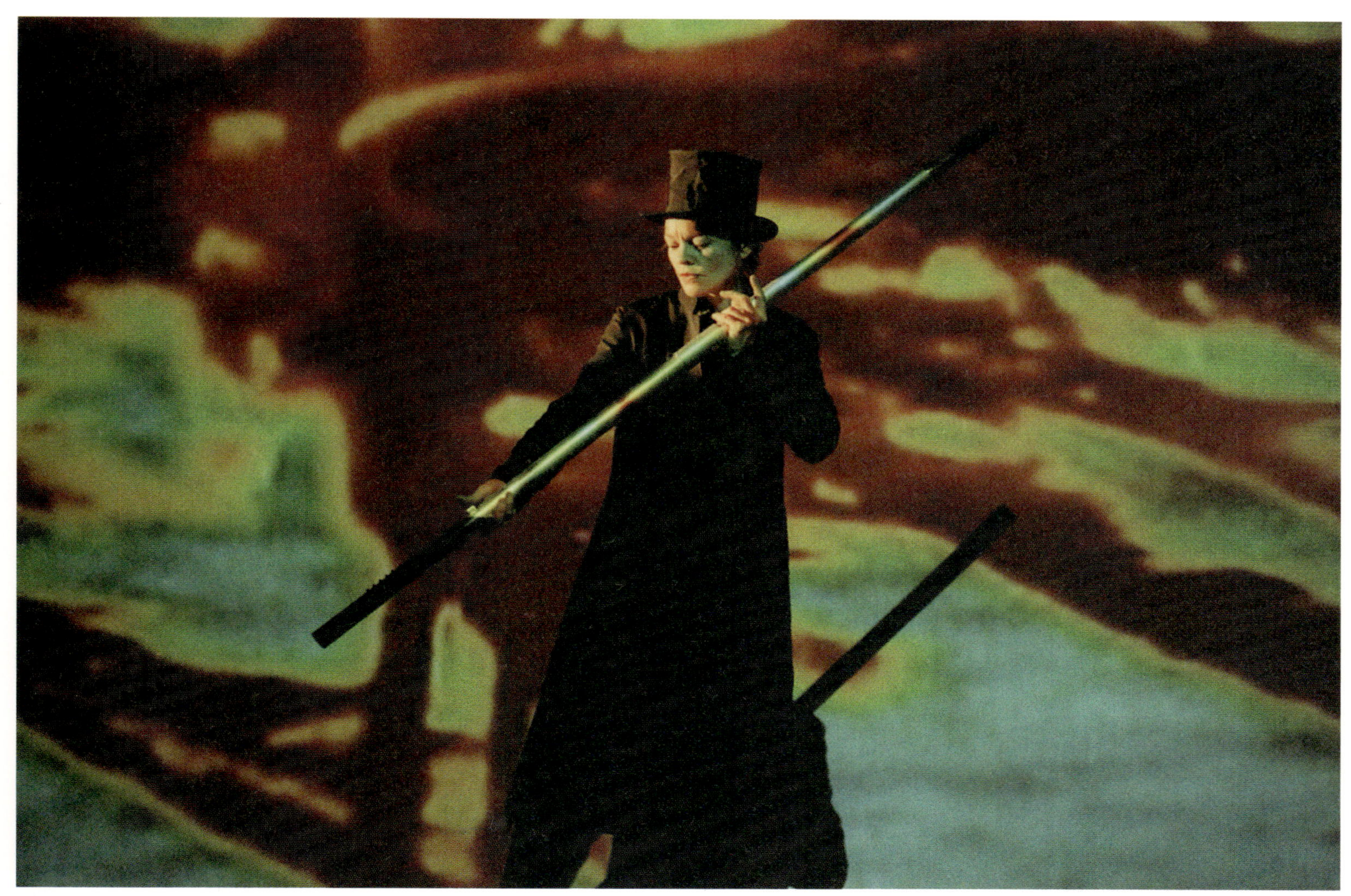

Production still from
'Hidden Inside Mountains'
2005
HD film, 25 minutes, produced for World Expo
2005 in Aichi, Japan
Written/Directed by Laurie Anderson
Produced by Cheryl Kaplan
Courtesy of the Artist
Photo Credit © Maggie Soladay

ANT

ONY

Antony and the Johnsons, a music ensemble based in New York City, was formed in 2000 by Antony. His unusual voice has been likened to "a cross between Nina Simone and Bryan Ferry", and has attracted collaborators such as Lou Reed, Marina Abramovic and Björk. Antony's voice and work exists between male and female, between darkness and light, power and vulnerability.

For his work in this exhibition, Antony has collaborated with Johanna Constantine, Dr. Julia Yasuda Ph.D, photographer Don Felix Cervantes, and Joie Iacono. Together they have created a series of portraits and images deriving from Antony's drawings. This collection entitled 'Leaves' reflects a world view that engages history, mythology and scientific prophecy. In this interview, Antony recounts his journeys since his early days performing in New York City nightclubs and references

WAS IT YOUR ENCOUNTER WITH MARTIN WORMAN AT NEW YORK UNIVERSITY THAT INSPIRED YOU TO FORM THE BLACKLIPS PERFORMANCE CULT IN 1992 WITH JOHANNA CONSTANTINE?

Martin was one of the main playwrights for the Cockettes, and he was teaching performance studies courses at NYU in 1991. He would take me aside after class and describe to me what he called our "family tree", which outlined the development of queer urban performance art, starting with Jack Smith, The Ridiculous Theatrical Company, Hibiscus, the Cockettes, The Angels of Light, Hot Peaches, Bloolips, and all the individual stars along the way… Ethel Eichelberger, Klaus Nomi and Joey Arias, the Pyramid scene, with all its bright stars, and more. He recognized my affinity and showed me this long under-

time in the city. In a weird way I felt like we embodied a part of the subconscious mind of the city, bubbling away in there so late at night. Half the players were on large quantities of drugs, and most of them were older than me. I was the self-appointed den mother to this very inspiring and motley assortment of somewhat scary geniuses.

WERE YOU ALREADY DOING MUSIC?

My inevitable role in Blacklips was to appear at the show's climax, recite a few lines, and sing one of my songs. I was always cast as God or the Devil, descending from the clouds to sing 'Love Letters' or 'Fist Full of Love'.

HOW DID YOU MOVE FROM BLACKLIPS TO ANTONY & THE JOHNSONS?

Blacklips dissolved after three years. It's a miracle it lasted so long, considering that

TOWARDS T

his visual and musical evolution. In parallel to NYC friends Devendra Banhart, CocoRosie and Kembra Pfahler, Antony shares a desire to voice intuitions, to challenge patriarchy and all its social and spiritual constructs, and to explore a notion of hope for the future.
— Born in 1971 in Chichester (UK), Antony now lives in New York City.

ANTONY INTERVIEWED BY AUDREY MASCINA

YOU BOUGHT YOUR FIRST RECORD, THE KICK INSIDE BY KATE BUSH, AT AGE 7 AND KNEW BY 12 THAT BOY GEORGE AND MARC ALMOND REPRESENTED SOMETHING MEANINGFUL TO YOU. WHY DID YOU INITIALLY GRAVITATE TOWARD EXPERIMENTAL THEATER CLASSES RATHER THAN MUSIC?

I started writing songs in my early teens. I didn't study music in university because my relationship to music felt so personal, and I was afraid that I might lose some part of my connection to it. I liked the mystery of it, like walking through the mist. The simple relationships were a source of inspiration to me. The head of the UCSC music department warned me that after he studied music theory he never wrote another song! So I got spooked and decided to leave it alone. Instead I studied other creative fields: performance art, theater, visual art, filmmaking, and photography. After classes I would put together these late-night musicals with friends, inspired by John Waters' early films. It was in this context that I first presented my songs.

ground tradition of things that came before me, none of which at that time were properly documented. So it was still very much an oral tradition, supported by various clippings and some memorabilia. When I was 20 my sole intention was to start a late-night club where I could sing torch songs at 3 a.m., bathed in a dark blue light. Something between Isabella Rosellini in Blue Velvet and the transvestite chanteuse in Soft Cell's song 'Torch'… My best friend and inspiration, Johanna Constantine, moved out to NYC to join me, and we started the Blacklips bar in an attempt to attract others of a similar mindset. Within a couple of months 13 of us had formed the core membership of the Blacklips Performance Cult. For a while it was a very wild and creative scene.

WHAT WAS THE IDEA BEHIND THIS COLLECTIVE?

At first I wrote a play for us to perform each week. Soon the others started writing plays and it evolved into a very rough, erratic, and exciting laboratory for all these marginal, hard-core people to act out their personal myths. There were many guest stars. We all did numbers and sang love songs and dressed up as monsters and human-sized maggots, and survived earthquakes, nuclear mishaps, and alien invasions, while pretending to chop off one another's heads… The shows were radically different from week to week, depending on the play's author that night. However, the group became an ensemble, and each performer had a strong stage presence that carried over from week to week. The audience would look forward to catcalling James F. Murphy's entrance as she whinnied showtunes like a singing horse, and they would gasp when Kabuki Starshine stepped onto stage, looking transcendental in six hours of makeup. I used to call it "auto-performance". We weren't interested in acting; we were presenting heightened versions of ourselves. It was kind of a dark

people were literally being paid five dollars a week. But for many of us at that time it was our raison d'être. Internal conflicts and diverging goals eventually led us to part ways. I wanted to focus more on my own work so I started a new group called The Johnsons, with Johanna and a couple of friends. The Johnsons was a platform for me to explore things I had been developing in my work at Blacklips. The Johnsons shows were heavily surreal and non-linear, filled with tableaux and spectacle, inspired by the mystical aspirations of The Angels of Light. We did a few plays in the mid- to late- '90s, at a club in the Meatpacking District and at an experimental theater venue in the East Village called PS122: Womb, Father, Love, Dusk, and Miracle Now. In 1997 I got a grant from NYFA and I decided to record an album. Shortly thereafter I assembled a band, which was the first time I had ever worked with other musicians. In the past I had always made my arrangements on keyboards and sung to pre-recorded cassettes. It was around then that I decided there was no future for me in experimental theater, and I began to focus solely on music.

44

YOU EVOLVED IN NEW YORK'S PERFORMING ARTS SCENE AT A TIME WHEN IT WAS HEAVILY AFFECTED BY AIDS. HOW WAS THAT REFLECTED IN YOUR WORK AT THE TIME?

At Blacklips many nights the show would end up with a pile of dead bodies onstage. I remember when Leigh Bowery died in 1993 and we did this spontaneous memorial. We literally just walked up onstage one at a time and made a huge pile of dead bodies while Diamanda Galas' 'Dark End of the Street' played in the background. Our final show was called '13 Ways To Die', in which we each acted out some death fantasy. Almost all of us had been affected by the spectre of AIDS in one way or another; HIV was definitely hanging around. The Blacklips shows were sometimes very gory and brutal, with cryptic humor. I used to say we were "camping in a graveyard". My songs from that period circled loss: 'Rapture', 'The Atrocities', 'River of Sorrow', 'Deeper than Love'… I took it very personally at that age. Arriving in New York as a 19-year-old felt kind of like marching home after a long war and finding your city in ruins.

THE COVER OF YOUR SECOND ALBUM, 'I AM A BIRD NOW', IS A PHOTOGRAPH OF CANDY DARLING, THE

le FEMININE

WARHOL SUPERSTAR, BY PETER HUJAR. YOU SAID HIS PHOTOGRAPHS SAY IN IMAGE WHAT YOU WOULD LIKE TO SAY WITH YOUR SONGS. WHAT DO YOU MEAN?

That photo shows Candy Darling lying in bed at Cabrini Hospital, dying of leukemia. She radiates a startling beauty from beneath the white sheets. She appears as a vision suspended between darkness and light, male and female, life and death, flesh and ghost, time and eternity. It's kind of like the Mona Lisa of underground photography. That portrait has been the centerpiece of my aesthetic altar for years.

YOU DID A COLLABORATION WITH VIDEO ARTIST CHARLES ATLAS, PORTRAYING 13 NEW YORK CITY "BEAUTIES". WHAT WAS THIS PROJECT ABOUT?

Charlie and I first staged Turning as a part of the Whitney Biennial in 2004 and later brought it to the capital cities of Europe, in December 2006. For me it was one of the most rewarding experiences of my creative life. During each song of the concert, a different model would stand on a turning platform. Charlie's crew would make a video of her face. The images were then treated, and projected onto a giant screen behind the musicians. The effect was hypnotic and extremely intimate. It was the first time I had witnessed something that I felt I could watch forever, these portraits of all these women who I adore. The theme in choosing the models was "everything moving towards the feminine" – something that I have been meditating on over the last few years. The models were a cross section of ages, backgrounds, and personal perspectives, all of whom have been a source of inspiration to me in their own ways.

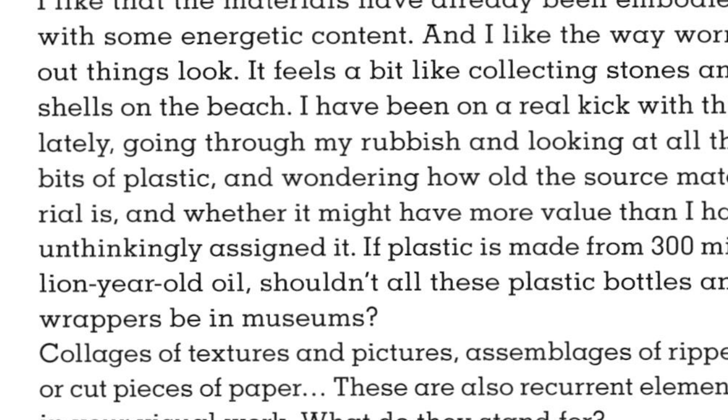

It is the relationship between things that is magic for me, the relationships between moments, songs, and images that transfix me. It is a process of continuous discovery.

YOU SAID THAT YOU ARE ALWAYS THINKING IN TERMS OF COLOR, LINE, SHAPE, AND MOVEMENT, WHETHER IT CONCERNS VISUAL ARTS OR MUSIC. HOW WOULD YOU DESCRIBE YOUR DRAWINGS?

For the last two years I have been very involved with drawing again. I used to draw a lot as a kid. I have been working on old newsprint and magazine cuttings, paper, ink, wax, charcoal, wax, white-out… anything I find, really. It's been sort of like brushing hair, waiting for it to grow, washing it, brushing it again. It's pretty intuitive. I've been trying not to censor myself. I try to follow the impulses of my hand as unconsciously as I can. The results can be quite abstract. The drawings seem to reflect aspects of my world, my internal world, human history, the natural world. In a second phase, I have been working with Don Felix Cervantes, someone with whom I have done photos in the past and who I really trust. We have been creating collages and combinations of these different source materials, and making a series of large prints. We are also working on several portraits of Julia Yasuda and Johanna Constantine – two friends of mine who I love to look at – and some images of me, which we intend to include in Brussels as well.

MANY OF YOUR WORKS ARE DONE ON OLD NEWSPAPER OR BOOK PAGES, CREATING LAYERS OF COLORS, WORDS, AND SHAPES, AND TRANSFORMING THE ORIGINAL MEANING INTO ANOTHER STORY. WHY DO YOU USE THESE PRINTED MEDIA AS CANVASES?

I like that the materials have already been embodied with some energetic content. And I like the way worn-out things look. It feels a bit like collecting stones and shells on the beach. I have been on a real kick with this lately, going through my rubbish and looking at all the bits of plastic, and wondering how old the source material is, and whether it might have more value than I had unthinkingly assigned it. If plastic is made from 300 million-year-old oil, shouldn't all these plastic bottles and wrappers be in museums?

Collages of textures and pictures, assemblages of ripped or cut pieces of paper… These are also recurrent elements in your visual work. What do they stand for?

Collage is very natural for me. In a way it is similar to directing a play. It is the relationship between things that is magic for me, the relationships between moments, songs, and images that transfix me. It is a process of continuous discovery.

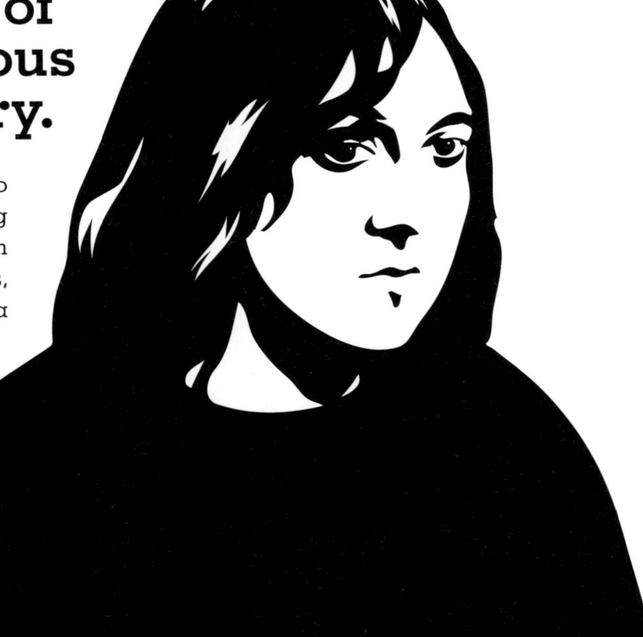

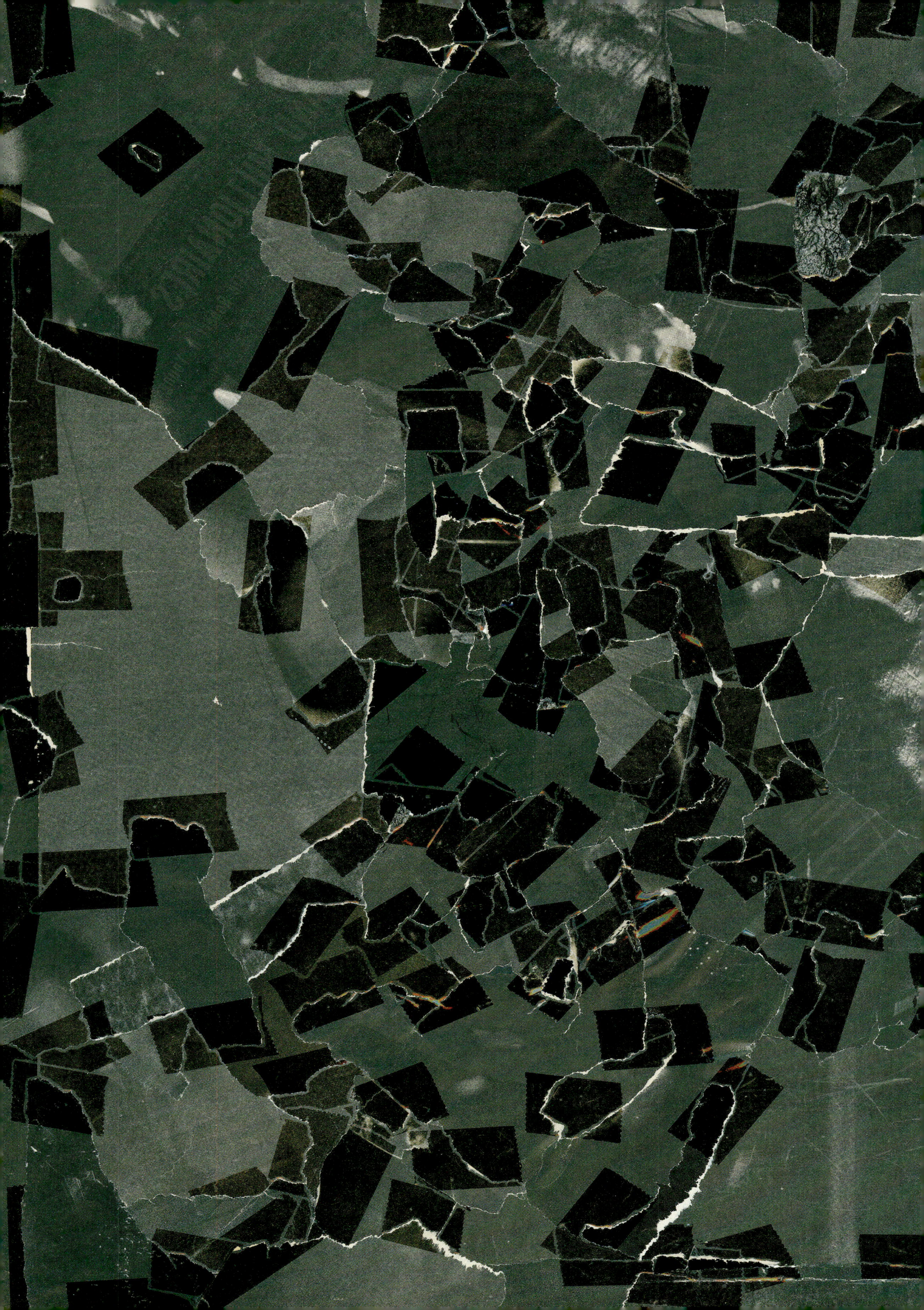

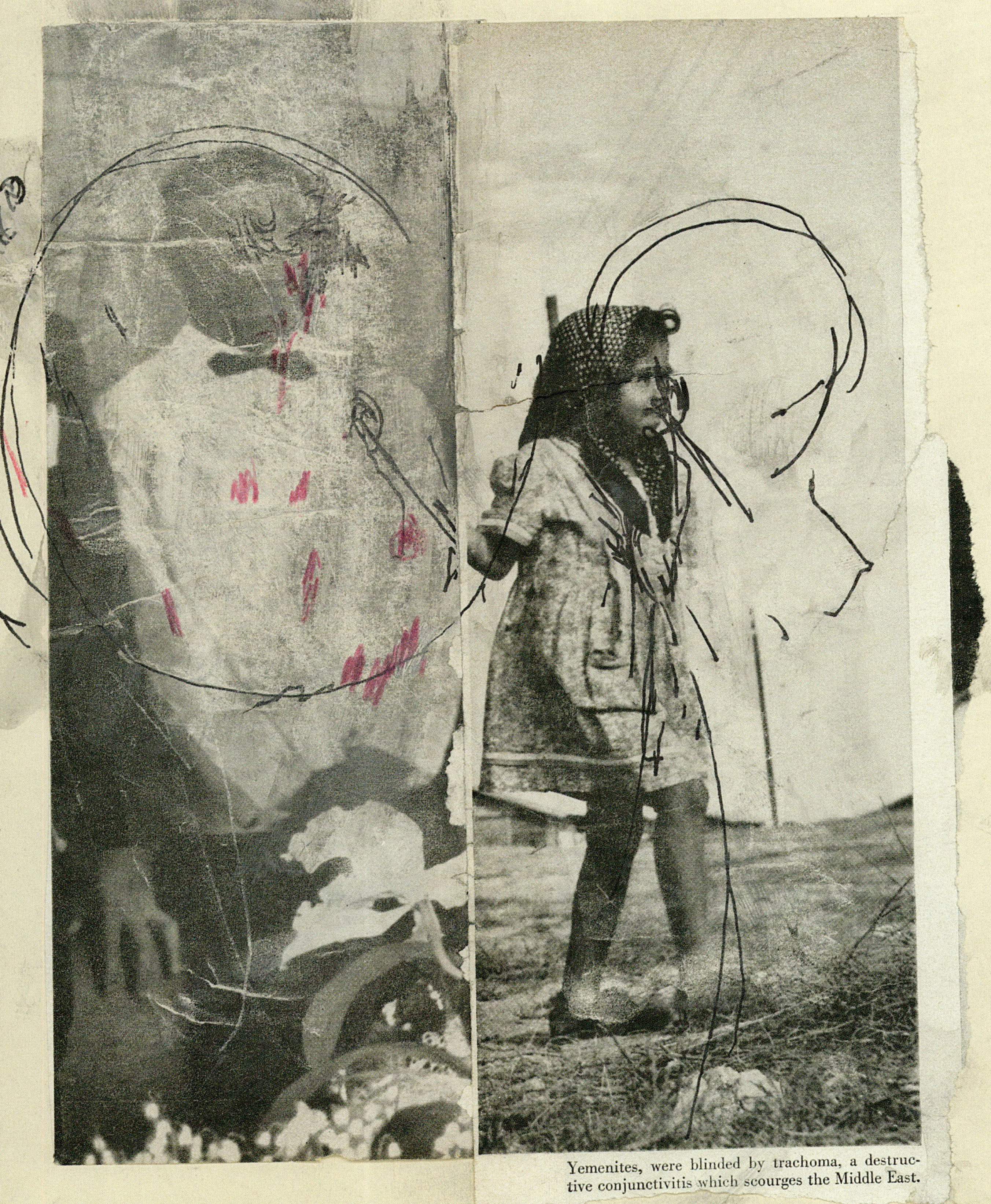

Yemenites, were blinded by trachoma, a destruc-
tive conjunctivitis which scourges the Middle East.

Page 46
Black Parts
2007
Card, newsprint, ink
43,2 x 35,6 cm
Courtesy of Antony

Page 47
Violetta
2007
Card, newsprint, ink
24,1 x 32,3 cm
Courtesy of Antony

Ghost
2007
Paper, pencil, ink
22,2 x 21,6 cm
Courtesy of Antony

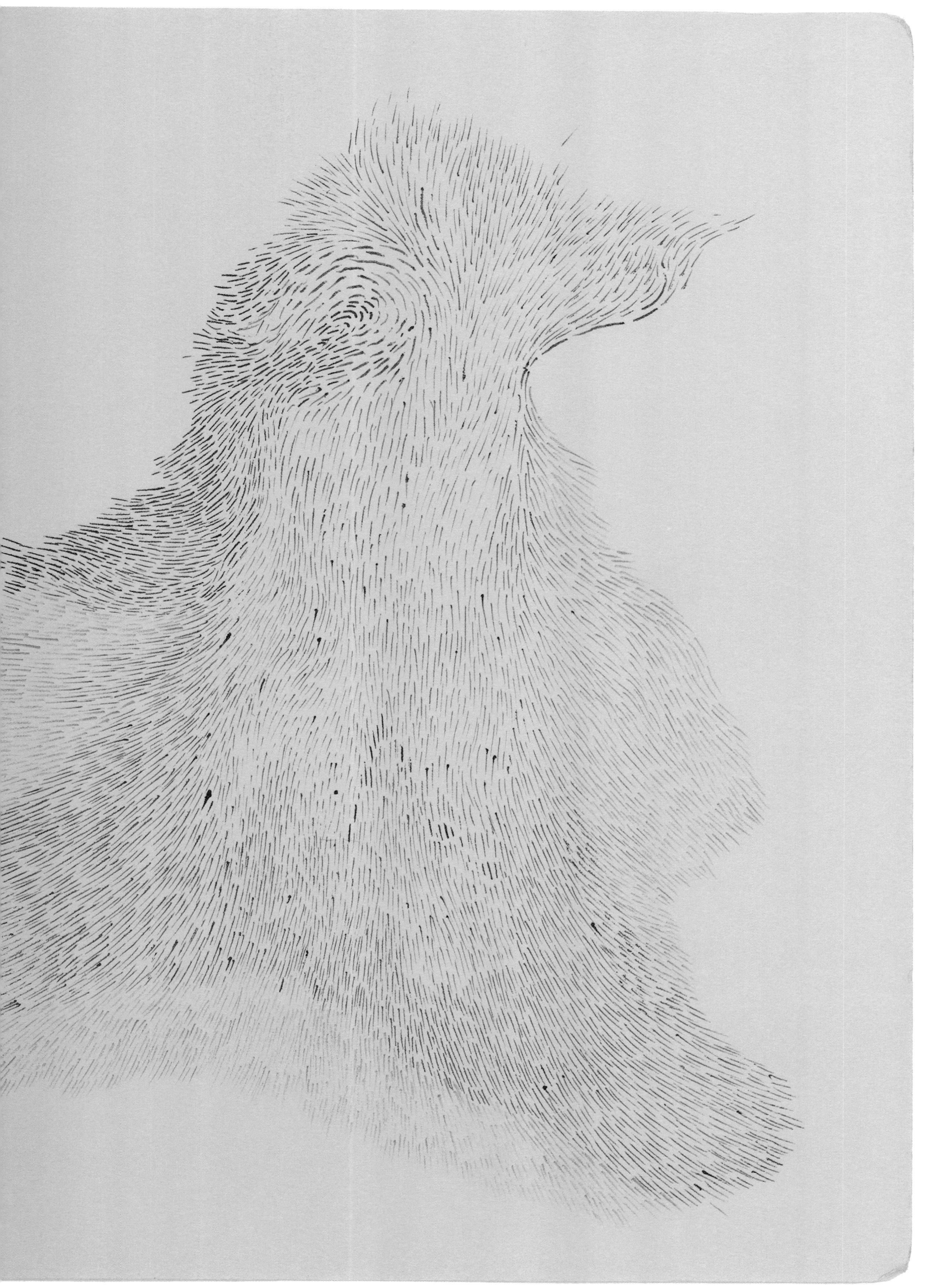

DeVeNDRA
BANI

ART

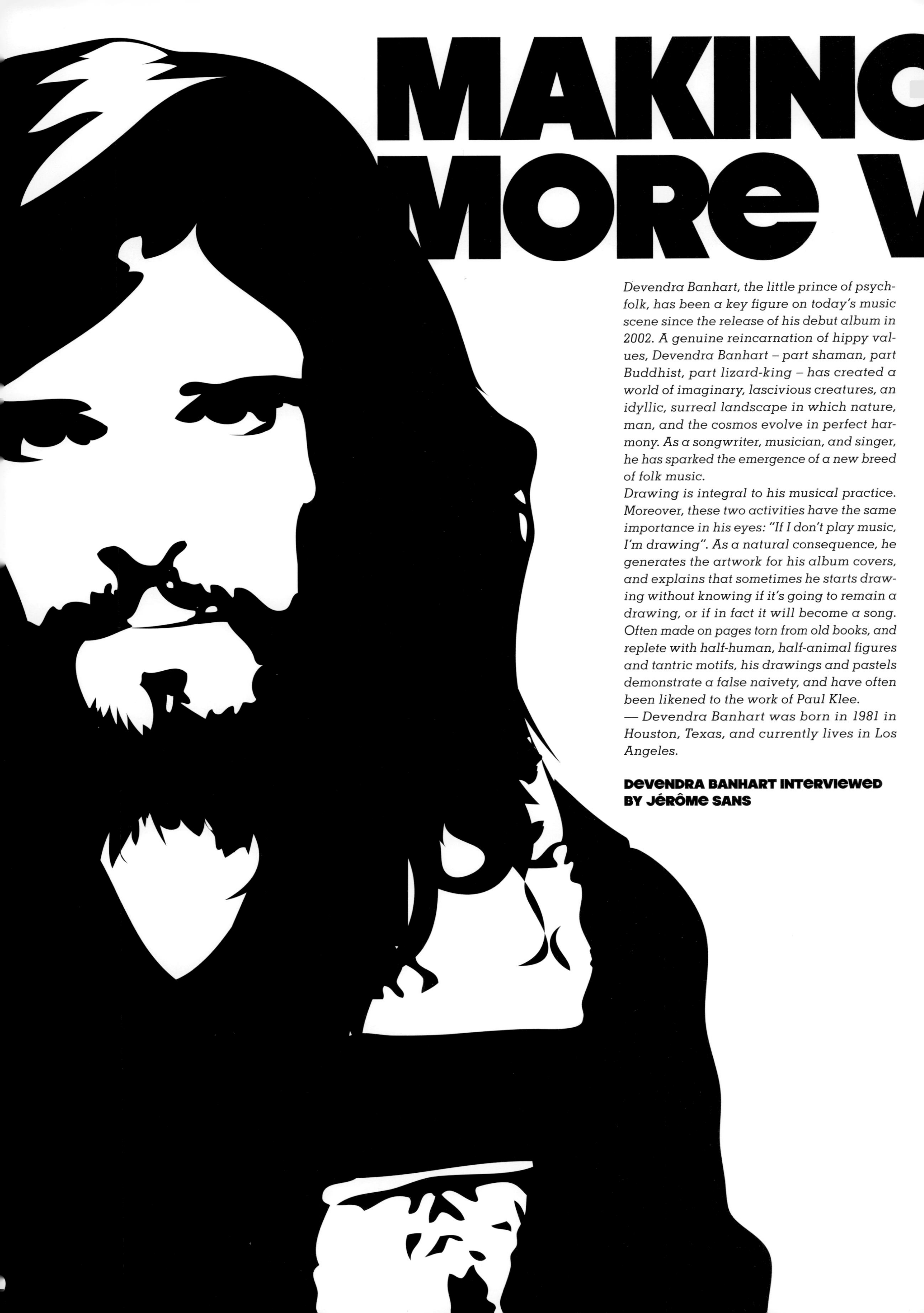

Devendra Banhart, the little prince of psych-folk, has been a key figure on today's music scene since the release of his debut album in 2002. A genuine reincarnation of hippy values, Devendra Banhart – part shaman, part Buddhist, part lizard-king – has created a world of imaginary, lascivious creatures, an idyllic, surreal landscape in which nature, man, and the cosmos evolve in perfect harmony. As a songwriter, musician, and singer, he has sparked the emergence of a new breed of folk music.

Drawing is integral to his musical practice. Moreover, these two activities have the same importance in his eyes: "If I don't play music, I'm drawing". As a natural consequence, he generates the artwork for his album covers, and explains that sometimes he starts drawing without knowing if it's going to remain a drawing, or if in fact it will become a song. Often made on pages torn from old books, and replete with half-human, half-animal figures and tantric motifs, his drawings and pastels demonstrate a false naivety, and have often been likened to the work of Paul Klee.

— Devendra Banhart was born in 1981 in Houston, Texas, and currently lives in Los Angeles.

DEVENDRA BANHART INTERVIEWED BY JÉRÔME SANS

ONeSeLF ULNeRABLE

YOU ATTENDED SAN FRANCISCO ART INSTITUTE FOR TWO YEARS. WHAT CLASSES DID YOU ATTEND THERE AND WHY DID YOU DECIDE TO QUIT SO FAST?

I was an interdisciplinary major thanks to the Osher Scholarship I was somehow – probably by mistake – kindly given. I split after two years once I realized that for me, the most fruitful of art-school tools was the library, and I had only to look like an artist to utilize it! I also split because I found myself skipping too many classes, to play music.

WERE YOU ALREADY DOING THE TYPES OF DRAWINGS YOU ARE DOING TODAY?

I was drawing repetitively, but mostly in ink, and the image was always minimal. For example: one bird drawn 500 times, very small, on a large piece of paper, etc.

HOW WOULD YOU DEFINE YOUR DRAWINGS AND THEIR CONNECTION WITH YOUR MUSIC, YOUR LIFE?

They were intertwined from the beginning. As time went on and I fell into "my thing", whatever the hell that is, they began to inhabit somewhat separate spaces, still linked but not dependent on each other.

YOU'RE MOSTLY DOING WATERCOLOR AND WORKS ON PAPER, INTIMATE ARTWORKS — LIKE YOUR MUSIC — DONE ON BOOK PAPER. WHY DID YOU CHOOSE THIS MEDIUM, THESE MATERIALS?

The Intimate element is key, and something I shoot for when writing a song or drawing, painting. The old paper/book pages is an aesthetic choice that, by its already having had a long history, forces me to be aware, delicate, and respectful of the materials. Something that hopefully will help the process of making oneself more vulnerable. It's the same with recording music and the equipment that is chosen. At least for me.

YOUR DRAWINGS APPEAR OUT OF HUNDREDS OF SMALL LINES. IS THIS LONG PROCESS A MEDITATIVE ONE THAT YOU DON'T HAVE WITH MUSIC?

> The old paper/book pages is an aesthetic choice that, by its already having had a long history, forces me to be aware, delicate, and respectful of the materials

It's very similar, because of that initial intuitive leap. Writing about it is very difficult, at least for me. Discussing instinct is not the coolest.

YOUR VISUAL WORK, YOUR WORDS, YOUR SONGS, THE WAY YOU DRESS OR UNDRESS… ARE ALL VERY MUCH IN TUNE WITH NATURE, AND CONNECTED WITH DIFFERENT ANCIENT CULTURAL MYTHS AND RITUALS, FROM HINDUISM, BUDDHISM, MEXICAN AZTEC KINGS, NATIVE AMERICANS… HOW DO YOU RELATE TO ALL THOSE SPIRITUAL INCARNATIONS?

The seed is always the same, and why not enjoy the sublime beauty of endless textures, colors, scents, and forever on and onward. This is the way I view religion. When I am open I'm the most human, and religion, myth, magic all require being in that state.

A COMMON NATIVE AMERICAN CULTURAL BELIEF IS THAT EVERYTHING HAS A SOUL, EVEN A TREE OR A STONE. WOULD YOU SAY THAT YOU GIVE A SPIRIT TO EVERYTHING YOU DRAW?

Not my drawings, but the greats, yes! The answer to the question, "Does this have a soul?" is a little more obvious when it's something clearly closer to us, like a portrait. But when it's a line – Cy Twombly – or a series of lines – Agnes Martin – there's so much soul radiating from it. Hot damn, that's it!

MOST OF THE CHARACTERS OR SHAPES YOU DRAW ARE, IN THE END, BOTH ABSTRACT AND FIGURATIVE. ARE ANY OF THESE RECURRENT MOTIFS IN YOUR VISUAL VOCABULARY?

Yes, and it's a struggle, a challenge to not repeat myself, just like songwriting. Unfortunately I keep drawing hands and singing about animals!

THERE ARE ALWAYS MANY GUESTS ON YOUR SONGS AND ALBUMS. WHO ARE THE VISUAL ARTISTS YOU FEEL CLOSE TO OR WOULD LIKE TO COLLABORATE WITH?

There's so many, so if I forget you, please forgive me! But I love and would love to work with: Keegan McHargue, Travis Millard, Alicia McCarthy, Adam Tullie, Jo Jackson, John Beasley, Chris Johanson, Marc Bell, Matt Leines, Matteah Baim, Amy Jo Diaz, Sarah Cain, Lucky Dragons, Maya Hayuk, Will Lemon, Ajit Chauhan, Scott Hewicker… There's so many more! My two current favorite no-longer-on-this-plane artists are Wallace Berman and Vali Myers.

WHAT ARE YOUR UPCOMING PROJECTS?

The first is a Megapuss album, and a festival aimed at raising money to stop uranium drilling… Save the rainforest, give instruments to impoverished children, raise money for AIDS research, and killer jams!

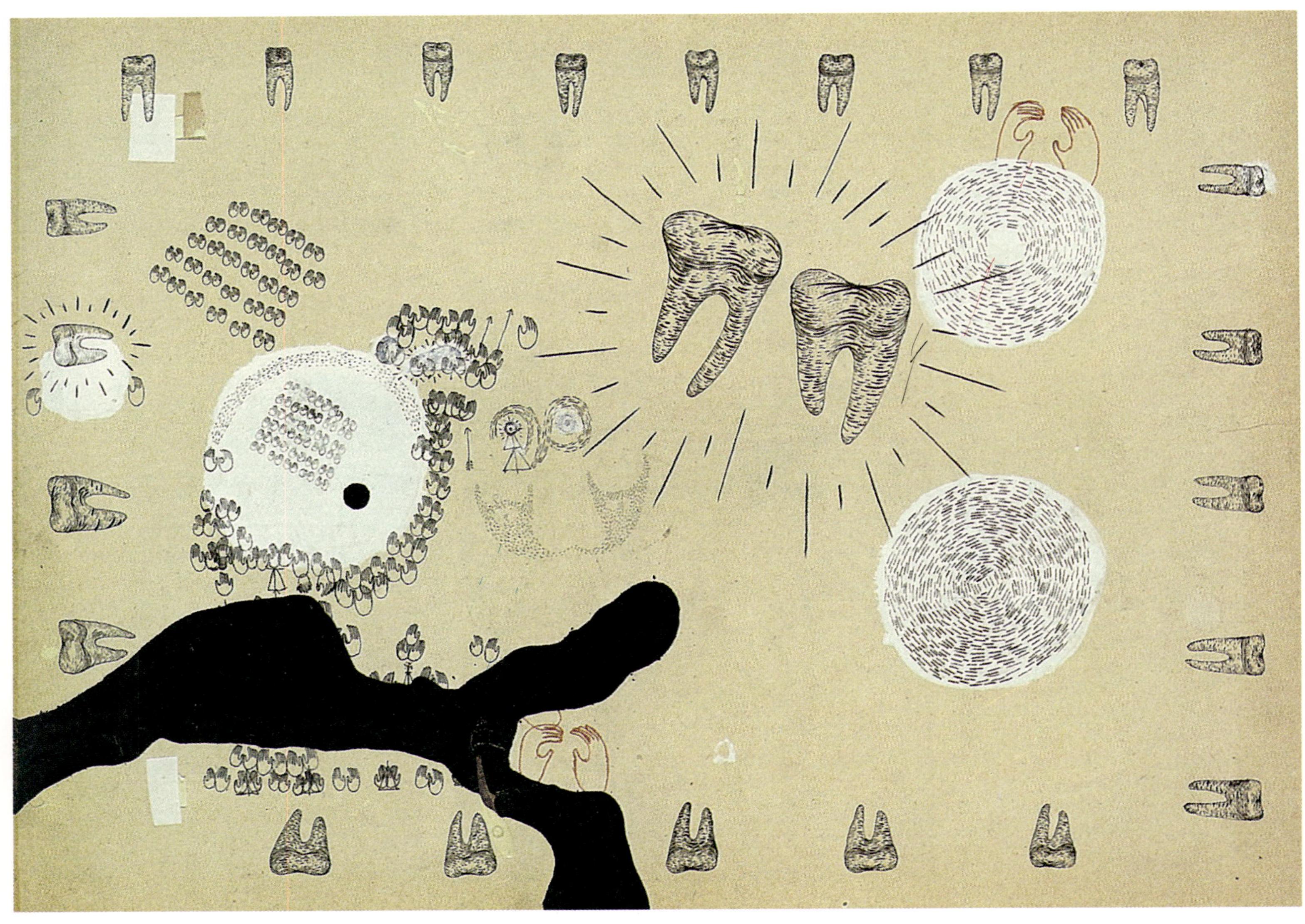

Untitled
2002
Ink and mixed media on found album board
35.56 x 48.26 cm
Courtesy of the Artist
and Deitch Projects, New York

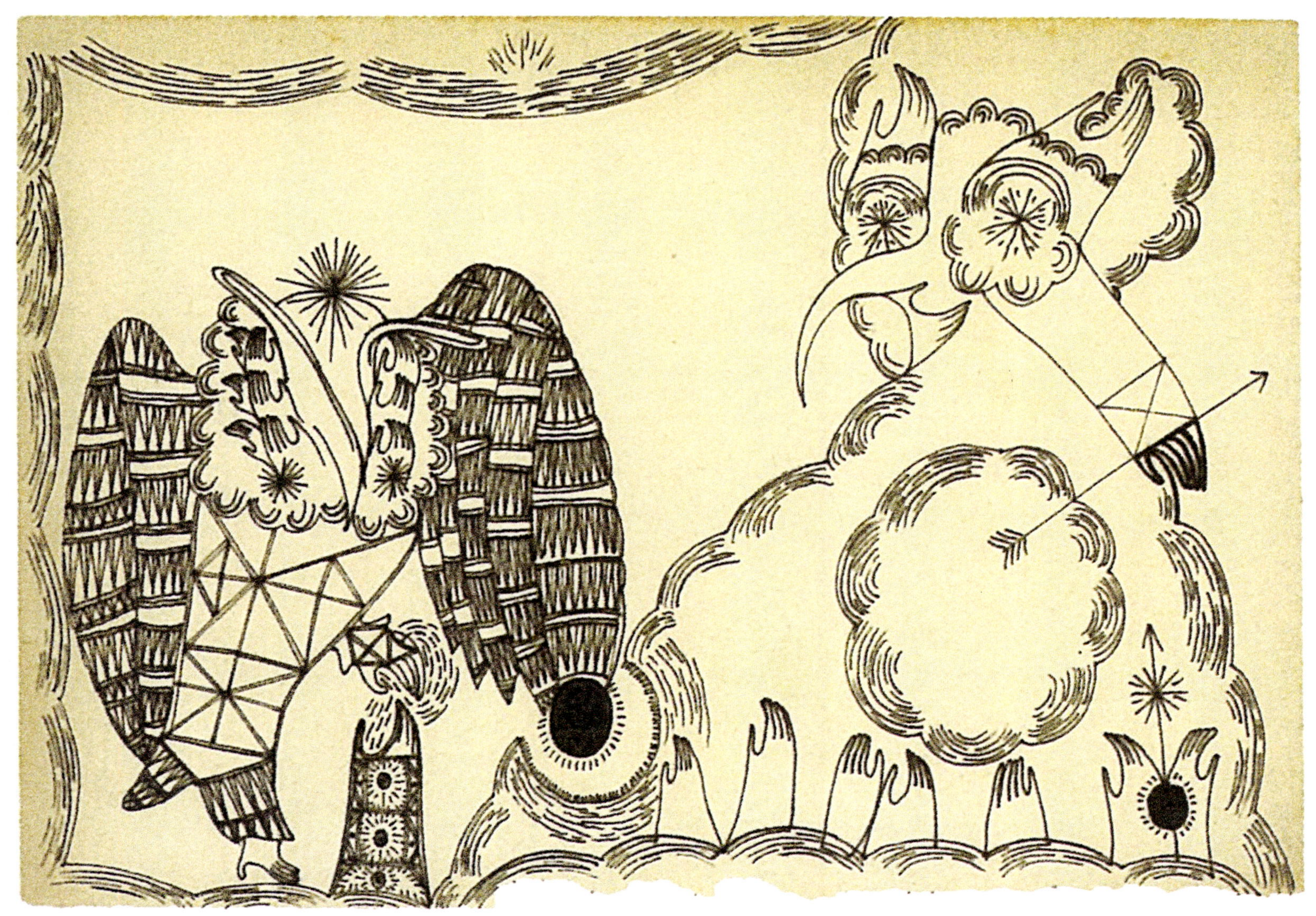

Untitled
2004
Ink on found book cover
13.7 x 19 cm
Courtesy of the Artist
and Deitch Projects, New York

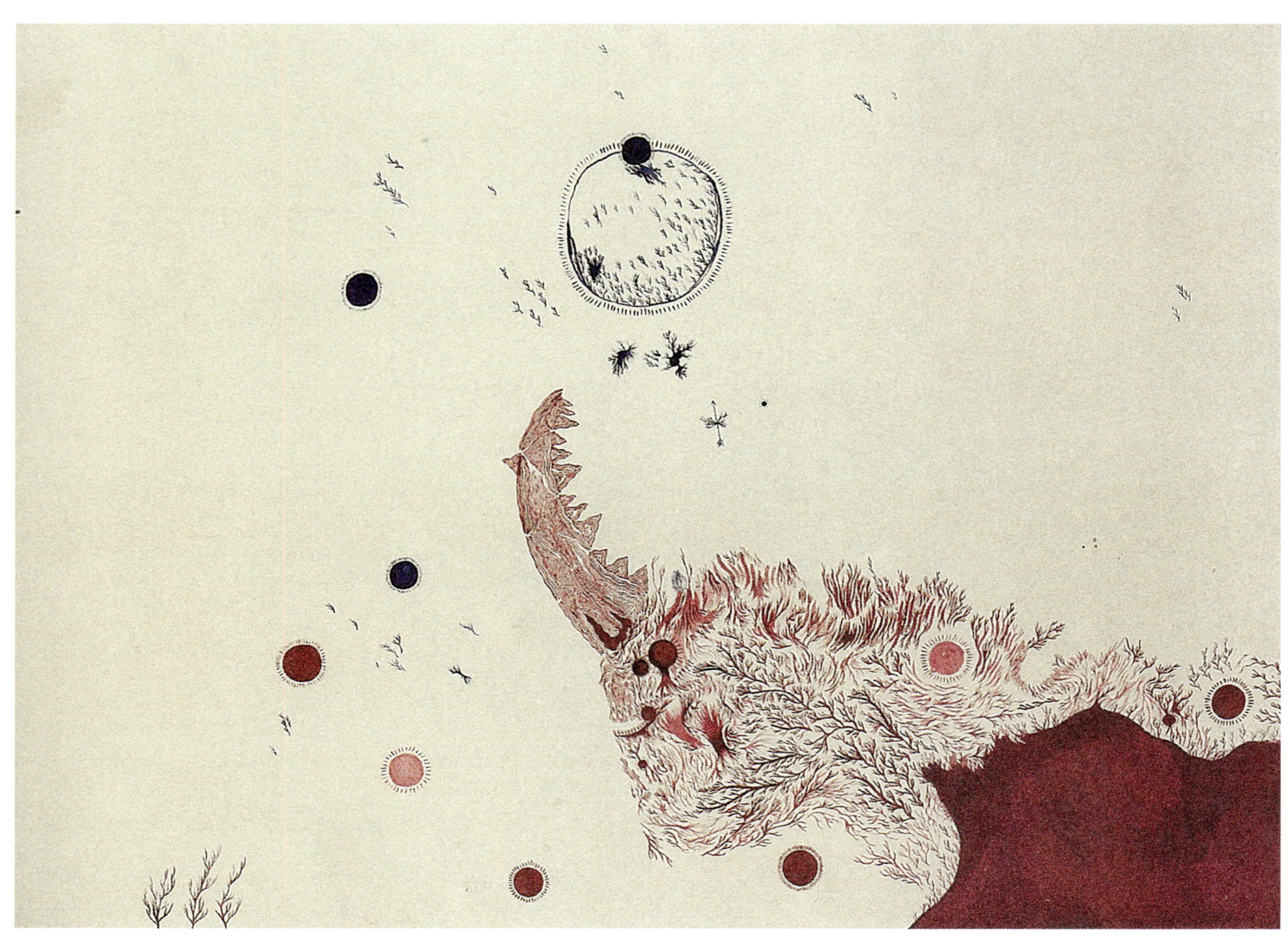

Untitled
2006
Ink on paper
56.39 x 75.44 cm
Courtesy of the Artist
and Deitch Projects, New York

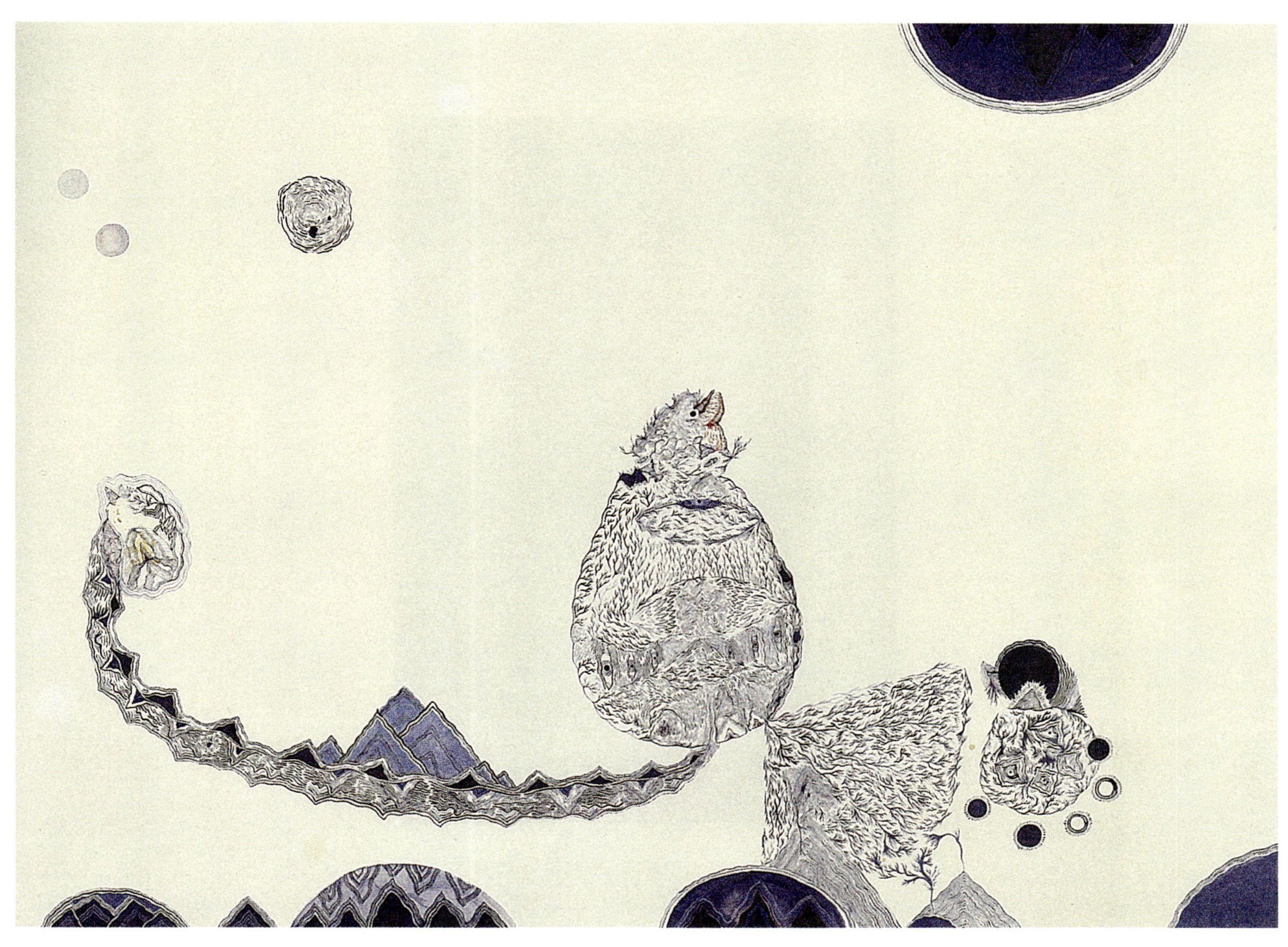

Untitled
2006
Ink on paper
56.39 x 75.44 cm
Courtesy of the Artist
and Deitch Projects, New York

DAVID BYR

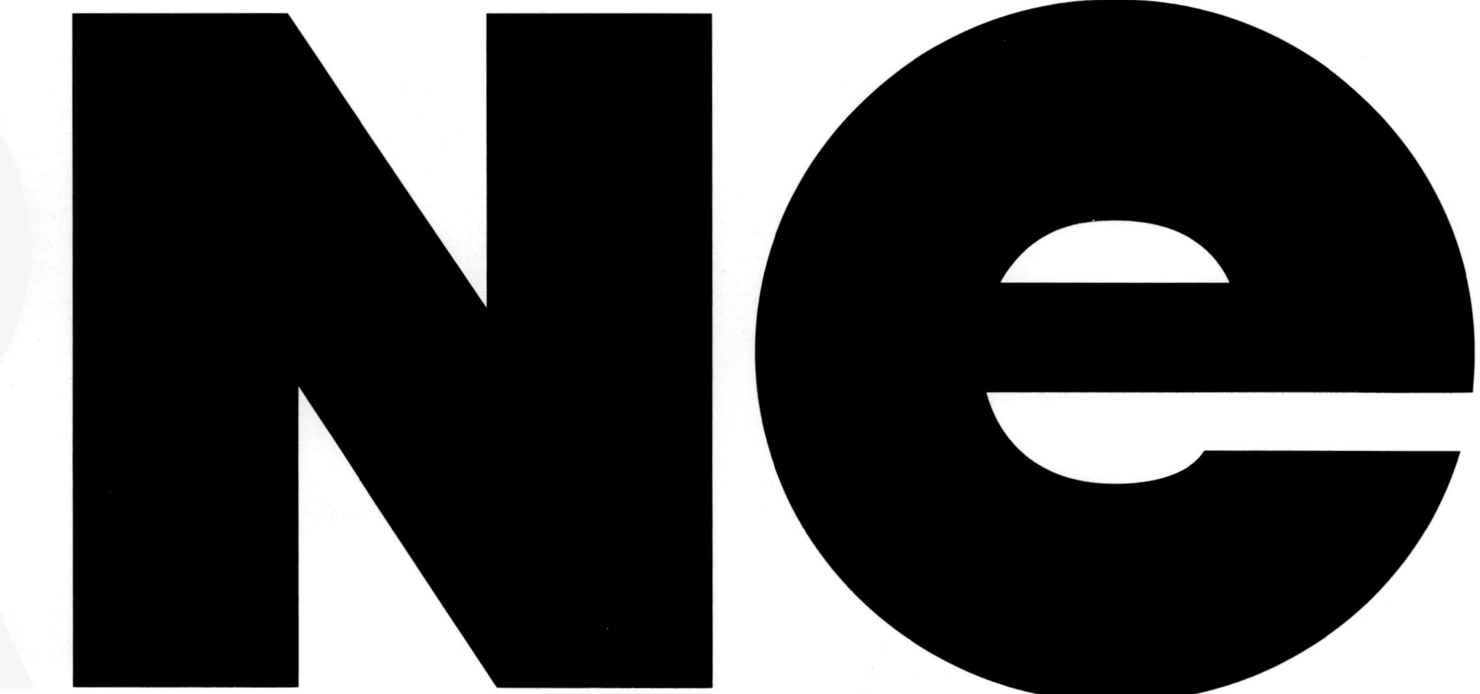

CRAZY HIDDEN TRUTHS

In 1974 David Byrne formed a band with two fellow art students. From the beginning, Talking Heads incorporated a striking visual component in their album art, performances, music videos, and stage design. The band went on to define pop music's new wave, and released a string of successful and critically acclaimed albums before splitting up in 1991. Throughout this period David Byrne worked on his own projects, as well as a variety of collaborations outside the band. 'My Life in the Bush of Ghosts', his pioneering 1981 album with Brian Eno, stands as an early example of sampling, and reflects his longstanding fascination with "world music" long before the genre label existed.

He has written scores for several films, including co-writing the score for Bernardo Bertolucci's 'The Last Emperor', which won an Oscar for Best Original Score in 1987.

As a photographer and artist David Byrne has exhibited in museums and galleries around the world. His visual art, like his music, transforms everyday objects into icons, raising the question that has been asked repeatedly throughout the 20th century: what is art? A strong emphasis on design and text in his artistic creations anchors them even further to daily reality. Byrne often exhibits in unconventional settings, exploring the link between public and private space. His most recent book, 'Arboretum', is a sketchbook facsimile of his 'tree drawings'; it was published by McSweeney's in September 2006.

— David Byrne was born in 1952 in Dumbarton, Scotland, and today lives in New York City.

DAVID BYRNE
INTERVIEWED BY DARIA DE BEAUVAIS

HOW WOULD YOU DEFINE YOUR MUSIC TODAY?

It depends on what project you're talking about. I did a score for a TV show that was based on Mormon hymns; a song cycle about Imelda Marcos, with Fatboy Slim; and a record of songs with Brian Eno. They're all completely different.

WHAT DO YOU FEEL IS THE FUTURE OF MUSIC?
Music will be fine. The traditional music business is in deep shit.

HOW IS MAKING MUSIC RELATED TO MAKING ART?
Obviously music is creative and bundles together ideas, emotions, craft, and technology, as does fine art. Those are the similarities. But there are huge differences. Fine art thrives on the rare, unique item. That is, for museums, collectors, and galleries, what makes it valuable and financially viable. Despite Walter Benjamin and the ideas of many others, the rarity and uniqueness of the art object is still what allows it to persist and thrive in the marketplace and elsewhere. That takes nothing away from art as a conveyer of ideas and emotions, but it makes it very different from music.

> Despite Walter Benjamin and the ideas of many others, the rarity and uniqueness of the art object is still what allows it to persist and thrive in the marketplace and elsewhere. That takes nothing away from art as a conveyer of ideas and emotions, but it makes it very different from music.

Music – not CDs or other fixed recordings – is evanescent. It's here and then it's gone. Not just hidden behind a wall or door, but gone forever. There's nothing left to buy or sell. Music is not fixed to the object that delivers it, in the way visual art is. The same music can be delivered in all sorts of ways, and it – the music – remains the same. Lastly, music is usually available to all and is more or less the same for all. No one can really own a musical experience and keep it for themselves.

YOU MAKE AND DRAW LOTS OF CHAIRS, AND SAID OF THEM RECENTLY, "MAYBE THEY ARE PORTRAITS, MAYBE SELF-PORTRAITS, MAYBE PORTRAITS OF MY INTERIOR STATE". WHAT ELSE IS THERE TO YOUR RELATIONSHIP WITH CHAIRS?

Chairs are so easy to anthropomorphize. They are more or less human-scale and they squat or crouch. We touch them and rub against them and they hug, cradle, and fondle us, or prod and attack us. I think drawing and making chairs is a kind of portraiture; whether self-portraiture or not I can't say.

YOUR PROJECT 'I LOVE POWERPOINT' IS QUITE FAMOUS NOW. HOW DID YOU COME TO CONSIDER THIS SOFTWARE AS A CREATIVE TOOL?

I realized it was a tool – a medium with limited but unique attributes – like any other. What makes it unique is the baggage it carries from the business and academic communities, where people use it every day and both love and loathe it. I began by trying to do a fake motivational speech, and realized the program could run on its own. Like a primitive kind of film or video medium.

CAN YOU EXPLAIN YOUR PROJECT, PRESENTED IN THE EXHIBITION 'ARBORETUM'?

I sensed that new ideas come out of logical leaps – connections made where there were none before. Often, connections are modeled in flow charts and branching tree-type diagrams, and I wondered whether, if I applied a non-rational logic to those forms, some deep connections and hidden connections might appear. Many were sketched and begun facetiously, but then sometimes some crazy hidden truths would emerge. Just recently I read a proposal that the drop in crime in the U.S. is related to the removal of lead additives in the gasoline. Turned around the other way, if one were to propose taking the lead out of gas as a way of solving the crime problem, they'd be viewed as a lunatic. But just like in this example, I sense there are connections that our intuition, senses, and heart know but that often remain invisible.

YOUR WORK CAN BE QUITE HUMOROUS, AND YOU SEEM TO BE AGAINST AN ELITIST VISION OF ART...

If art requires some prior knowledge to understand and appreciate, it limits itself to appreciation and consumption by an elite. I happen to like the taste of truffles, which are expensive, mainly due to their rarity. I know not everyone likes that weird, earthy flavor, so maybe that does make me elite, at least as far as my taste buds go. My parents, for example, might not like the taste at all. There are probably some artworks I enjoy that I only appreciate because I know their back-story. But mostly if it needs a theory or elaborate explanation to get it, then they can have it. Same goes with music. No doubt I have developed a taste for music that I didn't like as a teenager, but if you look, or listen, to my online streaming radio, I think my tastes have remained, for the most part, populist.

WHAT ARE YOUR CURRENT AND FUTURE PROJECTS?

Playing the Building and Voice of Julio. There is more information on current projects on my website, www.davidbyrne.com.

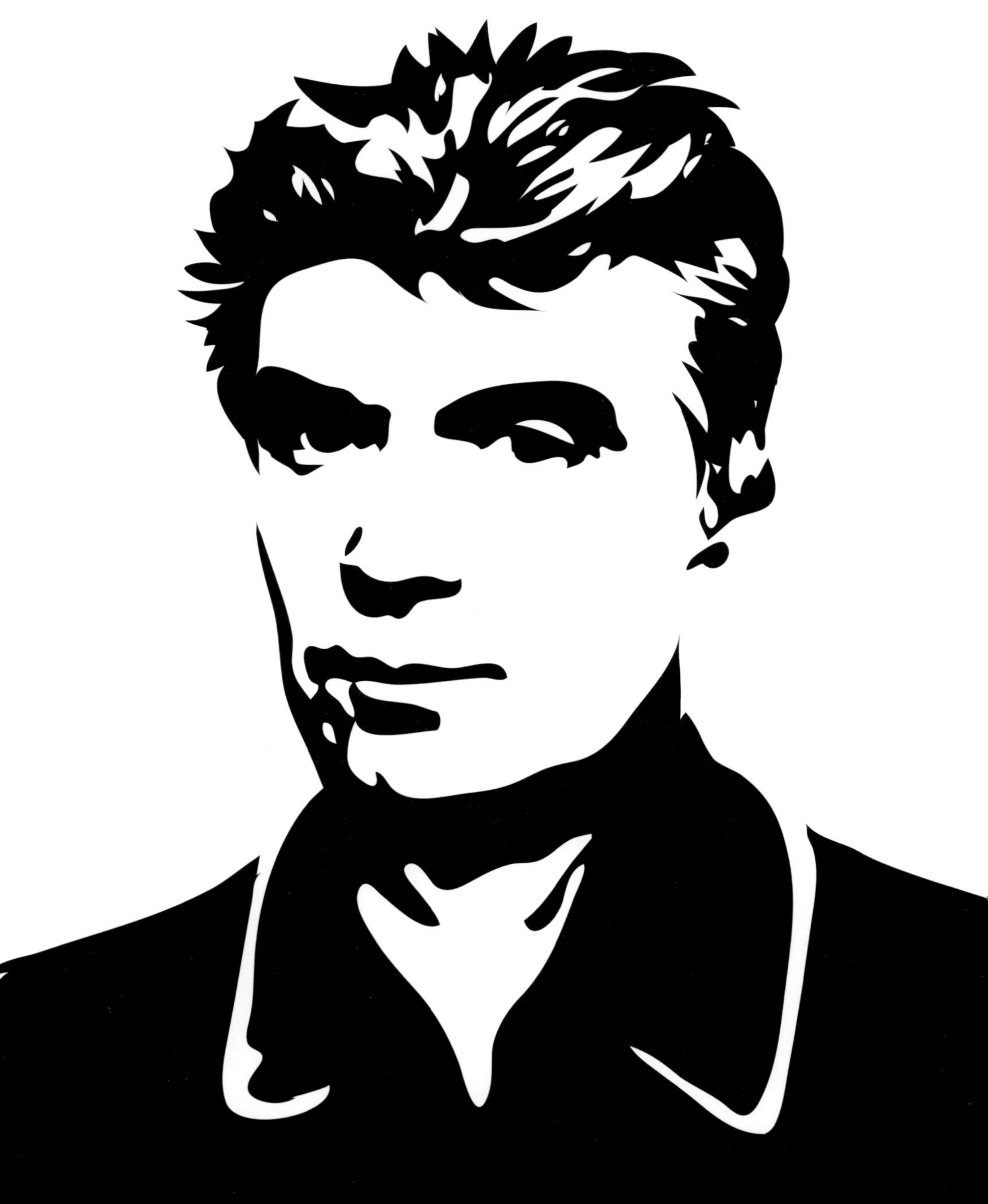

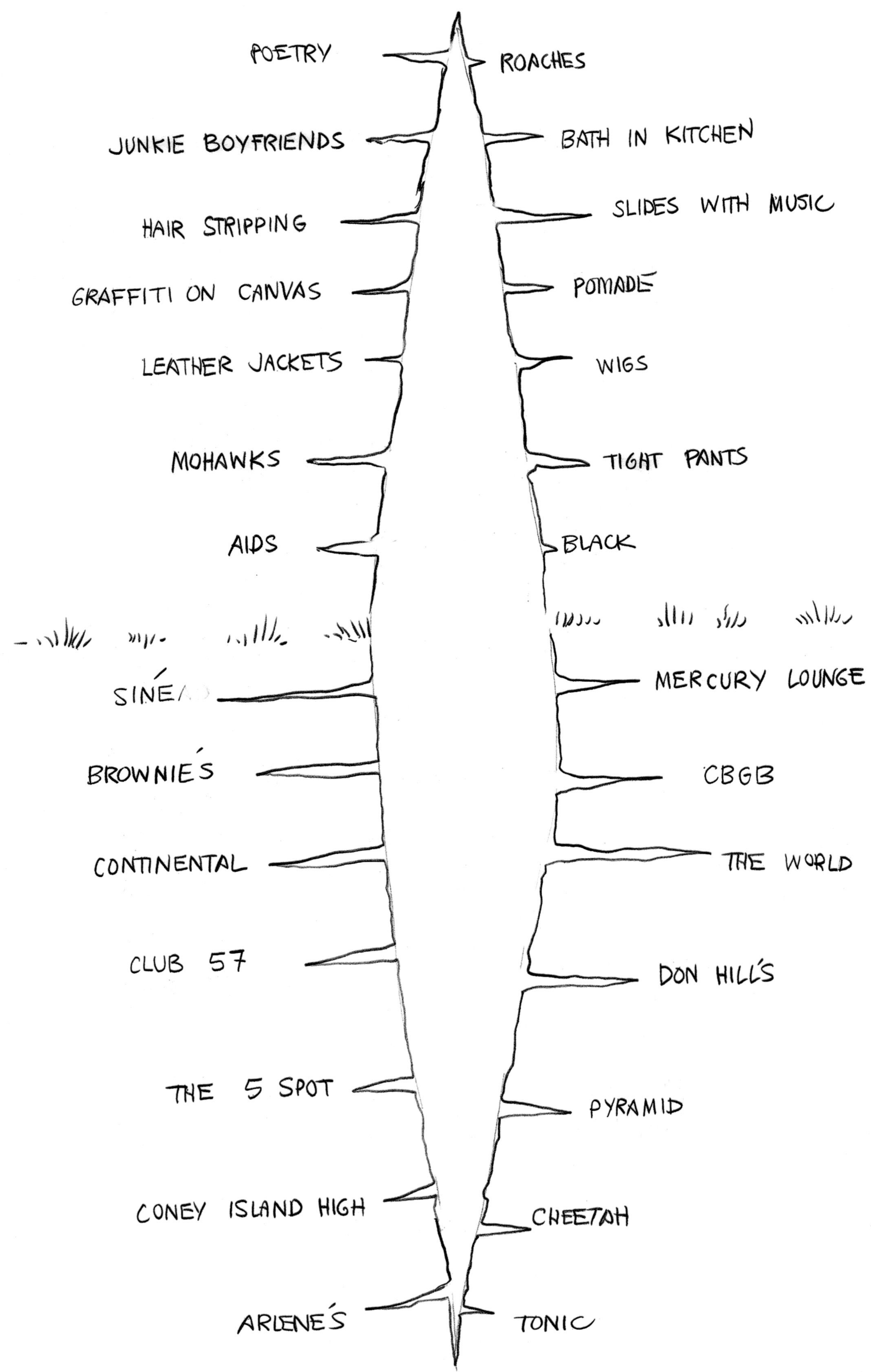

POETRY
ROACHES
JUNKIE BOYFRIENDS
BATH IN KITCHEN
HAIR STRIPPING
SLIDES WITH MUSIC
GRAFFITI ON CANVAS
POMADE
LEATHER JACKETS
WIGS
MOHAWKS
TIGHT PANTS
AIDS
BLACK
SINEAD
MERCURY LOUNGE
BROWNIE'S
CBGB
CONTINENTAL
THE WORLD
CLUB 57
DON HILL'S
THE 5 SPOT
PYRAMID
CONEY ISLAND HIGH
CHEETAH
ARLENE'S
TONIC

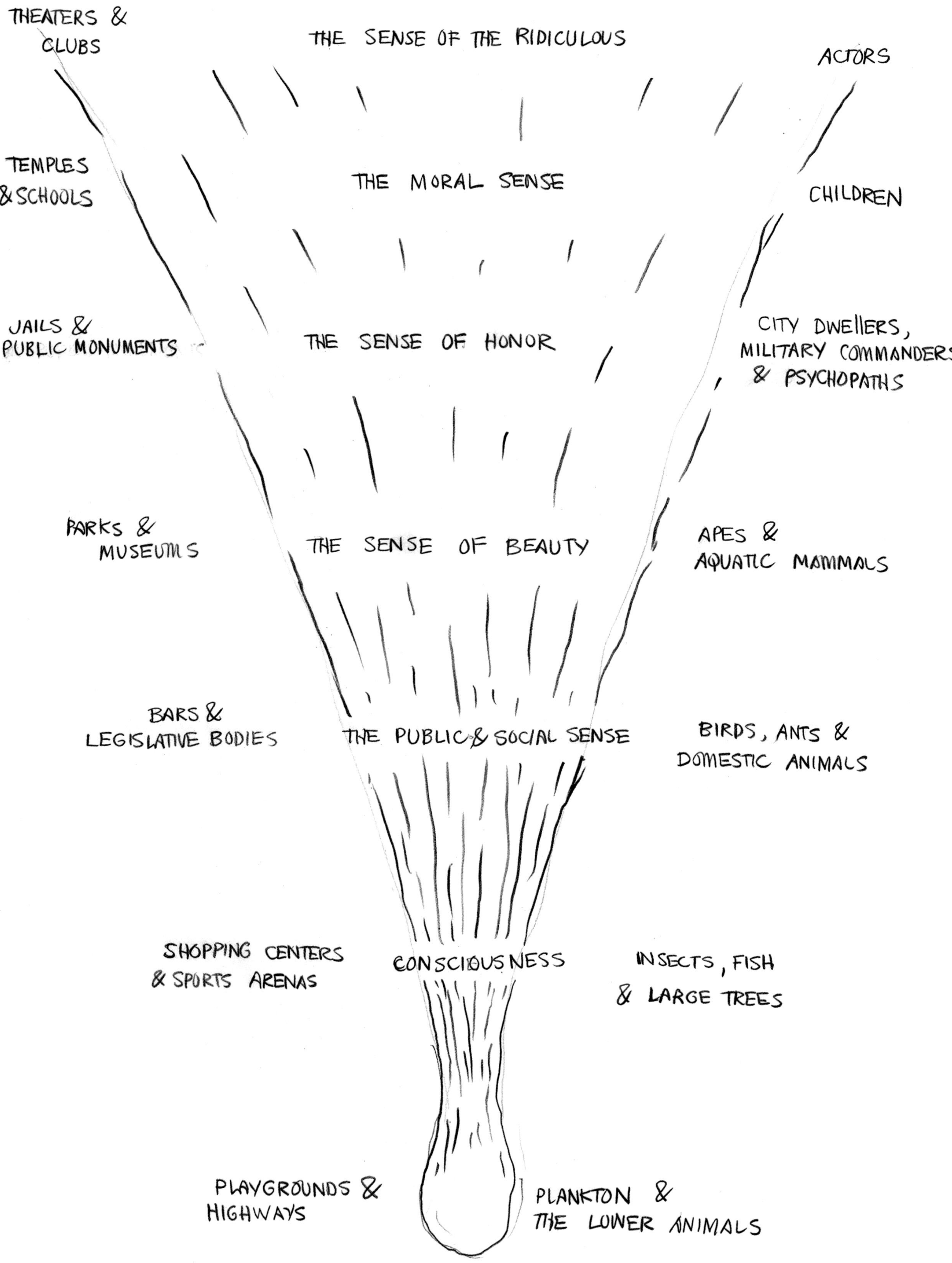

THEATERS & CLUBS
THE SENSE OF THE RIDICULOUS
ACTORS
TEMPLES & SCHOOLS
THE MORAL SENSE
CHILDREN
JAILS & PUBLIC MONUMENTS
THE SENSE OF HONOR
CITY DWELLERS, MILITARY COMMANDERS & PSYCHOPATHS
PARKS & MUSEUMS
THE SENSE OF BEAUTY
APES & AQUATIC MAMMALS
BARS & LEGISLATIVE BODIES
THE PUBLIC & SOCIAL SENSE
BIRDS, ANTS & DOMESTIC ANIMALS
SHOPPING CENTERS & SPORTS ARENAS
CONSCIOUSNESS
INSECTS, FISH & LARGE TREES
PLAYGROUNDS & HIGHWAYS
PLANKTON & THE LOWER ANIMALS

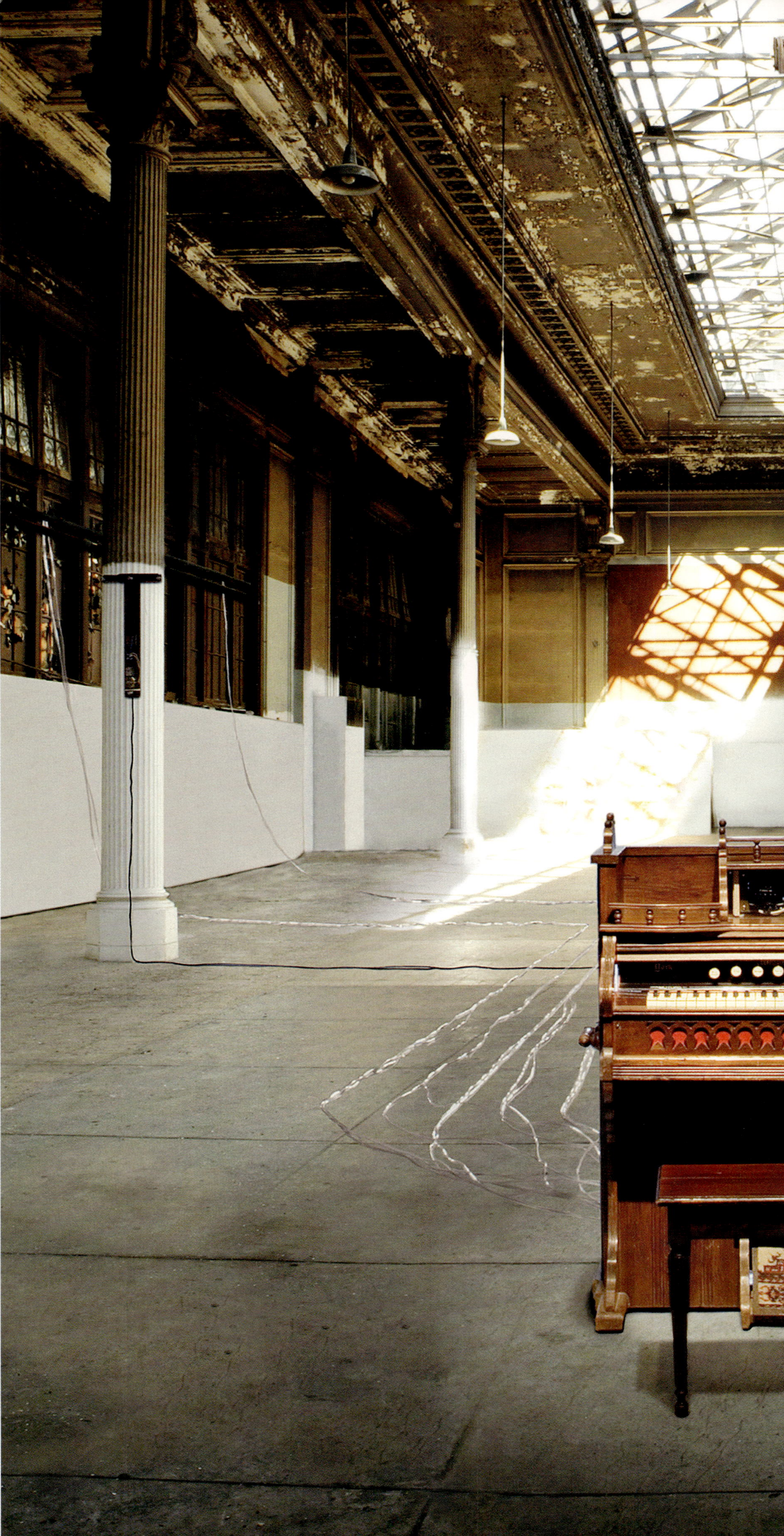

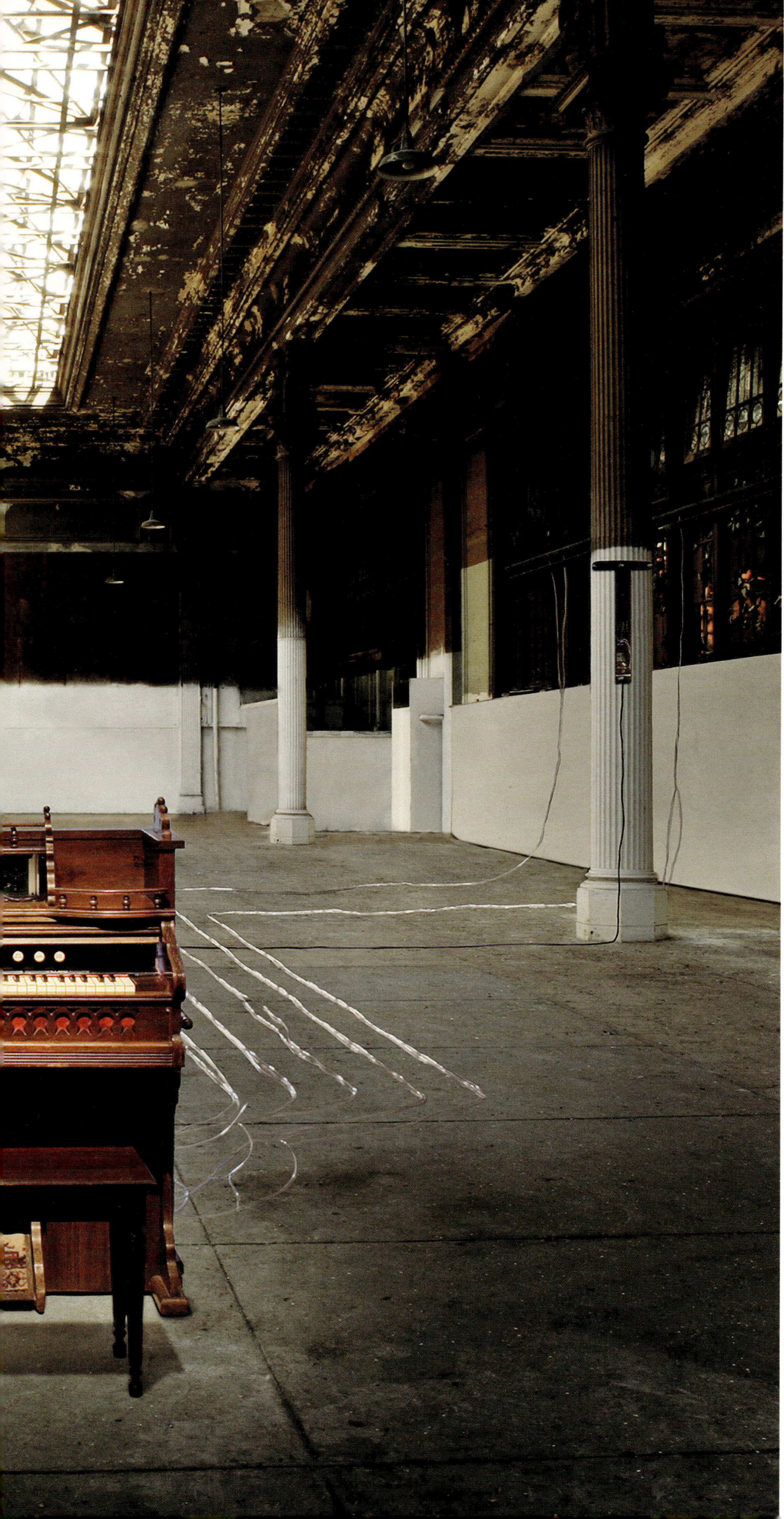

Playing the Building
2008
Digital rendering,
Courtesy Pace/MacGill Gallery, NYC
www.davidbyrne.com/art

BIANCA
CAS

ADY

I WANT A PENIS AND I WANT TO FLY

American sisters Bianca (Coco) and Sierra Casady (Rosie) form the musical duo CocoRosie, a psych-folk group (for lack of a better term) launched in 2003. Their highly poetic music is characterized by a unique mixture of lyrical song, gospel, and low-fi pop. Outside of CocoRosie, Bianca Casady pursues her own artistic practice. Her work encompasses a variety of mediums, including installations, performance, video, drawing, painting, and collages. "i assemble as I disassemble ancient values". In her colored compilations, human figures are placed alongside animals, the heads of corpses, balls – all recurring themes that constitute symbolic references to her own history, in which dreams play a particularly important and creative role.
— Bianca Casady was born in Hawaii in 1982, and lives in Paris.

**BIANCA CASADY
INTERVIEWED
BY AUDREY MASCINA**

YOU AND YOUR SISTER SIERRA DIDN'T SEE EACH OTHER FOR TEN YEARS BEFORE YOU VISITED HER IN PARIS. IS YOUR BAND COCOROSIE THE SYMBOL OF YOUR REUNION?
Our music created a marriage that at first I resisted, but as I have given in to it, it has brought so many gifts.

WHEN YOU STARTED RECORDING 'LA MAISON DE MON RÊVE' IN SIERRA'S BATHROOM IN PARIS DID YOU HAVE ANY PRECISE IDEA OF THE SOUND AND MUSIC YOU WANTED TO DO?
Only poetic images. We didn't consider what we were making [as] music. We were making little movies.

YOUR MOTHER IS A VISUAL ARTIST. DID THAT LEAD YOU TO BE AN ARTIST YOURSELF?
I'll never know what I would have been if my parents were accountants. I often wonder. My mother gave me my own section of the studio around the age of nine. I'm sure this gave me a head start.

DID YOU COLLABORATE WITH HER?
Yes, I do. She made the giant red bone in my recent show at Deitch. Also we made some videos together, and a few paintings. We share a world of beauty. I make the ugly stuff alone.

YOUR MOTHER IS A NATIVE AMERICAN, AND YOU SPENT MUCH OF YOUR CHILDHOOD ON AN INDIAN RESERVATION WITH YOUR FATHER. MOST OF YOUR DRAWINGS AND PAINTINGS SEEM TO RECALL BITS OF THOSE TIMES. WOULD YOU SAY THAT YOUR VISUAL WORK DRAWS ON THOSE MEMORIES?
My childhood was very diverse in terms of the climate. Nature and ritual was a part of my family life and has surfaced in a lot of my work, as well as memories of born-again Christian neighborhoods in the suburbs, etc. I work based on my dreams. Most of my installations are chaotic depictions of dreams and shattered memories, many things incongruous and inappropriate. Fantasy is always a little river running across my landscapes.

> Fashion and "identity" have always been the first mode of expression and self-exploration. "Am I a boy; am I a girl?" is a constant question. Is God a boy; is God a girl?

YOUR MUSIC AND ARTWORK ARE BOTH IMPRINTED WITH A CHILDLIKE ATMOSPHERE SOMEWHERE BETWEEN MAGIC, MYTHOLOGY, AND SEX. DO YOU INTEND TO MAKE ANY STATEMENTS THROUGH THOSE DIFFERENT SURFACES OF EXPRESSION?
Slowly pushing toward freedom, spiritual freedom.

BEYOND DRAWINGS, PAINTINGS, AND INSTALLATIONS, YOUR OWN TRANSFORMATION IN DIFFERENT CHARACTERS — OFTEN BOY ONES, LIKE MAD VICKY, RED BONE SLIM, WEE WILLY, GOLDEN BOY SLIM — SEEMS TO TAKE CENTER STAGE IN YOUR ARTISTIC PROCESS. WHAT ARE THE ROLES OF THOSE CHARACTERS?
Fashion and "identity" have always been the first mode of expression and self-exploration. "Am I a boy; am I a girl?" is a constant question. Is God a boy; is God a girl?

YOU'VE DONE THE COVERS AND ARTWORK FOR COCOROSIE. DO YOU WORK FOR OTHER MUSICIANS AS WELL?
Through my label, Voodoo-EROS, I have presented artists with aspects of my own art, and in collaboration with my label partner Melissa Shimkovitz. The whole world of Voodoo-EROS started with one of my drawings, which became the cover of the record The Enlightened Family.

WHO ARE THE VISUAL CONTEMPORARY ARTISTS YOU FEEL CLOSE TO?
Jim Drain, Henry Darger, Pierre et Gilles.

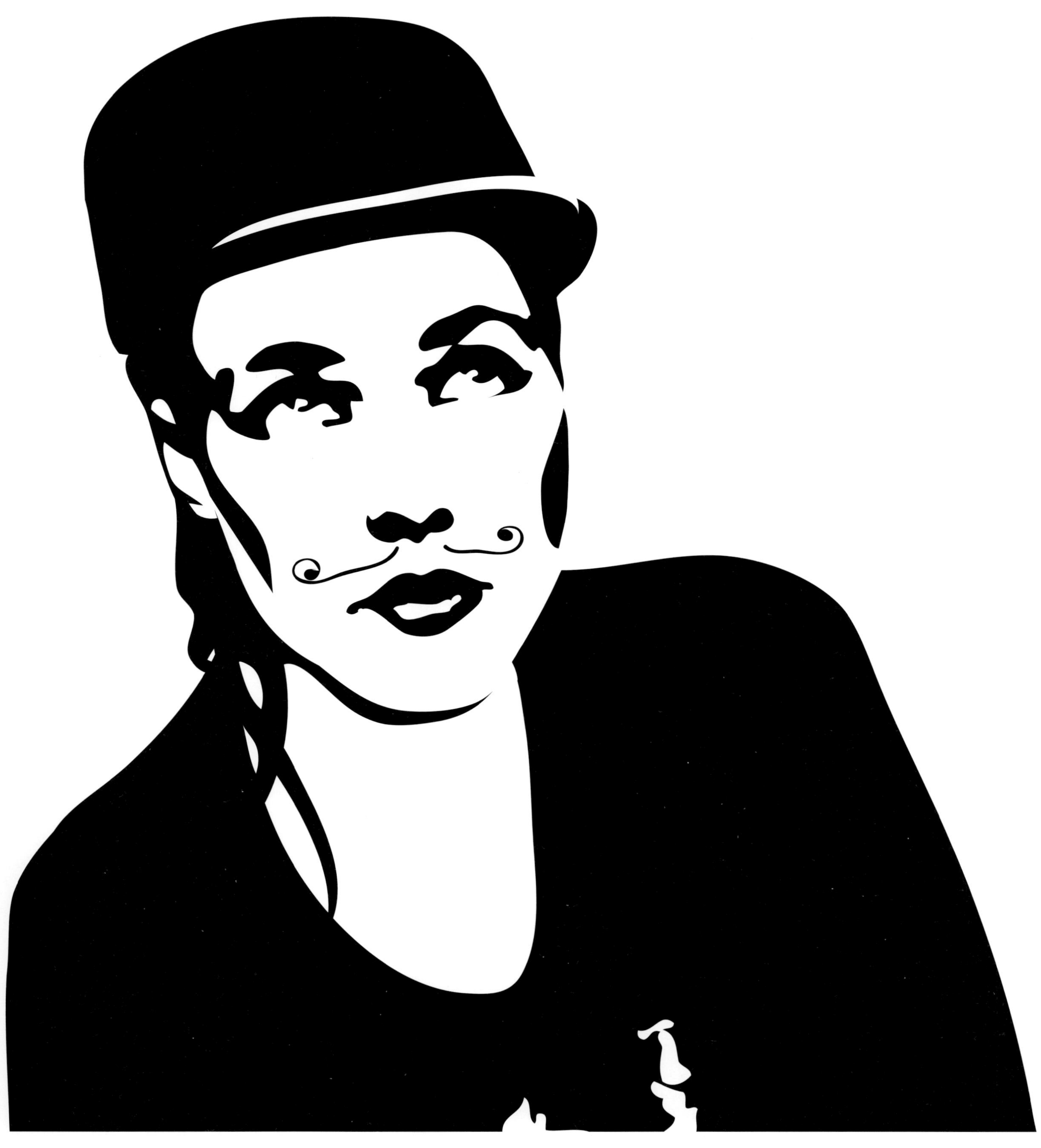

VOODO-EROS SIGNED YOUR SISTER'S NEW BAND, METALLIC FALCONS. WHAT IS YOUR GOAL FOR THIS LABEL? HOW MANY ARTISTS DO YOU REPRESENT?

We mostly represent trannies. They're always coming and going. The community is in constant transition.

YOU JUST OPENED A GALLERY IN PARIS CALLED MAD VICKY'S TEA GALLERY, WHOSE SPIRIT IS LIKE YOUR INSTALLATIONS — A GATHERING OF CLOTHES, OBJECTS, ARTWORKS; A REFUGE. BUT YOU ALSO HAVE A SPACE IN NEW YORK CALLED VOODOO-EROS MUSEUM OF NICE ITEMS, WHICH IS ASSOCIATED WITH YOUR RECORD LABEL. WHAT PROMPTED YOU TO OPEN SPACES ON YOUR OWN?

I've always wanted a clubhouse. A place for secret tranny discos. It was time.

DO YOU CONSIDER THOSE SPACES AS INSTALLATIONS?

Yes.

WHAT ARE YOUR UPCOMING PROJECTS?

CocoRosie is working on a fourth album… I'm working on a book of very personal work concerning the end of time and the cosmos… Mixing tea and having many gatherings and workshops at the new gallery… and I have a show in Italy in November.

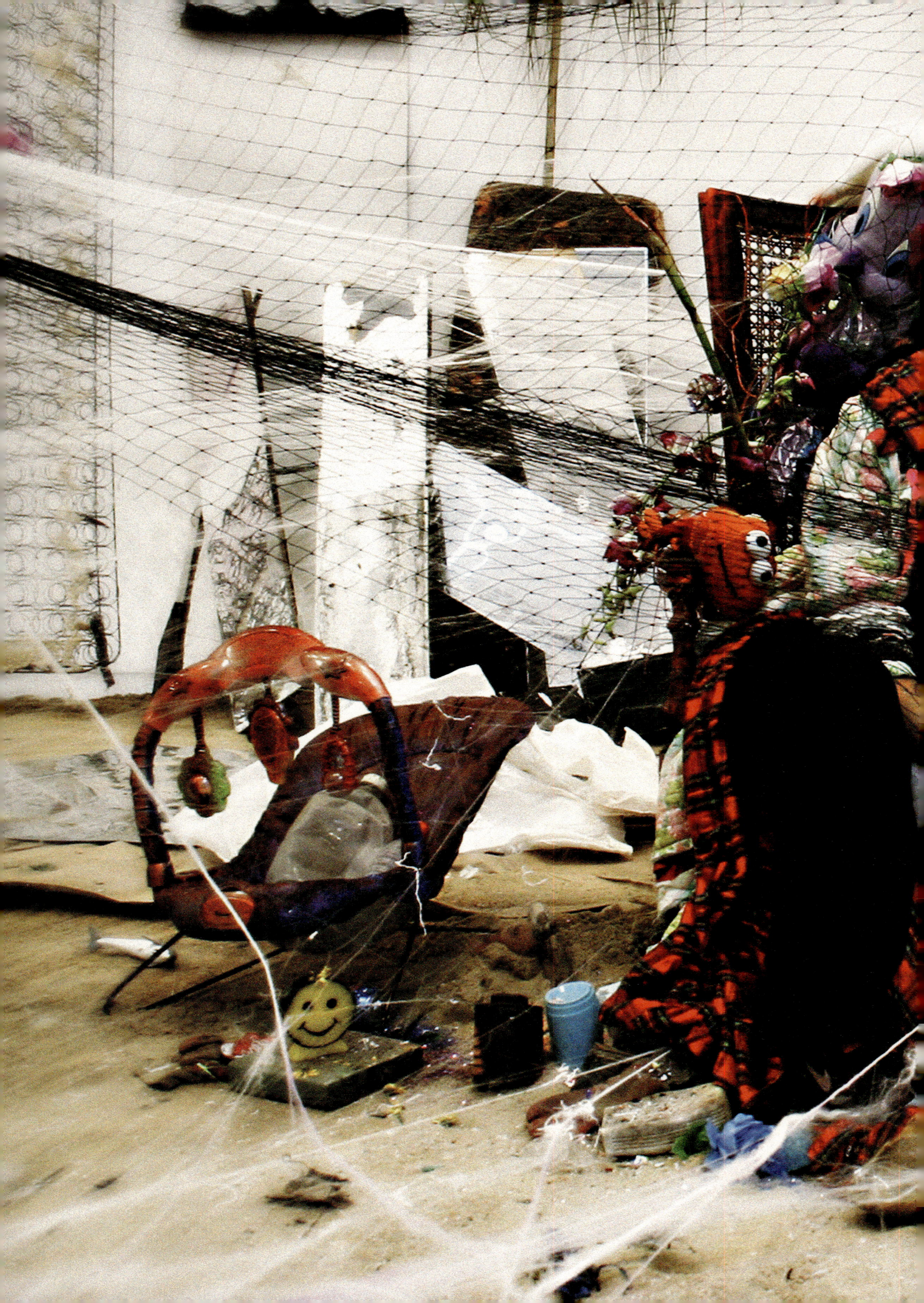

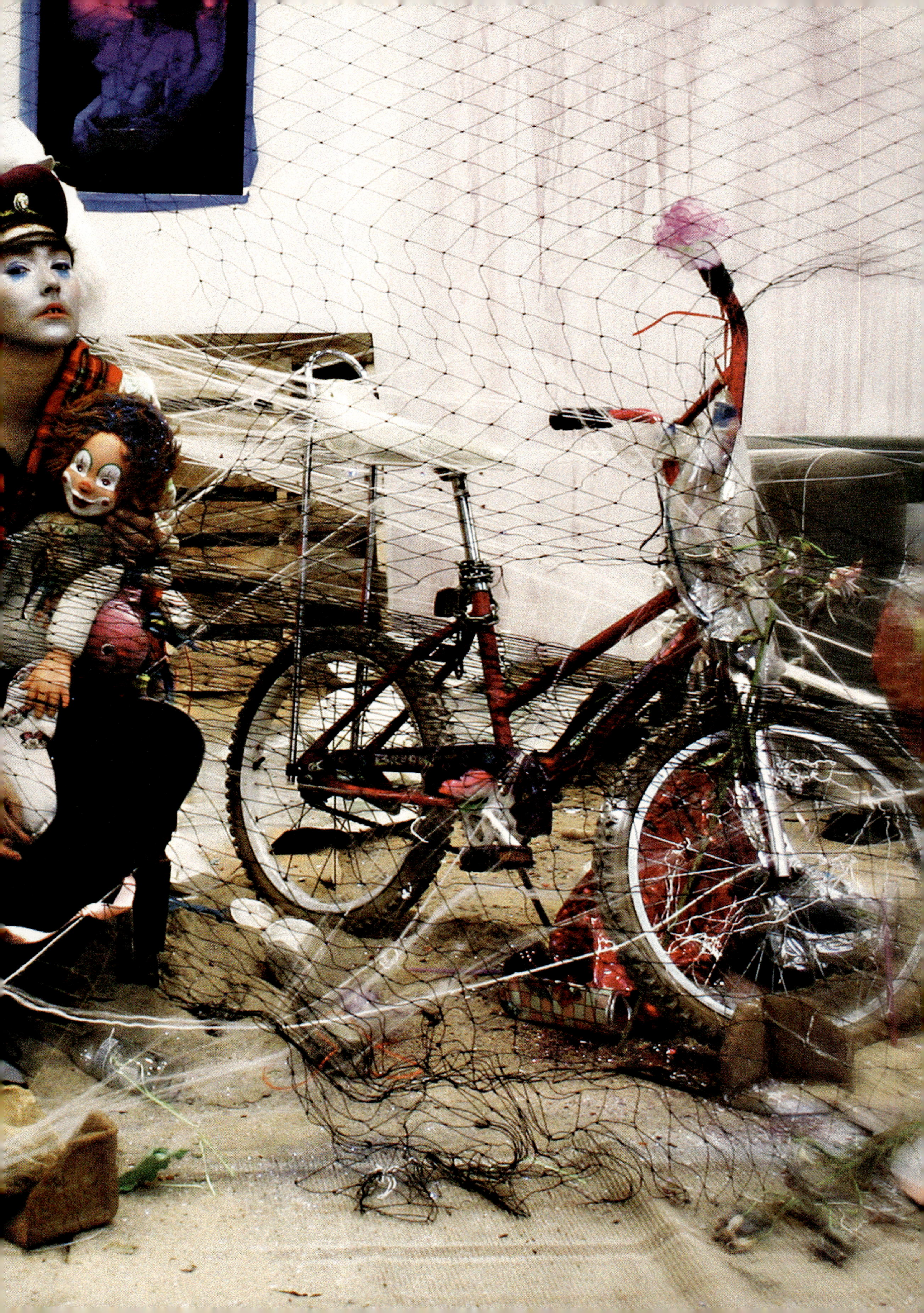

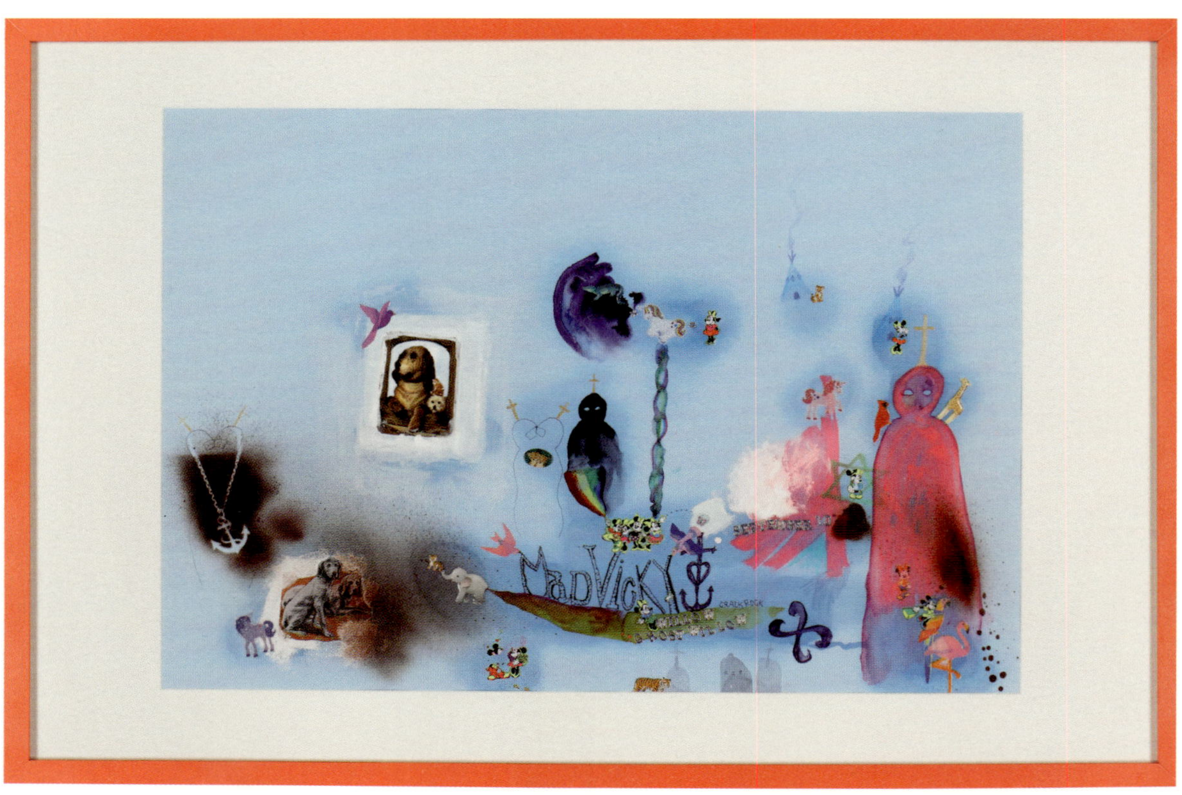

Page 70/71
Bianca Casady Portrait
Courtesy of the Artist
and Deitch Projects, New York
Photo Credit © Tom Powel Imaging,

Willow Ghost Willow
2007
Mixed Media
49.53 x 69.85cm
Courtesy of the Artist
and Deitch Projects, New York
Photo Credit © Tom Powel Imaging,

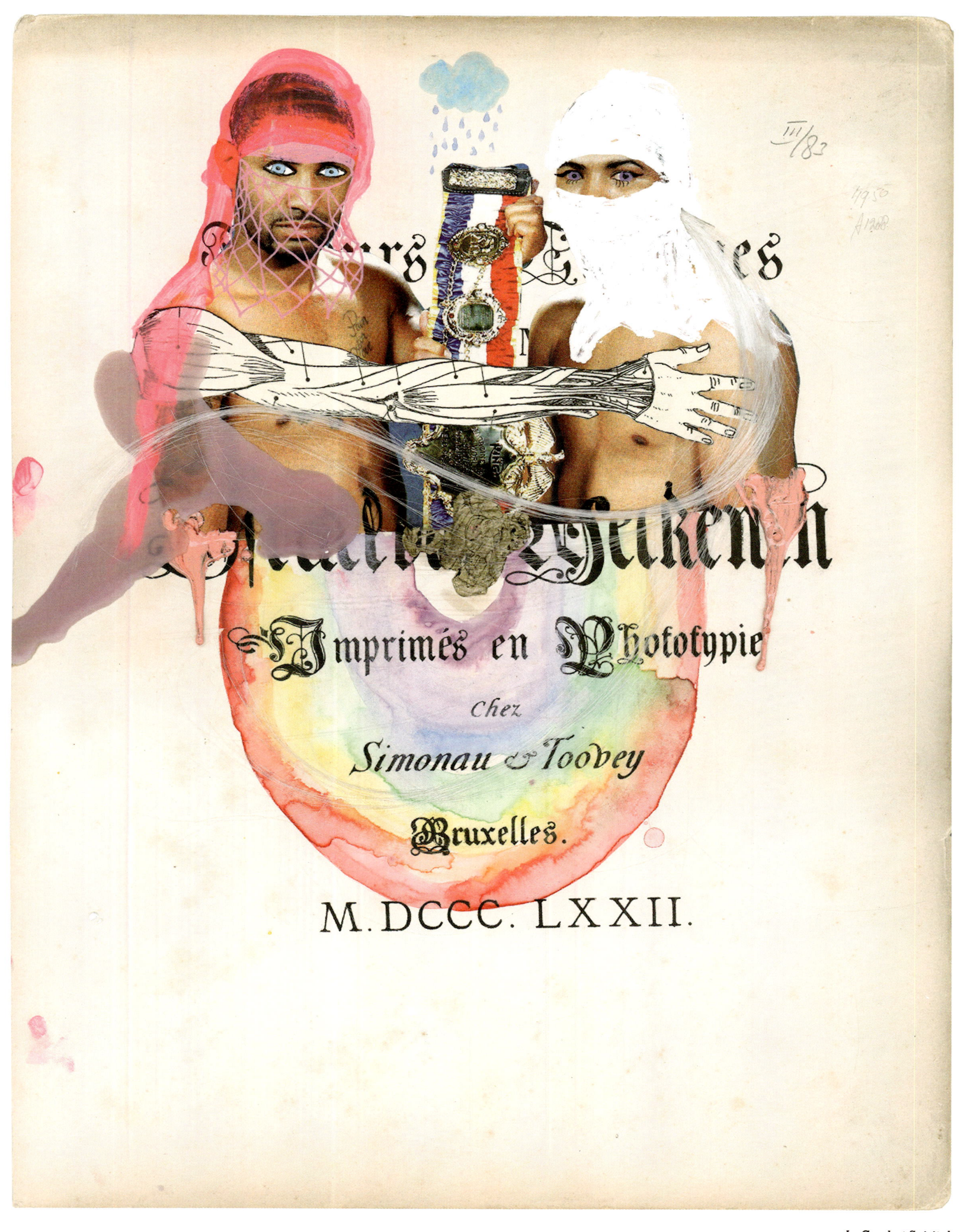

Le Combat Spirital
April 2008
Collage on cardboard,
mixed media and hair
35,9 x 27,4 cm
Courtesy of the Artist
and Stichting Wall House #2
Photo Credit © Bianca Casady

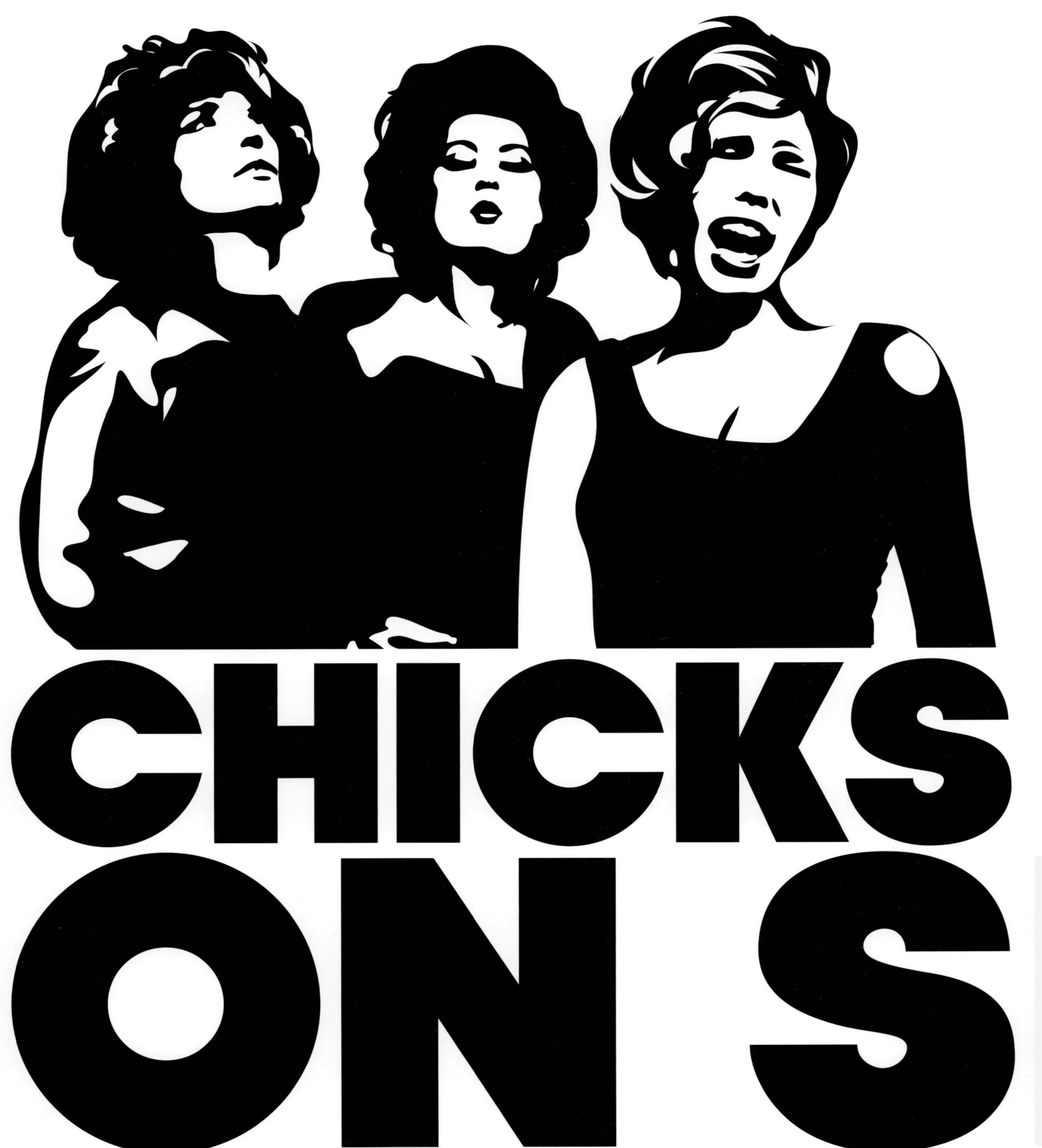
CHICKS
ON S

peeD

The international clan of creative collaborators called Chicks on Speed is centered around two main protagonists, Alex Murray-Leslie and Melissa Logan. Artists such as Douglas Gordon, Kathi Glas, Anat Ben David, and A.L. Steiner are current participants in the duo's free-spirited projects, and are very much "Chicks" in their own right. Formed in 1997 in Munich, where Melissa and Alex were studying fine art, the group has never stopped exploring new frontiers. As interested in music as in fashion and plastic art, the collective celebrates a cabaret spirit in which their roles and costumes know no limits. The DIY philosophy characterizes their creative process, and their indefinable music – as rock as it is electro – merges with their visual identity, inseparable from the production of their live shows. Visual work by Chicks on Speed includes video, photography, collage, textile banners, poetry, and sloganeering… the fine art on the edge of cottage industry, sculpture blobs on the verge of industrial design.
— Melissa Logan was born in 1970 in Spring Valley, NY (USA) and currently lives in Hamburg.
— Alex Murray-Leslie was born in 1970 in Bowral, Australia, and lives in Barcelona.

CHICKS ON SPEED (MELISSA LOGAN AND ALEX MURRAY-LESLIE) INTERVIEWED BY JÉRÔME SANS

AS A GIRLS' BAND, WHY DID YOU CHOOSE THIS NAME CHICKS ON SPEED?

Alex: Melissa and I met at The Akademie der Bildenden Künste München in 1997. Melissa was studying painting, and I was studying jewelry with Otto Kuenzli. Kiki [Moorse], whom we met one year later, was a stylist for Vogue/Conde Nast. We began working together as a way of survival in a very bourgeois, sometimes boring town. The necessity to bring people together in a socio-political party context was initially what pushed us to start Seppi Bar, followed by Chicks on Speed. The name: Melissa and I made a series of 25 watercolor/mixed-media collages in one night – the next day they were to be sold to a bank in Munich. We needed a group name; Chicks on Speed was the obvious choice!

Melissa: We didn't realize we were all girls at the time, and only later got in touch with the fact that just doing what you want can become political, and is the actual basis of politics. At the moment there is a strong focus on feminism. The name at the time was fun because the art scene in Munich was too serious. We definitely broke that. The art circuit was quite slow and we jumped onto the pop train, doing all the mainstream kitsch, then using the videos for installations, and exposing ourselves as an experiment, to be pulled into as diverse situations as possible.

The realms of music became more interesting to move within, rather than the white-box fine art gallery. The latter seemed elitist, confined, and secluded to the public eye. We decided to become a pop group. Our name was made for music and we had to go there. Not an arty-farty band, but one that would function in the music world.

HOW DID YOU START?

Alex: With limited editions, 7-inches [records], and tapes. As a foreign student in Germany, you really have to work to make a living, and I started working at Ultraschall, an electronic-

OPEN TO
OF CATAS

music nightclub. Melissa and Kiki would come by and help me stamp the hands of ravers. We got to know a lot of DJs. There was a total lack of female musicians, and this frustrated us and pushed us to start making music. We began collecting samples and sounds, and put them onto tapes as audio collages. Tape A was titled 'I Wanna Be a DJ… Baby', and we released it on Stop Records, our analog internet tape label at the time. We ended up working with many of the people we met in the beginnings at Ultraschall. Some of those people were Anthony 'Shake' Shakir, DJ Hell, Miss Kittin, Acid Maria, Upstart, Juergen Soeder, Tobi Neumann, Gerhard Potuznik, Christian Vogel, Christopher Just, and Fred Schneider (B52's).

WHAT IS CHICKS ON SPEED ABOUT?

Melissa: We started as an art clan, not a pop group, and never a band. With us it's spontaneous, and the hierarchy is not defined. It's something that is growing. With our show 'Chicks on Speed: It's a Project', at Deitch Projects in New York [in April 2004], we brought over a whole team of assistants who became part of the clan – even Jeffrey Deitch was a clan member – working intensively together for two weeks. It is imperative for us to work in a democratic way, even if we are the nucleus.

The group is open to editions and exploring unknown territories. The idea of working together is all about the project, the process, what one learns, and the way in which a group of individuals can influence culture and the betterment of the world. Actually, we start doing things and see where they lead. We are open to any kind of catastrophes.

IS THERE A MANIFESTO BEHIND CHICKS ON SPEED, OR ANY SPECIFIC ISSUES THAT YOU REACH?

Melissa: There are a lot of them but we don't like to define our patterns of thinking too much – when we do we usually contradict ourselves, because even our own "rules" are there to break. Parallel to this is the idea that we would limit ourselves to patterns and systems that already exist if we define what we are doing. We prefer to do – and especially to dare to do – things without understanding the outcome. We have learnt now that a lot of ideas behind sociology or philosophy are developed through doing, and then the theory gets worked out later.

Alex: We also think that if something can't be said in one sentence, it can't be sold. Fuck the rules! We may take off our skirts but we won't wear any guys' pants!

HOW WOULD YOU DEFINE YOUR MUSIC?

Alex: We see ourselves as a project, more than a band. Everything is possible; why stop with music? In music terms, you could say it's arty electronic-based pop, ranging from Euro-trash kitsch to difficult experimental sound-pieces, using handmade instruments and found sounds. Some music journalists like to refer to us as part of Larry T's "electroclash" movement from 2003, which is ok, too! We've been part of many different trends in art, music, and fashion over the last 11 years; that's part of the game! Our work as an entirety functions on diverse levels – as entertainment and as intellectual, political, social stimulation. Our recent works in performance art and live pop spectacles include living sculptures, super suits to wear which trigger sounds, giant-sized projected video loops, and hand-crafted, high-heeled shoe guitars. We're definitely into blurring the lines between cross-genre DIY performance, through our usage of art, fashion, video, pop music, DIY instruments, and architecture.

ARE YOU DEVELOPING A GLOBAL PROJECT?

Melissa: The word 'global' has become associated with the human-rights and environmental law abusers. Yes, we are international and ever-growing but our goal is not to become huge and take over; we concentrate on developing cultural expression. The intensity is more important to us than size. We see the Chicks on Speed as a mutating creative monster, a virus, spreading into all mediums as loudly and colorfully as possible.

IN YOUR LAST SINGLE, 'ART RULES', YOU MAKE FUN OF THE ART WORLD. IN YOUR PREVIOUS ALBUM, '99 CENTS', YOU CRITICIZED THE CONSUMPTION-DRIVEN NATURE OF FASHION. AND AT THE SAME TIME THE ART AND FASHION WORLDS SEEM TO INCLUDE YOU SOMEHOW…

ANY KIND TROPHES

Melissa: 'Art Rules' is an arty party song sticking out our tongue at the silly clichés of the art world. At the same time, it debuts at MoMA, Centre Pompidou, and Tate Modern. Of course we are not allowed to do this because we are part of it, a kind of Jean Baudrillardian twist using insider name-dropping and irony as the tools of demystifying and disempowering "inside trading" and elitism. Through this cheekiness, we are hoping for an openness to change. Stupid power structures should really be looked down upon and not just passed by as "oh that's just the way the art world works". This is our art world. We are the artists and curators, art dealers, and the institutions. We should be working together to bring out great work that will move humanity further, and not tolerate the institutes being marketing platforms for collectors. You know, in the U.S.A. a lot of the major institutions don't bother paying artists screening fees; they say – in this case, the New Museum – that it is good for the artists to show their work, as if the artists are a marketing ploy.

Alex: Craft plays an important role in the evolution of C.O.S. fashion and plastic arts. Activist crafting isn't a new concept: inspired by Jane Addams, late 1800's. We see ourselves as craftists, like folk musicians, reinventing craft and carrying on a tradition. We also see craft through a feminist perspective, a re-think of the 1970s equation that domesticity equals oppression. The patchworks we make are a celebration of feminism and craft, a lifeline thread reoccurring through our work over the last 11 years. Patchwork in sound, recycling and the construction of clothing, sloganeering banners – like on the cover of 'Fashion Rules', photographed by Karl Lagerfeld – to the super-sophisticated patchworks (made with Kathi Glas), now incorporated into all facets of C.O.S., from the Girl Monster installation banner to our exhibitions, homewares, and art outfits made for stage. After the fashion industry we needed to choose a new target. Art, which is even bigger and more

> We see the Chicks on Speed as a mutating creative monster, a virus, spreading into all mediums as loudly and colorfully as possible.

monstrous, was an obvious target. As Franz Liebl wrote, "it's always been part of C.O.S. subversive strategy to beat adversaries with their own weapons. They now fight the art market with art, and museums are their operating theatre". It's a love/hate relationship.

YOUR LIVE SHOWS RESIDE BETWEEN ART PERFORMANCES AND CABARET SHOWS. HOW DO YOU APPROACH YOUR CONCERTS?

Alex: For the moment it is more cabaret than performance, but it also goes back and forth. Sometimes it's mutating into a rock show. The visual side is actually totally cabaret, clownesque. It goes more and more in that way. Like in our book, we can play any role, any character. We can be actors or expressionist dancers. We want to mix up the roles.

YOU HAVE BEEN PARTICIPATING IN MANY GROUP AND SOLO EXHIBITIONS, AND DID A MAJOR ONE AT THE CAC IN VILNIUS LAST YEAR. HOW HAS YOUR VISION OF INSTALLATIONS AND EXHIBITIONS EVOLVED SINCE YOUR BEGINNINGS?

Melissa: The ideas we started working on in 1997 are still the same. Because of the large exhibition spaces and time spent on research and production, the scale is larger and technology is a lot more advanced. Early collage work has developed into 15-meter-long murals; our anti-instrument performances have become "object instruments"; videos have become eight-screen audiovisual triggered installations of tight loops and butt smacks. The love/hate relationship to fashion has became a shoe fuck, the channel logo a brainwashing device we use during lectures, for trend-hunters and futurologists. We use the audience as a performance tool. The exhibition space becomes a campground, clothes become a manifesto, the curator becomes the performer, and video becomes a spaceship slipping through the pile of bodies and cables, propelling the moment to be the future and the past at the same time. The moment sticks and you feel alive and finally can sense home.

YOU RECENTLY COLLABORATED WITH DOUGLAS GORDON, WHO BECAME A PROPER MEMBER OF CHICKS ON SPEED, WITH YOUR SINGLE 'ART RULES', A VIDEO AND A WHOLE LIVE PERFORMANCE. WHAT IS THE STORY OF THIS COLLABORATION?

Alex: I met Douglas at an opening he was having in Barcelona with Augustin Perez Rubio, head curator at the MUSAC in Leon, Spain. He [Rubio] said, "You have to meet Douglas", and dragged me across the stark white gallery space, where I found stylish Doug, dressed in a very fashionable trench coat, gold tooth, and pink checked shirt. I was a little shy, being such a big fan, but before I knew it he was lying on the floor and kissing my hand! We went to an after-party at Alfonso

Pons' home, where we all drank and looked at amazing art and art people! What a night that was. It was here that we cooked up the idea to work together. First stop: the MoMA in New York, where we played our first concert with Doug, and official release of 'Art Rules', the CD – a collection of 'Art Rules' songs made especially for the art stars and art market by Chicks on Speed, Douglas Gordon, and Christopher Just. So the idea grew and grew. In a sense, we're all playing roles of some sort in the performance. We're all pawns in the market, whether it be fashion, music, or art industries – something we try to blow up during our performances, literally! Douglas is the art star; the Chicks are the wannabe pop stars, deconstructing pop and jumping into the art. It's controlled chaos, with at least three things going on at once for one full hour. 'Art Rules' live is a sort of organic experiment in performance art, going in and out of a pop show, always collapsing, to reveal very uncomfortable situations. Some end up being big mistakes, but all part of the process in which we work.

DO YOU FEEL CLOSE TO OTHER VISUAL ARTISTS WITH WHOM YOU WOULD LIKE TO COLLABORATE?

Alex: Gorilla Girls, Hannah Wilke, Karl Lagerfeld, Lisa Walker, Jeremy Scott, Bless, 00I00, Bernhard Wilhelm, Planningtorock, Dandiwind, Third Draw Down, Nancy Spero, Cindy Sherman, Yoko Ono, Louise Bourgeois, Faye Dunaway, MAN and Marimekko, Sophie Kahl, Cosey Fanny Tutti, COUM Transmissions, Who Made Who… Karl Fritsch, and all things handcrafted.

Melissa: We dream of war with gelatin – girl clan versus boy group – wedding dresses for the gelatins, chicks in tuxedos. Weapons: Gelatins monster flowers; Chicks Champagne bottle corks, sling shots.

YOU FORMED YOUR OWN RECORD LABEL, CHICKS ON SPEED RECORDS. WHEN DID THIS START, AND WHAT MOTIVATED YOU TO START IT?

Alex: We started Chicks on Speed Records in 1997 with Peter Wacha, aka Upstart, and Juergen Soeder in 2000. We initially began the label as Go Records, releasing a series of handmade 7-inches in 1997 – 'Warm Leatherette', 'Euro Trash Girl', and 'Glamour Girl' – and in 2000 we began signing other artists. We realized in the beginning of our career: anything we wanted to do we'd have to organize ourselves or with friends. A record label wasn't going to take us at that time. We learned we'd have to go out there and do what we want to do and do it ourselves, as fast as possible. Our main motive was to rewrite women's musical history, through releasing cutting-edge music by women, and to give an account of the musical aspects of feminism. The label for us isn't just a record label; it's a medium that can project itself in as many forms as it desires, as with Girl Monster, an ongoing project which has mutated into events and investigative labs in museums, theatres… and all-girl stages at music festivals in Europe and U.S.A./Australasia in the near future. Chicks on Speed Records, and specifically the Girl Monster platform, enable us to find and meet with like-minded artists and make some *"feminasty" noise! (*term coined by A.L. Steiner)

HOW MANY ARTISTS DO YOU REPRESENT? WHAT IS THE ART DIRECTION OF THE LABEL?

Melissa: Running a record label has become a labor of love. It is part of the project that doesn't make sense financially but we decided to keep it alive by funding from other projects. We release, very selectively, daring and very special artists. Last year we released 'Girl Monster', a three-CD compilation which has become a series of performance art, theory, and video evenings at Kampnagel Theater in Hamburg. Chicks on Speed Records represents Gustav, Susanne Brokesch, Planningtorock, Anat Ben David, Le Tigre (for Europe), Kids on TV, Ana Da Silva, DAT Politics, and Chicks on Speed.

WHAT IS THE SPIRIT OF THE NEW ALBUM YOU WILL RELEASE IN MAY 2008?

Alex: 'Cutting The Edge', our fifth full-length album, is a mixture of art anthems and bubblegum pop, acting as a bridge between our newfound world of OBJEKTIFICATIONS – Chicks on Speed homewares – and ongoing fashion collaborations, and featuring advert-like songs celebrating and launching these product ranges into the world. A number of the songs even belong to actual physical products, such as 'Super Surfer Girl', which is the theme song to the girls' surfwear collection we created for the clothing label Insight, based in Australia, to be launched in 2009. Other song-like adverts we've crafted include 'Strip Song', made for the Designers Against AIDS campaign, launched with Hennes and Mauritz in 2008; 'Buzz', a song devoted to frequent flyers, which comes as inside travel pack, all part of OBJEKTIFICATIONS, The Electro Rock Homewares collection, available in all good museum shops.

— Interview originally published in LIVE exhibition catalogue, co-edition Palais de Tokyo and Cercle d'Art, Paris, 2004 Updated in March 2008

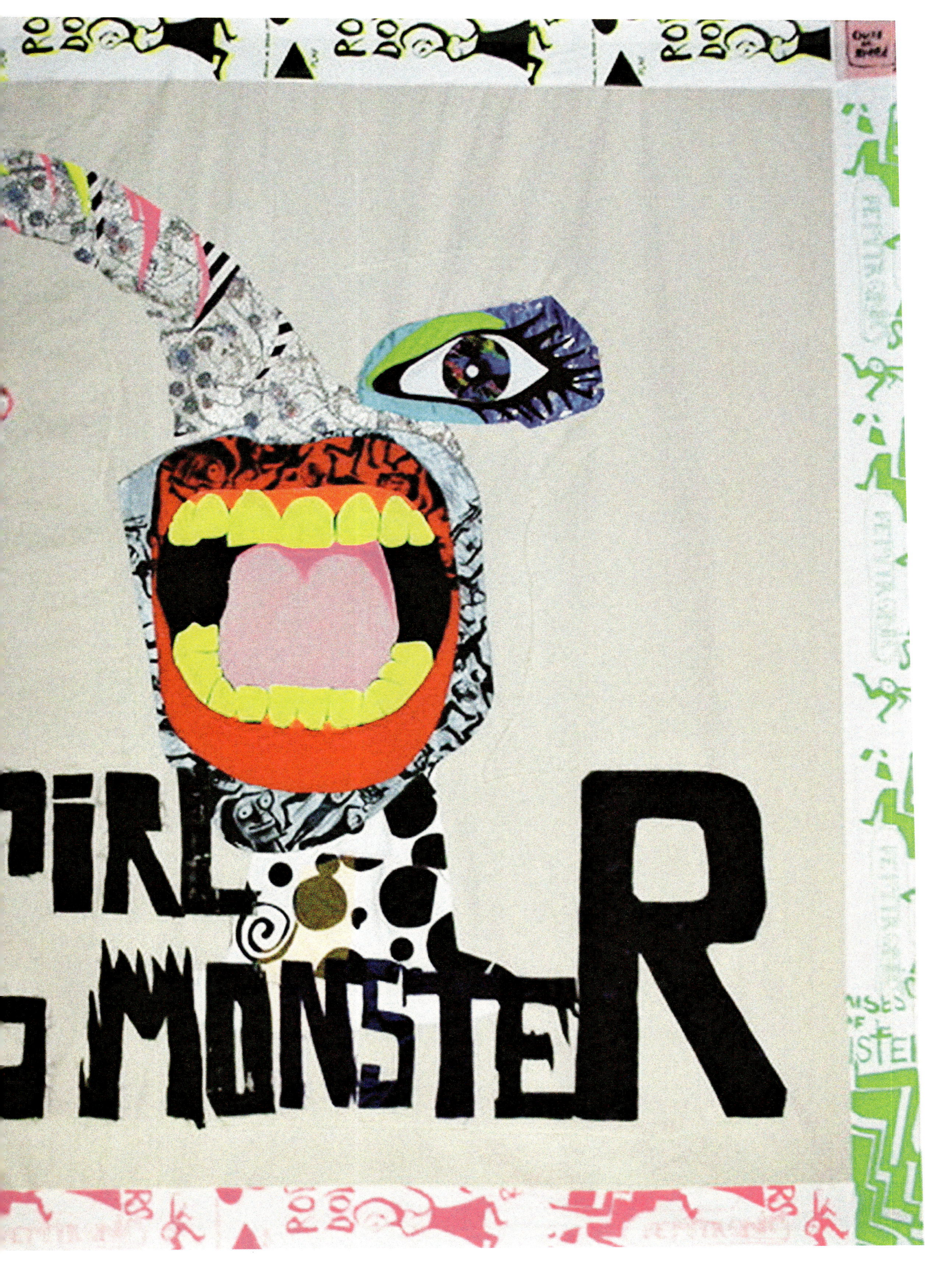
GIRL
MONSTER
R

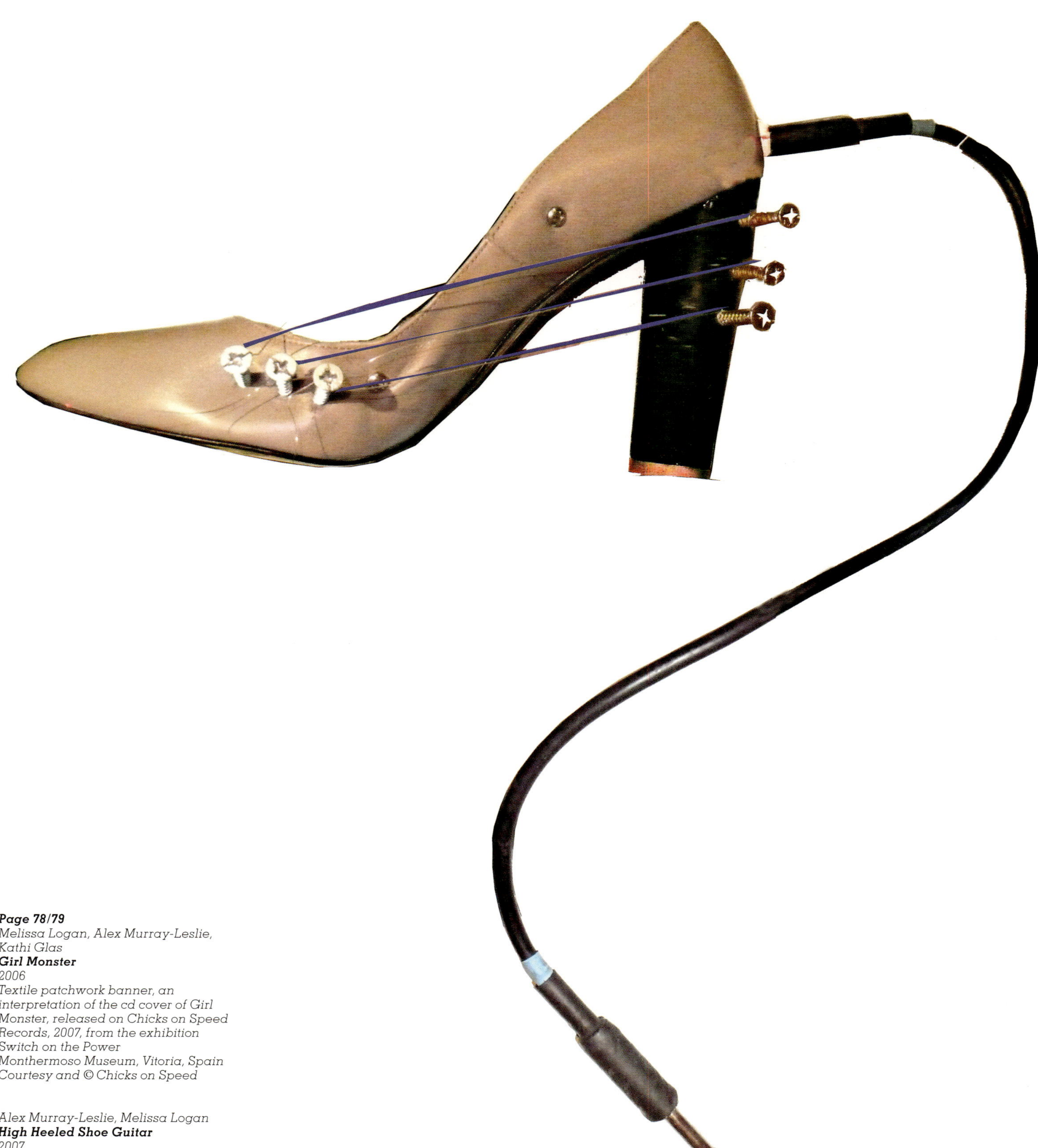

Page 78/79
Melissa Logan, Alex Murray-Leslie,
Kathi Glas
Girl Monster
2006
Textile patchwork banner, an
interpretation of the cd cover of Girl
Monster, released on Chicks on Speed
Records, 2007, from the exhibition
Switch on the Power
Monthermoso Museum, Vitoria, Spain
Courtesy and © Chicks on Speed

Alex Murray-Leslie, Melissa Logan
High Heeled Shoe Guitar
2007
Functional high heeled shoe guitar
Courtesy and © Chicks on Speed

Page 81
Melissa Logan, Alex Murray-Leslie
Shoe Fuck
2007
CAC Vilnius
Painting on canvas free hanging
and painting on canvas on cut out wood
2.20 x 5.50 m and 2 x 2.5 m
Courtesy and © Chicks on Speed

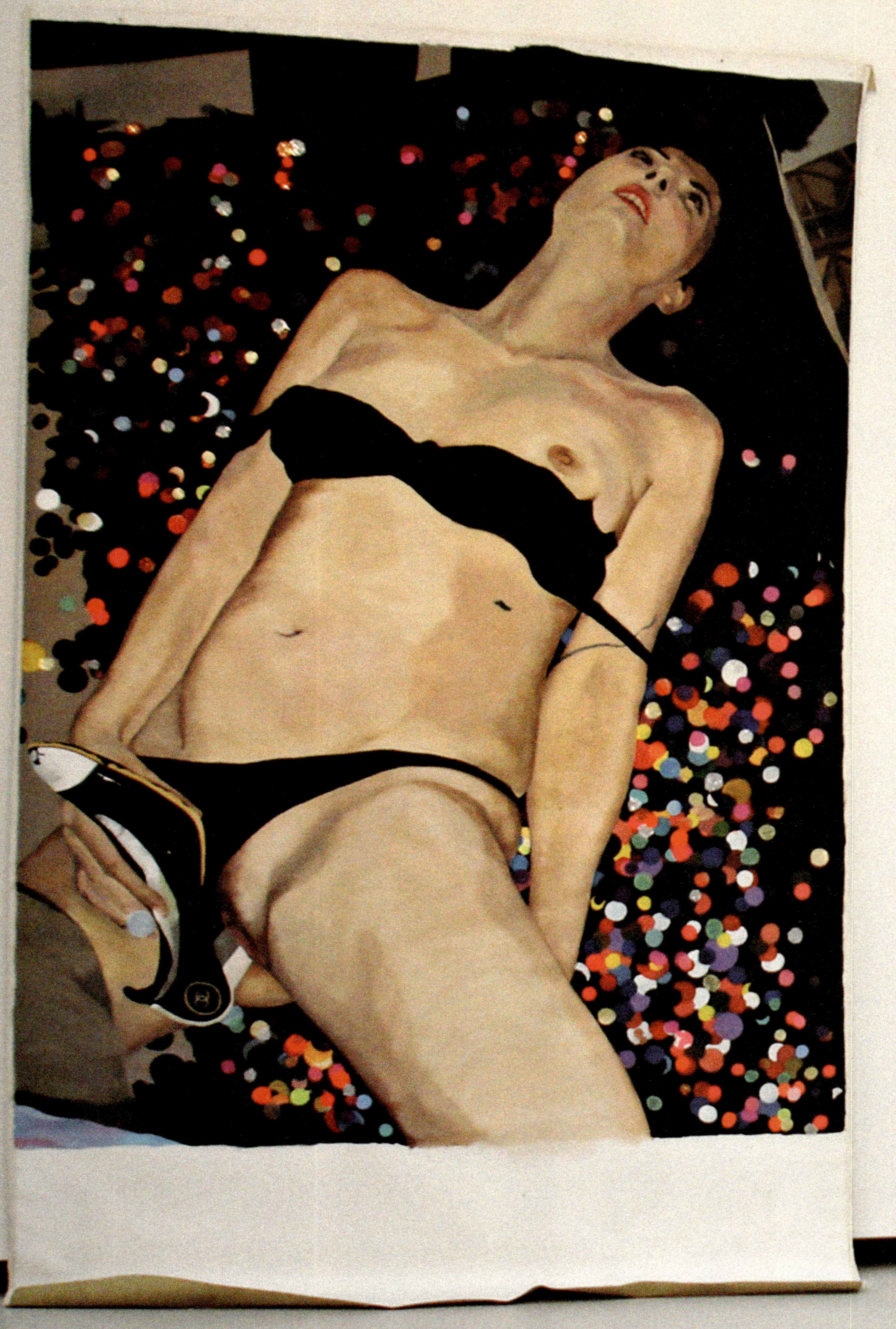

pete
DOHe

eRTY

...POET, PIRATE AND SELF STYLED LIBERTINE...

Immediately following the meteoric rise of his band The Libertines in 2002, Pete Doherty became a mythical figure of rock, incarnating all of the genre's attributes and excesses: "sex, drugs, and rock'n'roll". Charismatic and excessive, unpredictable and generous, untouchable but also accessible, Pete Doherty today fronts Babyshambles, a band with a dynamic, efficient style that shifts between rock, punk, ska, and jazz.

While not quite 30, Pete Doherty has already lived several lives. Alongside his musical career, he has consistently produced drawings and poetry, regularly appearing for public readings and recently, exhibiting his artwork. His latest series, drawn with his own blood, caught the imagination of many and launched his career as a visual artist. In 2007 he published his journal, 'The Books of Albion: The Collected Writings of Peter Doherty', which included his drawings, photos, and poetry.

— Pete Doherty was born in Hexham (UK) in 1979. He currently lives in London.

"All our dreams came true"
— Peter Doherty 2005

By definition, a libertine is one who frees himself from the shackles of "constraint, accepted morals, and forms of behaviour sanctioned by larger society". To apply these limitations to an artist's output – whether visual, verbal, or visceral – is to ignore artistic intent.

A true libertine, Peter Doherty is not restricted by medium. Whether through the shambolic verse of his diaries or the famously impromptu "guerrilla" gigs that serve as a testing ground for his new musings, what one invariably finds is an honest, offbeat, and charming voice, peppered with humour and a peculiarly British romanticism that is both familiar and distant. Peter's influences, from William Blake to Galton and Simpson, reflect a Britishness shrouded in a Union Jack of nostalgia that sets him apart from the current crop of art-school elite. One of Peter's great skills lies in his ability to share

Peter's vision is a twilight one that echoes the voices of Blake, Baudelaire, and Wilde

his personal dislocation with society in a way that makes his audience feel part of the conspiracy. Not since the early works of Peter Blake has an artist so perfectly captured the mood of his city.

One of Doherty's early artworks, 'Blackbird', references the McCartney classic and immediately lets it spiral into an altogether darker place. Yet it never loses sight of the song's tone, leaving the viewer unsettled but wryly smiling. Many of his "blood drawings" act as footnotes to his writings in 'The Books of Albion' – small sketchy figures occupying dark, half-remembered places. Peter's vision is a twilight one that echoes the voices of Blake, Baudelaire, and Wilde while somehow being completely of our time. He often revisits familiar themes both in his writings and artworks, re-exploring certain characters and places to give new flesh to his creations. One such theme is Albion, a ship that sails to Arcadia, a utopian society without rules and boundaries, where "Life trips along, pure and simple as a shepherd's song".

The output of any artist needs to be measured against its time and place. It is precisely Peter's sense of his own unique time and place that leads to his almost religious adoration. Through his refusal to be constrained in any aspect of his output, he leaves the door open for us to witness, from the comfort of our own lives, the existence of an alternative way, where a nostalgia and appreciation for working-class life is mixed with hedonistic abandon. Peter Doherty is perhaps the ultimate libertine, a character whose art reflects his life, a Dorian Gray for our times, whose self-destructive nature is matched only by his lust for life.

— Robin Barton, 2008

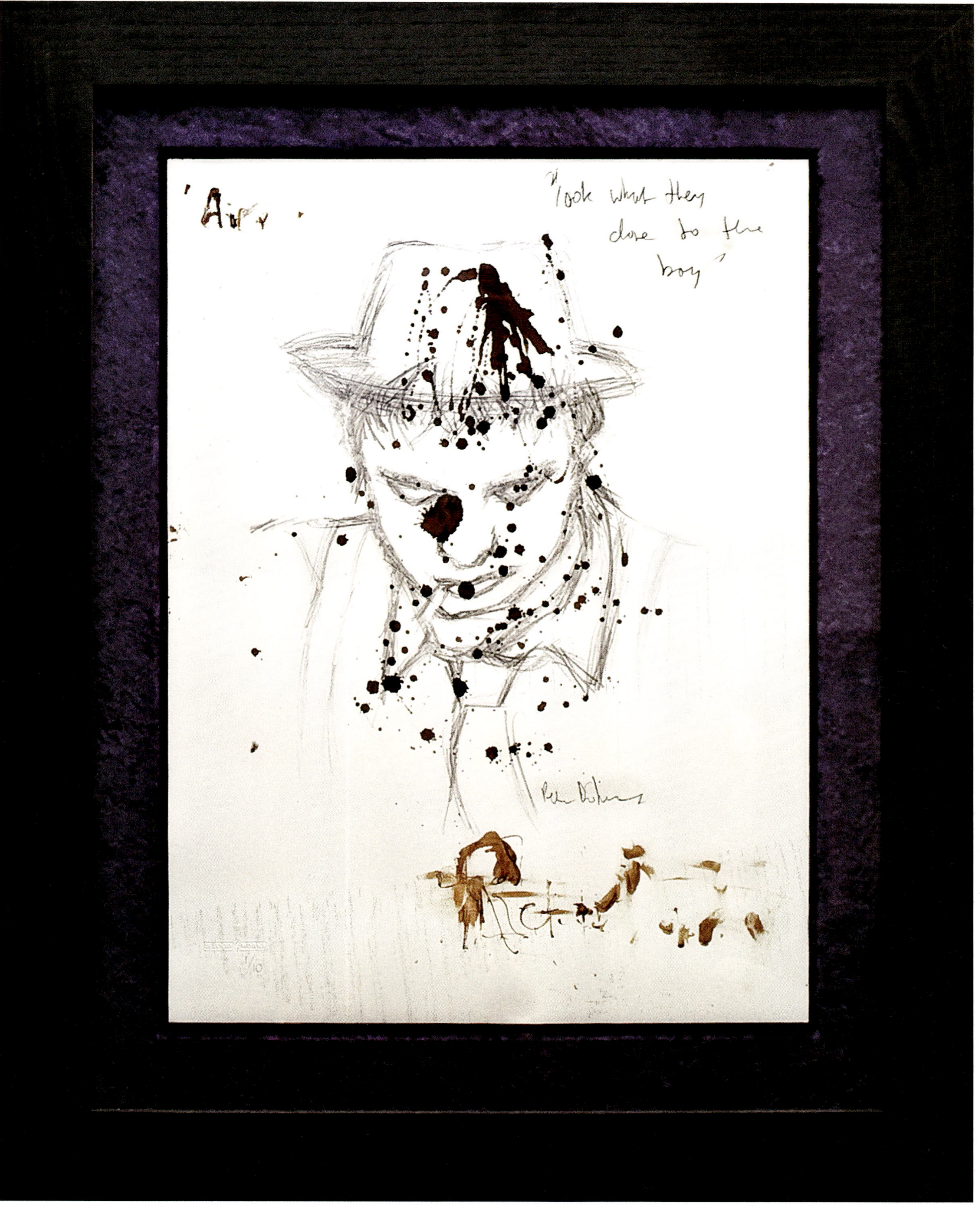

Look What They Done To The Boy
2007
Blood and pencil on paper
#1/10
83 x 64 cm
Courtesy of Bankrobber Gallery, London
Photo Credit © Tarik Briziz/MakeyourMark

85

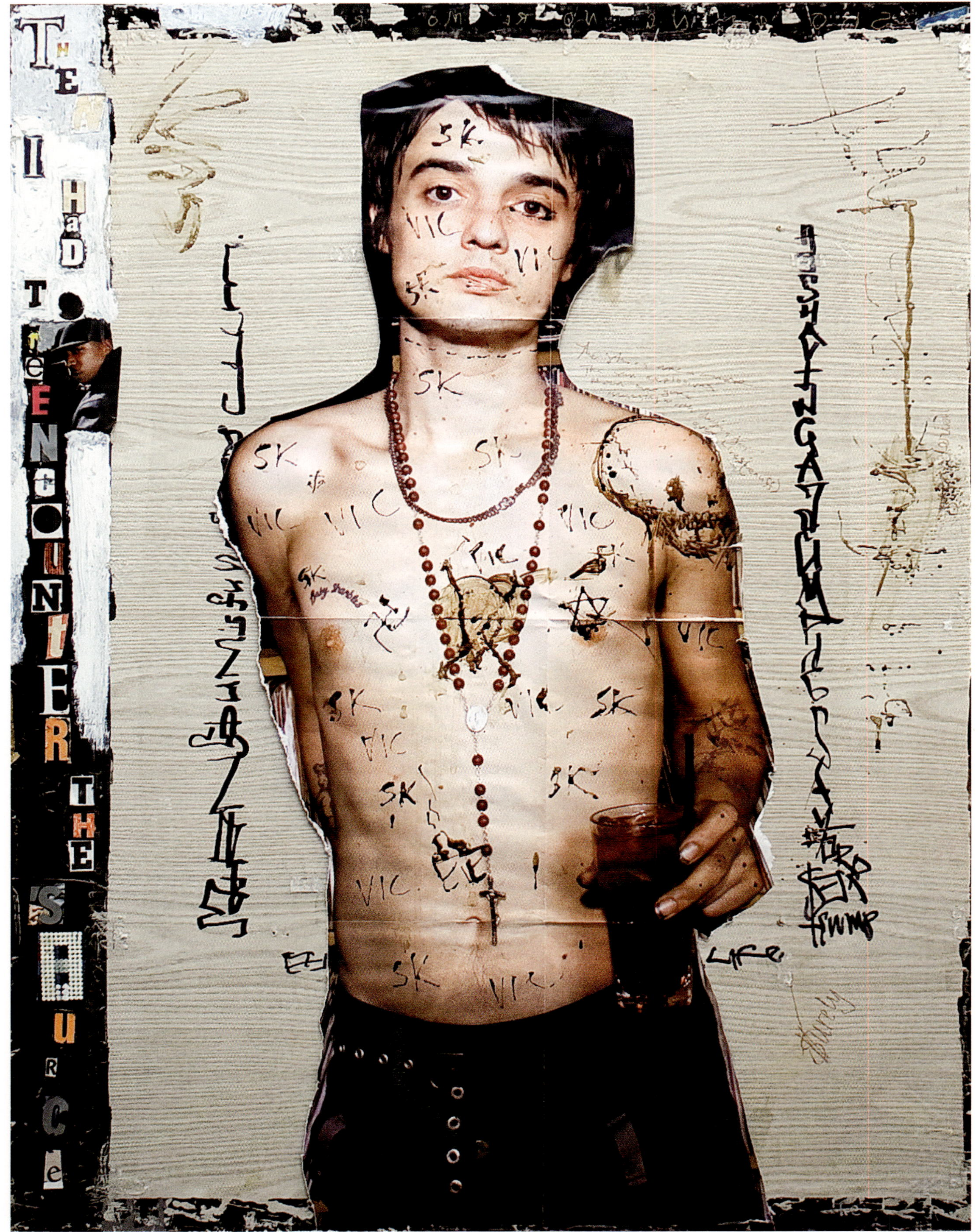

S.K.
2006
Photo, pencil and blood on board
113 x 97 cm
Courtesy of Bankrobber Gallery, London
Photo Credit © Tarik Briziz/MakeYourMark

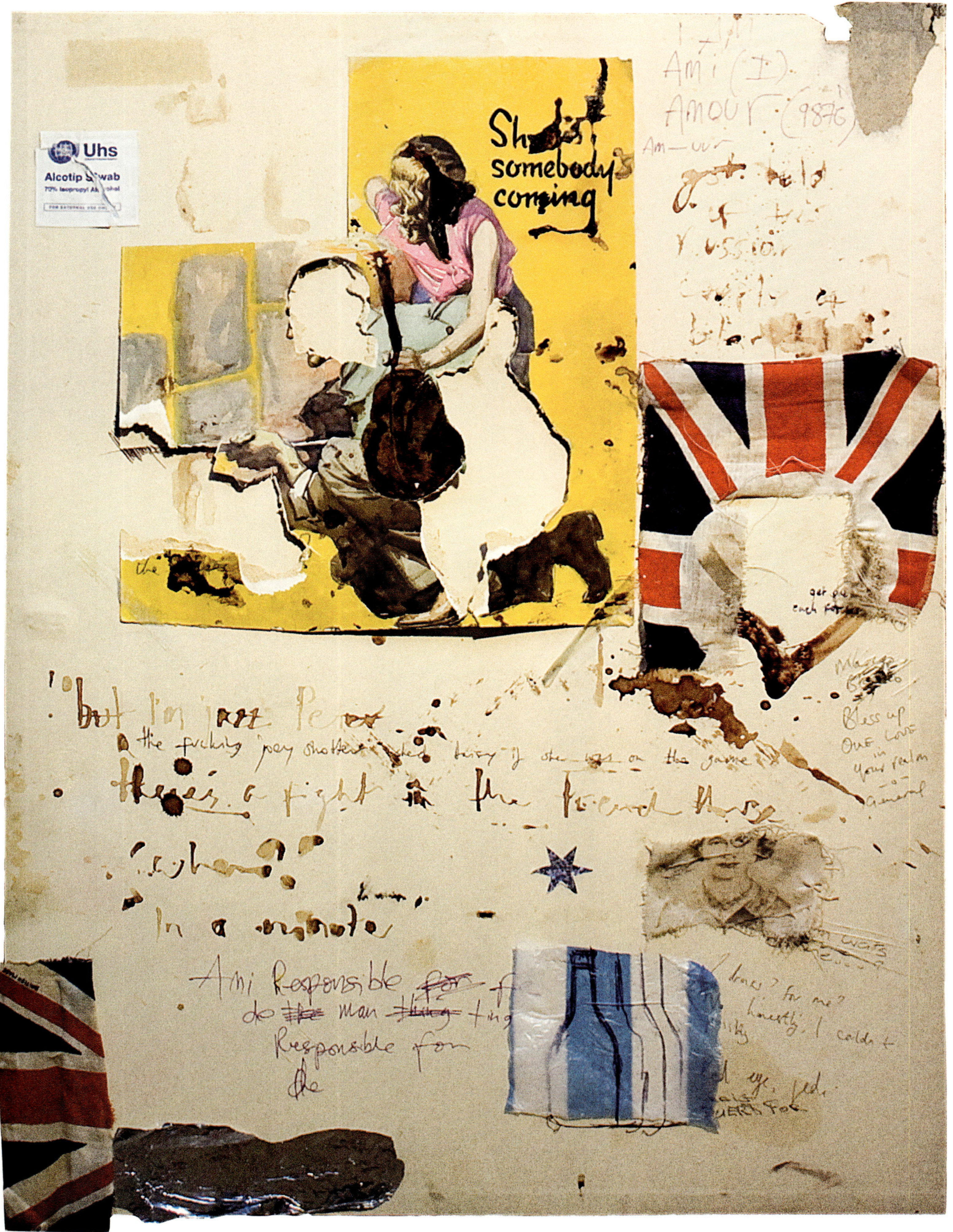

Flag
2006
Blood, pen and found objects on folio
85 x 70 cm
Courtesy of Bankrobber Gallery, London
Photo Credit © Tarik Briziz/MakeYourMark

Blood Clot Bilo
2006
Blood on paper
62 x 50 cm
Courtesy of Bankrobber Gallery, London
Photo Credit © Tarik Briziz/MakeYourMark

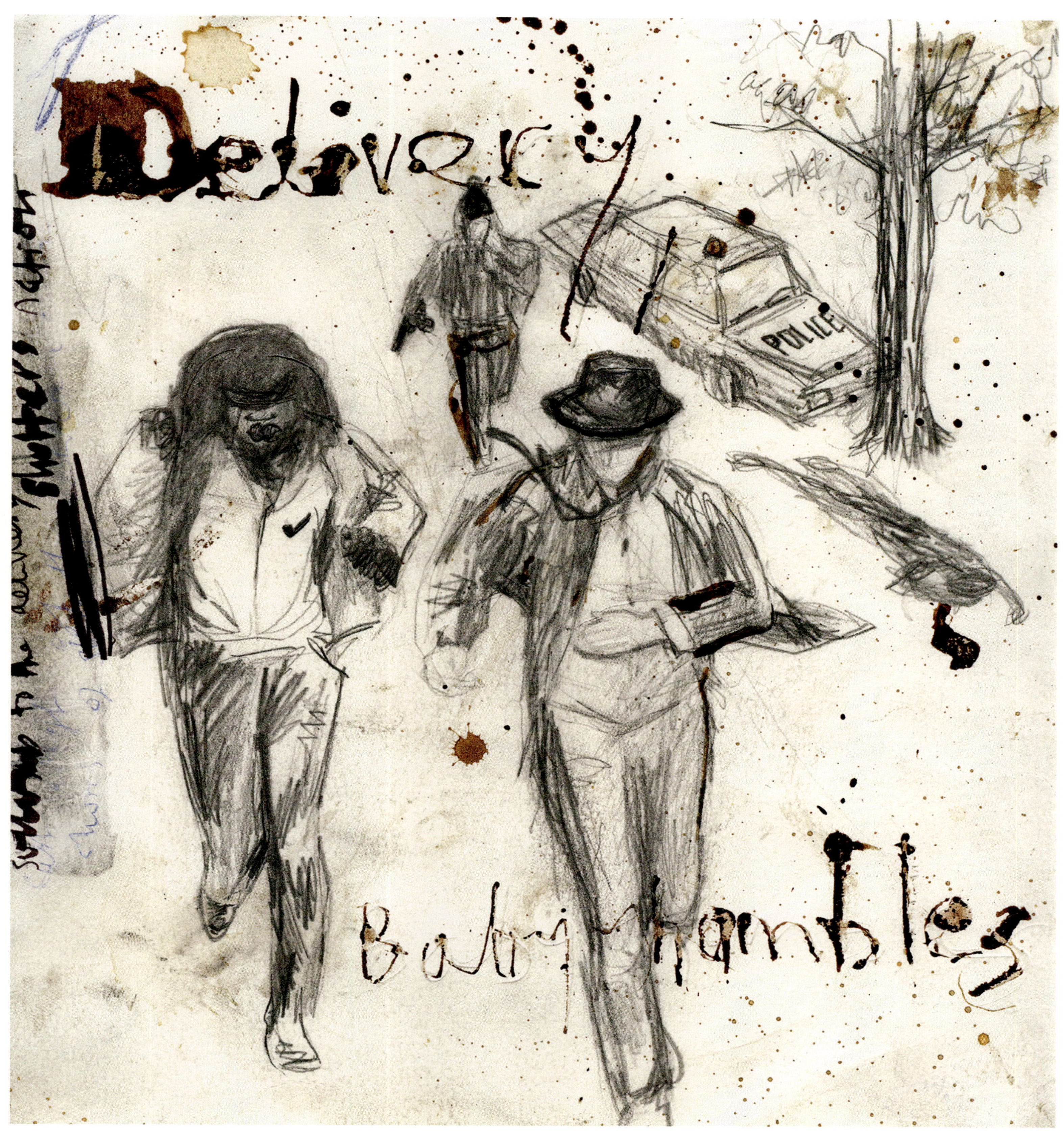

Delivery
2007
Blood and pencil on paper
Original single cover
24 x 22 cm
Courtesy of Bankrobber Gallery, London
Photo Credit © Tarik Briziz/MakeYourMark

BRIAN eno

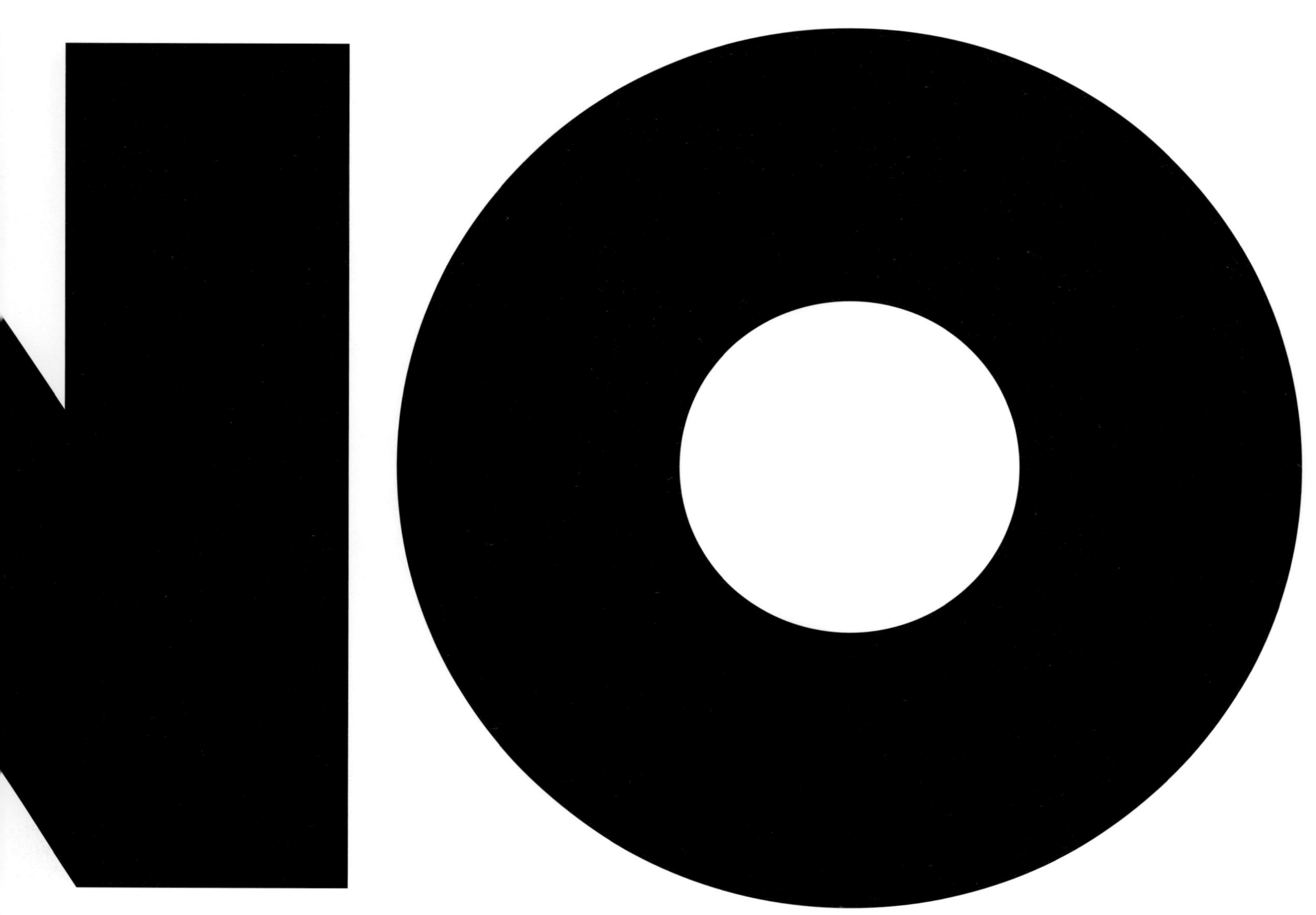

PAINTINGS THAT BEHAVE A LITTLE LIKE MUSIC

Following a degree in visual arts from Winchester School of Arts, Brian Eno embarked on a musical career that has seen the release of a number of solo albums as well as collaborations with artists such as U2, David Bowie, John Cale, Talking Heads, James, and Coldplay. However, throughout this nearly 40-year career in music, he never lost sight of his keen interest the visual arts, in particular the use of light sources to create videos, light sculptures, and 'paintings'. His visual and musical output has often centered around the idea of the piece being self-generative. This is particularly true with '77 Million' Paintings, a monitor-based piece that slowly changes before the viewer into countless random permutations, giving each viewer a unique visual experience.
— Eno is musician, theorist, producer, thinker, and ideas generator. He was born in Woodbridge (UK) in 1948 and now lives in Oxfordshire.

BRIAN ENO INTERVIEWED BY JÉRÔME SANS

HOW HAS YOUR ART-SCHOOL EXPERIENCE INFLUENCED YOUR THEORIES ABOUT CULTURE AND THE MUSIC YOU'VE BEEN MAKING?

At art school I studied with a number of professors who were as interested in what was going on in music as in painting. I came to know Cornelius Cardew, Gavin Bryars, Christian Wolff, Morton Feldman, and other influential composers of the era. I also thought that since music was intimately connected with process rather than object, it was closer to my interests at that time.

YOU STARTED DOING VIDEOS IN THE LATE '70S AND SAID THAT VIDEOS WERE MORE ABOUT MANIPULATING LIGHT THAN IMAGES. WHAT DID YOU EXPERIENCE IN THOSE EARLY WORKS?

I had been working with light since I was 17, and knew that it was a technologically clumsy game. The tools were under-evolved and expensive. But I was impressed by the potential of video – as the first really flexible and accurate way of controlling light – and utterly bored with television. I thought, "Here is a wonderful technology being poorly used". TV, having started life as the bastard child of cinema, which in turn began as the bastard of theatre, has always been wedded to a particular subset of video's possibilities – the use of light to form images and narratives. I was interested in the use of light to make pure pictures, perhaps analogous to the transformation that had happened in painting in the early 20th century.

YOU CALLED YOUR DIGITAL WORKS "VIDEO PAINTINGS". WHY?

They're not TV, not music, not narrative. They're two-dimensional visual objects, exactly like paintings are, with the qualification that they change.

DO YOU HAVE A DIFFERENT APPROACH OF CREATION WHEN MAKING MUSIC OR VISUAL ARTS?

We are used to the idea of paintings being still and music moving. When I started making ambient music, I was trying to make a type of music that approached the condition of painting, that approached a sort of stillness. Now I am doing the obverse of that: trying to make paintings that behave a little like music. I have always worked visually and musically. Neither my visual nor my musical directions would have taken the shape they did without each other. I make no distinction between the development of my visual and musical output, as the two have been growing together, feeding and informing the other. By the way, not so long ago, if you wanted to be in a rock band you would generally need to learn how to pluck guitar strings or construct piano chords, whereas if you wanted to be an artist, you needed to use a pencil or a chisel. The tools were exclusive to their area, and mutually intimidating. Now we are all using the same tool: the computer, which gives a visual artist a degree of empathy with how music is created, and vice versa.

YOU RECENTLY REALIZED A HUGE PROJECT CALLED '77 MILLION PAINTINGS', A GENERATIVE VIDEO AND MUSIC SOFTWARE THAT ALLOWS USERS TO CREATE, USING YOUR ORIGINAL PAINTINGS AND SOUNDS, 77 MILLION DIFFERENT COMBINATIONS OF YOUR ARTWORK AND MUSIC. WHAT WAS YOUR IDEA BEYOND THIS?

By its nature, '77 Million Paintings' is an abstract piece. It does have the occasional figurative element but these are rendered abstract by their context. Ideas of abstraction and realism are very much to do with the aesthetic and the content of the painting, and what is happening inside the frame. Much of the interest in 77 Million is what is going on behind the frame as well, in how the piece behaves and how it works. You are aware that what you are seeing is changing, and changing so slowly you can still relate to it as a conventional painting. But you as a viewer are also aware that you will never see the same painting again. In this sense, although the viewer is looking at abstract compositions, this is only part of the story as there is much more going on behind the scenes.

WHY THE NUMBER 77 MILLION?

The title of 77 Million was the result of some early calculations of the possible combinations which could be produced by the piece. It is actually a minimum figure, because it expresses only the nominal combinations of images; it doesn't take into account the different balances within those combinations. The actual figure would be much higher than this.

WAS THIS PIECE A WAY FOR YOU TO INVENT YOUR OWN TECHNIQUE AND METHOD FOR GATHERING ART AND MUSIC THROUGH A COMMON GENERATIVE PROCESS?

Working in a generative way is not a new idea, especially in music. It stretches back to Steve Reich, the California school of composers, to Cage and others. I like the idea of being someone who initiates a process, who builds the machine, provides the inputs, and lets the thing come into its own. The important thing is how you develop this idea. It is far rarer to work generatively in a visual medium, and it provides an equally rich set of possibilities and results as it does with music.

WHAT KIND OF RELATIONSHIP DO YOU EXPECT BETWEEN YOUR VISUAL WORK AND THE AUDIENCE?

The movement of the images is very slow. So when we did shows in Tokyo and Milan earlier this year, it was not immediately obvious to the audience that they were changing. People ended up going 'round the exhibition several times to check! Once they cottoned on to what was happening, their whole pace changed and slowed down, and they spent much longer, just sitting and watching. The result can be quite hypnotic, and some people stayed literally for hours in front of the same piece, while others returned several days in a row to look at them again. It is a painting which slows you down to its own pace. We are so used to seeing speed and action on screens that this can be a new experience.

YOU HAVE RELEASED '77 MILLION PAINTINGS' IN DVD, ALLOWING PEOPLE TO WATCH AND LISTEN TO YOUR ARTWORK AT HOME. DID YOU HAVE THIS IDEA IN MIND RIGHT FROM THE BEGINNING OF THE PROJECT?

Yes, this was very much an intention with '77 Million Paintings'. In the past my generative visual pieces have been projected installations in a gallery space. There were technological reasons for this: until recently it wasn't possible to make a home version of these experiences. The difference now is that the viewer has control over where the piece is placed, when it is viewed, what is happening around it.

> I was interested in the use of light to make pure pictures, perhaps analogous to the transformation that had happened in painting in the early 20th century.

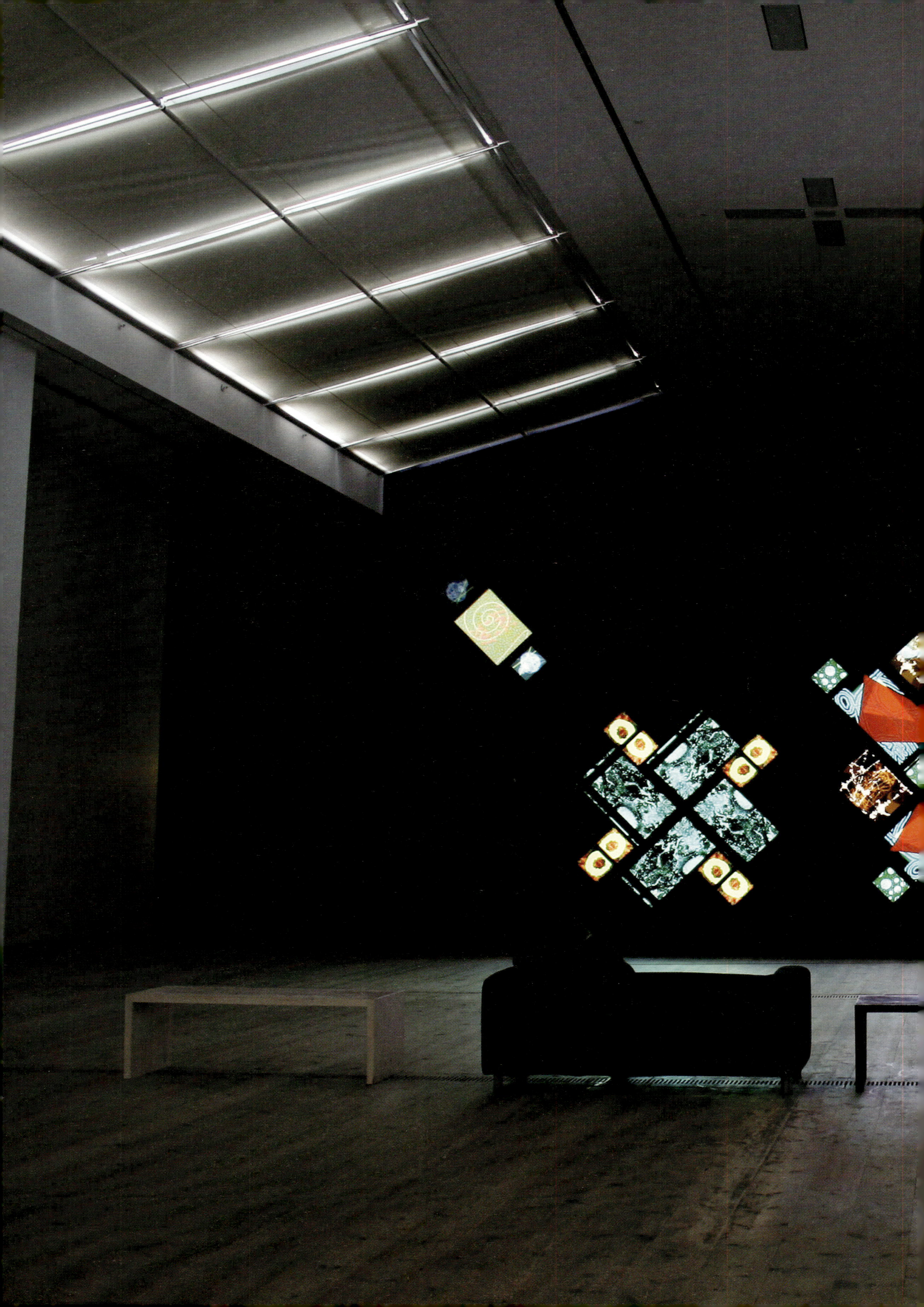

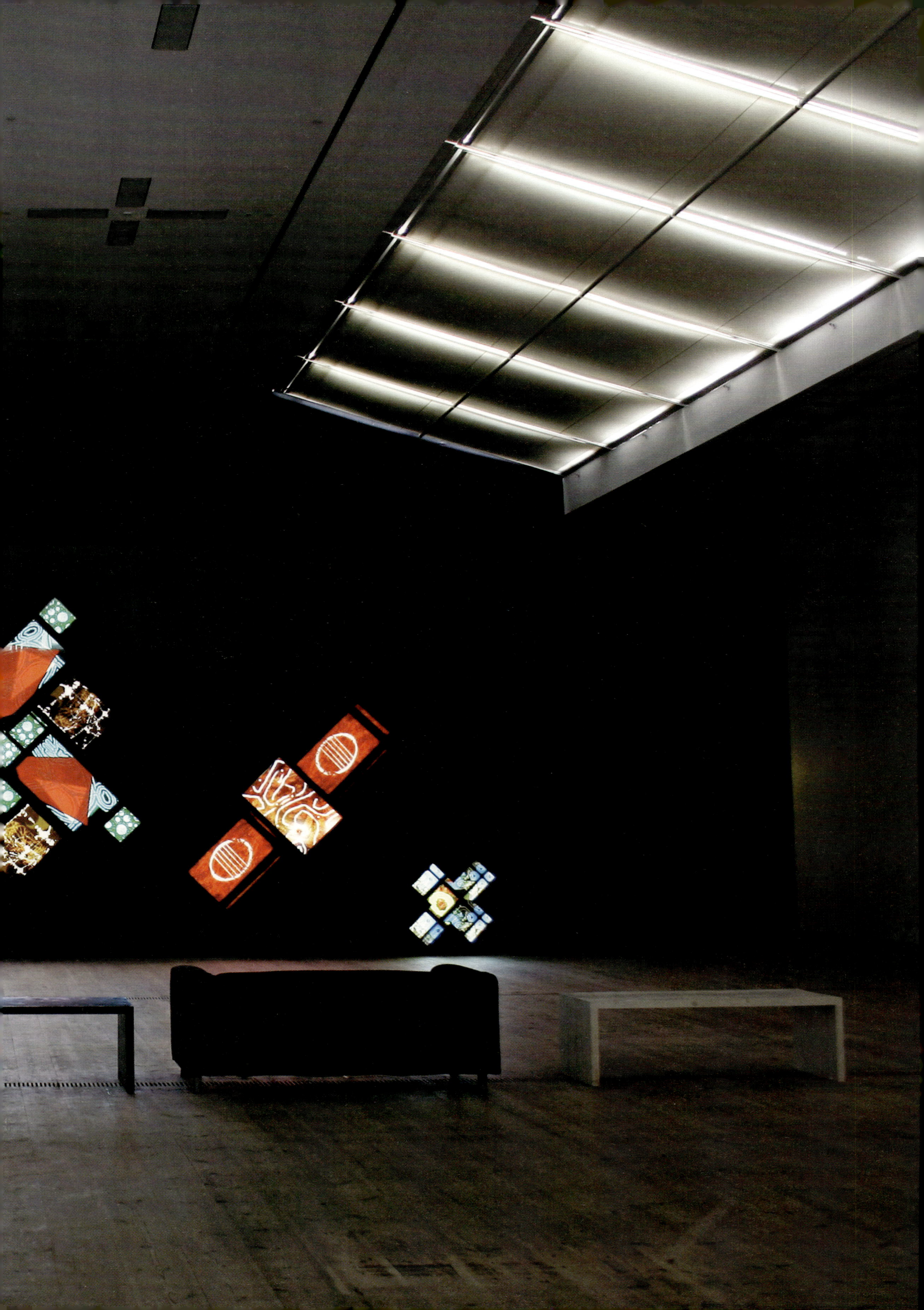

Page 94/95
Constellations
January – April 2007
BALTIC Centre for Contemporary Art
Photo Credit © Colin Davison

55 Million Crystals
Opened December 2007
Swarovski Kristallwelten
Permanent Installation

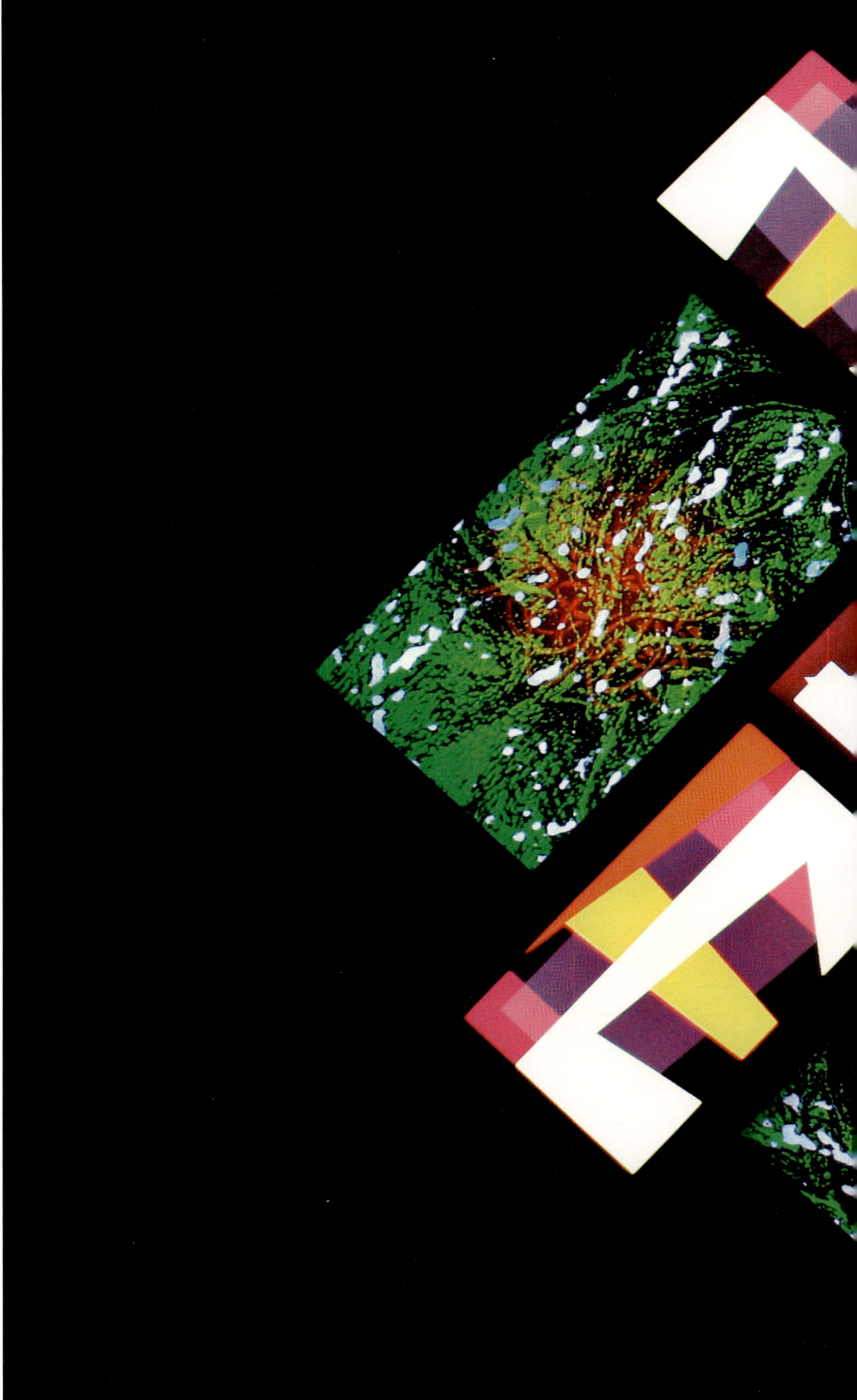

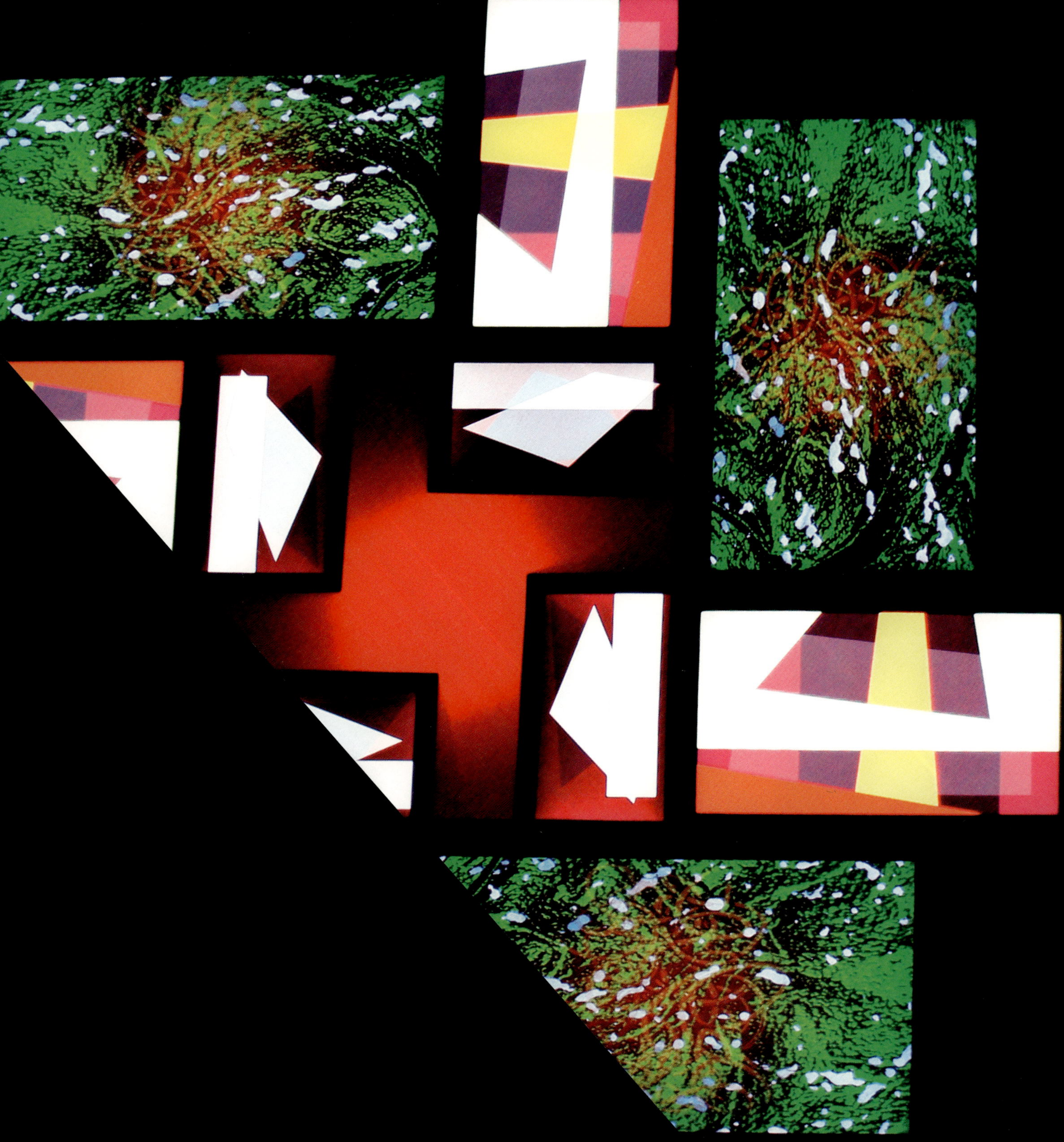

BRYAN
FER

RRY

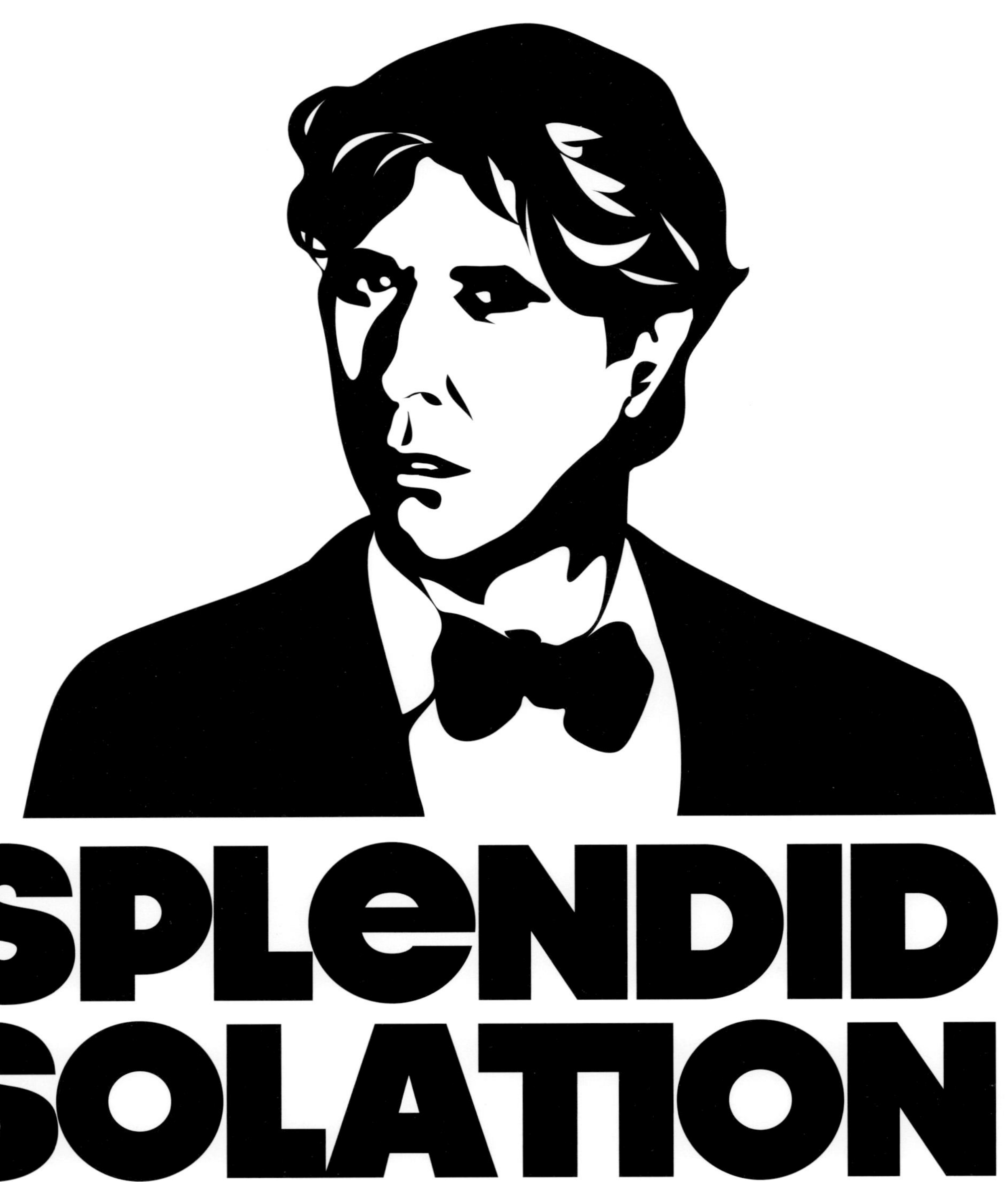

SPLENDID ISOLATION

Founding member and frontman of glam-rock group Roxy Music, Bryan Ferry is known for his gift of reworking existing songs. He explains this by pointing to the influence of pop art, a constant source of fascination and inspiration for him. He borrows from a variety of musical styles to craft his own sound collages. Marcel Duchamp was a major influence on this musician, who made reference to him in several songs during the '70s, notably in 'The Bride Stripped Bare'. The visual arts hold an important place in Bryan Ferry's musical constructions. A timeless dandy, he considers his eccentric choice of clothing and his live performances to be the visual translation of the spirit and soul of his music.
— Bryan Ferry was born in 1945 in Washington (UK), and today lives in London.

MICHAEL BRACEWELL TALKS TO BRYAN FERRY

RICHARD HAMILTON WAS ONE OF YOUR TUTORS WHEN YOU STUDIED FINE ART AT NEWCASTLE UNIVERSITY IN THE MID-'60S. WHAT DO YOU THINK YOU GAINED FROM HIM?

I think that there is a breadth of vision in his work that I found inspirational. You get the impression that some artists perfect one particular kind of picture throughout their career. Hamilton is much more diverse, and you get the sense of an intelligence leaping around. Some people found the work soulless but I didn't. My favorite paintings of his are those I find very lush and sensual, celebrating their subject matter in a good way. For me it was great, for someone who wanted to be an artist, avidly exploring the world of art, studying different periods and styles, and suddenly coming across someone like Richard, who seemed so incredibly modern. It was fantastic to find pictures where the inspiration was the shape of a modern motor car or Marilyn Monroe. It seemed very fresh and of the time that we lived in. And yet there was a sense of great skill there too. He was somebody who could obviously draw, and who was taking pains over something, which means that you take it more seriously. And that is something I quite like. I felt the same about Jasper Johns. Some of the more slapdash of the pop artists might not have impressed you so much in that way. What I learned from Hamilton, from work such as 'Just What Is It that Makes Today's Homes So Different, So Appealing', was very exciting to me. When I try to analyze my own work, certainly some of the early songs were very collage-like. I'd throw different styles of music into the same song, or try to.

To him, and in 'The Bride Stripped Bare', to Marcel Duchamp as well. I remember reading about the 'This Is Tomorrow' exhibition [at the Whitechapel Gallery, London, 1956] and thinking what a great title for a song it was. Sadly, that particular song wasn't quite up to the title but the thought was there. 'The Bride Stripped Bare' was just a conceit really. I thought that it was such a wonderful title – very curious in many ways, especially for the mass public – that maybe it would lead them into learning about something more interesting. When I took a song by somebody else and made my own version of it, I felt that I was adding my stamp to it, my signature. A song as a readymade, even though it was a sideline of mine, just as Duchamp felt that the readymades were a sideline. Something to keep your hand in, as it were, until the next great idea came along. But they're the works he's famous for now.

WHAT WAS YOUR OWN WORK AS AN ART STUDENT LIKE?

Well, it varied every year… [laughs] When I was just about to go to university, I remember doing a whole series of Francis Bacons – screaming heads and so on. I also did a whole series of stained canvases in the manner of Morris Louis, whom I also liked. And of course there was a Richard Hamilton period. Except that none of the pictures were any good, really. I hadn't found myself as an artist but I really enjoyed doing things. I was fiddling around with music while I was still there, so I wasn't as devoted a student as I could have been or should have been. Maybe my heart wasn't totally in it, although it was at first. But music is a very strong drug, and it became more and more clear to me that that's what I wanted to do, although it wasn't until after I graduated that I really knew. But I had a wonderful time dabbling at being an artist in the four years that I was at Newcastle.

ROXY MUSIC EMERGED IN 1972 WITH ITS SOUND AND IMAGE FULLY DEVELOPED. AS THE GROUP'S CREATOR, DID YOU HAVE A CONCRETE VISION OF WHAT IT WAS GOING TO BE LIKE?

Not really, other than that I knew I wanted it to be very eclectic stylistically. I wasn't conscious of wanting to create a style; I wanted the music to be very emotional – which some people never found it to be, but I did – and to take things from all the different kinds of music I was interested in, which was a completely open book. It ranged from experimental music – people like John Cage – through all the different strands of American music, the development of black music in America, mainly. The blues of Leadbelly, R&B, pop music from Detroit and Motown, the Stax musicians, who I thought were wonderful. And then all the jazz people, because I suppose the first concerts I went to were jazz concerts. I was a big fan of Charlie Parker, Billie Holiday, all the great jazz players. I absorbed masses of different kinds of music by a very early age – 10 or 11, which was when I started becoming obsessed by it. I read a lot about music because I used to deliver newspapers – the music weeklies and things, and they were all about jazz and blues. But what makes me different from a lot of the musicians who were influenced by the blues – like Van Morrison or Eric Clapton, who are from the same generation as me – is that I was interested in Fred Astaire and Gene Kelly and all the, let's say, "white music" of America from that period – Tin Pan Alley, Cole Porter, the great musicals – which was a more European-based music. It wasn't drawn from the cotton fields; it was more from Vienna. The Jewish émigrés from Austria, Germany, and so forth, meant that a lot of wonderful music drifted into New York in the 1930s. There is a whole other Broadway sound, or whatever you want to call it; I liked all that as well. There was a lot of music jumping around in my head, and when I started writing songs, all manner of weird influences came up, juxtaposed. The word "collage" does spring to mind: taking bits from here, there, and everywhere, and hopefully creating your own stuff from it. You have to bear in mind that I had five other people in the band whose strengths I was trying to play to as well, in the same way that Duke Ellington always tried to write to the strengths of his band. He had a fantastic sax player in Johnny Hodges; he had Harry Carney, the baritone player. I thought, great, Andy Mackay can play oboe, and so I can get a sense of Europe, or "proper" music, into some of the songs. Something like 'Sea Breezes' [on Roxy Music, 1972] has a very haunting oboe line and then suddenly the drums come crashing in with all those wild guitars. The thing about Roxy Music is that there was a larger than usual musical range in the group. We might not have been the best players in the world but the palette I had to work from was quite extensive. I think that that's what made some of the early Roxy stuff so satisfying: There was a richness to it. It wasn't just guitar, bass, and drums – which can be great, but I get bored with it after a while. You want other colors. It was wonderful to have Brian Eno there, who was able to transform the sound of all the regular instruments into sounds we hadn't heard before. There was a sense of looking back at previous musics, and also a sense of looking forward and creating something new as well. It was quite unique, and felt so at the time, I must confess. It was very exciting to be part of it, and to be, I suppose, the principal designer of it. But it makes me tired just talking about it… [laughs].

THE STAGING OF ROXY MUSIC CONCERTS HAS ALWAYS BEEN IMPERIAL, EXOTIC, AND SUMPTUOUS. HOW DID YOU APPROACH THE PROCESS OF PERFORMING LIVE?

The thing with Roxy Music was that the music should be played well, first and foremost. And then that the stage should be lit in an interesting way and the people on the stage wearing appropriate clothes, whatever that was at the time. I didn't really want to make a big deal of it or have it choreographed in any way, although on the recent Roxy Music reunion tour [2001] there were dancers who did a routine to a couple of songs. I thought it was a great way to present some of the songs – a kind of sideways look at Broadway.

I didn't want it to be like Kraftwerk, with black polo-neck sweaters; or like the anonymity of Pink Floyd, with just shadowy figures. Although there's something quite nice about that for a song or two but not for a whole show. You need to visually carry the mood of the music. A couple of times we have had grandiose-looking stage sets,

trying to do something reasonably interesting within the quite strict confines of what you can do on a stage. Because the reunion show was a traveling show, it had to work for 51 stages and fit into the parameters of different venues worldwide. Since we've never had a vast amount of money to play with, it's always been pretty simple and scaled-down. But we once had a huge eagle, and we once had a rather De Chirico open plaza. For 'Country Life' there were banners and I wore some military stuff, which Antony [Price] had designed: a black tie, and a strap across the chest. The banners seemed to go with this fascistic look, which was tongue-in-cheek but quite good to look at, I thought. I can't remember spending very much time over it, to be honest, other than saying, "Why don't we do it like this?" Usually these things are haphazard, and done at the last minute. If you look at the calendar of that period [the mid-'70s], there was an awful lot of material being made by Roxy Music, and by myself, and there wasn't really that much time to spend on such things. We did quite well, considering.

HOW AWARE WERE YOU OF THE RALLY-LIKE NATURE OF YOUR CONCERTS, AND THE HEIGHTENED IMAGE-CONSCIOUSNESS OF THE FANS?

Well, for a few years we were very popular. The albums were always Top Three, and the singles did very well considering that we weren't a singles band. There was a very strong following, not only in London but also in the provinces and internationally. Maybe the fact that I come from a provincial town [Washington, County Durham] also struck a chord with the northern, industrial cities, where we always seemed to have a really strong following, with boys as well as girls. In later years I think we maybe had a stronger female audience as the style of the music changed and became more lush. But yes, you did see people in the audience dressing up like us, and therefore each concert did have a sense of occasion. There were devotees out there.

THEY HONED IN VERY SPECIFICALLY ON THAT WEIMAR-DECADENCE-MEETS-GLENN MILLER LOOK, DIDN'T THEY?

The "matinee idol"… We didn't really dictate a style so much as favor certain styles. It was a way of playing around style, rather than defining one. Generally I would favor tailored clothes as a rule, thus ending up looking like a character from a movie or something. We were perhaps the most cinematic-looking band. Apart from myself, Andy Mackay is quite a dandy figure, very interested in clothes, and he developed a particular look that was rather splendid. Phil Manzanera had a certain Latin look with his dark features and white suits. Paul Thompson, in the background, was quite down-to-earth, a genuine musician.

YOUR OWN IMAGE WAS SEIZED ON QUITE EARLY AS THAT OF A STYLE ICON. THE PICTURE OF YOU WEARING A WHITE TUXEDO ON THE COVER OF YOUR SECOND SOLO ALBUM, ANOTHER TIME ANOTHER PLACE (1974), WAS CONSIDERED ONE OF THE MOST ICONIC POP IMAGES SINCE ELVIS PRESLEY IN A GOLD LAMÉ SUIT. HOW DID YOU FEEL ABOUT HAVING A REPUTATION FOR SUPREME STYLISHNESS?

I think that most people tend to favor wearing things that they are comfortable in, and which they feel show them off to their best advantage [laughs]. You may also have a certain penchant for a particular period, and therefore you want to emulate it. I liked the way Jimi Hendrix looked, but it wouldn't be something I could pull off! Hendrix lived the rock 'n' roll lifestyle, among rock 'n' roll people. If you're sleeping all day long and only going out at night to a club where you're playing, then you can look like a fabulous troubadour gypsy. In any other circles that's going to attract a lot of attention. I quite like the anonymity of dressing almost like Philip Marlowe. I was always fascinated by men's clothes, although they didn't determine my life. Working in a tailor's shop for two or three years when I was a teenager had some impact on my taste in what to wear and my knowledge of what to wear. I suddenly knew about three-button, single-breasted suits with side vents [laughs], or which buttons you were supposed to fasten and which you weren't, and all the rest of it. Apart from that, there was the interest I had in different musicians from different times. I always liked the cool ones. [laughs] Miles Davis and Charlie Parker, the Modern Jazz Quartet or Chet Baker. They all had a sense of being quite chic. I felt that I wasn't doing anything particularly new, just taking bits from here and there that I liked, and assembling my own doctrine.

WAS THE WHITE TUXEDO FOR 'ANOTHER TIME, ANOTHER PLACE' JUST ONE OF A LIST OF OPTIONS FOR THE COVER SHOT?

I can't remember. I just remember sitting with Antony Price and saying, "What do we do next?" He's always loved men in uniform, so we thought there's nothing more of a uniform than a dinner jacket. It can either be black or white, and a white dinner jacket has quite a strong look. In some countries they said I looked like a waiter [laughs], which wasn't the desired effect. But in England and America it brings out connotations of the great cruise liners and a bygone age of people dressed in a very sophisticated way to go out in the evening. It could make you think of casinos and the movie Casablanca; a lot of interesting connotations that are romantic, sexy, exclusive – things that we thought were interesting at the time. As you say, it's a very strong image, and it did stick for a long time. I was resentful of it in a way but now I tend to think it was quite a good thing.

THE LAST LINE OF THE FIRST ROXY MUSIC ALBUM IS "SHOULD MAKE THE COGNOSCENTI THINK". IS THIS AN APT SUMMARY OF YOUR ARTISTIC AMBITION?

At the time it was. More than to sell vast numbers of records; I hadn't thought about that really at all. It was more a case of just making a record, making a statement, and creating something that could make some kind of mark and make people think. Especially smart people. We thought that if it's going to appeal to anyone, it's going to appeal to people who are bright, smart, with it. That's the crowd we wanted to touch. The first record was exciting to make because it had so many different flavors. I thought, well, it would make me think if I heard it [laughs].

IS IT FAIR TO SAY THAT YOU'RE AN ARTIST IN THE TRADITIONAL SENSE BUT THAT YOU'VE CHOSEN TO WORK IN THE MEDIUM OF STARDOM?

It's a very strange medium to work in because it's so wide and all-embracing. The art world – the world of picture-making, sculpture, video, and event-based art – is quite small. I was asking for trouble, really, in trying to work in a bigger world than that, one that is less special and where you have to try and sell your art to a mass public. It's quite nice to think of making your work for a small and more discerning kind of audience again. But once you've sold in large numbers to a mass market, it's very hard to go back the other way. Because there's also a snobbery of a certain kind that people have about artists: that if somebody is popular, then they can't be any good. I would hope that it didn't apply to me, but I don't know. It would be nice to do something again that was quite demanding to the listener.

DO YOU THINK THAT YOU'VE ALWAYS BEEN INTERESTED – SINCE MOD ONWARDS, PERHAPS – IN THE IDEA OF ÉLITES?

Yes, I probably have. I remember that when I left school I very much wanted to go to university rather than art college. At that time there was quite a difference. There were only about three universities where you could study fine art, and you felt you were going to be with people who were more interested in the thought and theory of it. Whereas if you went to art school you'd be with people who were good at drawing rather than good at thinking. That's how it seemed to be. It was more difficult to get into university but I suppose that you'd meet a better class of person [laughs]. I guess I had a fairly élitist view of what I was interested in, and that's a good example of how you're probably right. I suppose I've always been a bit stuck up. I like being with smart people rather than those who aren't. I wanted to be with people who would get me going, and not only at university. When I was living in Newcastle for those four years, you'd want to go to the clubs where the best-looking girls or the coolest people were. There were cliques and élites wherever you looked. I noticed that when I came to London as well. Although I can't say that I ever graduated to becoming a part of any particular group. I've always felt outside, and that's one characteristic of me I suppose. I've always been on the outside looking in. Or the inside looking out.

The work of Bryan Ferry was not represented during the exhibition at the Centre for Fine Arts in Brussels

— This interview was first published in Frieze, issue 80, January/February 2004

> I've always felt outside, and that's one characteristic of me I suppose: I've always been on the outside looking in. Or the inside looking out.

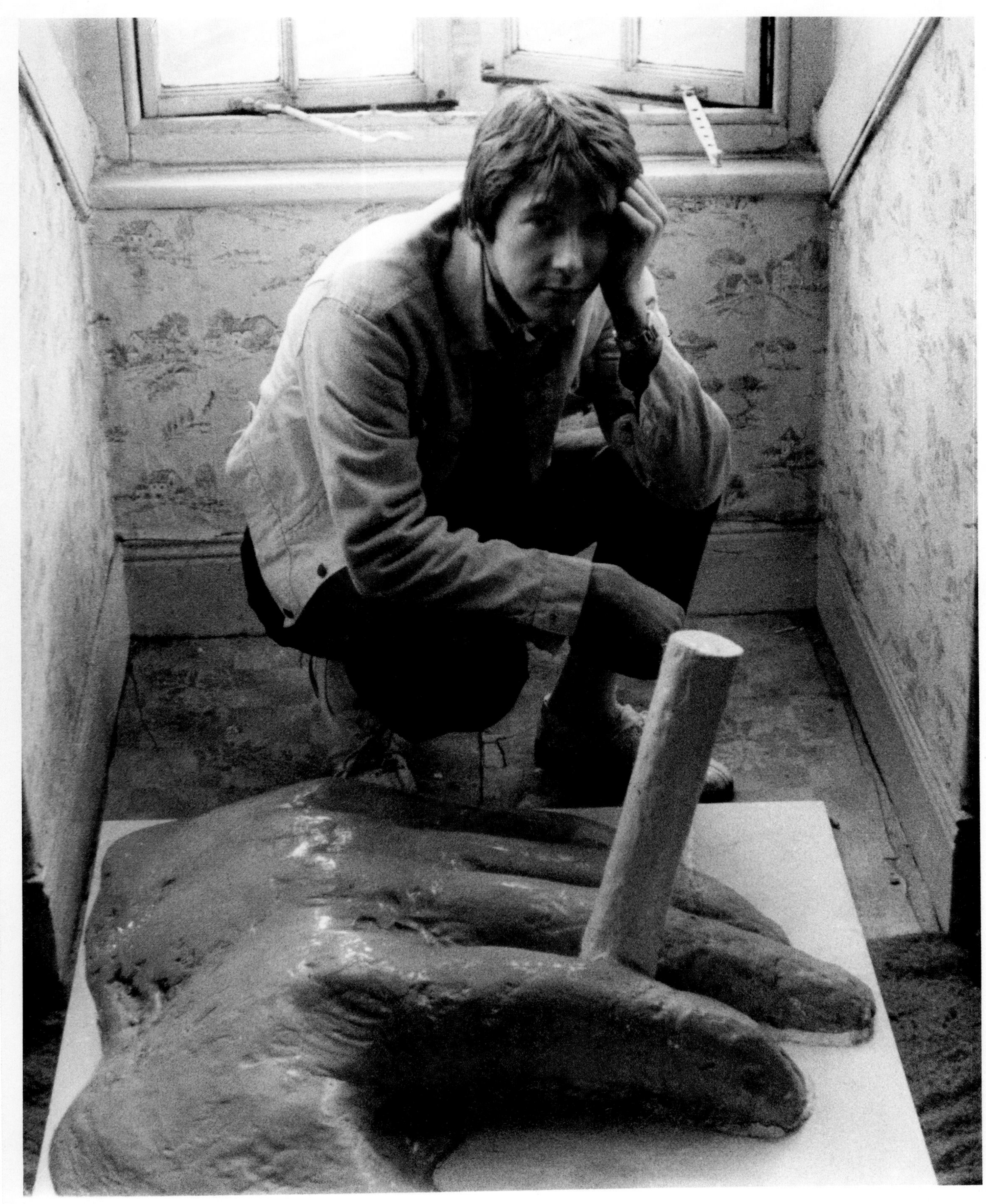

Photo by Michael Brick
Permission Bryan Ferry

Page 104/105
Photo by Michael Brick
Permission Bryan Ferry

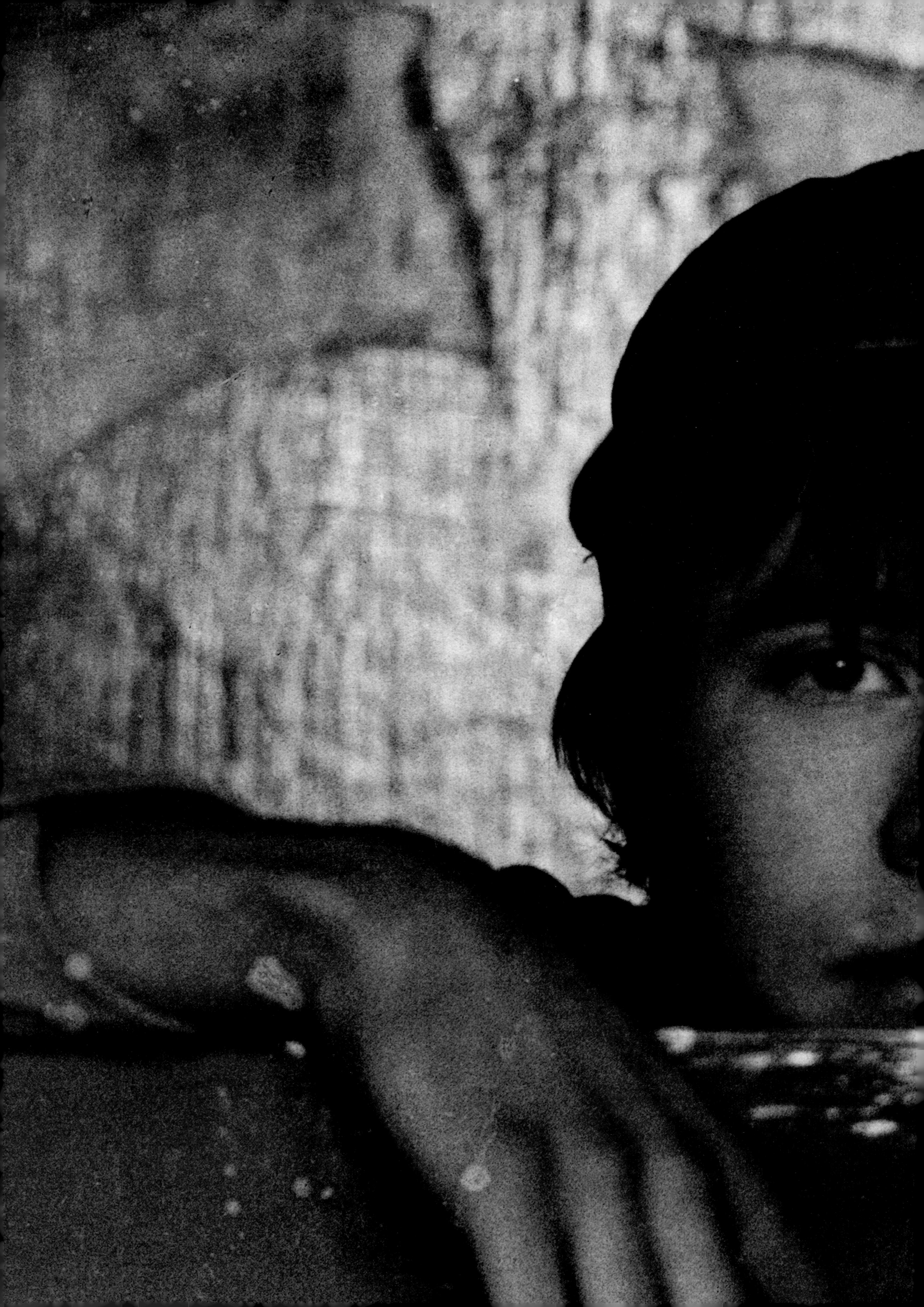

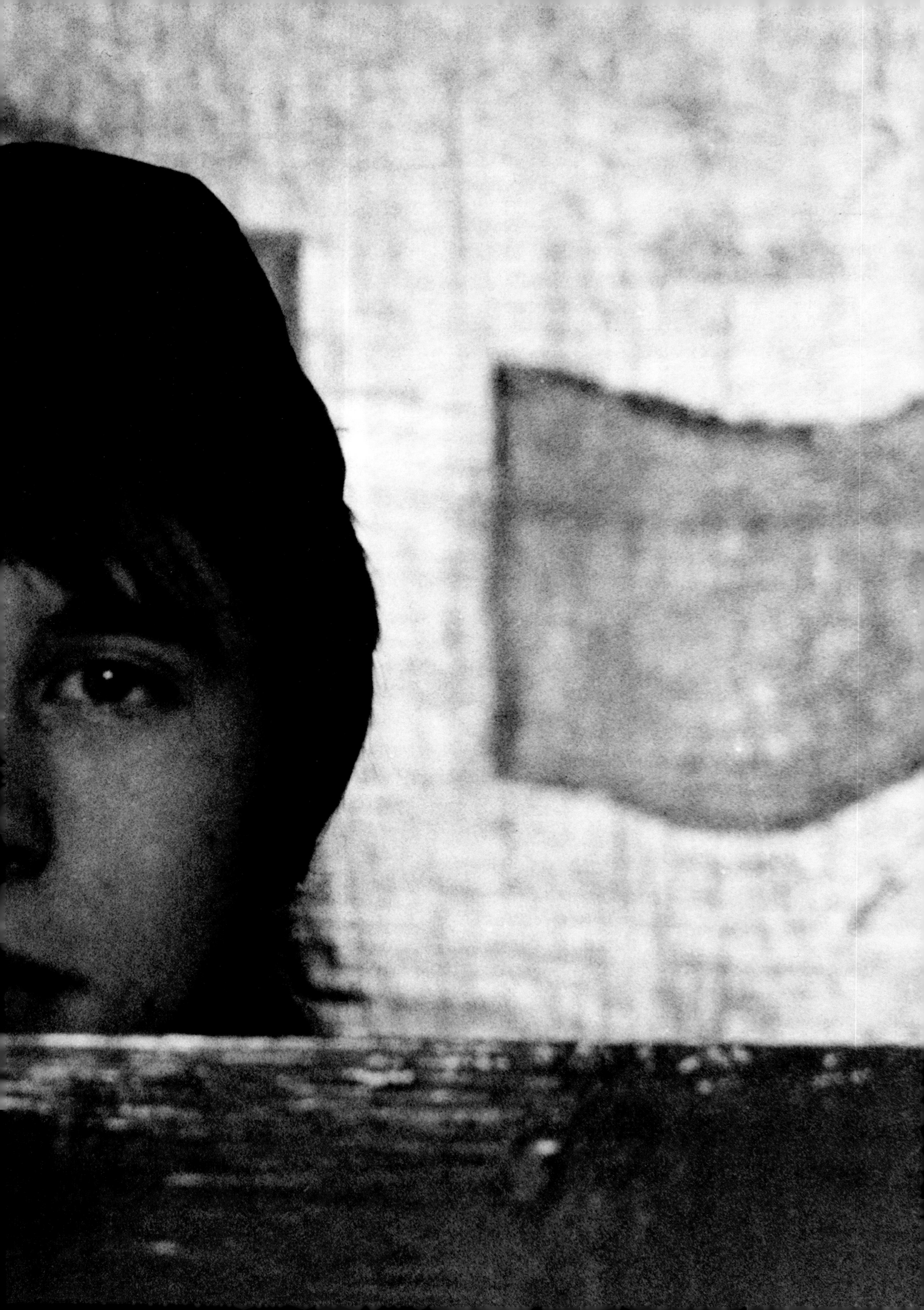

KYLe Fle

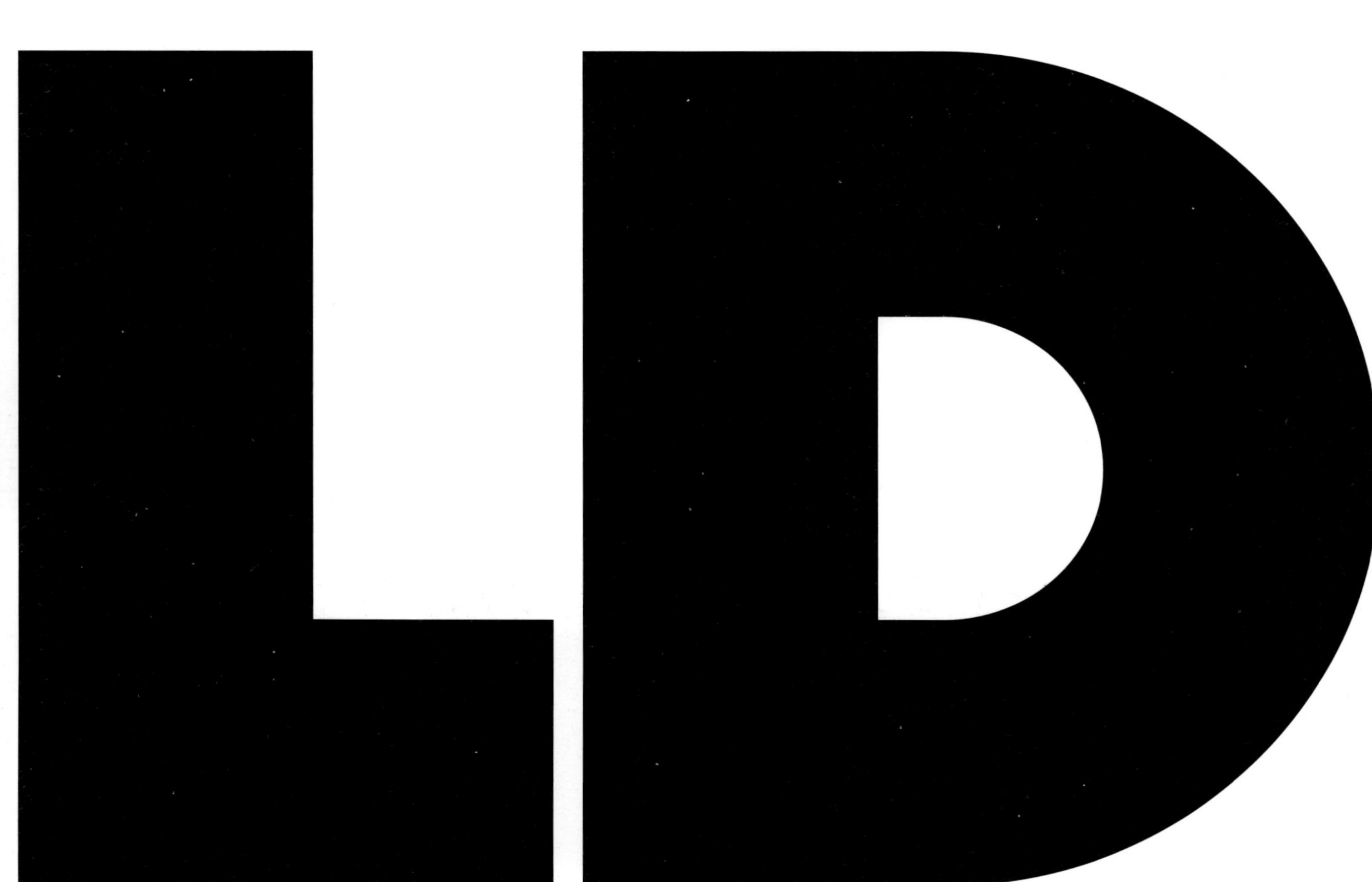

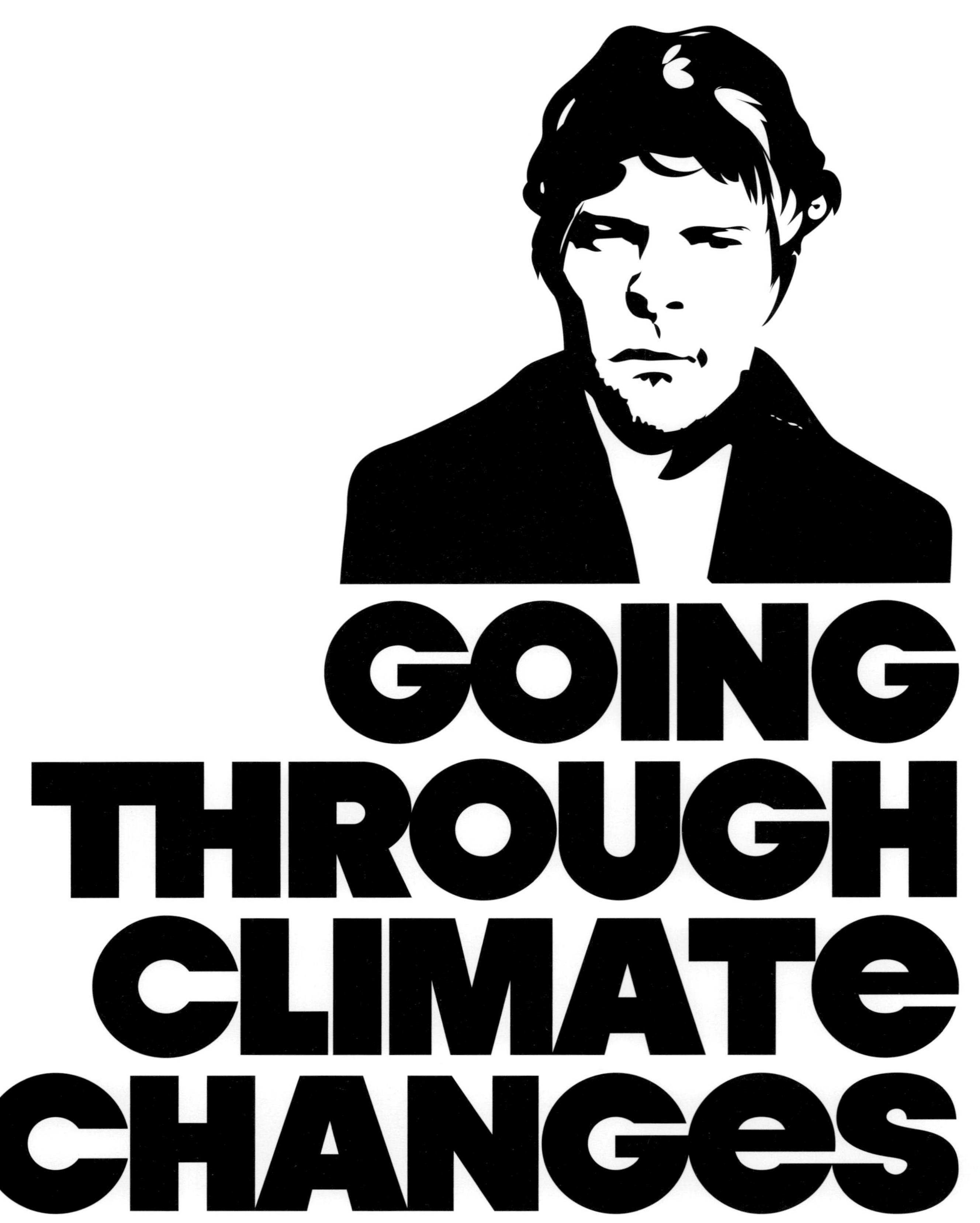

GOING
THROUGH
CLIMATE
CHANGES

Kyle Field is an artist, surfer, and musician, and his daily life is dominated by these activities. Under the pseudonym of Little Wings, this self-proclaimed "strolling minstrel" has created his musical alter ego, and collaborates frequently with a revolving door of musicians that has included M. Ward, and Jason Lytle of Grandaddy. In 2002, Little Wings' Light Green Leaves' album (K Records) was released on CD, LP, and cassette, in a different recorded version of the album for each format. Incorporating homemade instruments he has discovered along the way, Field "paints" his songs, creating a distinctive audio-palette and a personal, neo-folk sound he is constantly reinventing.

Kyle Field's visual work often deals with the theme of memories. His drawings can be recognized by their delicate lines and soft colors – a subtle combination of pastels and ink – and are peppered with his poetry. His visual universe shares a folk aesthetic with the musical and visual work of contemporaries such as Devendra Banhart and CocoRosie. 2007 saw the release of his eighth album and his first book of drawings, released on the Ahornfelder label.

— Kyle Field was born in 1973 in Alabama (USA). He currently lives in California.

KYLE FIELD INTERVIEWED BY JÉRÔME SANS

WHEN DID YOU START MAKING DRAWINGS?

As a baby and a child and young man I would like to lay on the kitchen floor and stick my tongue out and let it explore my lips, and listen to the music my parents were always playing, and try to stay in a creative mood.

HAVE YOU BEEN TO AN ART SCHOOL?

I have been to a few different art schools. The next-door neighbor had a good one. Then art lessons, lots of lessons in technique early on. I started showing real promise when I was 16, and won 250 dollars for a "say no to drugs" poster contest, and my folks really thought it was great I could make a bit of money on my art. The money changes everything.

HOW AND WHY DID YOU START MAKING MUSIC?

I started playing bass guitar as a teenager. I wanted to make music because I love music so much. I wanted to learn how to do it, you know, and I have ended up meeting a lot of people and going to a lot of places, neither of which I might have seen without this outlet. I feel excited about that, thinking about it, really.

HOW DO YOU RELATE YOUR ART PRACTICE TO YOUR MUSIC?

I am not sure that they are related. I just have to keep busy and doing many things. Like sleeping away from home… going through climate changes… continually refreshing your vision. I feel like you shift from one to another naturally.

SURFING AND THE BEACH SEEM TO PLAY IMPORTANT ROLES IN YOUR EVERYDAY LIFE. DOES THIS EXPLAIN THE PIECE YOU MADE FOR AN EXHIBITION IN POITIERS AT LE CONFORT MODERNE — A LITTLE BEACH CABIN WITH A VIDEO OF THE SEA PROJECTED INSIDE?

Exactly! I wanted to share a favorite spot in the outdoors with a new spot indoors. I have always enjoyed water my whole life, and surfing and stuff involved is part of my subculture that I have grown up with and I am proud of.

WHAT IS THE PROCESS IN MAKING YOUR DRAWINGS? IS IT CLOSE TO THE MAKING OF YOUR MUSIC?

I like sitting comfortably and trying to do my best. I'm a new man now!

HOW WOULD YOU DEFINE YOUR DRAWINGS AND YOUR MUSIC?

They are really like diaries in some way, and sort of personal, reflecting on thoughts or feelings about what is happening always.

ARE THE WORDS APPEARING IN YOUR DRAWINGS THE LINK BETWEEN BOTH?

I don't think so. There are so many things in the world. I am drawing web lines between them all – not just between my things – and my things.

WHAT IS THE STATUS OF THE WORDS?

It is poetry!

> **I just have to keep busy and doing many things. Like sleeping away from home… going through climate changes… continually refreshing your vision. I feel like you shift from one to another naturally.**

DOES THE MAKING OF A DRAWING INSPIRE YOU TO MAKE A SONG, OR VICE VERSA?

Yes, all the time. I go back and forth between all practices, and the newness inspires.

WHY 'LITTLE WINGS' AS THE NAME OF YOUR BAND?

It just sort of happened that way.

WHAT ARE YOU REFERENCES IN ART AND IN MUSIC?

My books are 'Lord of the Flies' (William Golding), 'The Outsiders' (S. E. Hinton), 'Big Sur and The Oranges of Hieronymus Bosch' (Henry Miller); movies are 'Deliverance', 'The Shining', 'Big Wednesday'. I was born in the South and absorbed some of that, and have gotten to mix it in with the West Coast.

WHICH ARE THE ARTISTS YOU FEEL CLOSE TO AND WHY?

I check in with the following people: Barrett Gentz, Jake Longstreth, Jay Nelson, Jeffrey Manson, Andrew Kidman, Thomas Campbell, Erik Bluhm, Tim Bluhm, Lee Baggett, Ashley Corbin, Rachel Corry, Creative Moving Eyes, and other people that I will certainly forget to mention here. I also collaborate with musicians more recently, such as Lee Gull, White Rainbow, Swanny' Prince' Richard and Tommy Mc Donald of Marin Headlands Bicycle Guides and all of the people at Mollusk in San Francisco where I live now.

DOES YOUR VISUAL ART APPEAR IN YOUR LIVE MUSIC PERFORMANCES?

Yes, on record covers… at the souvenir stand… in my facial expressions, some of which are intentional and intended to inspire or entertain.

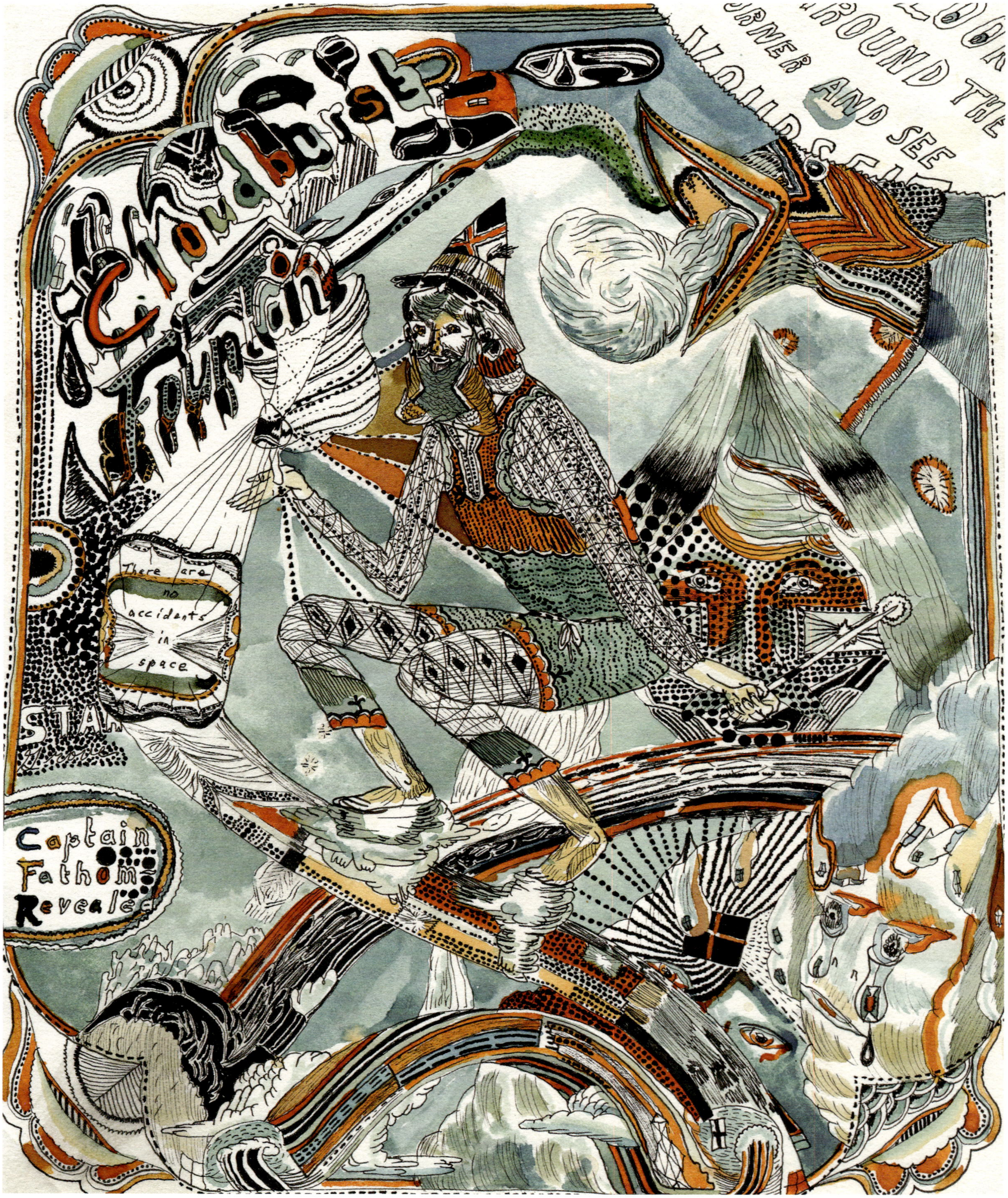

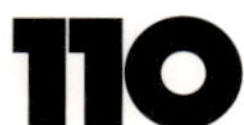

Cloudburst Fountain Toward Horizon
Aiming True
2004
Ink and watercolor on paper
20 x 24 cm
Collection of Jane Whitfield
and Jens Keumle, Paris
Courtesy of Cardenas Bellanger
© Kyle Field

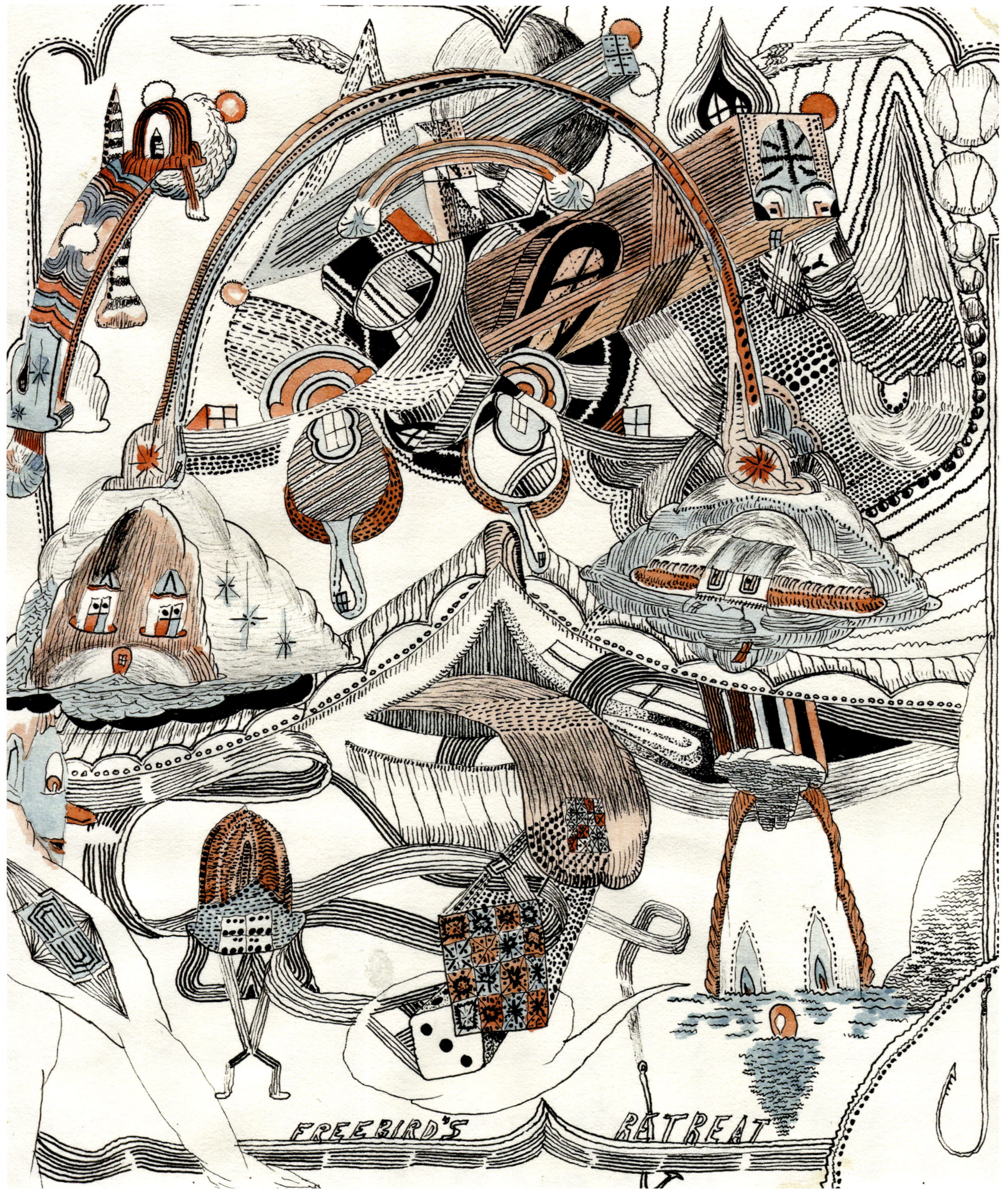

Freebird's Retreat
2004
Ink and watercolor on paper
20 x 24 cm
Collection of Jane Whitfield
and Jens Keumle, Paris
Courtesy of Cardenas Bellanger
© Kyle Field

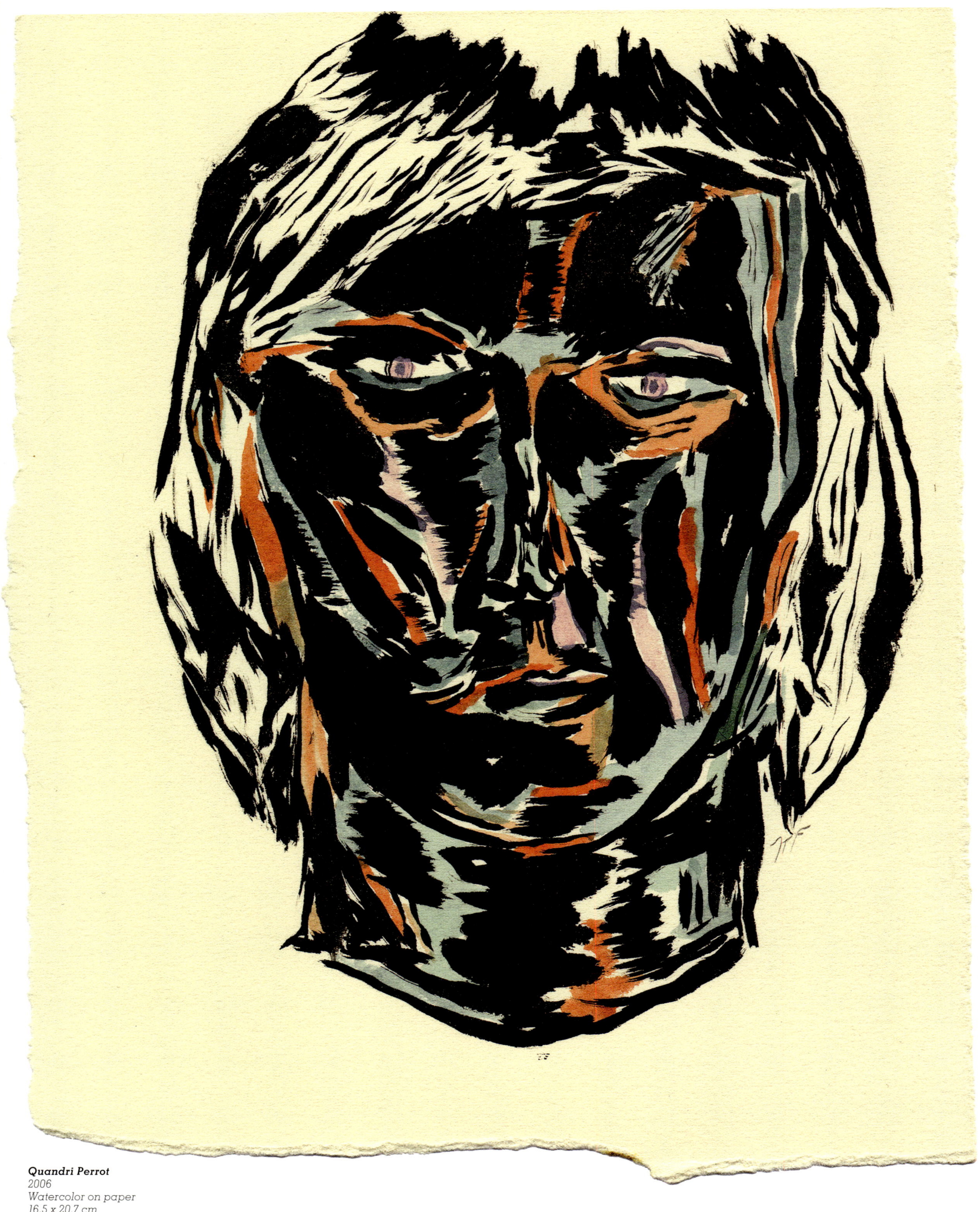

Quandri Perrot
2006
Watercolor on paper
16,5 x 20,7 cm
Private collection, Paris
Courtesy of Cardenas Bellanger
Photo Credit © Kyle Field

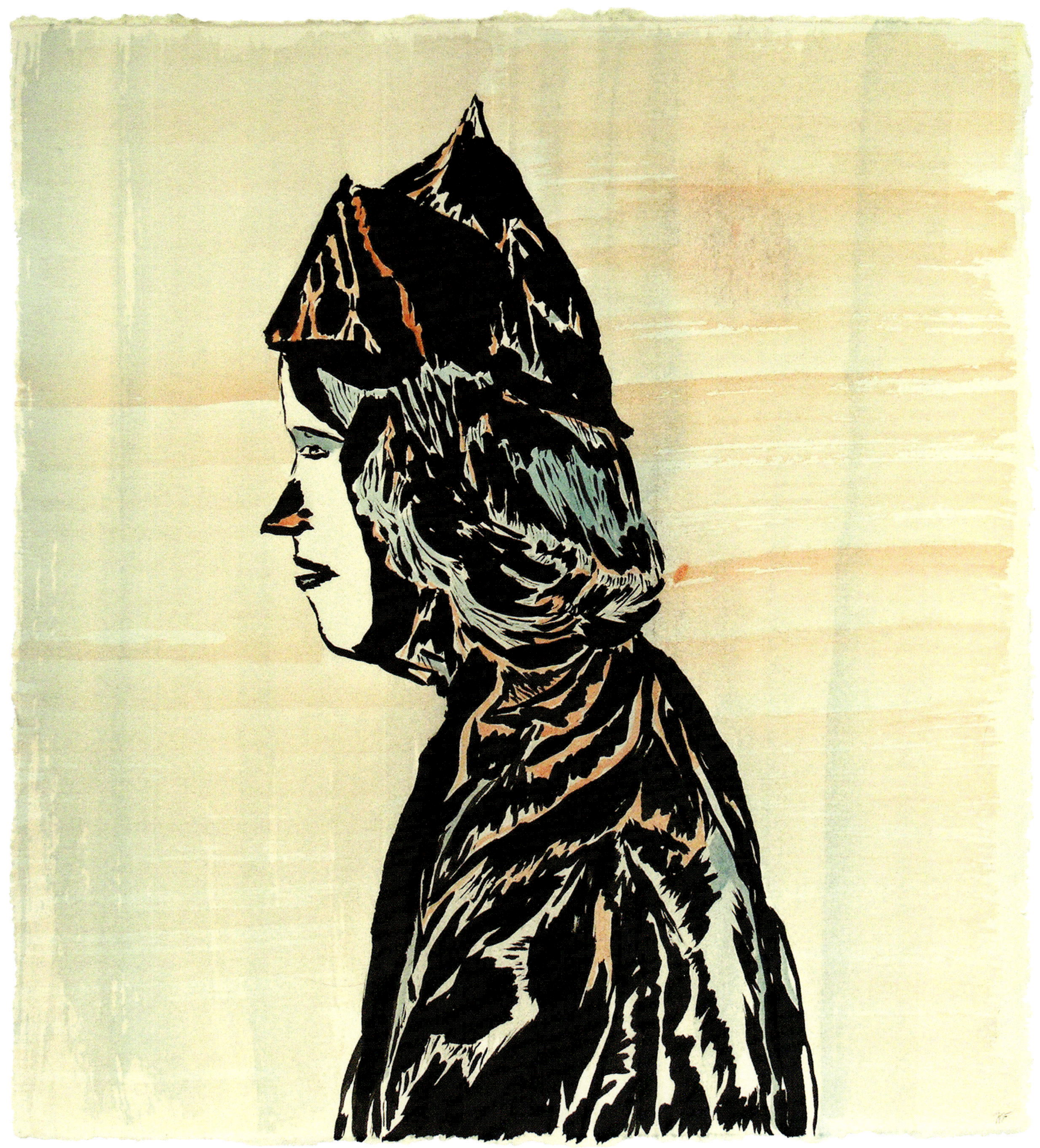

Kaysle Finn
2006
Watercolor on paper
27 x 31 cm
Collection of Bernard Crespiw, Paris
Courtesy of Cardenas Bellanger
Photo Credit © Kyle Field

FISC
SPOC

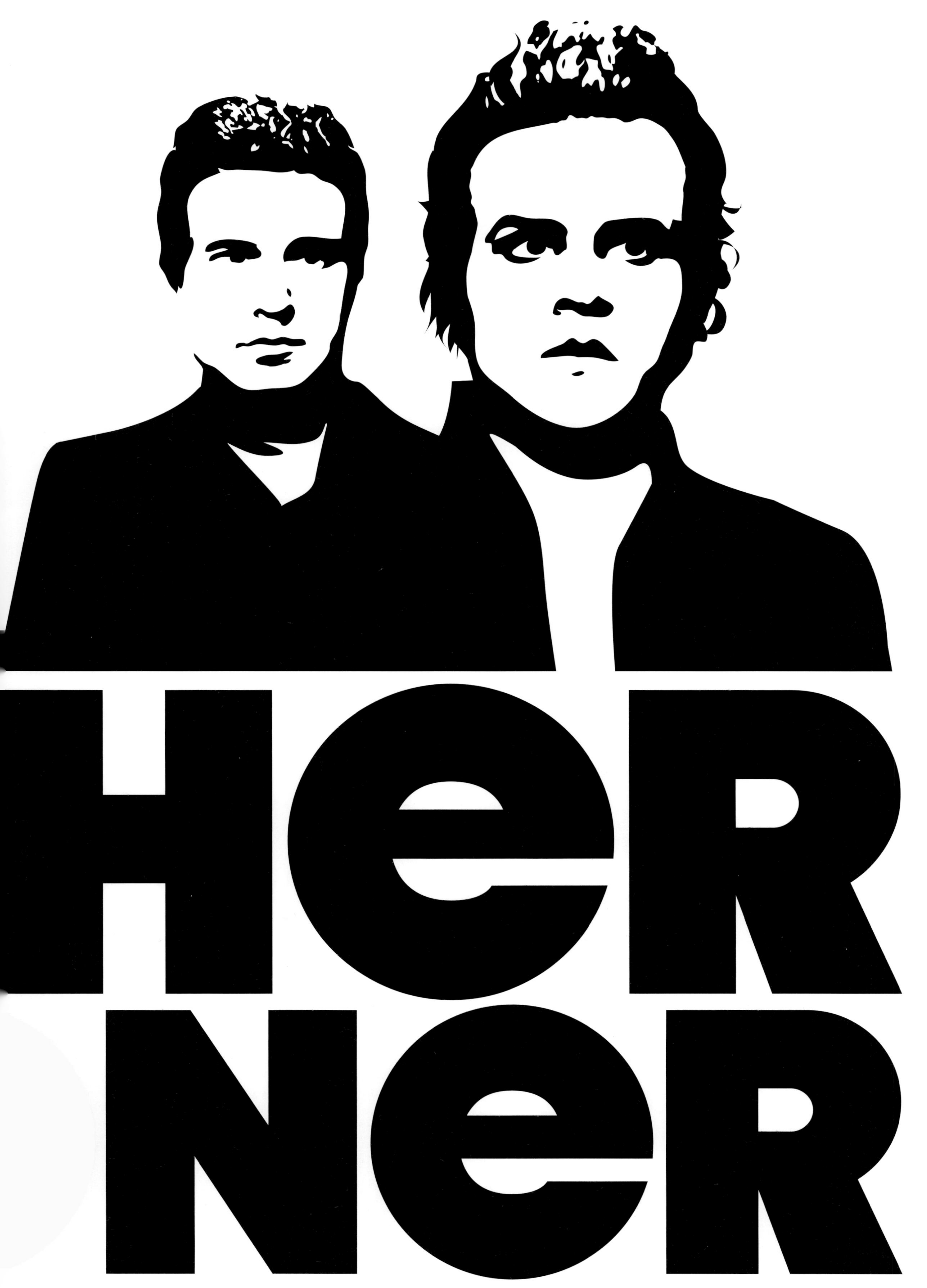

HER
NER

For the last ten years, Fischerspooner has been stretching the limits of art and music to provide pure, unabashed entertainment. Stemming from an initial idea of an artistic project about entertainment, the duet was formed in 1998 by Warren Fischer, musician, and Casey Spooner, performer. Originally composed for performances or video projects, their unique brand of electro-pop and new wave was to find its niche after a debut concert at Starbucks in New York City's Astor Place. With the release of their first album, in 2000, Fischerspooner quickly established themselves as a unique band straddling two worlds of expression. Their hit 'Emerge' from that album solidified their reputation in the international music scene.

Experimental versus mass culture, Fischerspooner does not seek to select but rather to transpose codes to reach the widest possible audience. Casey Spooner's background in experimental theater – combined with the mechanical, electronic beats produced by Warren Fischer – provides the main ingredient of their live shows – visual, theatrical, grandiose style. Fischerspooner released two singles in early 2008 and are currently working on their third full-length album.

— Casey Spooner was born in Athens, Georgia (USA) in 1970, and lives in New York City.

— Warren Fischer was born in Los Angeles, California (USA), in 1968, and lives in New York City.

CASEY SPOONER OF FISCHERSPOONER INTERVIEWED BY JÉRÔME SANS

YOU ATTENDED THE ART INSTITUTE IN CHICAGO, WHERE YOU MET WARREN FISCHER. AT THAT TIME WERE YOU ALREADY DOING PERFORMANCES?

I started as a painter but all my painting teachers said that the best part of my work was when I described my motivation behind the paintings. They encouraged me to explore performance. I met Warren in a video class, and we actually ended up doing a couple performances together; I did spoken word and he played violin.

HOW WERE YOUR PAINTINGS?

They were all different. I painted for many years. In high school I went to a special school for the arts. I was doing lots of different things, such as ceramics, sculpture, printmaking, painting, and photography. I went through many different styles and ideas. I can't remember the last painting I made, but I remember that I was trying to do portraits of people from memory.

WHO DID YOU HAVE IN MIND AT THAT TIME IN TERMS OF PERFORMANCES?

I always loved Laurie Anderson, Spalding Gray, and Grace Jones. I grew up in a conservative Southern town. My only access to cultural information was through magazines and television. It was difficult for me to find artists that I could relate to. I had always had an interest in performance but I didn't know what to do with that interest. I didn't fit in with the theater kids or the musicians. I was a visual artist with a strong interest in performance.

DID YOU FEEL CLOSER TO THE ART WORLD OR DID YOU HAVE ONE FOOT IN ART AND ONE IN MUSIC?

I went to the University of Georgia for my first year of college, and I met lots of very interesting musicians. I went on the road with one band called 'The Chickasaw Mudd Puppies'. I got this crazy idea to create a marketing plan, something called "performative merchandising". I created a character with a costume and used a microphone; I was a sideshow character and I sold T-shirts. Then I met an experimental theater director, Erika Yeomans. She invited me to do a show with her company, 'Doorika'. I worked with the company for nine years, until 1999. This was the real beginning of my performance career. The year before I started Fischerspooner I joined a band called 'Sweet Thunder', in 1997, as a singer, and also played the tambourine. Ultimately, I was always on the arty side of music. I found musicians a little too serious and a bit conservative. And I think they always felt my ideas were a little too uncool and weird.

HOW DID THE STORY OF FISCHERSPOONER START?

Warren Fischer, his wife Karen, and I were working on a film project. It was supposed to be a pitch for a television show. The show got axed but we ended up with a lot of film footage. We didn't know what to do with it. We kept cutting it and I suggested Warren should create a soundtrack. We ended up going in a totally different direction – ditching the film and making a song about a dirty cab driver. My friend Kelly Kuvo was organizing a showcase at Starbucks in New York, and she heard we were working on a song and she invited us to perform it. This is how we did our first performance, just Warren and I, and a CD. This one-song performance was a breakthrough for us. It was exciting to do something really experimental in a public space. I had been doing theater and music for years, but it was not reaching many people. All of a sudden I felt like I was doing something relevant, reaching a new audience. It was an audience that wasn't really an audience. It was people who were just buying coffee in a corporate/public space. I felt like I was doing social outreach. It was exciting and wrong.

HOW WOULD YOU DEFINE FISCHERSPOONER?

It is a portrait of entertainment.

DO YOU FEEL LIKE THE ART WORLD IS AFRAID OF ENTERTAINMENT?

Of course they are! It is a kind of evil empire, a very dangerous machine to play with. There are all these issues about reproduction and access in the art world. Dealers want to control access to the product. Artists are supposed to create works out of passion, not to produce a work in order to supply the demand of collectors and

ARE YOU ENTERTA

museums. Entertainment is about creating a product and making it as accessible as possible to as many people as possible. The underlying business of entertainment is typically what the business of the art world is trying to conceal. Value and commerce are defined very differently in these respective worlds.

IS THAT WHY YOU TRY TO ESCAPE THE TRADITIONAL CONTEXT OF ART, INVENTING YOUR OWN CHARACTER AS A PERFORMING ARTIST, A CHARACTER MORE RELATED TO THE FIELD OF ENTERTAINMENT?

It's not always that conscious. The

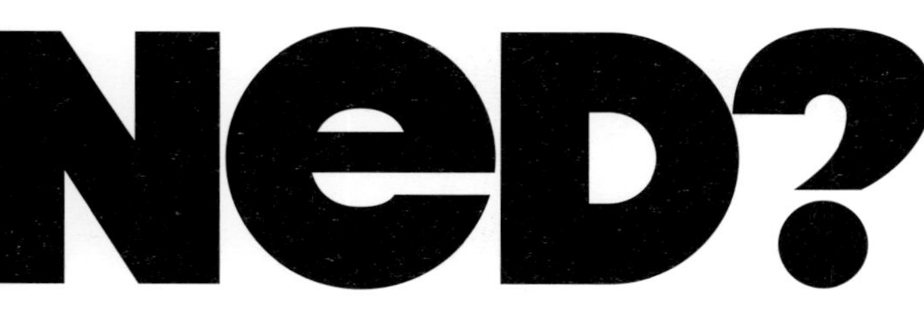

most exciting thing about this project is to make something about entertainment which ultimately can be entertainment. Creating confusion between what is art and what is entertainment, and asking what is the line between the two. I see it as a real challenge, a real opportunity, to participate in these commercial systems that are ultimately at odds with each other. I am able to be an outsider and an insider. But I feel like a person with no place. It can be terrible because you feel totally torn apart and misunderstood.

IT IS THE BEST PLACE SOMETIMES TO HAVE EVERY PLACE BUT NO ROOM.

It is definitely a very exciting and unusual place to be. It brings uneasiness and forces you to be alert.

IT IS THE MOST INSPIRING PLACE BECAUSE IT FORCES YOU TO BE CREATIVE TO STAY ALIVE.

Exactly. But it can be very frustrating. The art world is very supportive, and an amazing place to work, but as Fischerspooner became more and more popular and part of entertainment, lots of people of

the art world didn't think of it as art anymore, even if the material was the same. It is a very interesting journey for sure – the popular versus the elite, in a way.

I SAW YOUR LIVE PERFORMANCE AT THE POMPIDOU CENTRE IN 2003. I WONDER WHETHER THE MUSIC WORLD WOULD HAVE ACCEPTED THE STAGING OF SUCH A SHOW IN A TRADITIONAL CONCERT HALL OR CLUB…

This was the show that we performed in support of our first record for years. We took this production out on the road and played in music venues all over the world. And it was received very well. But the audiences were always divided; some people loved it and some people hated it. This always thrilled me. It felt like we were doing something provocative, something against the grain. We had always avoided performing in music festivals or doing shows with other bands because we were using all pre-recorded music. Then in 2003 at 'The Coachella Music Festival', we agreed to share the stage with more traditional music acts. It was a big turning point and the show was a success. It didn't matter if the music was created live or not; it was more about an exciting performance. When the time came to do the next record it was very difficult to create a new show within the traditional corporate system of a major label. It was all about having a proposal, presenting that proposal, presenting a budget… It takes us a long time to develop a show, and the music business wasn't interested. We kept saying we aren't a band; we can't just go out and play. It is a show. What we do always takes time. We worked on a music video once for a year. By traditional entertainment standards, that's ridiculous.

IS THAT WHY YOU GATHERED SUCH AN AMAZING CAST OF COLLABORATORS, RANGING FROM LINDA PERRY TO SUSAN SONTAG, DAVID BYRNE TO MIRWAIS?

Working with a major label gave us access to people we would never have been able to work with otherwise. We could work in big studios with the best technicians in the world. We were legitimized in a way. It was about trying to bring worlds together: the avant-garde, the intellectual, and entertainment. We chose a broad range of people that were unique, and represented our interests. From the biggest hit-writer to a famous intellectual.

WHICH CONTEMPORARY MUSICIANS OR VISUAL ARTISTS DO YOU FEEL CLOSE TO? WHICH CREATORS FROM OTHER FIELDS?

I've been working with the 'Wooster Group' a lot.

THE 'WOOSTER GROUP' IS FOR ME AN UNDERGROUND GROUP FROM THE 1970S DOING PERFORMANCES IN NEW YORK. WHAT IS YOUR RELATIONSHIP WITH THEM?

This is my background; it is the company I always wanted to work with. It is part of the tradition of performance that I had always dreamed to be a part of. I was surrounded

by a world I didn't understand and that didn't understand me. I went to the 'Wooster Group' for safe harbor. Right now they are more or less the only artists I feel close to. There is a combination of sound, image, and performance, which is complicated and layered. It is a very special company, that I have great respect for.

WHAT ABOUT THIS NEW VERSION OF 'HAMLET' DIRECTED BY ELIZABETH LECOMPTE? WHAT IS YOUR ROLE?

I play a couple of different characters: Laertes, Rosencrantz, Guildenstern, and The Player King. All the actors have multiple roles. Warren and I also made music for the show. Warren contributed instrumental music, and we wrote two songs using Shakespeare's text.

IS IT A NEW DIRECTION YOU INTEND TO DEVELOP IN THE FUTURE?

It is great for me to work with people I respect, and to learn from them. The thing is, I have never been able to find a mentor. I always wanted to interact with an older generation of artists. It is very difficult and it is not a tradition in contemporary art; there is not this idea of the atelier and the old master. I enjoy learning from someone else and doing something together in a nontraditional way. Now 'Hamlet' is almost done and we are finishing up the new record. The 'Wooster Group' is helping us develop the next FS performance. We are also partnering with producers to build a show that can live in a theater for a long period. So I guess I am moving more towards theater. But we always end up somewhere in between.

WHAT WILL BE THE DIRECTION OF THE THIRD ALBUM, WHICH YOU'RE WORKING ON?

It is more electronic. It is, in a way, a perfect combination of the first and second record. It is a return to a more synthetic sound but with stronger songwriting. Now we are going to Brazil to find a location for the São Paulo Biennial. I also want to return to more performance-driven shows, more experimental, unusual, and unique.

YOU ARE ALSO WORKING ON A BOOK?

Yes, we are working on a book. I have been very busy organizing the archives. We have a lot of visual material, starting in 1998, that has never been seen. It is very early stuff, when we were constantly changing and experimenting. We are focusing on the period 1998–2003. It is a beautiful arc from a very small performance-art project into "real" entertainment.

WHO IS GOING TO PUBLISH IT?

We don't know yet.

> The most exciting thing about the project was to make something related to entertainment which ultimately became entertainment; creating confusion about what is art and what is entertainment and asking where is the limit between the two.

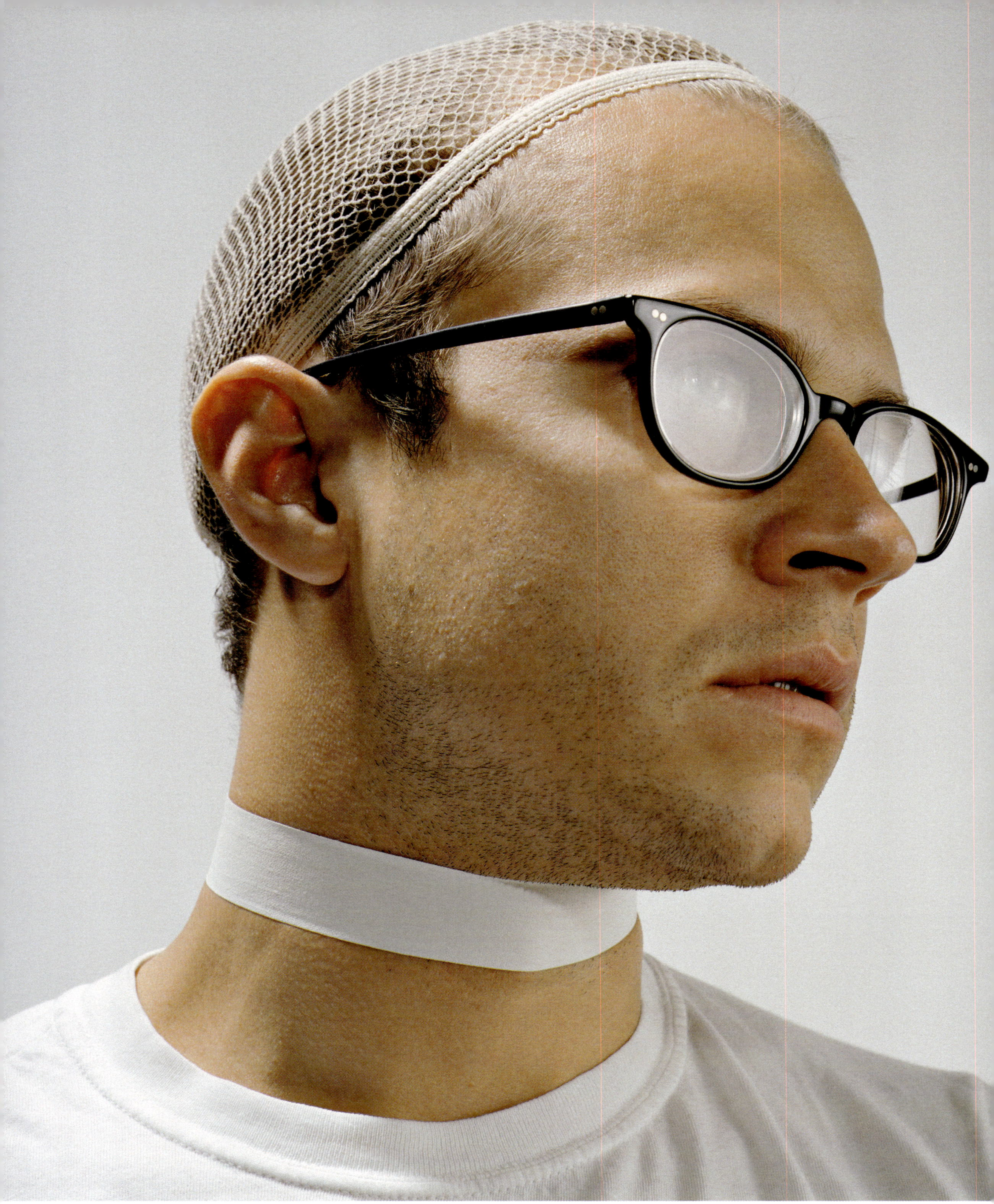

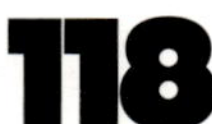

Monster
2003
Five images, C-print
Edition of 3
127 x 130,81 cm
Courtesy of Deitch Projects, New York
Photo Credit © Roe Ethridge

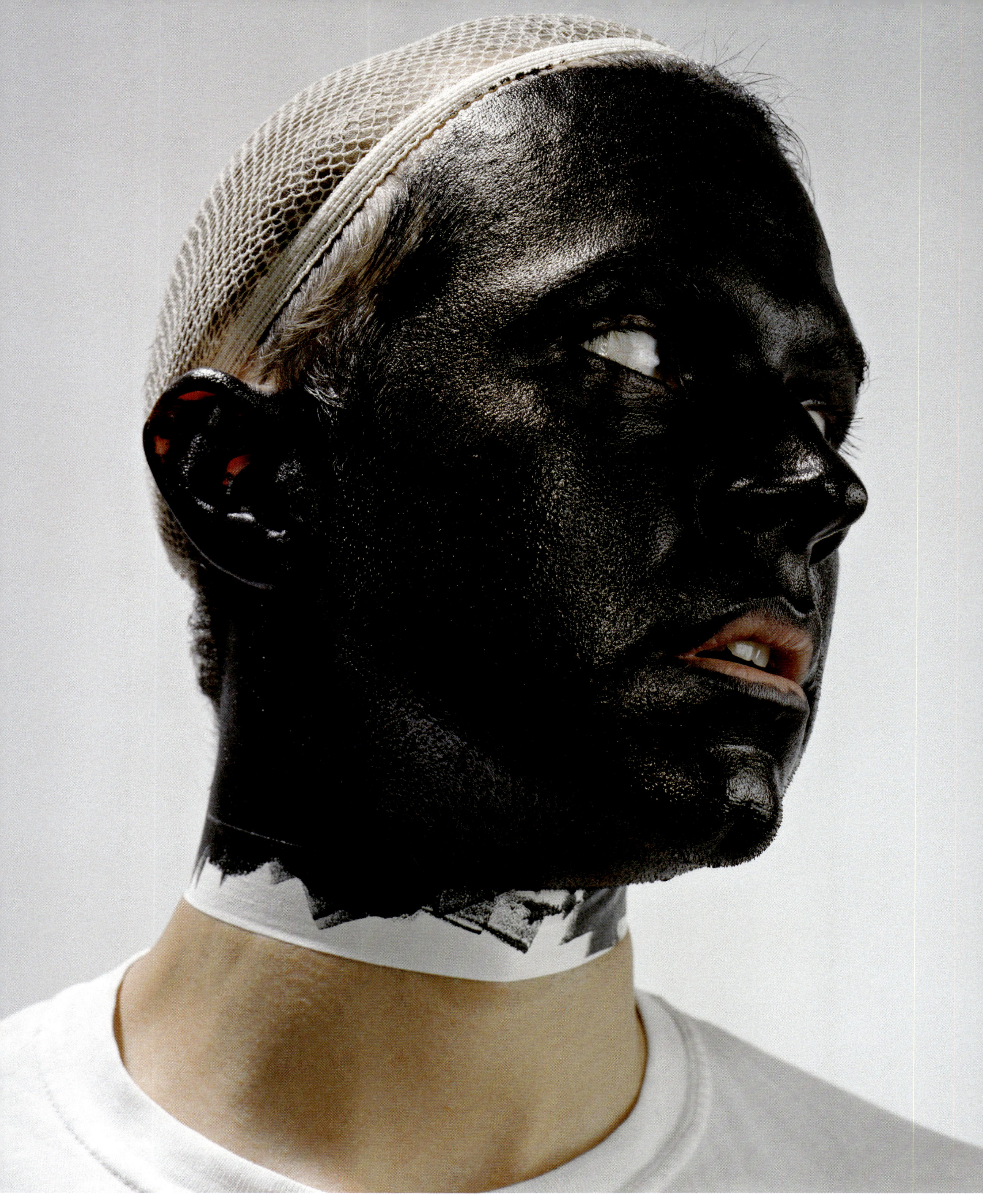

Monster
2003
Five images, C-print
Edition of 3
127 x 130,81 cm
Courtesy of Deitch Projects, New York
Photo Credit © Roe Ethridge

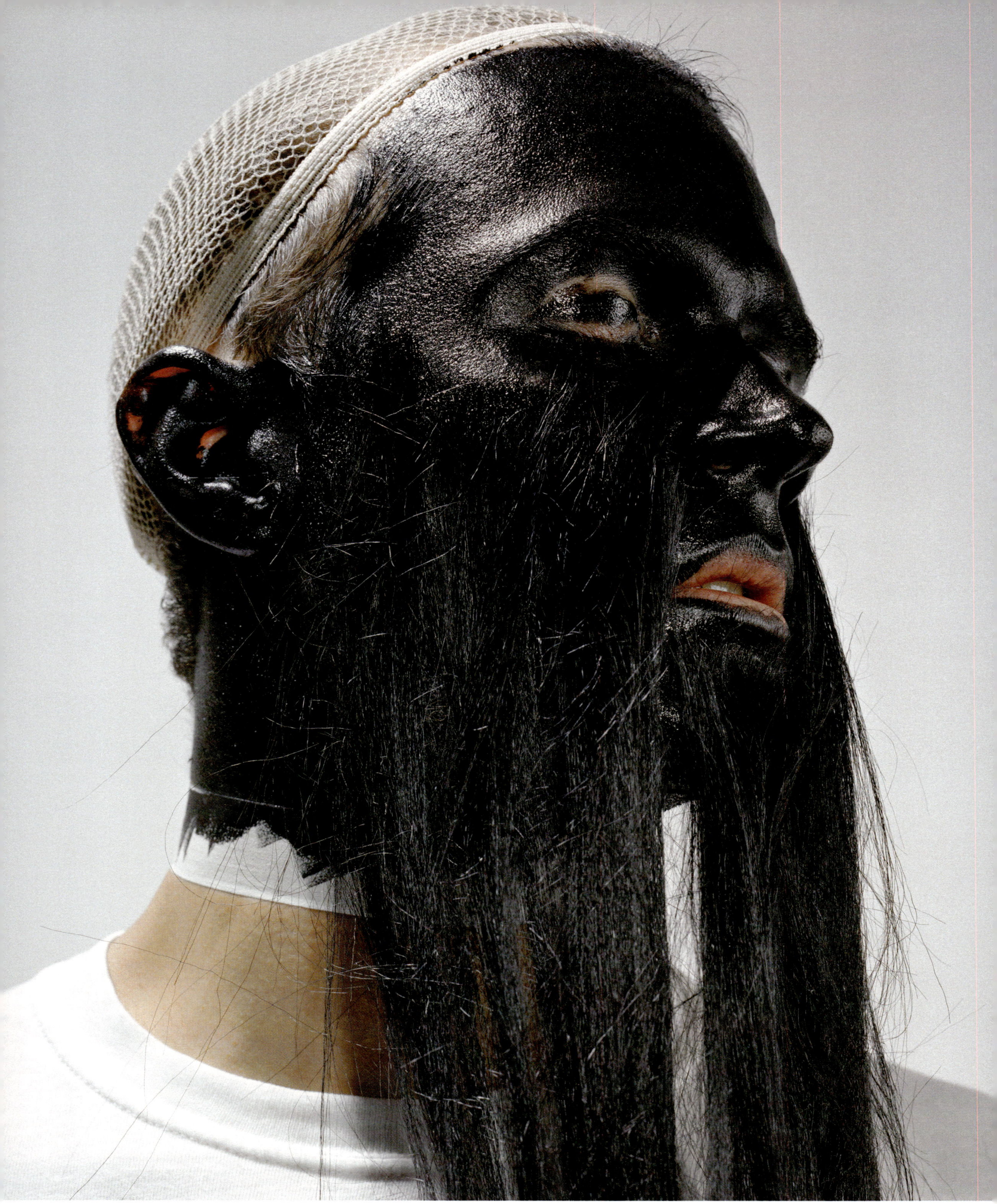

Monster
2003
Five images, C-print
Edition of 3
127 x 130,81 cm
Courtesy of Deitch Projects, New York
Photo Credit © Roe Ethridge

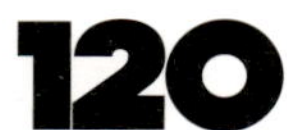

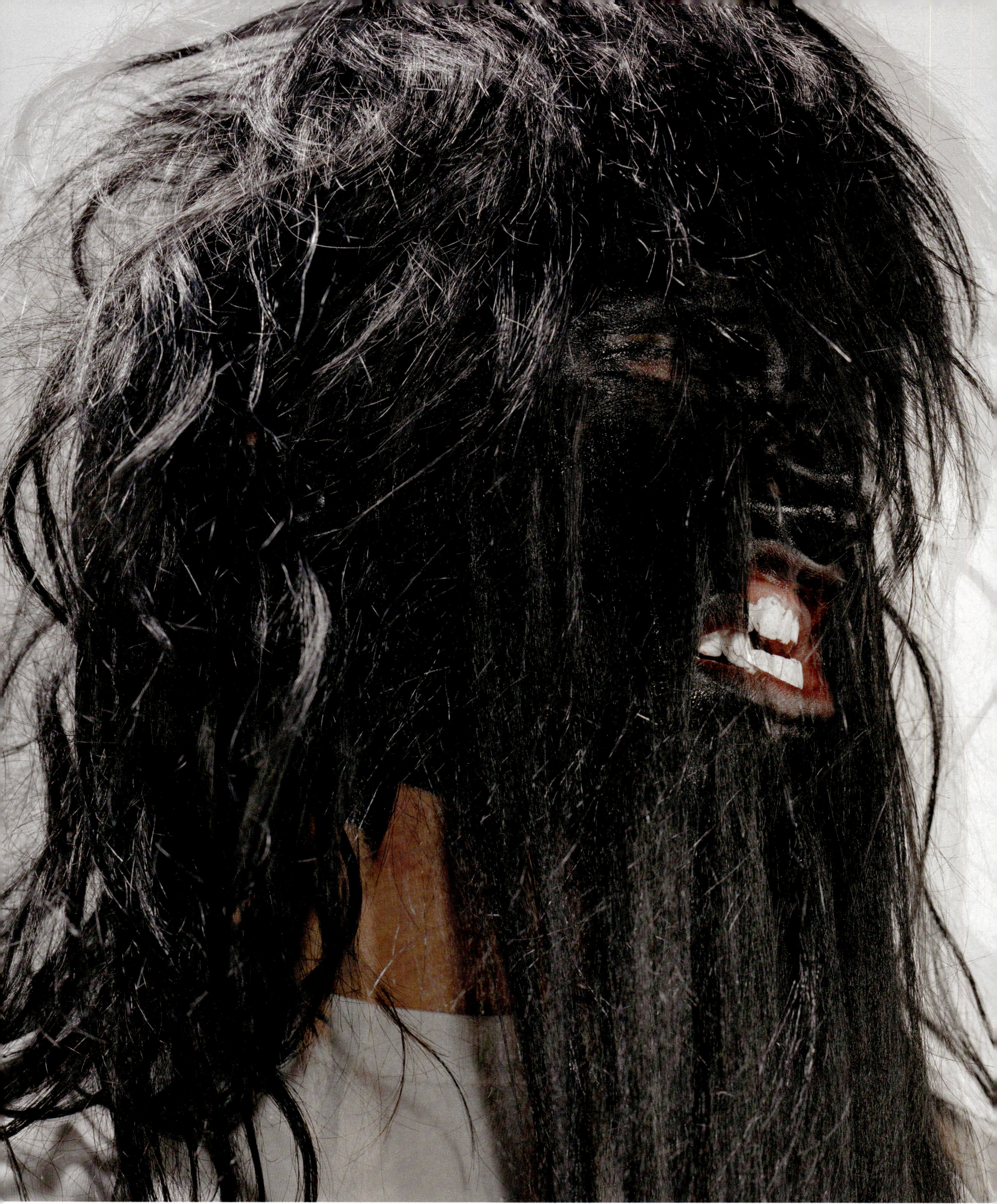

Monster
2003
Five images, C-print
Edition of 3
127 x 130,81 cm
Courtesy of Deitch Projects, New York
Photo Credit © Roe Ethridge

THE KI

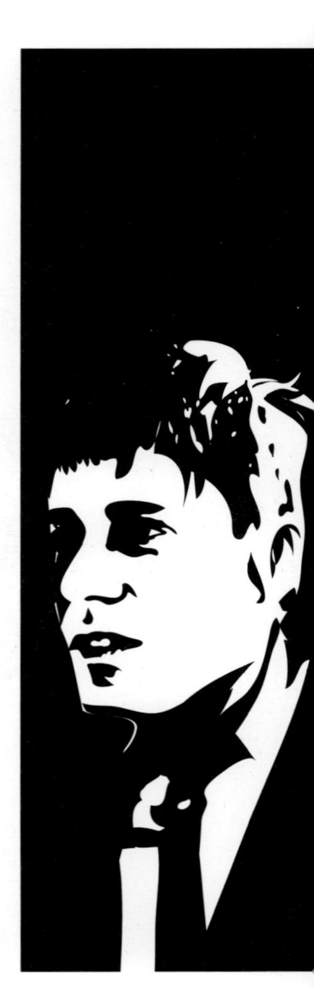

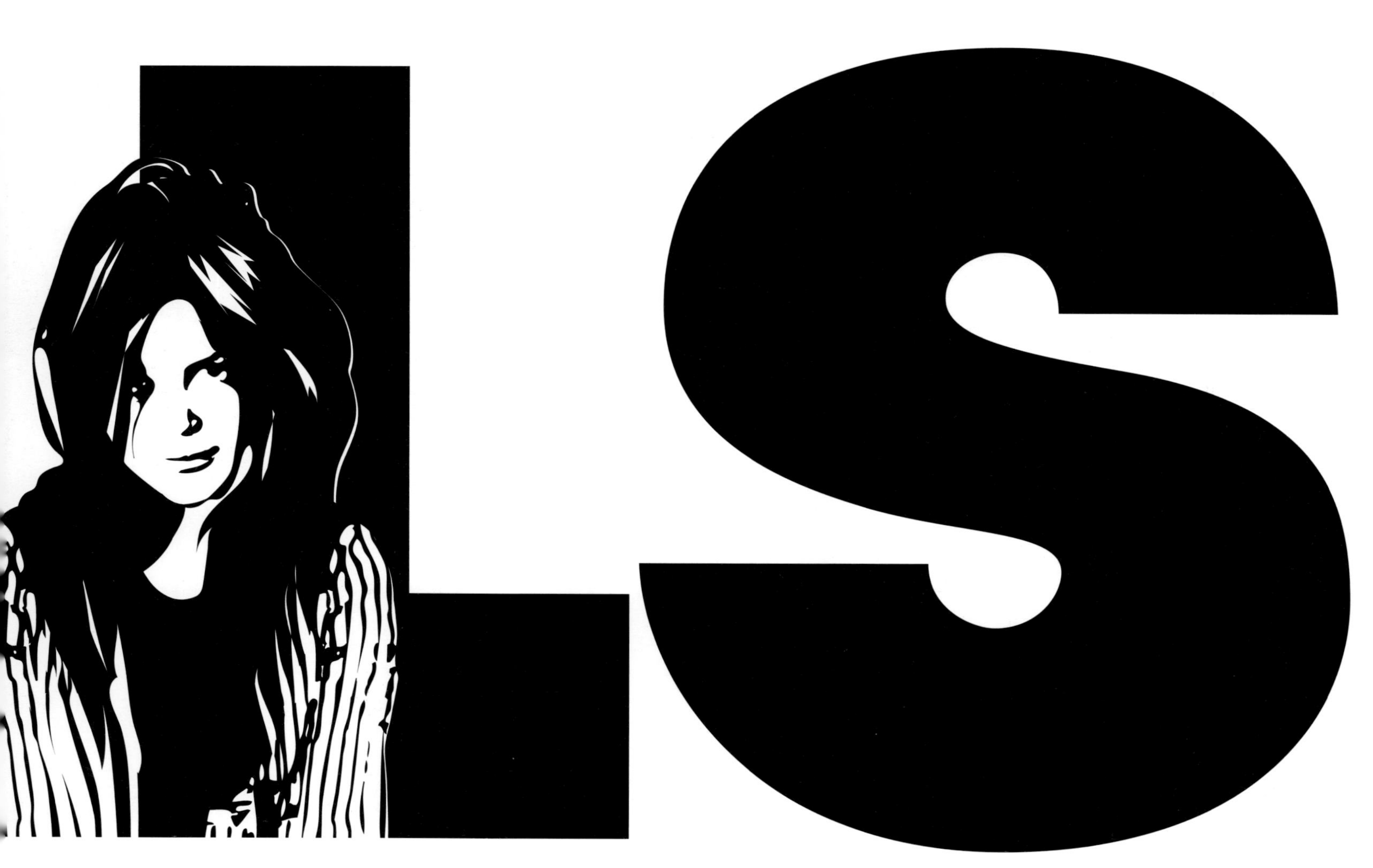

When you cross Florida with England you get The Kills. Two soul mates whose paths first crossed in London, Alison Mosshart and Jamie Hince – also known as VV and Hotel, respectively – form with The Kills something beyond merely a rock duo. Eight years and three albums in, their raw, primitive, bluesy punk-rock has given rise to an extended body of visual work.

Their band is their life, the space between them, the energy that fuels their songs. In their journeys they record not only music, but everything, documenting their lives through polaroids, drawings, films, and sketches. Strongly influenced by Warhol and Dada, The Kills open up the doors to their private playground, with a patchwork of their memories. Their third and latest album, Midnight Boom, was released in March 2008 on Domino.

— Alison Mosshart was born 1978 in Vero Beach, Florida (USA), and lives in London.

— Jamie Hince was born 1968 in Newport Pagnell (UK), and today lives in London.

ALISON MOSSHART AND JAMIE HINCE OF THE KILLS, INTERVIEWED BY JÉRÔME SANS

HOW DID YOU CHOOSE YOUR NAME 'THE KILLS'?

Alison: We sat on the floor, each with a typewriter, and typed out lists of names. We wanted something that sounded timeless. The Kills was on Jamie's list. When we finished recording our first roll of tape – at Toe Rag, for our Black Rooster EP – we needed a name to write on the box. So we wrote The Kills.

Jamie: It was the last name, typed after hundreds of names on dozens of sheets of paper, and we just stopped after I read it out loud. It was a day of dueling typewriters and The Kills was the last one standing. That was it.

HOW DID THE BAND START? WHAT WERE YOUR BACKGROUNDS?

Alison: We had both been playing music for years in other bands. I had grown up in Vero Beach, Florida. There wasn't much going on there. A small retirement community – a lot of Cadillacs, white hair, bingo… Zero youth culture. My mother was an art teacher, my dad a used-car dealer. I grew up around cars and paintings. We decided to start a band with some guys I was skateboarding with. I was about 14. When I was 18 or 19 I met Jamie in England when I was on tour. We became a little sort of social club, the two of us. We talked about books; he played me records I had never heard – Captain Beefheart,

> **When he picked me up from the airport, we said we didn't want to have a band in our lives anymore; we wanted our life to be a band, an artwork, an all-encompassing nightmare… pleasure… everything.**

when we first met, part of scenes we weren't really connecting to anymore. Jamie lent me a four-track cassette recorder to take on the road. I took it away and brought it back to him with tapes full of noise, talking, German radio, and some songs. That's when he started adding stuff to what I had done. I went back to Florida and we sent music to each other by mail – four-track tapes, art, long letters, drawings, photographs. I had found someone to share my secrets with. I was in art school at the time, and suddenly everything I did had a purpose. I had someone that mattered to me, to show things to. I dropped out of school, quit my band, and moved to England to hang out with Jamie. We played our first show together on Valentine 's Day, 2002.

HOW WOULD YOU DEFINE YOUR BAND? IS THERE A MANIFESTO BEHIND THE KILLS, OR ANY SPECIFIC ISSUES THAT YOU REACH?

Alison: I don't really think of The Kills as a band. We never intended just to play music. It has always been about an attitude, about art, about life. When he picked me up from the airport, we said we didn't want to have a band in our lives anymore; we wanted our life to be a band, an artwork, an all-encompassing nightmare… pleasure… everything. We decided if we were going to start something, it would involve our heartbeat, our breathing, our sleeping, our fighting, our habits, our insecurities… everything, just everything. And there would be no such thing as career or a job, those submissive adult cornerstones people feel the need to gravitate towards in order to feel relevant in society, to be taken seriously. It fucks up art. The mind is better naïve and full of mistakes – open ended. That's what we talked about.

Jamie: There was a pact and a few vows but not a manifesto. Things change far too fast for manifestos. Mostly it was about making something happen that hadn't happened yet.

HOW WOULD YOU DEFINE YOUR MUSIC?

Alison: I guess it is the combined energies of the two of us. I think that more than guitars and drums and vocals, what you hear is what's happening between us, what's happening in that space. We're not trying to be accomplished songwriters or even learn our instruments that well; that's not important to us at all. Great songwriting has never been our intention. It has always been about a triumph of ideas over ability, and embracing an attitude and an energy instead of a genre or a type of sound.

Jamie: In old blues circles they used to talk about music and voodoo in the same breath. Like, they acknowledged that it wasn't the notes

HAPPY ACCI
AMONGST T

PJ Harvey, old blues, Television. We talked about Edie Sedgwick, The Chelsea Hotel, New York… that scene – the late '60s, early '70s – like it was our heritage, and that's what we wanted to see again, be part of. We were both looking to start over, whether at the time we were conscious of it or not. I don't think either of us were very happy people

or the rhythms or even the words that made a song electrifying, but something else, like a raw power and a primitive sexual thing that was in the attitude of the people playing it. I think that's what we always recognized as the most precious thing in music, and I suppose that's what we're chasing.

SINCE THE BEGINNING OF THE BAND, YOU HAVE PRODUCED MOST OF THE IMAGERY AND MUSIC VIDEOS FOR THE KILLS. IS THIS A WAY TO CREATE A GLOBAL ARTWORK?

Alison: Perhaps… Or maybe we just need to control everything, by our nature. I don't think anyone can represent us better than we can. We love every aspect of what we do. It feels like cheating ourselves by relinquishing control of any aesthetics, visually or audibly. The few times we have, in my opinion, have been a disaster.

Jamie: For me it's not intended as a "global artwork". In fact I'm put off by those two words combined; they don't appeal to me at all. It sounds like the equivalent of "world music" or something the National Lottery would fund. We've been documenting The Kills in this haphazard, hurricane kind of a way since the very beginning, and I don't think the sum of its parts should need to be coherent for anybody. One thing's for certain: It's our thing and we would be doing it regardless of whether anyone got to see it or not.

YOU HAVE ON YOUR WEBSITE AN ART SECTION, WITH YOUR OWN DRAWINGS, COLLAGES, AND POLAROIDS. WHAT IS YOUR RELATIONSHIP WITH ART?

Alison: At the moment, our relationship with art is quite documentary. Because we travel so much, so extensively, our artwork in the past few years has become small and fast – Polaroid photographs, sketches, collage in notebooks, and writing. It's our way of remembering what we've done and where we've been.

WHAT IS THE STATUS OF THOSE PIECES?

Alison: They are our memories. They are really dear to us. It's new to us to see our private thoughts hung in a gallery. We walked around our house and dug though the drawers, swept the floors and gathered all the Polaroids we could find, put them in a box, put them in the mail. And all of sudden our private thoughts are public thoughts. It's a wild transition. When we saw our Polaroids hanging in the

Baltic Gallery, I felt confused, embarrassed, and then quite elated. You never imagine anyone is going to find these things of interest, I guess. Life is full of surprises.

Jamie: There are a lot of things you put in jeopardy when you live like this. Always on the road, always putting a life-and-death slant on music and art. It's an impossible life, absurd when you stop to think about it. Friendships, relationships, your home, your bills, your lovers… they all take a beating when you're on the road. Things that most people protect as the most precious and personal things in the world, you end up testing to breaking point when you live like this. I think that all the sketches and collages and writing and photographs, all those patched-up notebooks that come out of it, are a real antidote.

HOW DO YOU RELATE THESE WORKS WITH YOUR MUSIC?

Alison: I think they go hand in hand. What we see and experience inspires our music. And what we see and experience we usually take a photo of, or write about, or capture in some way.

Jamie: It's difficult because what tends to happen is that people analyze and intellectualize all these things. And to be truthful, that kind of meaning is rarely put into a song or a sketch or a roll of film or whatever. I have no idea what the relationship between the two things is. I just like the whole chaos and randomness of it. It makes it a lot wilder and satisfying when you find happy accidents amongst all the mess. Where two or three or however many different things fit together perfectly, when they were never intended to…

IS ONE OF YOU MORE COMMITTED TO THE ART PART?

Alison: Not really. We both do our equal share in art and photographs. I tend to put together the booklets and covers for the records but we edit together and choose what to use together, picking from a big pool of our images.

Jamie Hince: Alison's a lot more disciplined than me, and more prolific in what she presents. I tend to be secretive about it; I can't stand people's views about it!

HAVE YOU COLLABORATED WITH VISUAL ARTISTS?

Alison: Yes, we collaborated with Sophie Muller on our last two videos. The process is a bit strange to explain. She arrived with the know-how, and we arrived

with the ideas. We would discuss how we wanted it to look, and then she would turn the cameras on and we would freely do whatever came to mind in front of the camera. We did that for 'U.R.A. Fever' and 'Cheap and Cheerful'. The videos are really different but both capture an incredible, unscripted energy, similar to Warhol films and John Cassavetes

movies. She took the footage and edited it all together – eight hours of us running around and having fun, down to 4 minutes – and we wouldn't want to change anything. And at the moment, I'm talking to Brad Kahlhamer about working on some drawings with him. I'd love to do that, but that's quite a way off from happening just yet.

ANDY WARHOL AND RICHARD HAMILTON SEEM TO BE MAJOR INFLUENCES ON YOU. WHAT ARE YOUR REFERENCES IN CONTEMPORARY ART? WHICH ARTISTS INFLUENCED YOU?

Alison: Don Van Vliet (Captain Beefheart), Patti Smith, Velvet Underground, Andy Warhol, William Burroughs, Sonic Youth, Brad Kahlhamer, John Cassavetes, Leos Carax, Christian Marclay, Jem Cohen, Basquiat, Billy Name, Bridget Berlin, Nobuyoshi Araki, The Rolling Stones, Dick Jewel, Franz Gertsch, Niagara, Lawrence Ferlinghetti, Robert Frank.

Jamie: Francis Picabia, Max Ernst… I love how the Dada movement combined beauty, ugliness, and the absurd, all for no reason. Somehow they managed to have this sense that they were a political movement that threatened to bring down society when, at the root of it, there was no real agenda or politics behind it at all. Even their so-called manifestos were deliberately stupid and non-sensical. People are so stumped by things that have no meaning; it's a pretty powerful weapon. I love Jake and Dinos Chapman for the same reason.

ARE YOU WILLING TO DEVELOP MORE ON THE VISUAL SIDE?

Alison: Yes, I hope we are developing all the time. Certainly everything around us is changing and becoming more quick and throw-away. Maybe I'd like to develop backwards – throw my computer away and only do long, slow, precious things from now on. But we'll see.

DOES THE ART CONTEXT GIVE MORE FREEDOM THAN OTHER SCENES OR PLACES?

Alison: Of course. At the moment it seems more pure than music for us, because we're not working with anyone who's trying to sell it. As soon as you start selling things, that's when things get a little hostile.

HOW DO YOU SEE THE FUTURE OF THE KILLS?

Alison: We don't think much about the future. But I imagine we'll do a lot more music, a lot more art, and we'd like to do books at some point. Art books, books of writing, etc. I'd like to do something with film, either make one or act in one. I'd like to think the future of The Kills will consist of plenty of "first times"…

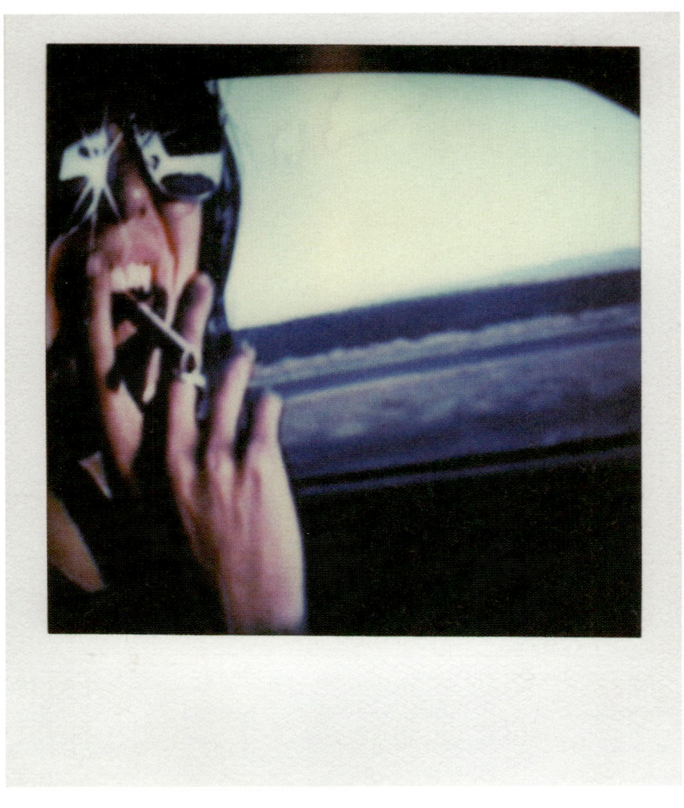

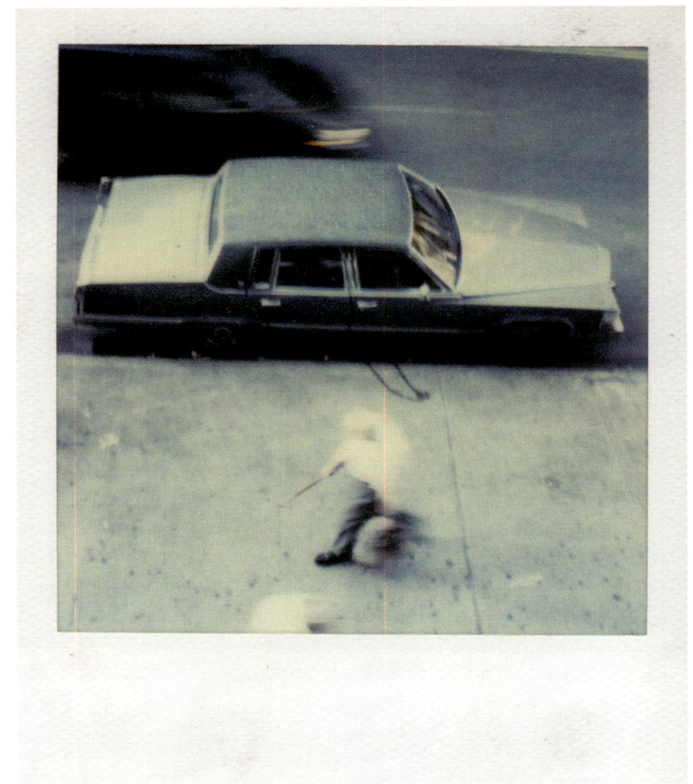

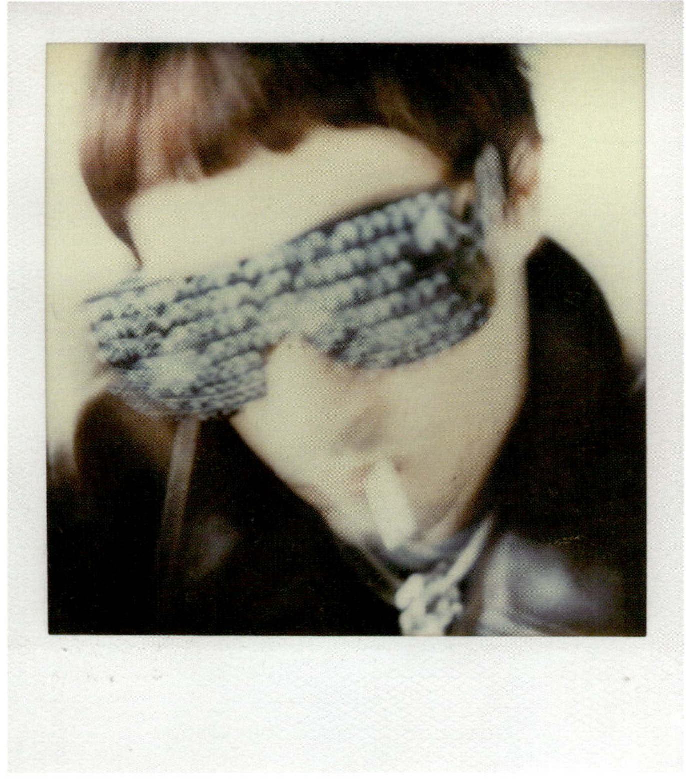

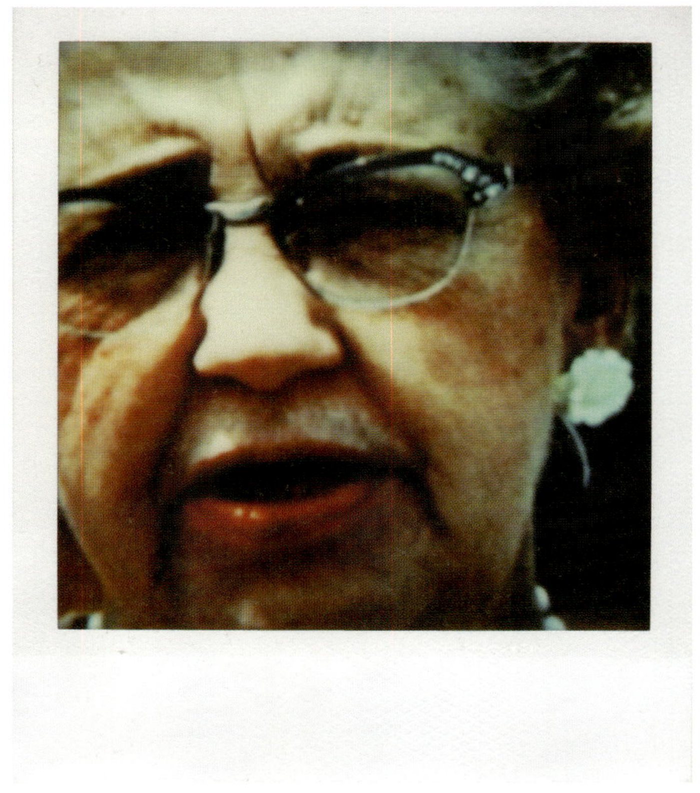

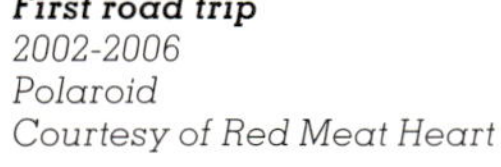

First road trip
2002-2006
Polaroid
Courtesy of Red Meat Heart

Sonic states
2002-2006
Polaroid
Courtesy of Red Meat Heart

View from the Chelsea Hotel
2002-2006
Polaroid
Courtesy of Red Meat Heart

Sour old woman
2002-2006
Polaroid
Courtesy of Red Meat Heart

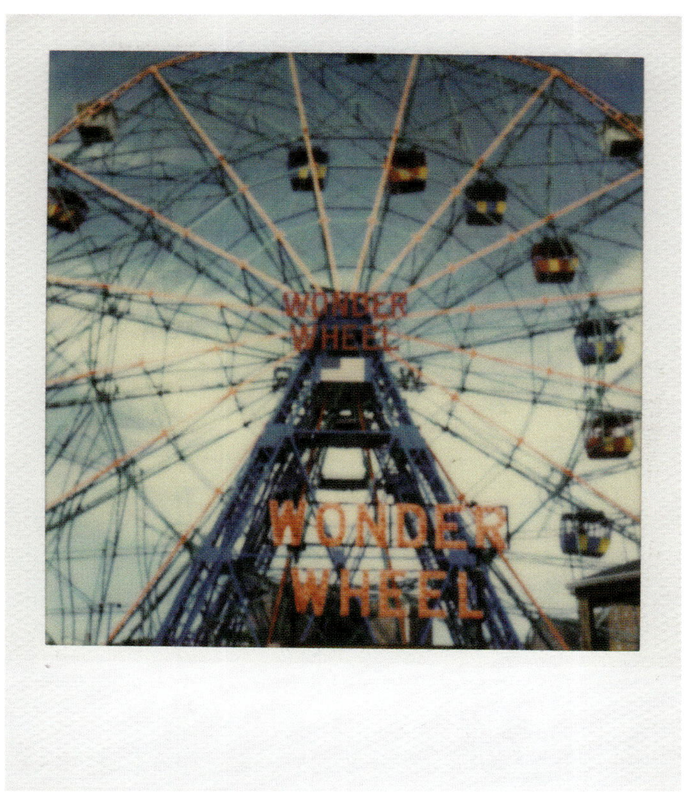

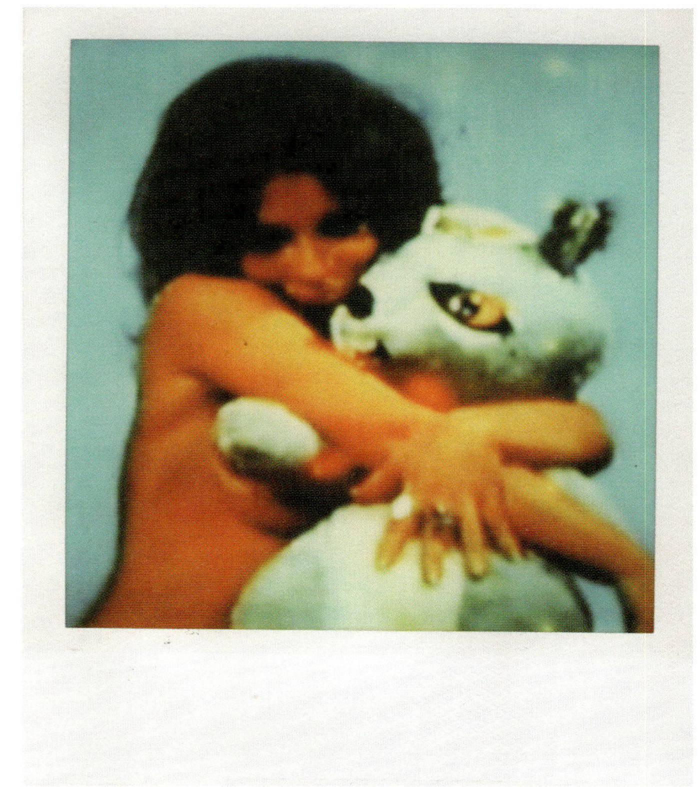

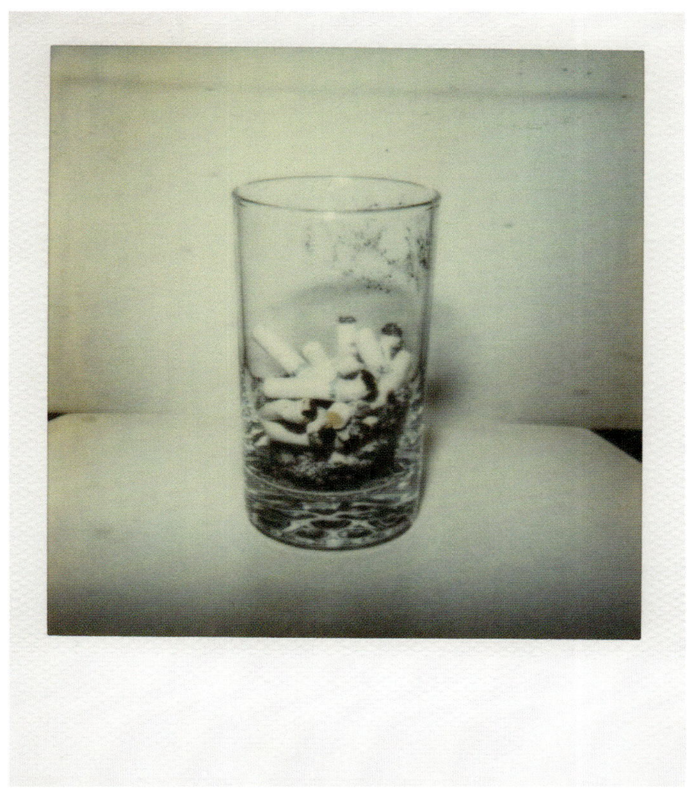

Coney Island Wonderwheel
2002-2006
Polaroid
Courtesy of Red Meat Heart

Hotel ashtray
2002-2006
Polaroid
Courtesy of Red Meat Heart

Chipmonk
2002-2006
Polaroid
Courtesy of Red Meat Heart

Sky
2002-2006
Polaroid
Courtesy of Red Meat Heart

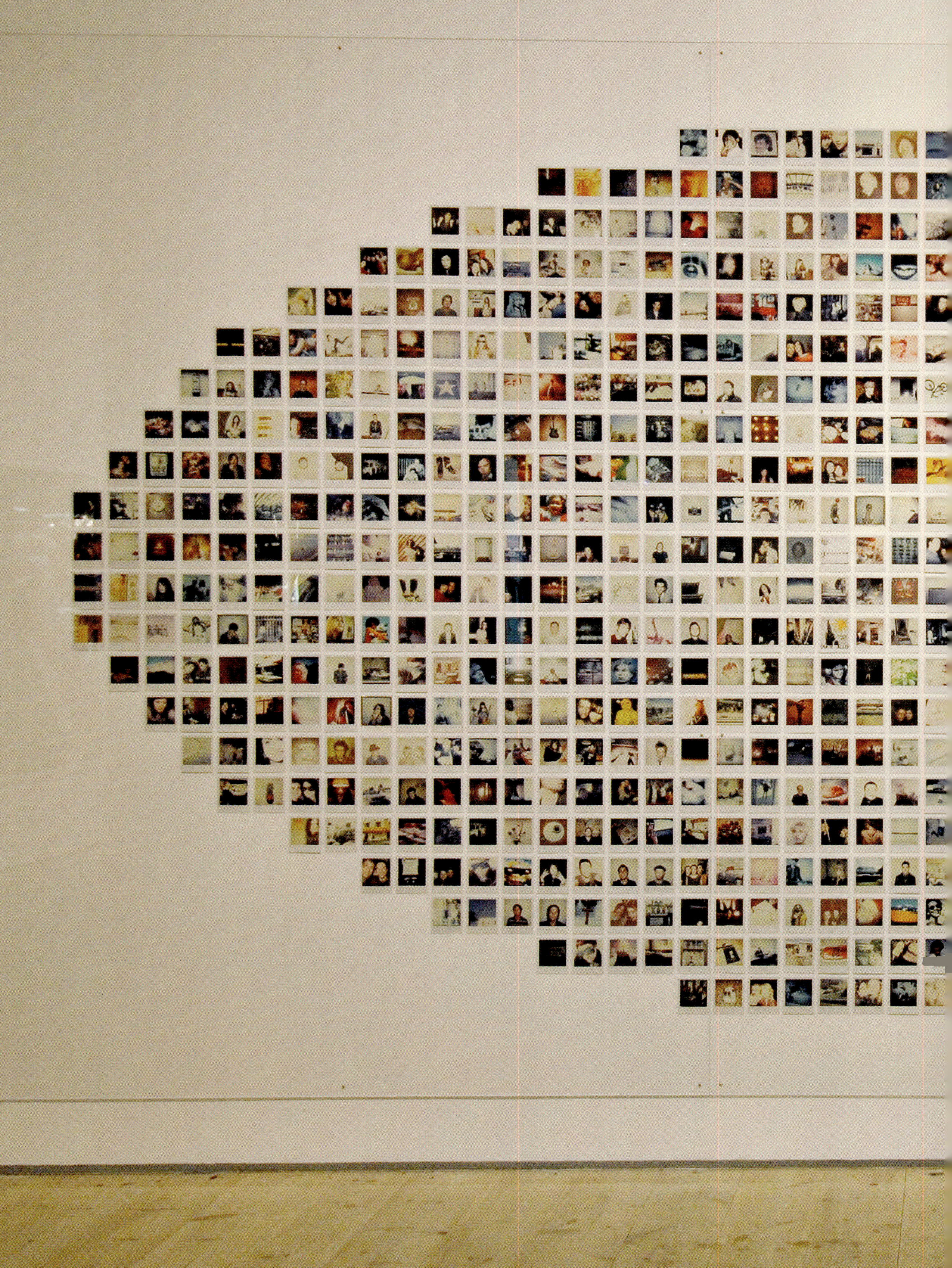

Polaroid Collection 1
all photos taken by
Jamie Hince and Alison Mosshart
1999 – 2007
400 Polaroids
Courtesy of Red Meat Heart and BALTIC,
from the exhibition Dazed & Confused Vs
Andy Warhol, 2007 at BALTIC Centre for
Contemporary Art
Photo Credit © Colin Davison

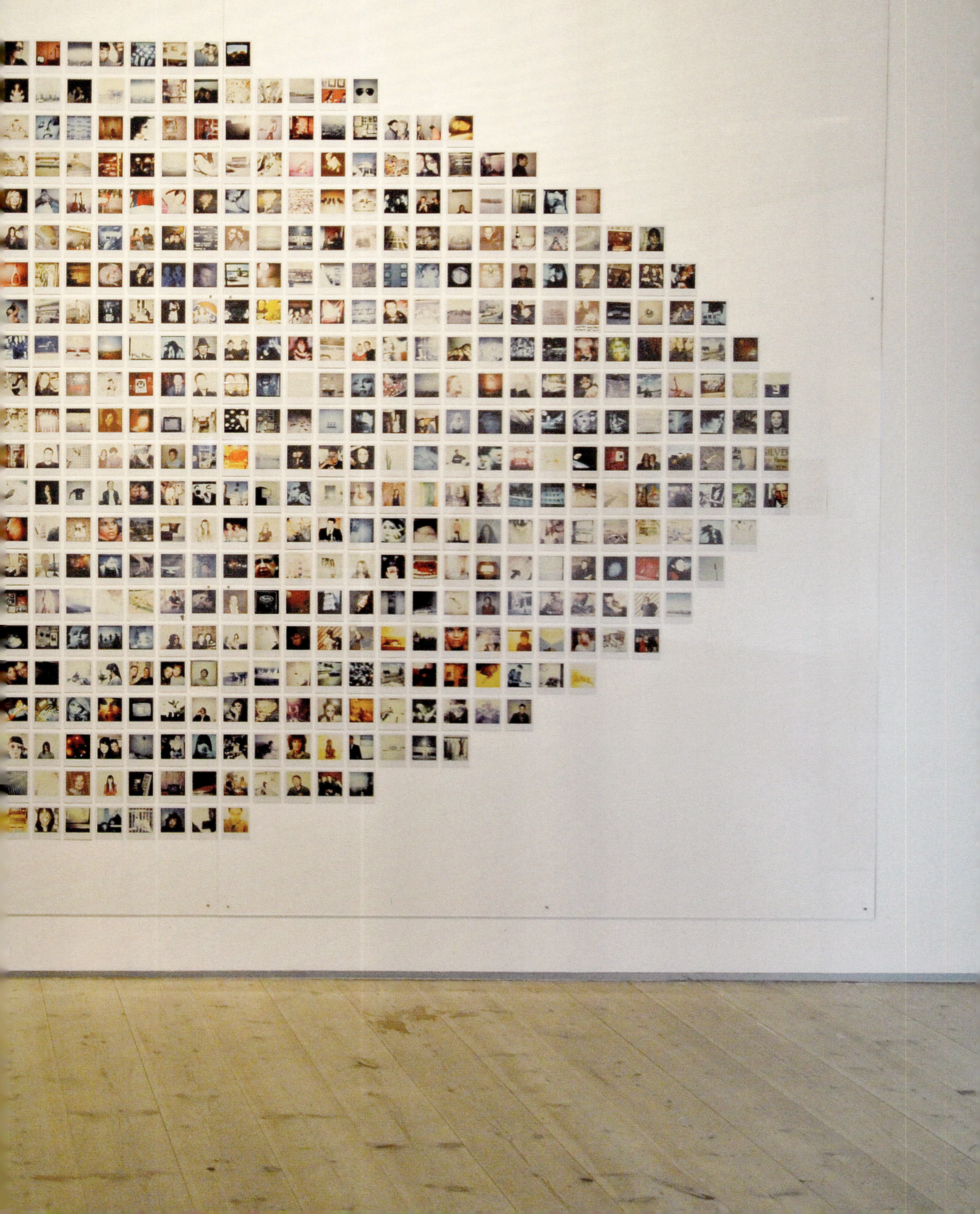

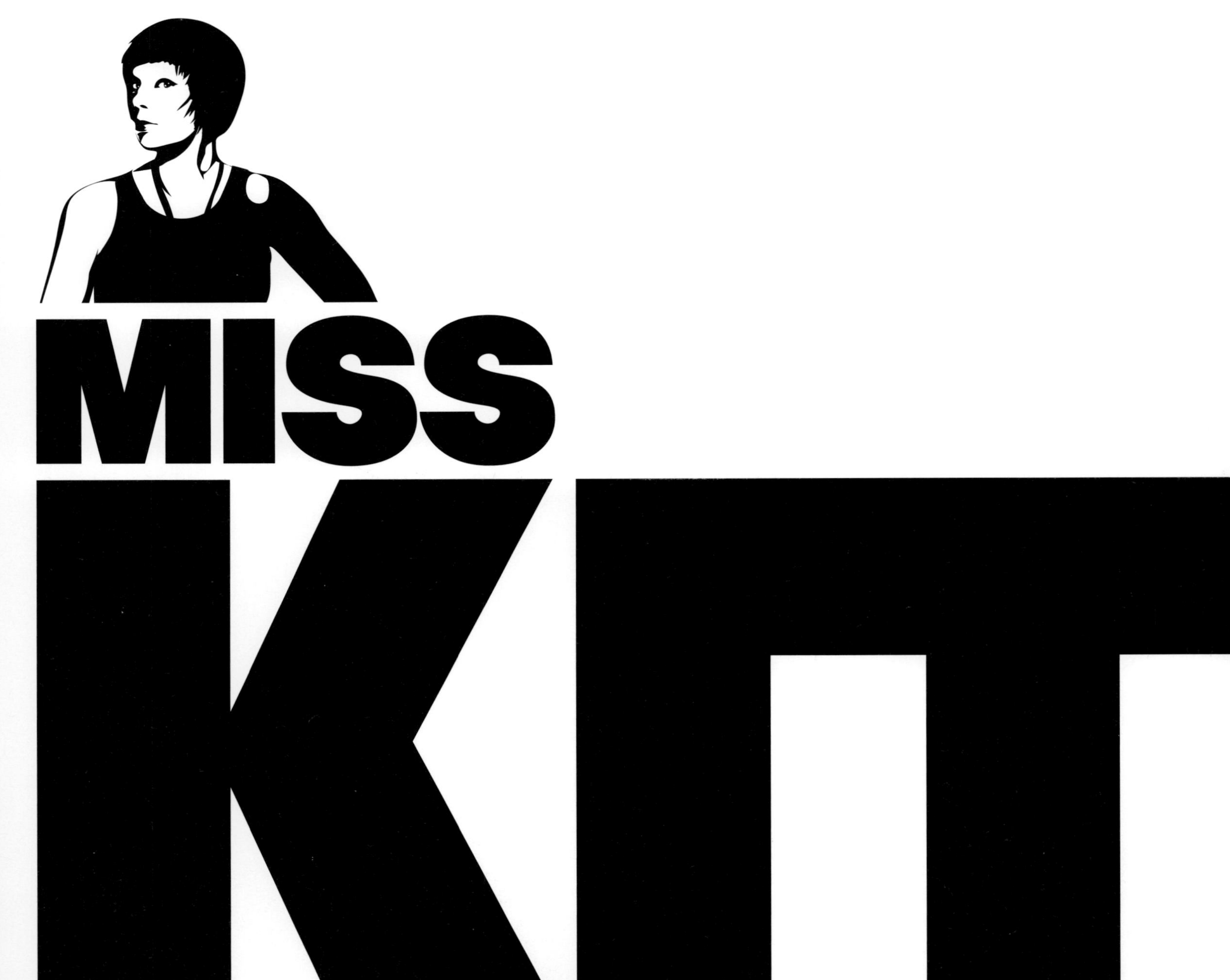
MISS
KIT

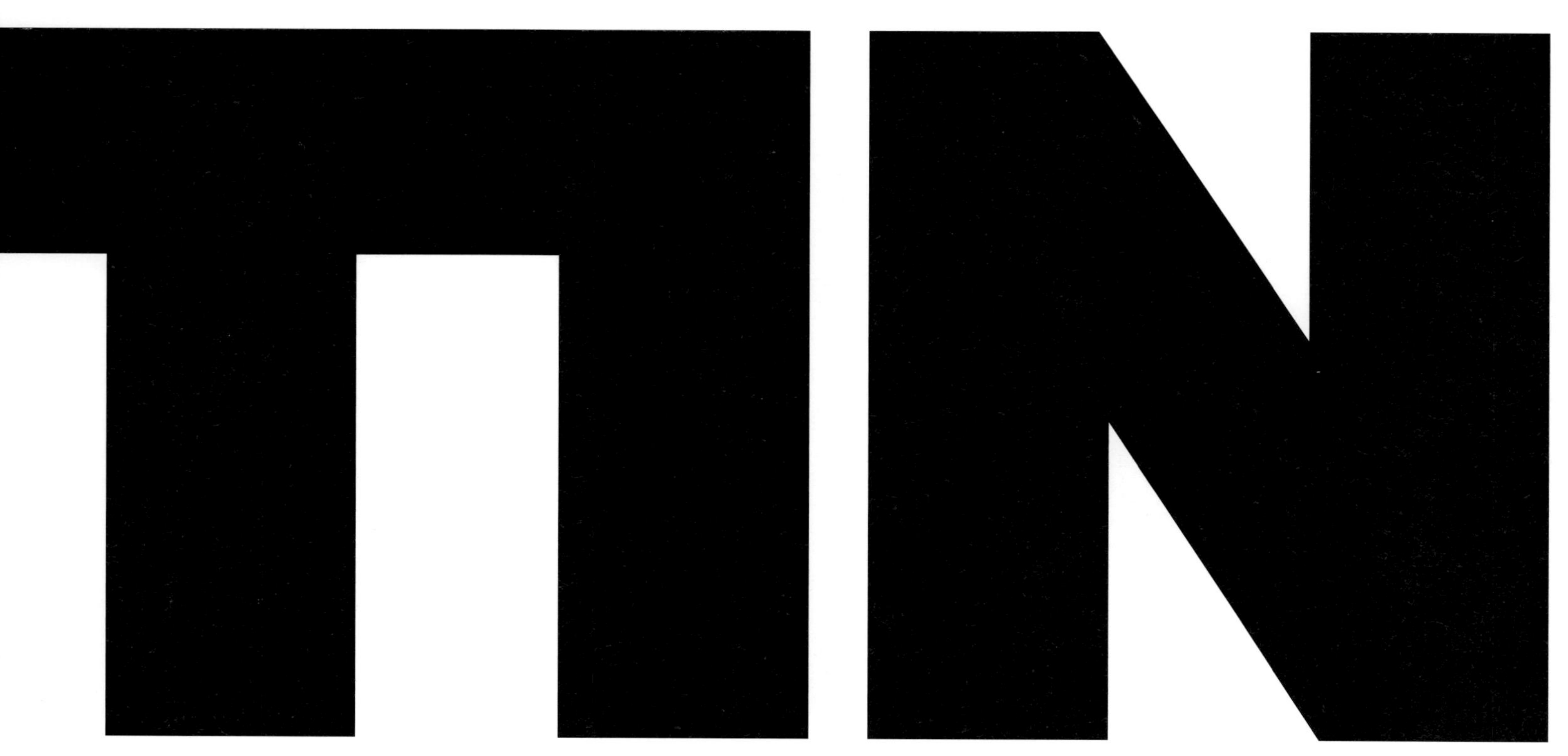

KICKING THE BOX

A former fine arts student of Grenoble and Amiens universities, Caroline Hervé, under the moniker Miss Kittin, has established herself as a major player on the international electronic music scene over the last 10 years. Born out of the effervescence of early raves, and meeting collaborators The Hacker and DJ Hell, Kittin's provocative mixture of techno and new wave came to the fore in 1998 with the hits '1982' and 'Frank Sinatra', which catapulted The Hacker and her into the limelight. She went on to work with Felix da Housecat, Sven Väth, Golden Boy, and the Detroit Grand Pubahs before releasing her first album, 'First Album', with The Hacker in 2001. Following inclusion on several compilations, including Electroclash in 2002 and Radio Caroline in 2003, Kittin released her first solo album, 'I Com', in 2004. A world tour and several delirious dancefloors later, the simultaneous release of her new solo album, 'Batbox', and a new opus with The Hacker, tells us that a new electronic earthquake is imminent.
— *Caroline Hervé was born in Grenoble in 1973, and lives in Paris.*

MISS KITTIN INTERVIEWED BY AUDREY MASCINA

WHAT IS THE ORIGIN OF THE NAME MISS KITTIN?

During my time at the Grenoble Fine Arts University, a few friends and I formed an association called Swift Tuttle to create different décors for party-nights so we could party and get into clubs for free. Then we started to organize our own events in empty buildings, where we squatted all night. I started to mix at that time because I'd been asked to play in one of the venues that we called The Chill-out. I had to find a pseudonym because it was awkward to use my own name. I don't know how I chose the name "Kittin". It's not derived from the English word 'kitten', and it's not a spelling mistake either, like many people think. "Kittin'" comes from the expression "kick into something". At the time, there was no "Miss" in front of the word.

WHO TRANSFORMED KITTIN INTO MISS KITTIN?

When I first had a few small contracts with DJing, the promoters used to put "Miss" because they thought it sounded cooler. At first it bothered me; I couldn't see any advantage in them doing that. I really insisted that they should drop it, but I came to see that it wasn't possible. Now I just accept it and use it to my advantage. On the cover of my new album, Batbox, the Miss has been reduced to a "M" and a "S" by Rob Reger, who did the cover design.

HOW DID YOU FIRST START WORKING IN A MUSIC SETTING?

I left home at 17 and started to work in a club in Grenoble called Magic, just to earn a bit of money. It was the place where all the new-wave fans used to meet. I loved dancing, and I had heard people talking about go-go dancers in Ibiza. I offered to do performances to get things moving and get people onto the dancefloor. For me it was an ideal way to go out, dance, and see my friends while being paid at the same time. It was also there that I met The Hacker, a lot of DJs, and that I heard about the first raves. The club was renamed Factory when techno first started.

WHAT LED YOU TO STUDY FINE ARTS?

Initially I wanted to do interior architecture, design, or dress-designing. I couldn't decide what to choose between these different options but I wanted to work in an artistic field. After my baccalauréat I therefore attended an école préparatoire [two-year intensive foundation course] in applied arts in Marseille so that I could then attend either the École Boulle or the Berçot Studio. But my application was rejected, so I returned to Grenoble to start an arts degree. I hardly attended the lectures. I was really bored. I was more excited by music, clubs, and raves. It was at that time that I really discovered electronic music and that at the Magic, I met Vidya Gastaldon, a visual artist who has become my best friend. She was the one who encouraged me to apply for the fine arts course in Grenoble, where I was accepted.

COULD YOU DESCRIBE SOME OF THE WORK YOU PRODUCED WHILE IN YOUR FINE ARTS COURSE?

We always had to produce work based on a given topic. Fortunately I was always given good subjects. One project involved producing an item of clothing to reflect the image of an artist whose name we pulled out of a hat. By chance, I picked out Damien Hirst. I produced a body bag. Instead of producing it in dull black, mine was transparent, with small holes so you could breathe inside it. It was my first piece of work and it set me apart in the class from the outset. I can also remember an exercise designed to give us a liking for painting, so that we wouldn't forget this medium, since at that time the majority of artists were producing videos. The approach itself was interesting but the subject was completely absurd. We had to choose an artist and produce a painting using their style. I chose Niele Toroni. I bought sponges and slates to do the same thing as him, using circular designs. I saw absolutely no point in doing this exercise and I explained to the artist who was doing the lessons – the painter Bernard Piffaretti – that if the other students needed a guiding hand, it wasn't so in my case. I was finally allowed to do a different painting – a Super Mario with a mushroom on a square – because if the exercise is designed to have you follow an artistic trend, I felt closer to pop art, to the street.

DID YOUR FINE ARTS EXPERIENCE INSPIRE YOUR APPROACH TO MUSIC, AND VICE VERSA?

I have always kept music and art separate. Undoubtedly because throughout my school years I was bullied because I listened to techno.

WERE YOU CRITICIZED FOR WANTING TO DEVELOP TWO PARALLEL ACTIVITIES, ART AND MUSIC?

I have always been perceived as being a disturbing influence, whereas I thought I was doing the right thing. And most students wanted to be in the same workshop as me because there was always music around. I was a very hard-working student, but I was dismissed at the end of my second year. I didn't have bad marks – quite the opposite – but I didn't match the profile that the school was looking for. I was transferred to Amiens, because the director thought that my work was closer to graphic design than contemporary art.

> What I like about music is not the show, but the search for absolute truth in a world that is so focused on outward appearance. That's why I was so drawn towards music, without having really looked for it.

WERE YOU ALREADY A DJ AT THAT TIME?

Yes, but I'd only just bought my turntables, paid for by working at Leclerc supermarket for three months as a cashier. The teachers used to mockingly refer to me as "the DJ". I explained that it was so that I could finance part of my studies.

HOW DID YOUR CAREER IN PLASTIC ARTS DEVELOP AT AMIENS?

The fact that I was transferred to Amiens, and that it was decided for me that graphic design would be better for me, removed any desire I might have had to pursue plastic arts. I found myself with students who had spent three years in front of a computer screen, whereas I'd had no previous training in this at all. In a sense I was humiliated. That year in Amiens turned out to be a nightmare. Fortunately I was able to take refuge in my music. For the lessons on object design, each student had to design an electrical object. As a deliberate provocation I presented a dildo project, in black latex covered in tiny stars, that was entitled 'Oh my God'. The teacher said to me, "You just couldn't help producing a techno object could you?" To which I simply replied, "Do you really think a dildo is techno?". That summer I went on a mixing tour. At the end of the holidays I decided to leave the course at Amiens. I would rather eat pasta all my life and live off my music than stay in that particular artistic environment.

WHICH ARTISTS DO YOU IDENTIFY WITH?

Wolfgang Tillmans, from whom I bought a photograph. I try to buy a work of art once a year. It's a means of supporting and helping the artists that I appreciate. I keep up-to-date with the world of art thanks to Vidya Gastaldon, but I just can't take it seriously.

WITH WHICH MUSICIANS DO YOU FEEL AN AFFINITY?

Peaches is someone who I greatly respect. When people make comments about her she knows how to deal with them, and always replies with incredible honesty. That's one of the hardest knocks you can take. What I like about music is not the show, but the search for absolute truth in a world that is so focused on outward appearance. That's why I was so drawn towards music, without having really looked for it. I'd never thought of being a musician. I had opportunities, I seized them, and that was my escape route. Music welcomed me with open arms. I never had the impression that I was struggling with problems; it was destiny. But that's not to say that it's always easy. There are many pitfalls to avoid. I could have fallen for drugs or continued to produce songs with Felix Da Housecat about limos, sex, and champagne. Everyone thinks that I'm fascinated by these things, whereas I'm not. On the contrary, it's a complete satire on the whole celebrity thing.

WOULD IT BE TRUE TO SAY THAT WHAT YOU WEREN'T ABLE TO EXPRESS AT ART SCHOOL FOUND FULL EXPRESSION IN THE CHARACTER OF MISS KITTIN?

No, I don't consider either my music or my life as being a work of art. I am not a made-up character. Maybe the public see me as such, but I express who I am and I certainly don't have the impression that I'm playing a role; that doesn't interest me. It's already hard enough to be true to yourself without having to take on other character traits. My goal is to be as incorruptible as possible. The change of name was to separate my professional life from my private life. Everyone, even the record companies I was with previously, would like to see me mutate into a kind of Kylie Minogue, Pink, or Goldfrapp. There is this fascination with inaccessible characters. The public see me as having a bad character, of being domineering. In a sense, this perception suits me because it keeps me safe. I don't particularly want my public to know who I really am. The fact of being seen as glamorous or fashionable isn't a problem to me. On the other hand, I don't want to be a party to other people's fantasies. I'm extremely repulsed by the idea of being seen as an object, an alibi, or a social cause. In my heart of hearts I'm a perpetual rebel, so that I can't be pinned down or put in a convenient box. Every time that I feel imprisoned I do everything to escape.

BACK THEN THERE WERE NO ELECTRONIC TRACKS WITH VOCALS. WHAT TOOK YOU DOWN THAT PATH?

It was just a joke to be different from everyone else. It wasn't at all premeditated.

WHAT'S THE STORY BEHIND THIS FAMOUS TRACK, 'CHAMPAGNE', THAT ESTABLISHED YOUR REPUTATION WITH THE HACKER?

The DJ agency with whom I'd just started working had asked me to produce a track for a compilation. Most of the other tracks were very straight techno pieces, and I only had one day to come up with something. Unlike the others I didn't have a studio or any material, so I immediately decided to write something completely different, even if it meant it couldn't be played in the clubs. I called my friend The Hacker, who had a studio above the record shop where he worked, so I could record the track. Our inspiration was a record by Dopplereffekt called 'Scientist' that we'd found in a shop in Lyon. At first no one understood the track because everyone was expecting me to write something harder, like I had been playing up till then. DJ Hell then discovered this compilation and asked me if I'd write other tracks for his record label. That's when The Hacker and I wrote 'Frank Sinatra'.

WHAT DO YOU THINK OF THIS TERM "ELECTROCLASH" THAT IS USED TO DEFINE YOUR MUSIC AND ALL THE OTHER GROUPS THAT HAVE FOLLOWED YOUR LEAD?

Like Blondie and the punk movement, The Hacker and I are the pop side of the electro underground. When the term "electroclash" was first used, it was a name that sounded very pejorative to us, because we've always associated electro with the Detroit sound – somber music that is neither fashionable nor attractive.

HOW DID YOUR COLLABORATION START WITH ROB REGER, THE CREATOR OF EMILY THE STRANGE, FOR THE COVER OF YOUR NEW ALBUM?

It happened by chance at the right time. He wanted to design an album cover, which he almost did for Green Day's American Idiot, but it didn't work out. Emily The Strange is a character that I love and find very relevant. It's the first time that one character is the fantasy of every rock 'n' roller. She's an adolescent Betty Page, a little perverse because she's young. She's the symbol of the fascination with young girls.

HAD YOU WORKED WITH OTHER ARTISTS FOR THE COVERS OF YOUR PREVIOUS ALBUMS?

I had never previously made a real priority of this phase of album production, as if I was running away from my image and what I could represent. I didn't want to play the game of image control or to be obliged to be always faithful to a perfect image. That's why I don't pay much attention to my covers, and also why I don't appear in my clips. The less I'm seen, the better.

HOW WOULD YOU DEFINE THIS NEW ALBUM?

It's my coming of age to the adult world, an adieu to the '20s. I've got fairly clear ideas about who I am and where I'm going; I am less of a tortured soul. I've made peace with my darker side, which is the best way to reinvent yourself, to be free, and move towards inner peace. For me, this album is the incarnation of all that. It's a demonstration of taking a long look at yourself, and being willing to explore where it hurts. It's something wonderful and liberating. I have always sought confrontation. If I'm living a lie it never lasts long because I have to say it as it is, including to myself. So many people are afraid to face themselves; they prefer living with a victim-mentality. It's easier to stay in a familiar context. My album is proof to the contrary, that you have to shake yourself up, even if it's scary. It's like reading an adventure story.

BORED IN M
WHERE IS ROYKSOPP?
TESTING PUB'S NECTAR?
PLAYSTATIONNING IN DA TOUR BUS?
NO FOOD IN THIS HOLE!
BAD PIZZA SMELL & CEREAL SAMPLERS 0!
I'M TRIPPIN' ON A TRIP!
A CRAZY NYMPHO TRIP
CAN WE KISS U ON THE LIPS
FIRE INSIDE...
...3°C OUTSIDE
PS

DCHESTER
NT BALL WAR
THE PARKING
PLACE ?
SOMEONE SAID THEY
WENT 2 THE MOVIES...
MISSING MY BEST FRIEND
& MY MANAGER
STAYED HOME...
BAD KARMA
4 X-MAS...
inhale
exhale
IT'S SOLD OUT
KITTN 12·2002

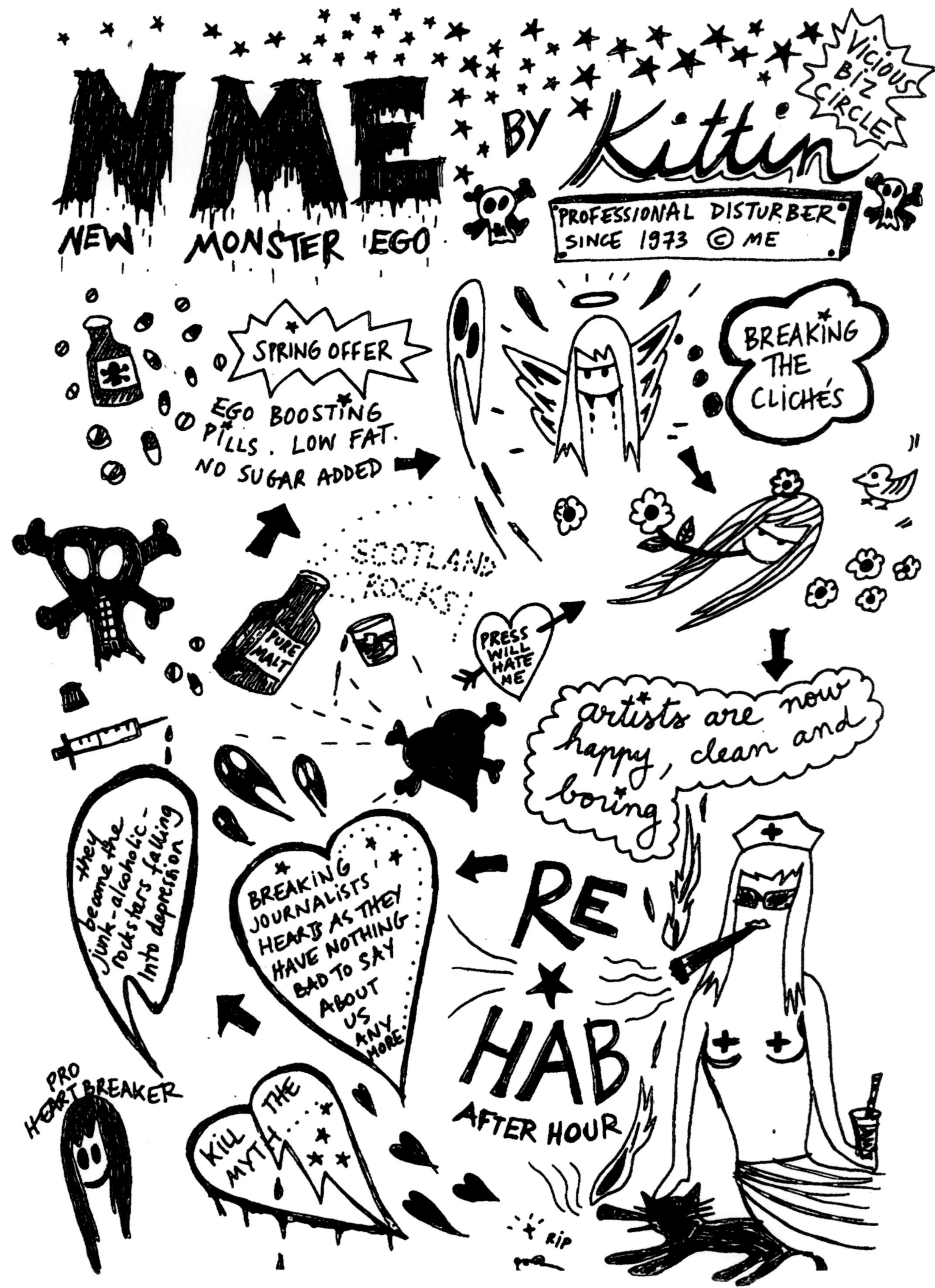

NME
NEW MONSTER EGO
BY Kittin
VICIOUS BIZ CIRCLE
PROFESSIONAL DISTURBER SINCE 1973 © ME
SPRING OFFER
EGO BOOSTING PILLS. LOW FAT. NO SUGAR ADDED
BREAKING THE CLICHÉS
SCOTLAND ROCKS
PURE MALT
PRESS WILL HATE ME
artists are now happy, clean and boring
they became the junk-alcoholic-rockstars falling into depression
BREAKING JOURNALISTS HEARTS AS THEY HAVE NOTHING BAD TO SAY ABOUT US ANY MORE
PRO HEARTBREAKER
KILL THE MYTH....
RE HAB
AFTER HOUR
RIP

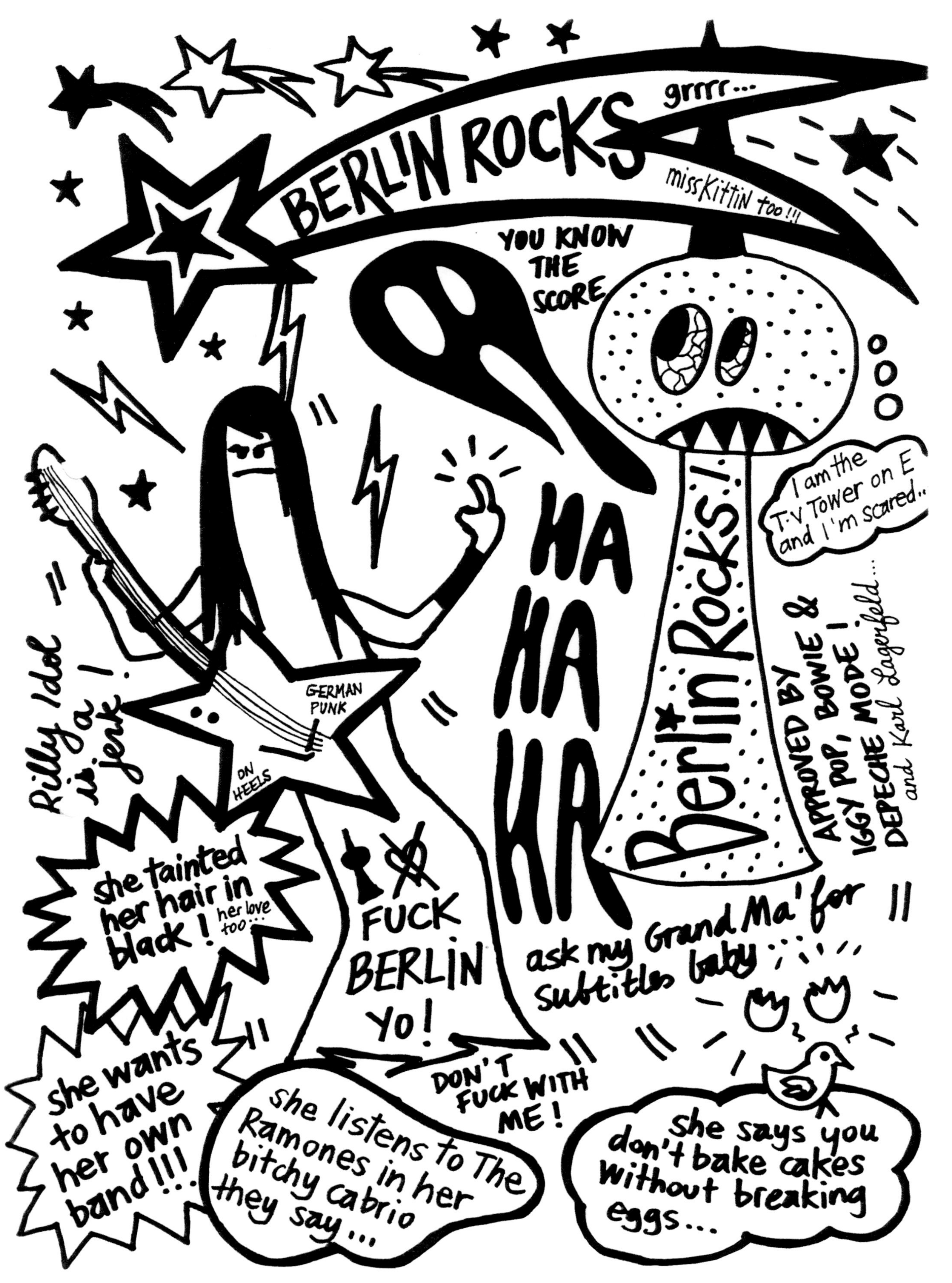

Berlin Rocks
2002
Drawing
© 2002, Miss Kittin

YOKO ONO

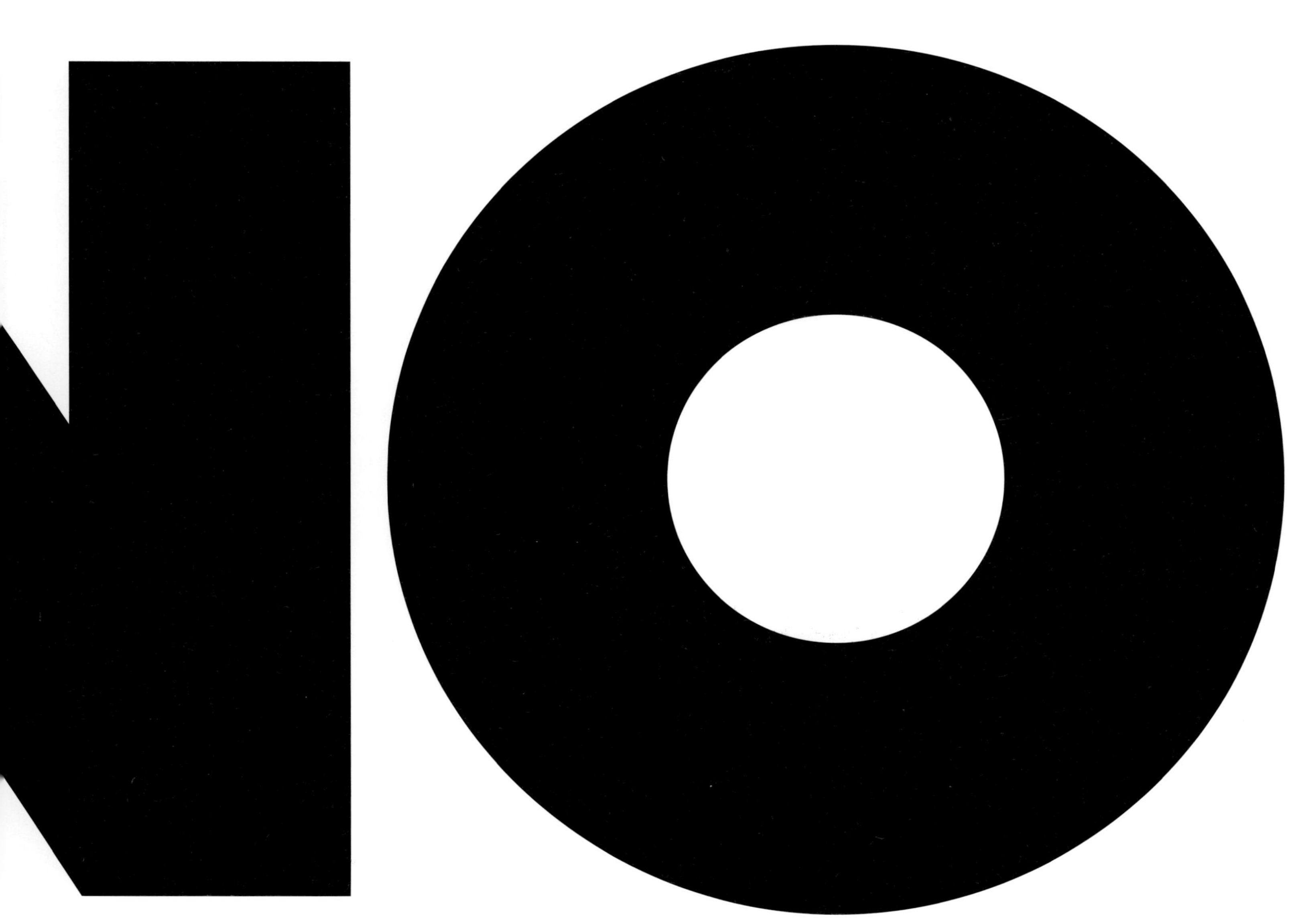

Since the early '60s, multifaceted Yoko Ono has worked as a visual artist, performance artist, singer, musician, composer, performer, author, and film producer. Drawing on the strengths of her native Japanese and adopted Western cultures, she has created a unique identity and an enduring body of work. A founding member of Fluxus and a close friend of John Cage, she is a truly nonconformist figure whose work has continually reflected the times. Her meeting with John Lennon in 1966 led to the creation of a mythical couple always in the public eye. Their joint artistic endeavours, such as their philosophy of Bagism, the bed-ins in support of world peace, or any of their musical collaborations, have an amazingly modern appeal even today.
Between musical hits, and exhibitions in the world's largest museums, Yoko Ono has dominated the international cultural scene for over 40 years. Her influence can be seen everywhere from Björk to Pipilotti Rist, and her perspective on women and the human physique in general continues to resonate. Her visual, plastic art, with its conceptual influences, is often based on interaction with the public and has stood as a mirror of the times from the '60s to the present day.
— Yoko Ono was born in 1933 in Tokyo. She currently lives in New York.

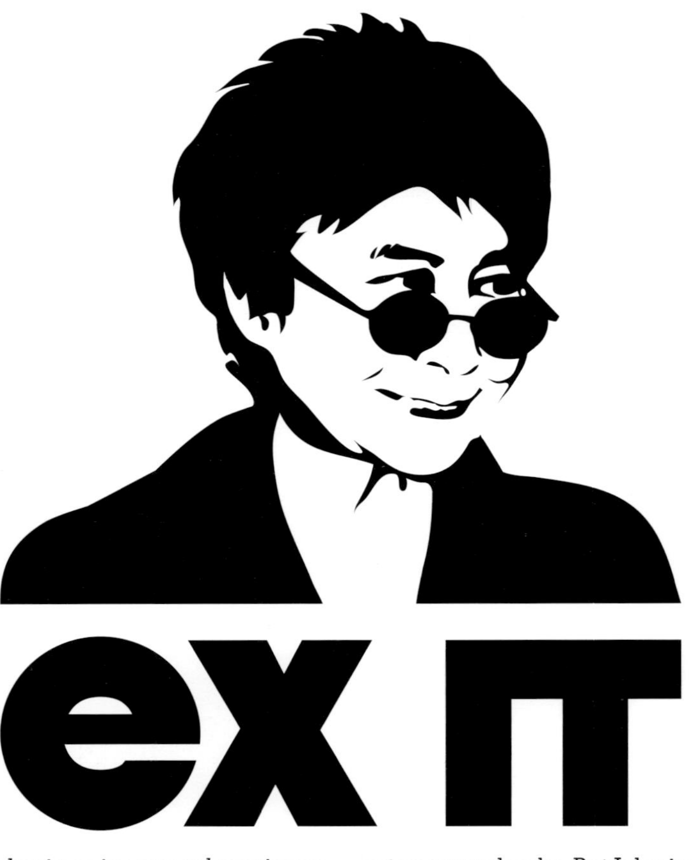

YOKO ONO INTERVIEWED BY AUDREY MASCINA

WOULD YOU SAY THAT YOUR FLUXUS EXPERIENCE HAS CLEARLY IMPRINTED YOUR ARTISTIC AND MUSICAL PHILOSOPHY IN THE SENSE THAT YOU HAVE ALWAYS DEFIED CONVENTIONAL DEFINITION IN ART AND RELATIONSHIPS WITH YOUR AUDIENCE?

Fluxus has received benefit from my sense of defying conventional definition in arts and relationships with the audience, not the other way around. Together with artists such as La Monte Young and George Brecht, I was at the inception of Fluxus, and before.

HOW WOULD YOU DEFINE YOUR WORK?

Conceptual romanticism.

WHY DID YOU USED TO DESCRIBE IT AS SOMETHING ORGANIC?

Because it was and is.

WHETHER FILM, INSTALLATION, OR PERFORMANCE, YOUR WORK HAS ALWAYS PLACED THE VIEWER IN A PARTICIPATIVE, INTERACTIVE, RESPONSIVE POSITION. IS THE VIEWER THE SECOND HALF OF THE WORK FOR YOU?

The future is my second half.

IS YOUR ART A WAY TO PROMPT IMAGINATION?

I am hoping that it will give people inspiration, encouragement, and love for life, with a sense of fun.

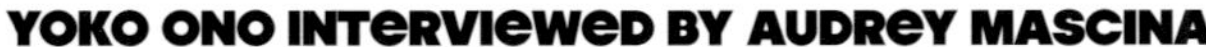

> I don't limit myself to one mode of creativity. I just dish out what came into my head so as to clear my head.

FREEDOM OF THE SPIRIT, LIBERATION OF THE BODY AND SELF, DEMYSTIFICATION OF THE SEXUAL AURA... THESE ARE THEMES CENTRAL TO MOST OF YOUR CONCEPTUAL EVENTS, FILMS, PAINTINGS, AND MUSIC. HAS IT BEEN A FIGHT TO SUSTAIN THOSE IDEAS IN YOUR WORK AND LIFE?

We have three candidates for the President of United States now: one coping with ageism, one with sexism, and one with racism. I had and still have all three to cope with.

YOUR MUSIC AND VOICE HAVE OFTEN BEEN DESCRIBED AS "PRIMAL SCREAM". IS THERE FOR YOU A DIFFERENT OUTPUT, A LOUDER MESSAGE, IN MUSIC THAN IN ART?

"Primal scream" was a phrase coined by Arthur Janov. The book was sent to us, to John and to me, when we lived in Ascot, England. We used to get so many books. But John immediately picked this one up and said, "Jesus, this is you". And that made him read it. The rest is history. Now, some people label my music as "primal scream". If it is that for you, then I guess it is that for you.

YOU HAVE REFORMULATED SOME OF YOUR EARLY WORKS LIKE CUT PIECE AND IMAGINE PEACE. IS YOUR WORK AN OPEN FIELD YOU CAN REACTIVATE IN DIFFERENT FORMS?

I don't limit myself to one mode of creativity. I just dish out what came into my head so as to clear my head. I'm not concerned if the form happens to be a re-formation of something I did before or not. The work has to be strong, and appropriate for that time.

WHAT ABOUT YOUR LATEST WORK, THE IMAGINE PEACE TOWER IN REYKJAVIK?

I am most pleased and surprised that it has actually been built. What a thing to happen!

AFTER 'GIVE PEACE A CHANCE', IS 'GIVE EARTH A CHANCE' YOUR CURRENT POLITICAL AND ARTISTIC COMMITMENT?

I certainly think that we have a chance. By IMAGINING. Let's imagine, and give Earth a chance.

WHICH YOUNG CONTEMPORARY ARTISTS DO YOU FEEL CLOSE TO?

All artists of today. I think art and music are very important components of the PEACE INDUSTRY. We should bless all artists who have decided to be artists, and who are.

DO YOU PLAN TO RELEASE A NEW ALBUM SOON?

I wish.

WHAT ARE YOUR NEXT PROJECTS?

I don't think about my next project. I am always just busy with the project of now. I ask you to IMAGINE PEACE with me. It's a strong mantra that will help to save the world.

Thank you, and I love you! Yoko Ono.

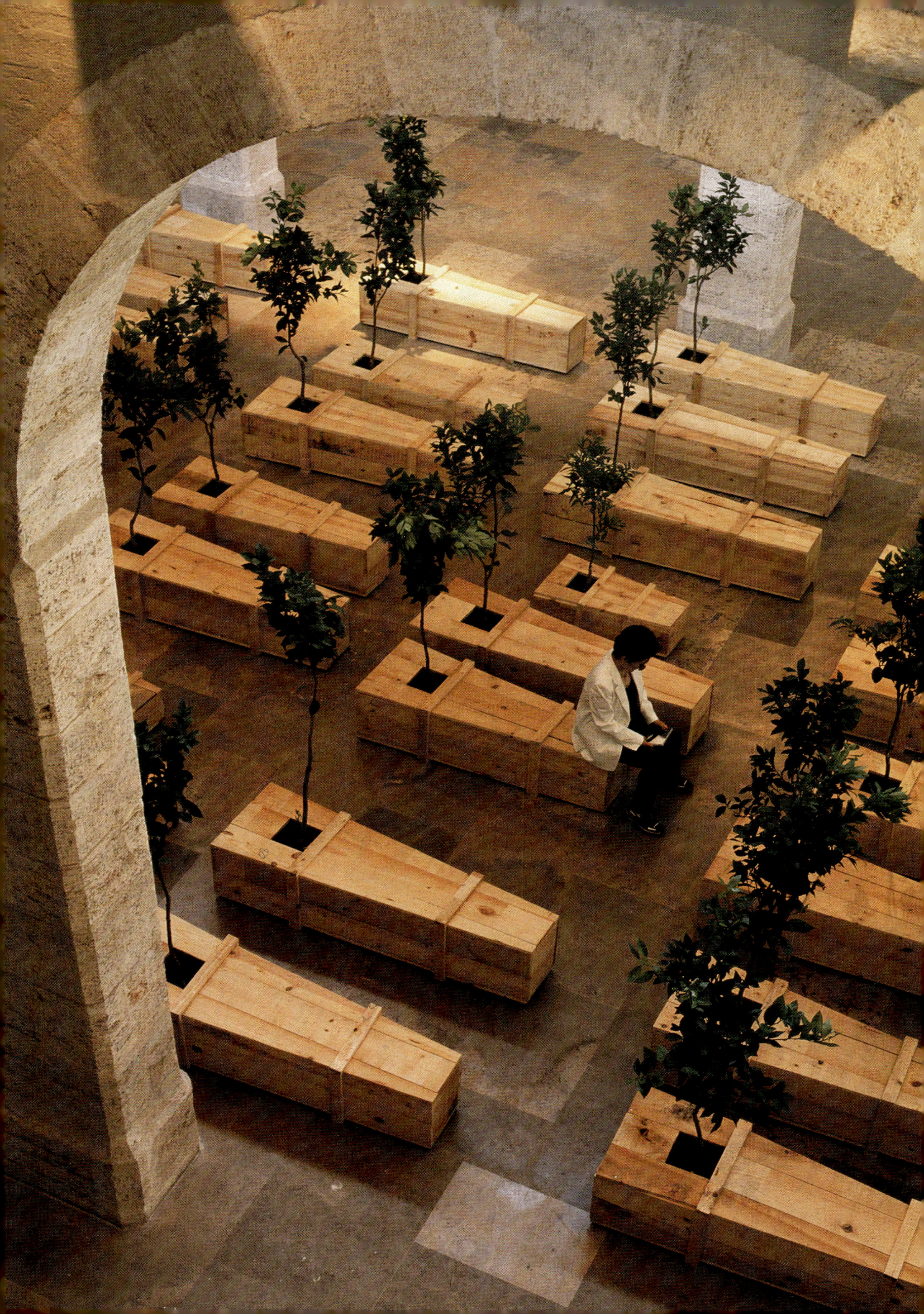

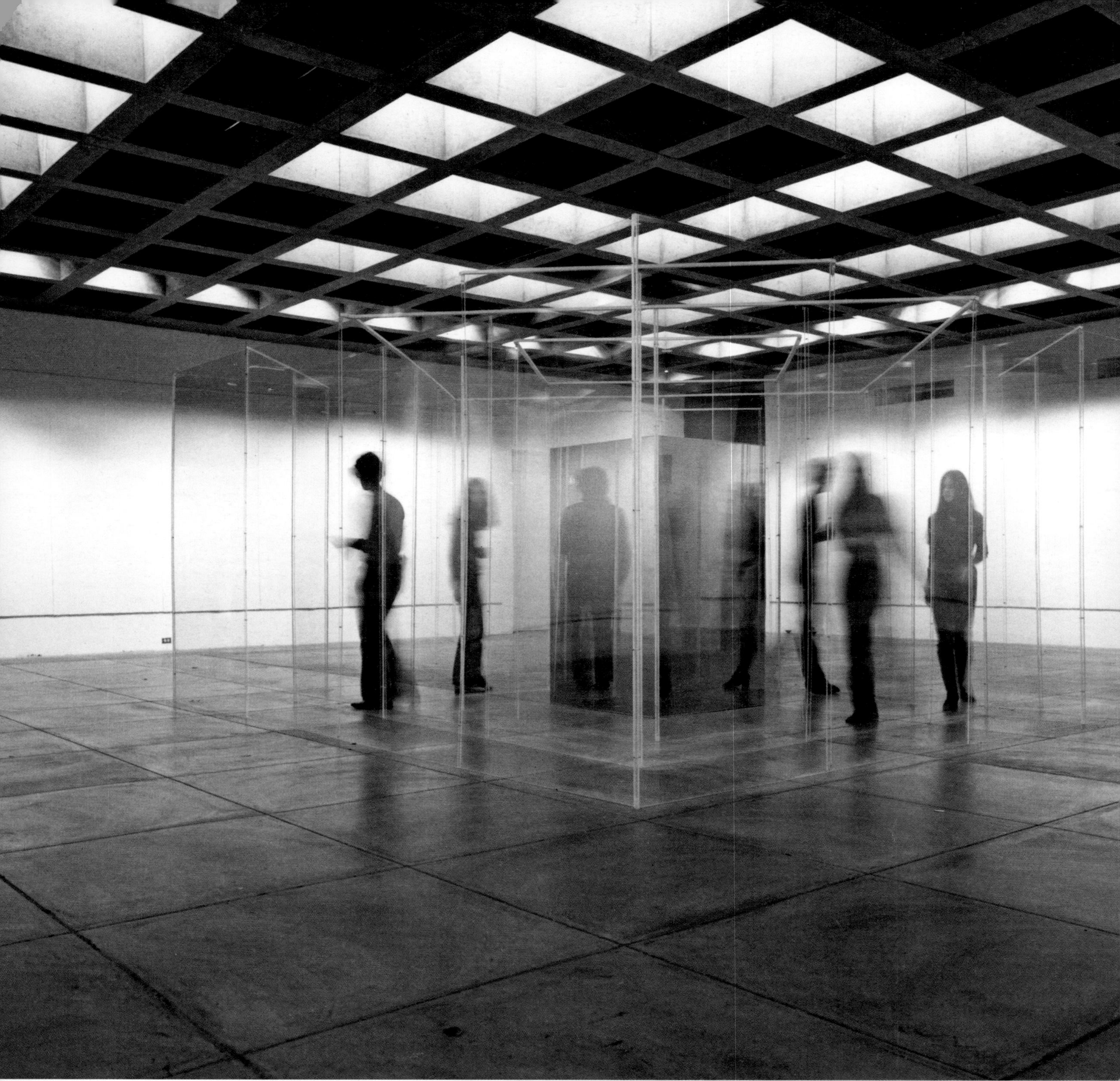

Page 141
Yoko Ono installing 'Ex It'
En Trance – Ex It, June 23 – July 25, 1997
Lonja del Pescado, Alicante, Spain
Courtesy of Lenono, Photo Archive and
Photo Credit ©Miguel Angel Valero
Generalitat Valenciana

A Maze
1971
Everson Museum, Syracuse, NY 1971
Plexiglass maze installed
at This Is Not Here exhibition
October 9-27, 1971
Photo Credit Iain Macmillan/ © Yoko Ono

Page 143
Cut Piece
Performance by Yoko Ono
March 21, 1965
Carnegie Recital Hall, New York City, NY
Courtesy Lenono, Photo Archive
Photo Credit © Minoru Niizuma

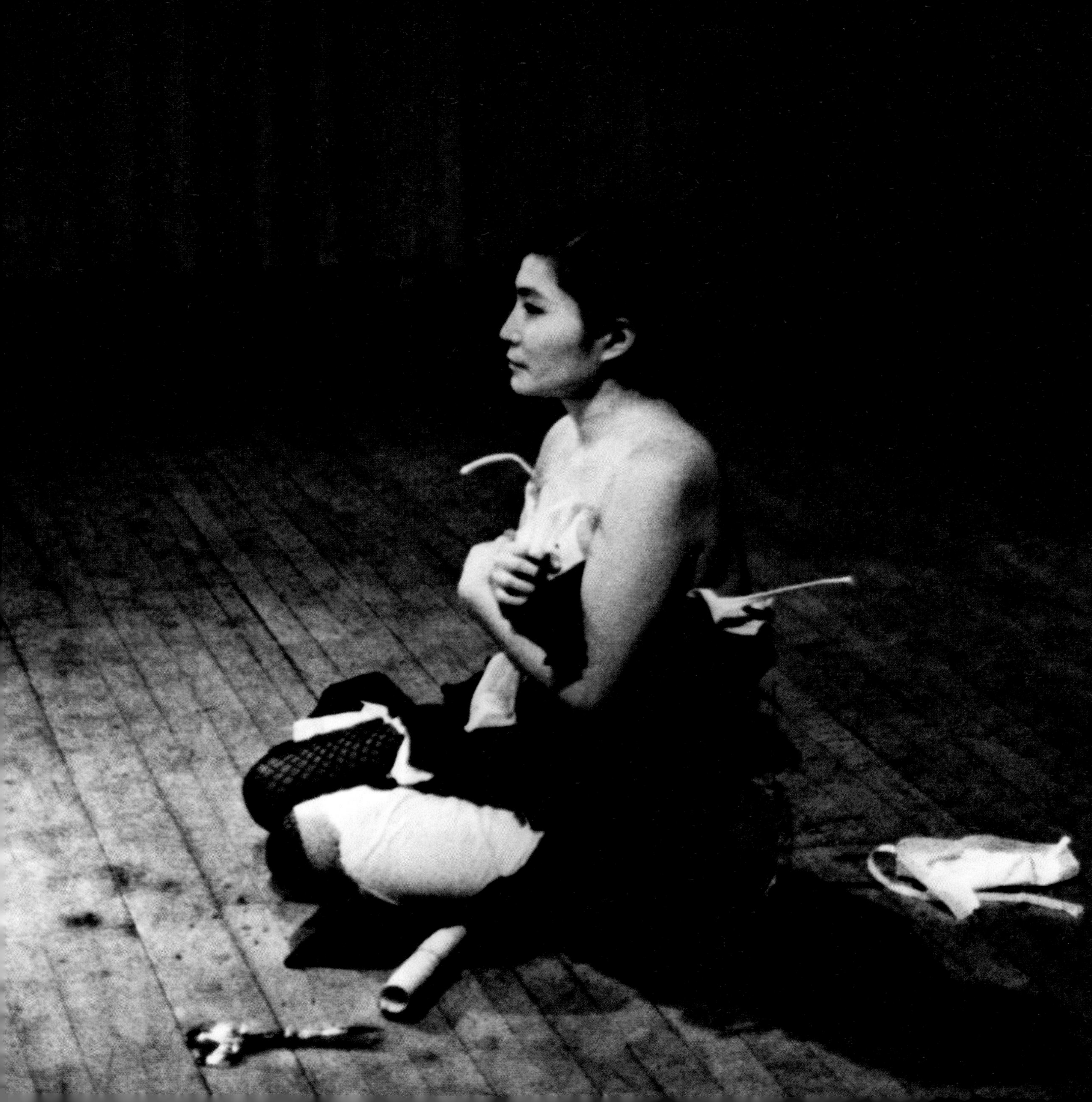

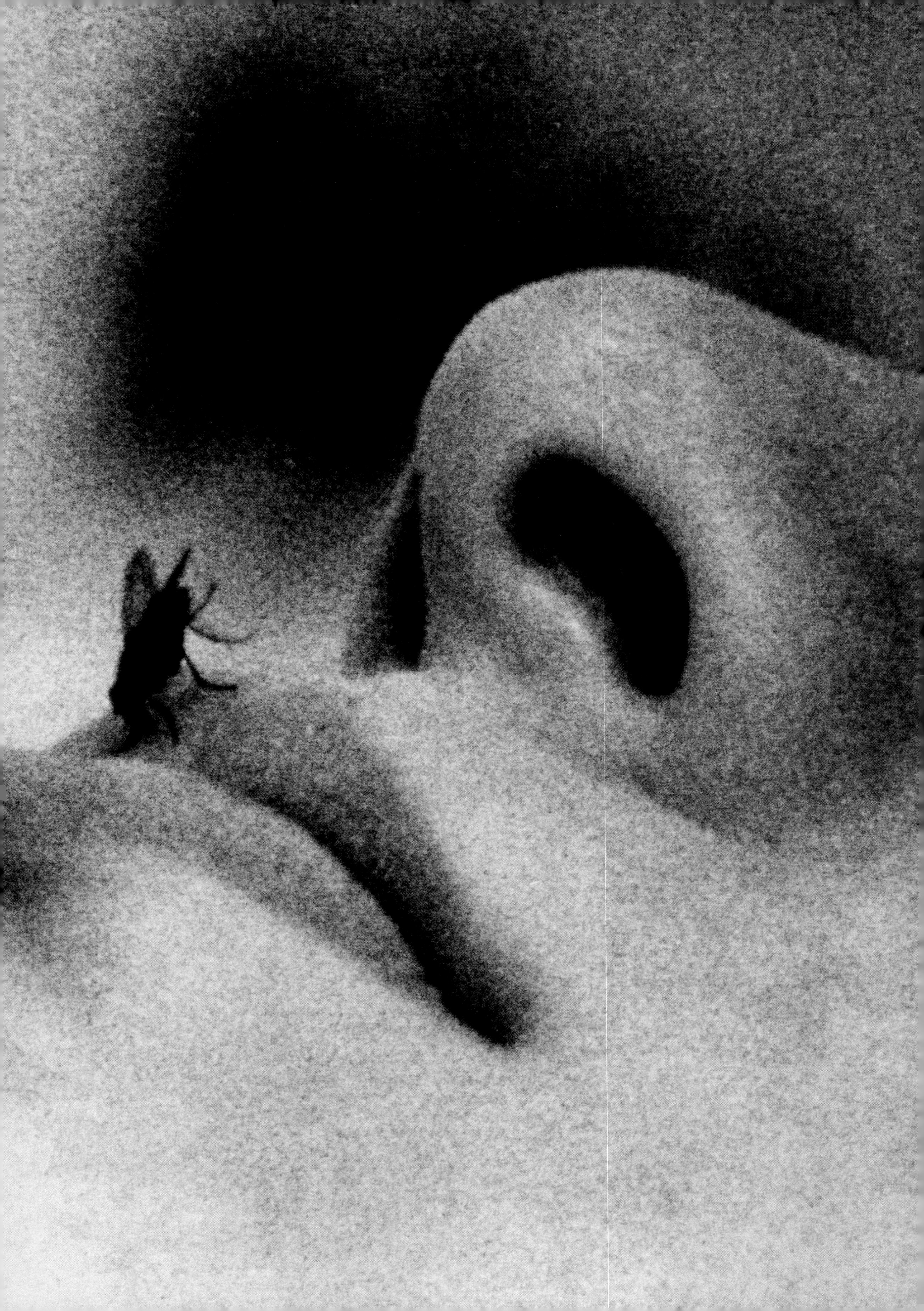

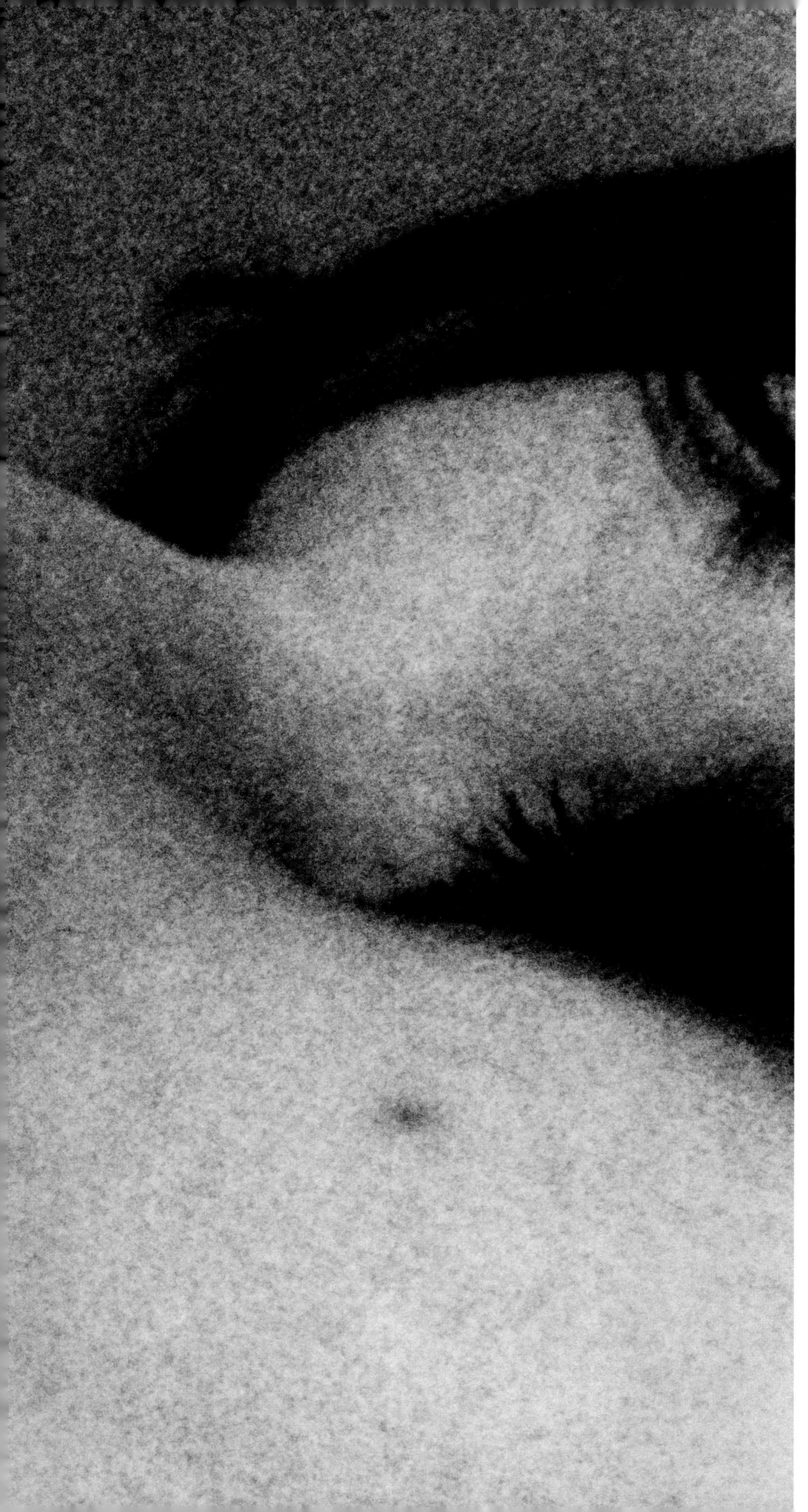

Film Still from FLY
1970
Directed by Yoko Ono
Courtesy of Lenono, Photo Archive
Photo Credit © Yoko Ono

145

KEMBRA PFAF

LeR

Kembra Pfahler is an American performance artist and the lead singer of the heavy goth/punk band The Voluptuous Horror of Karen Black, which she formed in 1990 with her then-husband, guitarist Samoa. Her claim to fame is her philosophy of "availabism" – making the best creative use of whatever materials are available – and her guiding vision of "anti-naturalism".

Pfahler's dark, theatrical, world began with Super 8 horror films and performance art, and today includes photography and installations. There is no hierarchy of creative mediums in her work. Her live performances are actually "in-motion" installations gathering objects, low-tech sets, and props, made according to the principles of availabism. Naked, her body fully painted in blue, pink, or yellow, and wearing a witchy black wig, Kembra, with her Karen Black girls, delivers a foxy, transgressive take on gender and sexuality.

Kembra Pfahler was featured in the 2008 Whitney Biennial via her "Sit Ins", a series of paintings made by sitting on paper with her Karen Black body paint on, as a tribute to Vienna actionism and the work of Yves Klein.

— Kembra Pfahler was born in 1961 in Hermosa Beach, California. She currently lives in New York City.

KEMBRA PFAHLER INTERVIEWED BY JÉRÔME SANS

HOW DID YOU GET INVOLVED IN THE PERFORMANCE ART AND EXPERIMENTAL FILM SCENE IN NEW YORK?

I got involved in performance in the early '80s in New York because friends in the Lower East Side would have events and art exhibits where the curation was a bit spontaneous and feral. I was walking down the street one day and a writer from the East Village Eye asked if I wanted to do a performance at a place called Armageddon. I said yes. I didn't have a band or any notion at all of what I'd do. It had to be short. I went home and in my empty apartment I had a couple of eggs in the refrigerator. I decided it would be impactive if I stood on my head and had my friend Donald Miller from the noise ensemble Borbetomagus crack an egg on my vagina. I just used the tools available to me: my body and a couple of eggs. That's when I started to use the term "availabism" – making the best use of what is available.

WHAT PROMPTED YOU TO COMBINE YOUR PERFORMANCE ART AND MUSIC, AND CREATE THE VOLUPTUOUS HORROR OF KAREN BLACK?

When I was a child in Santa Monica, California, I was doing performance art but I didn't know it. What I did was drowning in blood in the bathtub, nude driving on the Pacific Coast Highway, hanging upside down on the street signs and stuff. Mostly out of boredom and because we smoked a lot of pot.

WHY DID YOU NAME YOUR BAND AFTER ACTRESS KAREN BLACK?

By accident, sort of. I always loved that movie she did called Trilogy of Terror. Also, the legendary filmmaker Mike Kuchar described one of my early-'80s film-shows-with-live-performances as "voluptuously horrific". Later, in 1990, Samoa and I – he was my husband and artistic collaborator – decided to start a band. The name The Voluptuous Horror of Karen Black just sounds right.

WHAT DEFINES THE CONCEPT OF THE BAND?

The band uses the same kind of imagery I had been doing without music in the '80s. I guess it's called "anti-naturalism". Growing up in Los Angeles and having parents with very good musical taste has imprinted my consciousness. Classic rock, metal, in the manner of verse-chorus-verse-chorus-verse-chorus-guitar solo-verse-chorus-out.

YOU HAVE DESCRIBED YOU MUSIC AS "SIMPLY ROCK, MEAT AND POTATOES". WHY?

That's just my indigenous music. I think if I had made really complex, freestyle music with the images coming out I'd probably have a nervous breakdown.

YOUR BAND IS RENOWNED FOR ITS HIGH THEATRICALITY AND AMAZING LIVE SHOWS – SOMEWHERE BETWEEN LEIGH BOWERY, ALICE COOPER, AND THE ROCKY HORROR PICTURE SHOW. HOW WOULD YOU DEFINE YOUR APPROACH TO STAGING YOUR MUSIC?

Thanks for those comparisons. Whoa it's like illustrating a story with props and costumes for each song. Or hiding in plain sight, if you analyze it, really. But I don't, really.

DO YOU CONSIDER YOUR LIVE MUSIC PERFORMANCES AS ARTWORKS?

I don't believe there's a hierarchy of creative mediums.

HOW DO YOU RELATE ALL YOUR PRACTICES – MUSIC, PERFORMANCE, VISUAL ARTS, FILMMAKING?

They are all related like a family. Cousins, babies, aunties…

YOUR MUSIC PERFORMANCES AND FILMS SHOW A CLEAR MIX INFLUENCES – FROM ACTIONISM TO HORROR FILM AND GOTH AND GLAM. HOW

> When I was a child in Santa Monica, California, I was doing performance art but I didn't know it. What I did was drowning in blood in the bathtub, nude driving on the Pacific Coast Highway, hanging upside down on the street signs.

WOULD YOU DEFINE YOUR AESTHETICS AND VISUAL WORKS?

Beautalist, anti-naturalist, availabist, and sometimes really fun.

YOUR VISUAL WORK SHOWS A CRUDE TAKE ON WOMANHOOD. WHAT KIND OF STATEMENT DO YOU INTEND TO DRAW?

I didn't know it was crude. I think we look glamorous, and far from indecent.

IS THERE A SPECIFIC FACET OF YOURSELF THAT YOU EXPOSE IN YOUR VISUAL ARTS THAT ISN'T CLEAR IN YOUR MUSIC OR PERFORMANCE ACTS?

Not really. It all sort of matches.

YOU OFTEN DEFINE YOUR WORK AND YOUR WORLD AS "ANTI-NATURALIST". WHAT DO YOU MEAN?

Anti- but natural… contrarian… transformative… modernistic but pre-Christian.

YOU'VE COLLABORATED WITH PHOTOGRAPHERS BRUCE LABRUCE AND RICHARD KERN. WHICH OTHER CONTEMPORARY VISUAL ARTISTS DO YOU FEEL CLOSE TO?

Bruce is one of my favorite artists, as are Antony & The Johnsons, Rick Owens, CocoRosie, Andrew W.K., The Vienna Action Group, Samoa, Scott Ewalt, Manowar, Ron Athey, Vaginal Creme Davis, PTV3, Kenneth Anger, the Screamers, Gyda Gash, Diamanda, Matthew Barney, Luther Vandross, Vampira, Bambi Magal, Dave Weston, Armen Ra, Danzig; my brother's band, Jawbreaker, The Great Cardone, Louise Bourgeois, Julian Schnabel, Martin Luther King, Louisa May Alcott, Lou Reed, Rainer Maria Rilke, John Fante, Danilo Donati, Joe Coleman, the girls of Karen Black, who are Bijoux Altamirano, Anne Hanavan, Jackie Rivera, Alana Amram, Alice Moy, Laure Leber, Constance Brantly. They all have their own separate art practice beyond Karen Black as well. Bruce Brown, surf filmmaker, La Petite Versaille. Also working with Deitch Projects, I had my palette exploded seeing things I wouldn't have known about, from artists like E. V. Day, Kehinde Wiley, Kathy Grayson, Julie from BluPrint clothing and Leslie Rosa. Jeffrey Deitch is very open and positive. It helps my darkness.

WHAT ARE YOUR UPCOMING PROJECTS?

For my upcoming projects I am going into what I call the "beautalist" phase. I might stay in Paris this spring – in Bianca Casady's new gallery, Mad Vicky's Tea House – and do some "beautalism". But that might come later. I'd like to have a test tube baby, buy a house for my mother and father, learn how to speak more languages, and possibly join a gym.

148

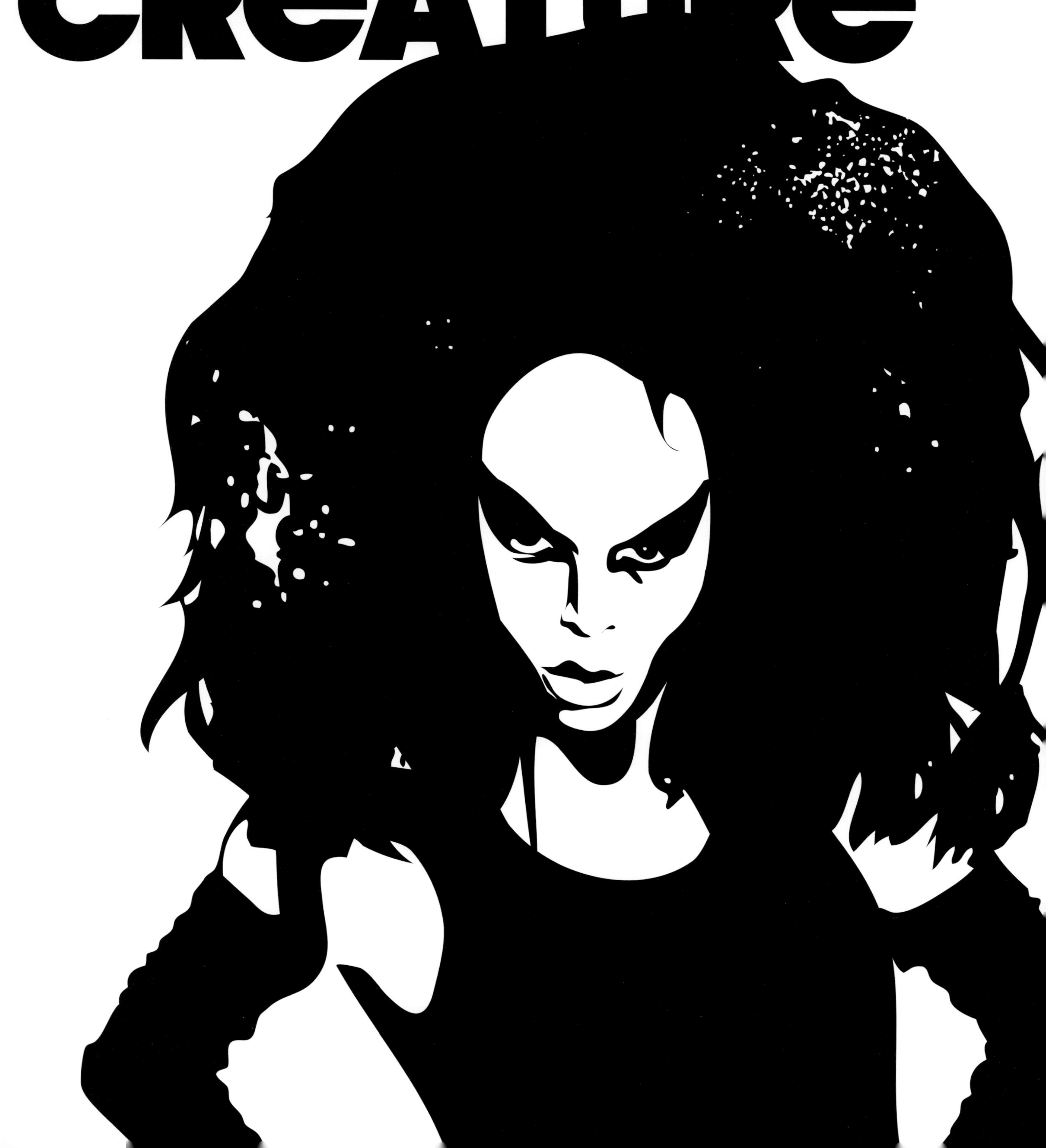
THE
BEAUTALIST
CREATURE

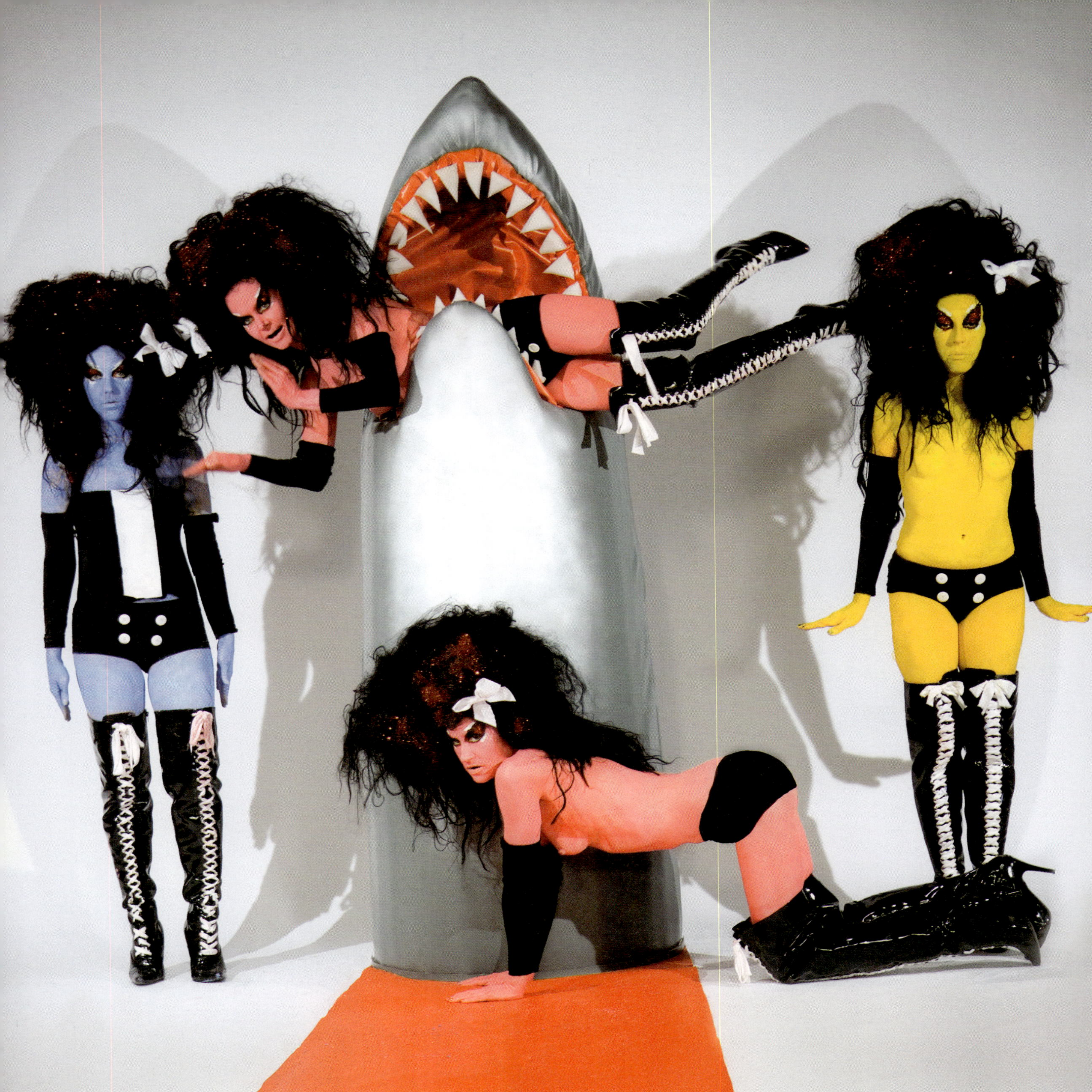

The Voluptuous Horror of Karen Black
During filming of 'i believe in Halloween'
for the IFC
2007
Courtesy of the Artist
and Deitch Projects, New York
Photo Credit © Kristy Leibowitz

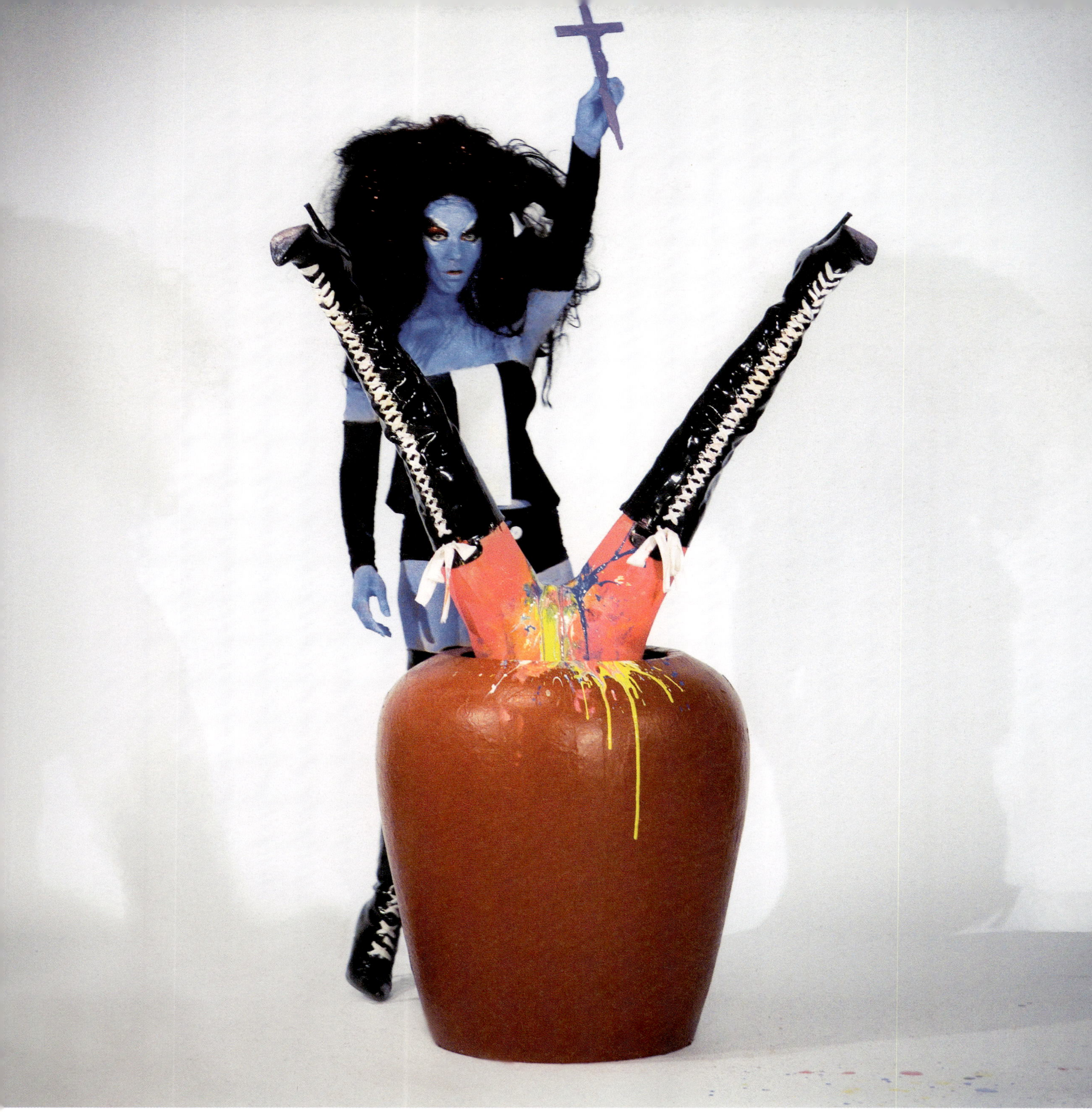

The Voluptuous Horror of Karen Black
During filming of 'i believe in Halloween'
for the IFC
2007
Courtesy of the Artist
and Deitch Projects, New York
Photo Credit © Kristy Leibowitz

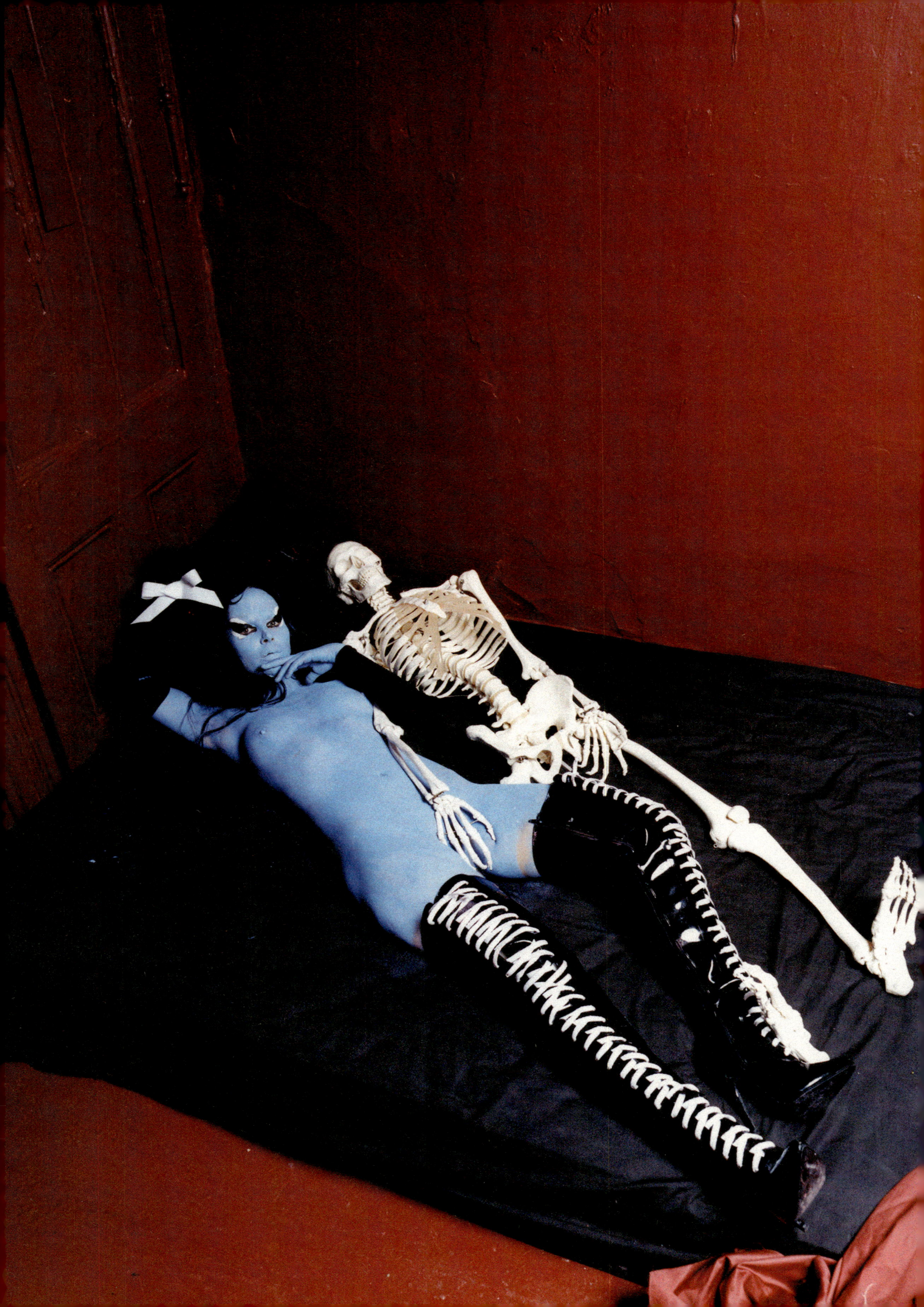

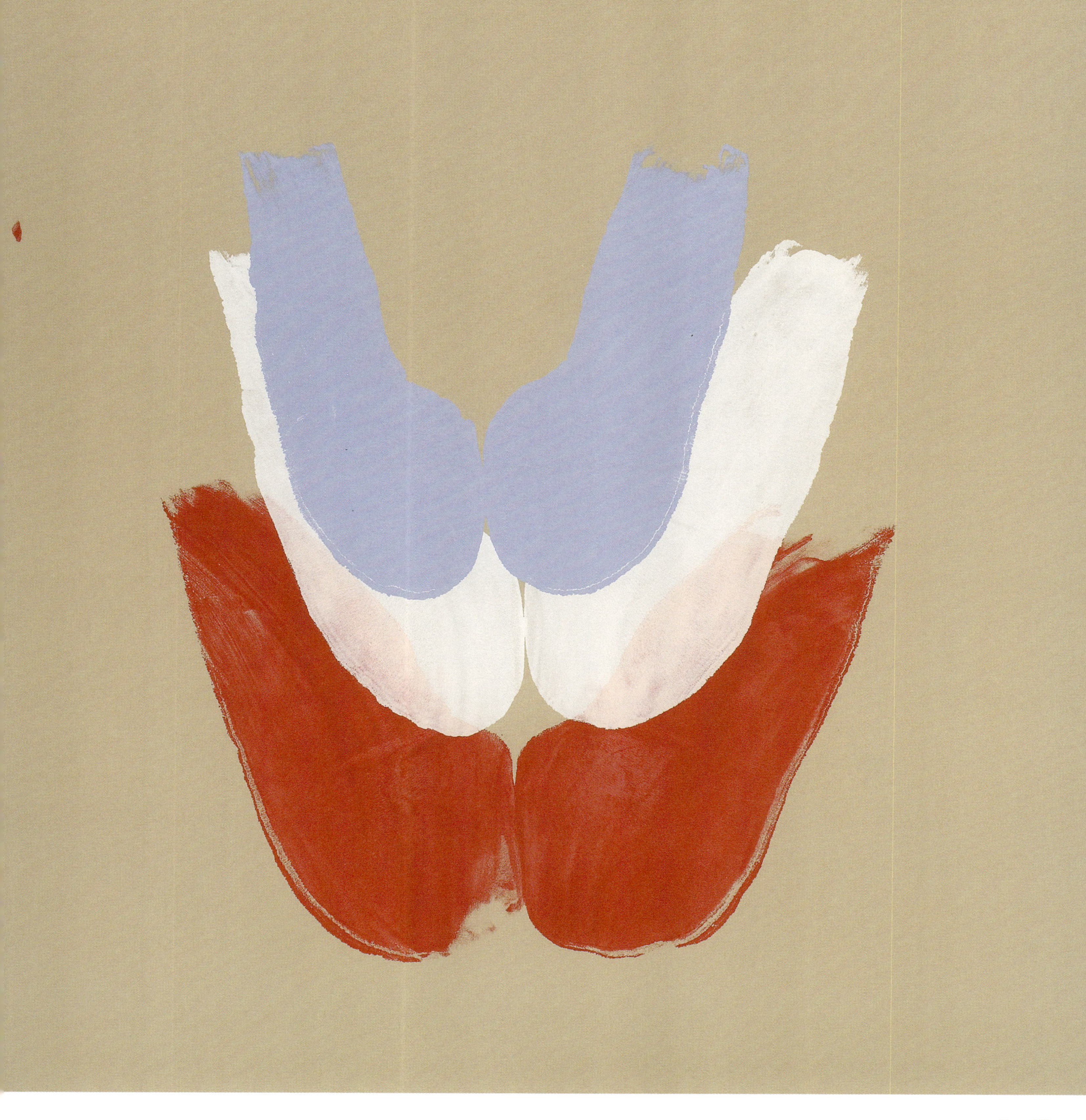

Page 152
Skeleton Fornication
2006
Photo by Katrina del Mar
Photograph
Edition of 4
55,9 x 45,7 cm
Courtesy of the Artist
and Deitch Projects, New York
Photo Credit © Tom Powel Imaging

America USA
2008
Water-based body paint on paper
76,2 x 76,2 cm
Courtesy of the Artist and Deitch Projects,
New York
Photo Credit © Tom Powel Imaging

THE
RESID

eNTS

PART PROGR AND PART e

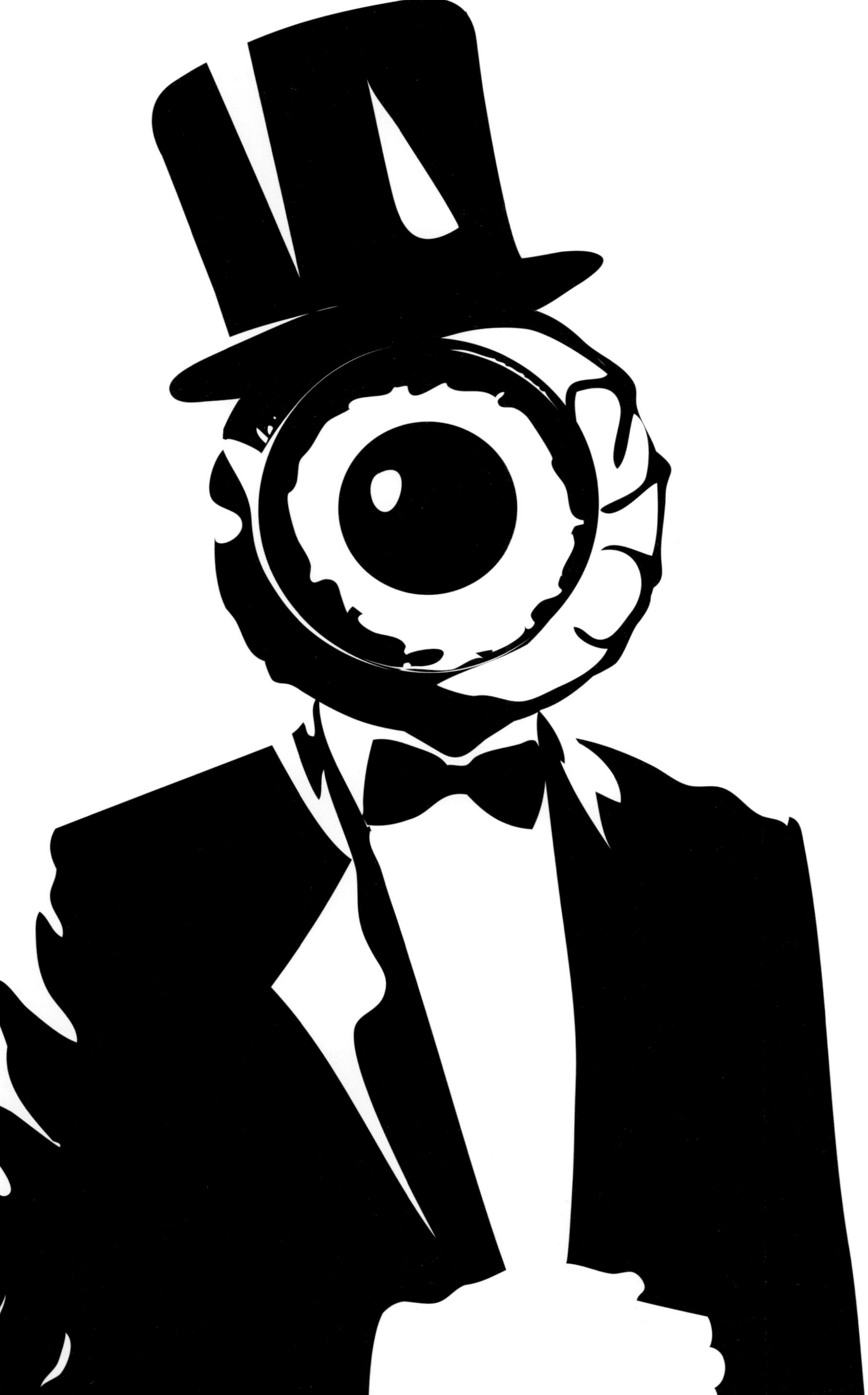

Legends despite remaining consistently anonymous, an entity rather than a group, The Residents have haunted the world of music since 1972. Its four members are still unknown to this day, and use the mystery surrounding them to perpetuate their mythology. They refuse all interviews and appear in public dressed in dinner suits and top hats, and disguised in giant eyeball masks. Their nonconformist and indefinable work defies description and demonstrates that there really are no rules in music.

In visual art, too, The Residents have developed a truly iconographic repertoire that is both fictional and full of humor. For them, their art is more important than their music – as their manager often says: "Without art, there would be no Residents". Producers of hilarious video clips and extravagant performances, these highly imaginative West Coast masters of the absurd have developed a lasting identity, both visual and musical, weaving lies, rumors, interpretations, and half-truths into a rich creative legacy.
— The group was founded in 1972.

HOMER FLYNN AND HARDY FOX (MANAGERS) FOR THE RESIDENTS INTERVIEWED BY DARIA DE BEAUVAIS

...essive ...xistential

HOW WERE THE RESIDENTS FORMED?

The Residents were created by people who had become bored by the music being produced in the early '70s. These consumers had followed music as it had progressed from the decadence of pop music in the mid-'50s to the rebellious attitude of rock 'n' roll through the British Revolution of the early '60s and the psychedelic movement that followed a few years later. But by the early '70s, the importance of experimentation and change had faded, at least as far as popular music was concerned. With the field wide open, The Residents moved in. And it's still wide open. But there is a lot of interesting music being created these days.

HOW WAS THIS NAME CHOSEN, AND WHAT WAS THE IDEA BEHIND IT?

The Residents have always seen themselves as part progressive and part existential as far as their values are concerned. Their name, which came from the mailing label of a demo tape returned to them from Warner Music in 1971, illustrates the existential side.

WHY SUCH ANONYMITY? WAS IT A WAY OF AVOIDING THE STATUS OF THE "ROCK STAR", A REAL CLICHÉ IN THE '70S?

The Residents have preferred to be seen as a group rather than a collection of individuals. This group identity is much easier to maintain behind the facade of anonymity.

CAN YOU TELL US MORE ABOUT THIS IDEA OF THE RESIDENTS CONSIDERING THEMSELVES AS A GROUP MORE THAN A BAND?

It relates to the underlying essence of music and musicians. A band is an aggregation of humans that are primarily musicians. The Residents are not musicians, but instead, a group that attempts to manipulate music – as well as other sounds – in an artistic way. But they're not musicians. Musicianship is a skill and one which has definitely not been cultivated by the group. From their perspective, real musicians should be offended at being grouped together with amateurs like The Residents.

WHAT IS THE MYTHOLOGY OF THE RESIDENTS? IS EVERYTHING EXPLAINED IN THE TRUE STORY OF THE RESIDENTS, WRITTEN BY MATT GROENING IN 1979?

The mythology of The Residents is a collection of lies, misinterpretations, half-truths, fiction, and absurdity, mixed in with the occasional tidbit of truth, which has accumulated over a period of 35 years. At this point it is impossible to summarize its entirety in an interview. Matt Groening did an admirable job of capturing the essence of The Residents' œuvre in 1979, but now, almost 30 years later, his version is missing quite a few chapters.

WHAT ARE THE CRYPTIC CORPORATION AND POOR KNOW GRAPHICS?

The Cryptic Corporation is the entity that deals with business and public relations on behalf of The Residents. According to the mythology, such mundane activity would be beneath the dignity, as well as the competence, of the restless, creative, and irresponsible genius inhabiting The Residents. Poor Know Graphics is The Residents' personal design functionary.

HOW WOULD YOU DESCRIBE THE RESIDENTS' MUSIC?

The music of The Residents is the sound of grim frivolity, darkness and light. It's the black cloud blocking out the silver lining, the old joke gratifying a new audience, a donkey shitting on the president's foot. Beyond that, it's difficult to describe.

WHY HIDE BEHIND GIANT EYEBALL MASKS?

The eyeball mask is actually a mirror.

> **Without art, there would be no Residents.**

THIS BIG EYE ICON – TOGETHER WITH THE PRESENCE OF A BIG BROTHER CHARACTER ON THE RESIDENTS' OFFICIAL WEBSITE – IS REMINISCENT OF GEORGE ORWELL'S PREMONITORY IDEA, "BIG BROTHER IS WATCHING YOU". HOW DO THE RESIDENTS FEEL ABOUT THIS THEME?

While The Residents watch the world, they don't really see that the world watches them, or at least not very much. And that's okay. When the group started, they were much enamored with the "theory of obscurity", an idea stating that an artist does his or her best work while sheltered from the influence of an audience. This concept still has great value for them.

A WHOLE ICONOGRAPHY WITH A VERY STRONG IDENTITY, BOTH HUMOROUS AND FICTIONAL, HAS BEEN DEVELOPED OVER THE YEARS BY THE RESIDENTS. WHAT IS THE ROLE OF ART IN THEIR PRACTICE?

Without art, there would be no Residents, only an oily residue consisting of poorly played music, thinly veiled lies, and underdeveloped concepts held together with pretense and folly. This lofty idea – art, or at least a commitment to making decisions with artistic intent – has always held a high position in their mythological world.

WHAT ABOUT THE PERFORMANCES?

More theater than concert, The Residents' performances are usually viewed as events. Enhanced by strong visuals and the excitement of real-time creativity, the group's performances are often more emotionally direct than their recordings.

WHAT ARE THE RESIDENTS' UPCOMING PROJECTS?

The group is currently involved in an ambitious new project consisting of three primary parts: a new album, a tour, and an interactive internet component. The internet portion will begin in the summer of 2008, while the album and tour will surface in October and November of this year (2008).

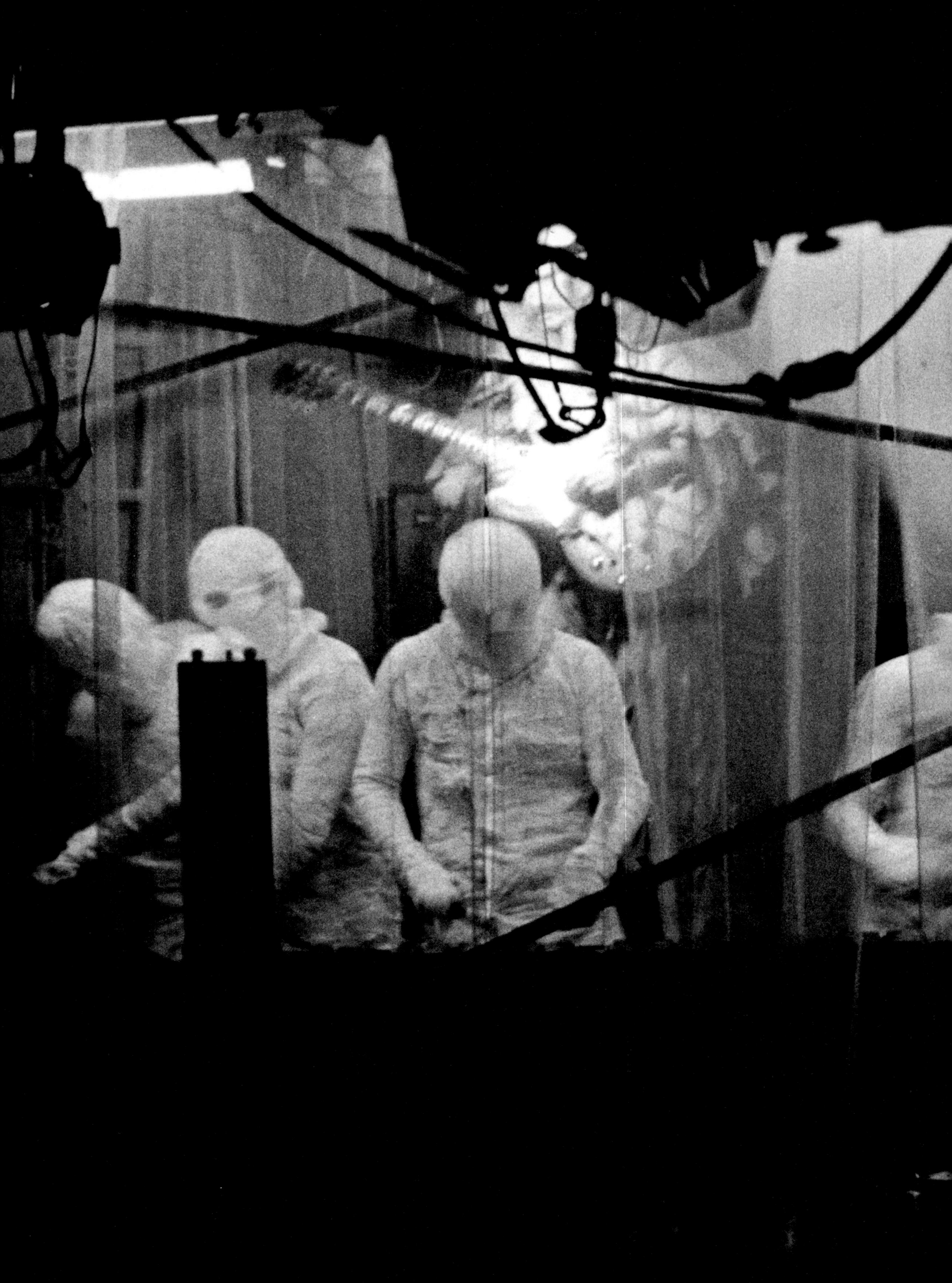

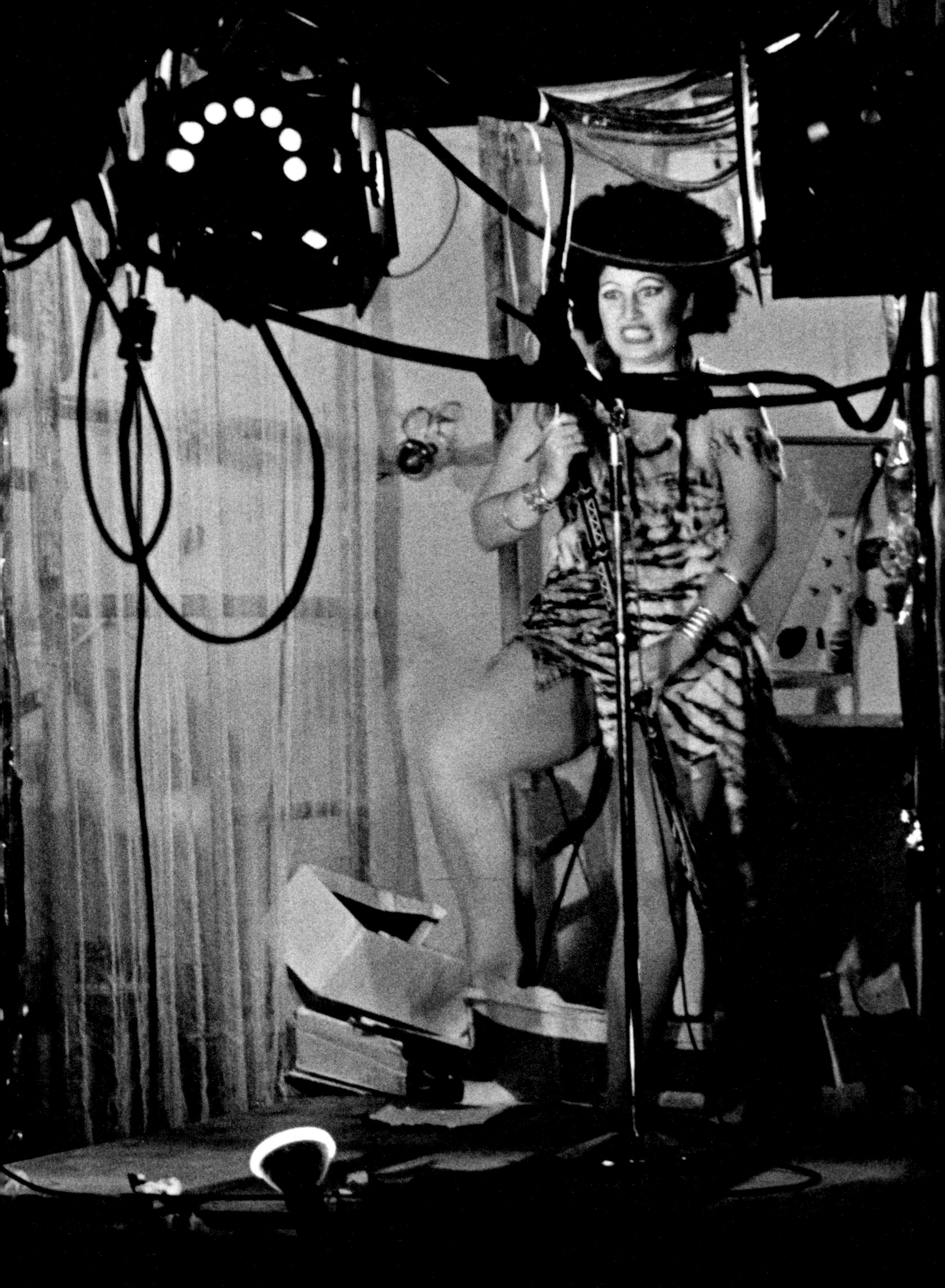

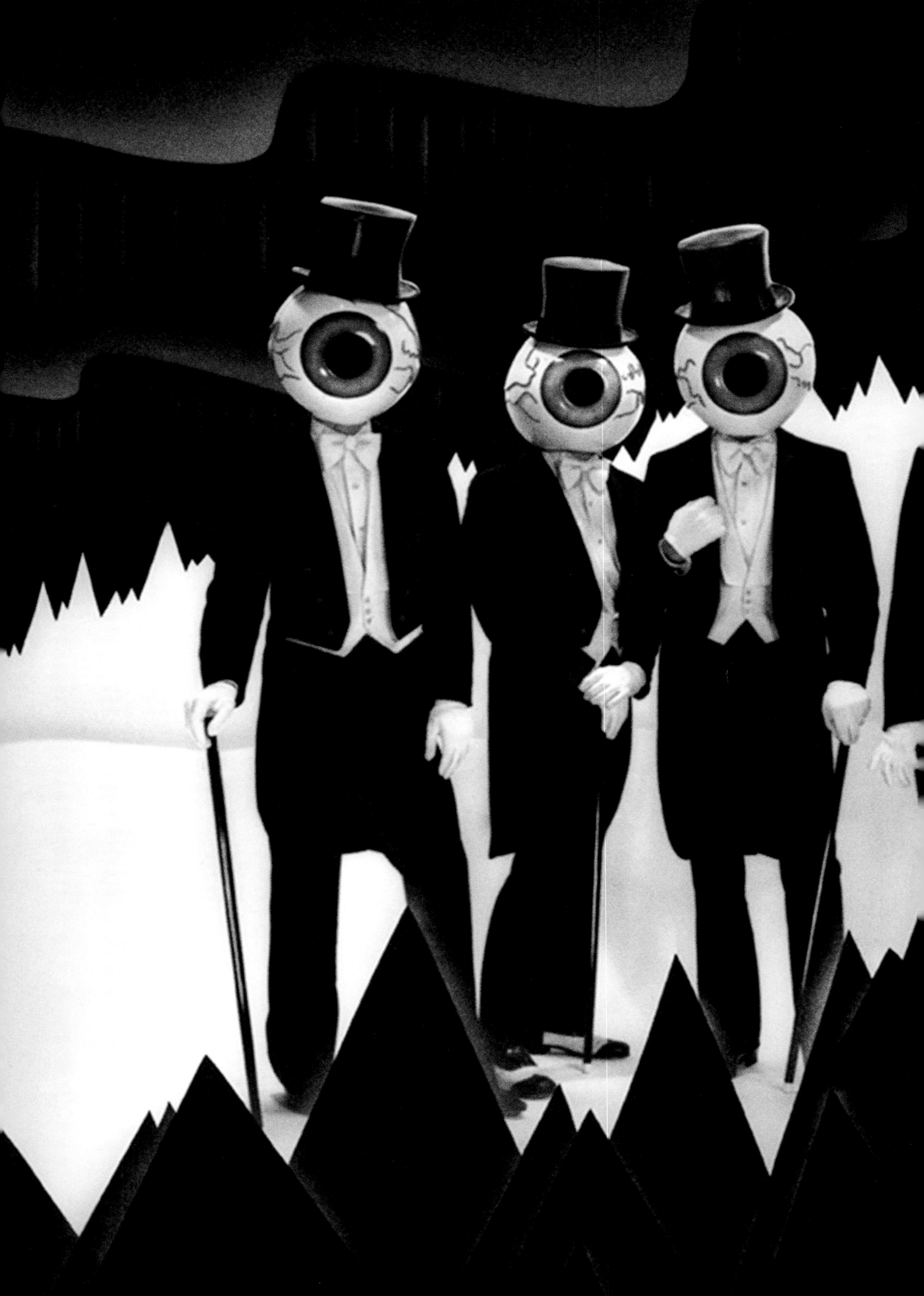

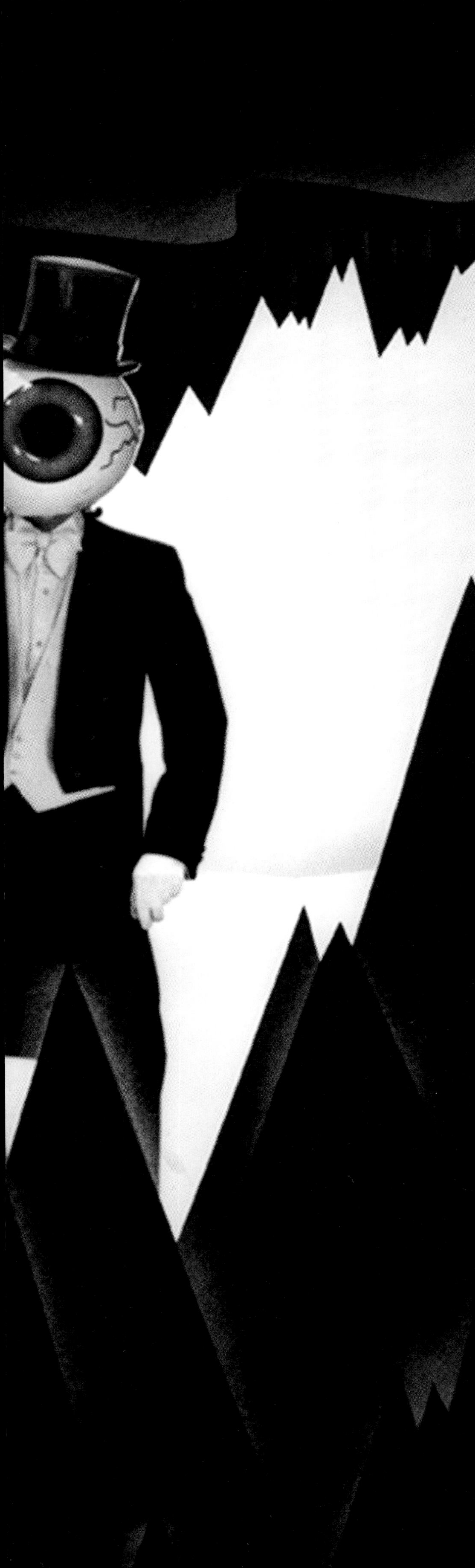

Page 158/159
The Residents appearing at the Long Branch
Saloon in Berkeley, CA
1976
Courtesy of The Cryptic Corporation
Photo Credit © Richard McCaffrey

The Residents 'ESKIMO'
1979
LP Cover
Courtesy of The Cryptic Corporation
Photo Credit © Poor Know Graphics

RICEBOY SLE

eps

Drummer Boy
June 2003
Stencil
102 x 48 cm
Courtesy of the Artists,
Gallery Turpentine, Iceland and
The Agency Gallery, UK

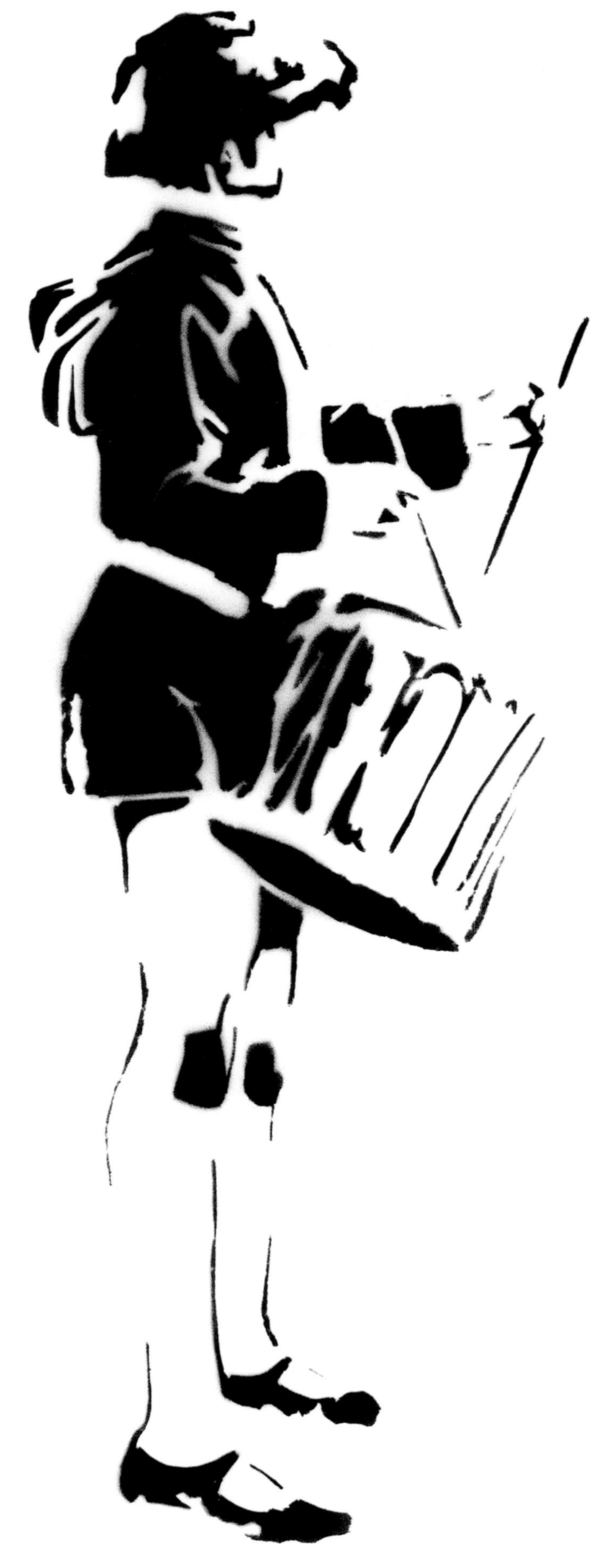

SMALL MOMENTS IN LIFE

Behind the pseudonym Riceboy Sleeps is the Icelandic duo of Jónsi Birgisson and Alex Somers. In addition to being known for their artistic collaborations, both are familiar figures in the music world. Jónsi Birgisson is singer and guitarist with the group Sigur Rós, and Alex Somers, together with Scott Alario, make up Parachutes. The music of Riceboy Sleeps is characterized by atmospheric soundscapes that are typically Icelandic and evoke the geography of their creators' native land. What began as a musical collaboration, Riceboy Sleeps has become a two-headed feast at which art and music are both fed and consumed on a daily basis. Imagined as a collage of eras and histories, a family album of an anonymous family, the artistic creations of Riceboy Sleeps combine old photos with newer originals, interspersed with sketches, poems, and pages from ancient tomes. Taken together these elements make up a mysterious universe, sleep-inducing and dreamlike, a reflection of their particular Icelandic nature.

—Jónsi Birgisson was born in 1975 in Reykjavik, Iceland, where he resides today.

—Alex Somers was born in 1984 in Baltimore, Maryland (USA), and currently lives in Reykjavik.

ALEX SOMERS OF RICEBOY SLEEPS INTERVIEWED BY JÉRÔME SANS

YOU BOTH HAVE YOUR OTHER MUSIC PROJECTS — JÓNSI, WITH SIGUR RÓS, AND ALEX, WITH PARACHUTES. HOW AND WHEN DID THE ART COLLABORATION RICEBOY SLEEPS START?

Riceboy Sleeps started a little over four years ago, soon after we first met. It started with us just making songs. Then somewhere along the line, after we were living together, we began making video pieces together and drawing and painting and everything else.

WHERE DOES THE NAME RICEBOY SLEEPS COME FROM? WHAT DOES IT MEAN?

Jónsi used to call me Riceboy because for some period of time I was only eating rice, just because I was a bit poor. And I did sleep a lot. Riceboy Sleeps was originally the name of one of our songs, then somehow we ended up calling everything Riceboy Sleeps.

HOW DOES YOUR COLLABORATION FUNCTION? DO YOU DO EVERYTHING TOGETHER OR DOES EACH OF YOU WORK ON A PARTICULAR PART?

We are both really involved in everything. Of course sometimes one of us will do more or less in one particular stage, but for each whole artwork or song we are both very involved. Even when we draw, after one of us finishes we often trade drawings and let the other add to it or change it. We have the same sense of what is beautiful, and because of that we rarely disagree about what works and what does not.

HOW DO YOU RELATE YOUR ART PRACTICE TO YOUR MUSIC?

Making art and music is really similar for us. We do not have a studio. So we make most of our art and music at home in our living room and kitchen. It has become a part of daily life. The art and music is really coming from the same place. We just enjoy creating an atmosphere that feels right to us, in a picture and in a song.

HOW WOULD YOU DEFINE YOUR ARTWORK?

Our art is an honest expression of our ideals. It is our imaginations playing with moments from our lives, and fictional moments we create.

YOU WORK WITH DIFFERENT MEDIA — DRAWINGS, PHOTOGRAPHS, PAINTINGS. WHAT ARE THESE DRAWINGS OR PHOTOS ABOUT?

Small moments in life. Finding the beauty in climbing a tree or listening to the wind. All these things Jónsi and I share. Sometimes it's things you can forget about…

LAST YEAR YOU EXHIBITED IN THE GERTRUDE CONTEMPORARY ART SPACE (MELBOURNE, AUSTRALIA) AND IN GALLERY 801 (ARKANSAS, USA). FOR THESE TWO EXHIBITIONS YOUR WORKS WERE INSTALLED IN OLD WINDOW FRAMES. WHY?

It just happened. We were taking a drive in the countryside and we stopped and decided to go for a walk. After walking for a long time we came across a huge pile of very old, beat-up windows. We both had the same idea right away: These windows could make beautiful picture frames. So we collected as many as we could and took them home.

HAVE YOU BEEN TO ART SCHOOL?

I am currently studying in The Icelandic Academy of the Arts, in the visual arts program. I also studied music at Berklee College of Music, in Boston.

WHO ARE THE CONTEMPORARY ARTISTS YOU FEEL CLOSE TO?

Ingibjorg Birgissdóttir, Sindri Már Sigfússon, Marguerite Keyes, Scott Alario, Sally Mann, and Marcel Dzama and The Royal Art Lodge.

WHAT ARE YOUR FUTURE ART PROJECTS?

This year we plan to release our first album. Then we hope to finish another picture book, and maybe a recipe book. We love food. We also recently took some black and white photographs then painted them in with watercolors… We would like to do more of that. Now we are collecting antique maps and we are going to do something with them soon. And Jónsi is pretty busy with his band Sigur Rós; they are working on their fifth album now. And I am also making music of my own with my best friend Scott, and we are also slowly putting together an album of our own.

> We just enjoy creating an atmosphere that feels right to us, in a picture and in a song.

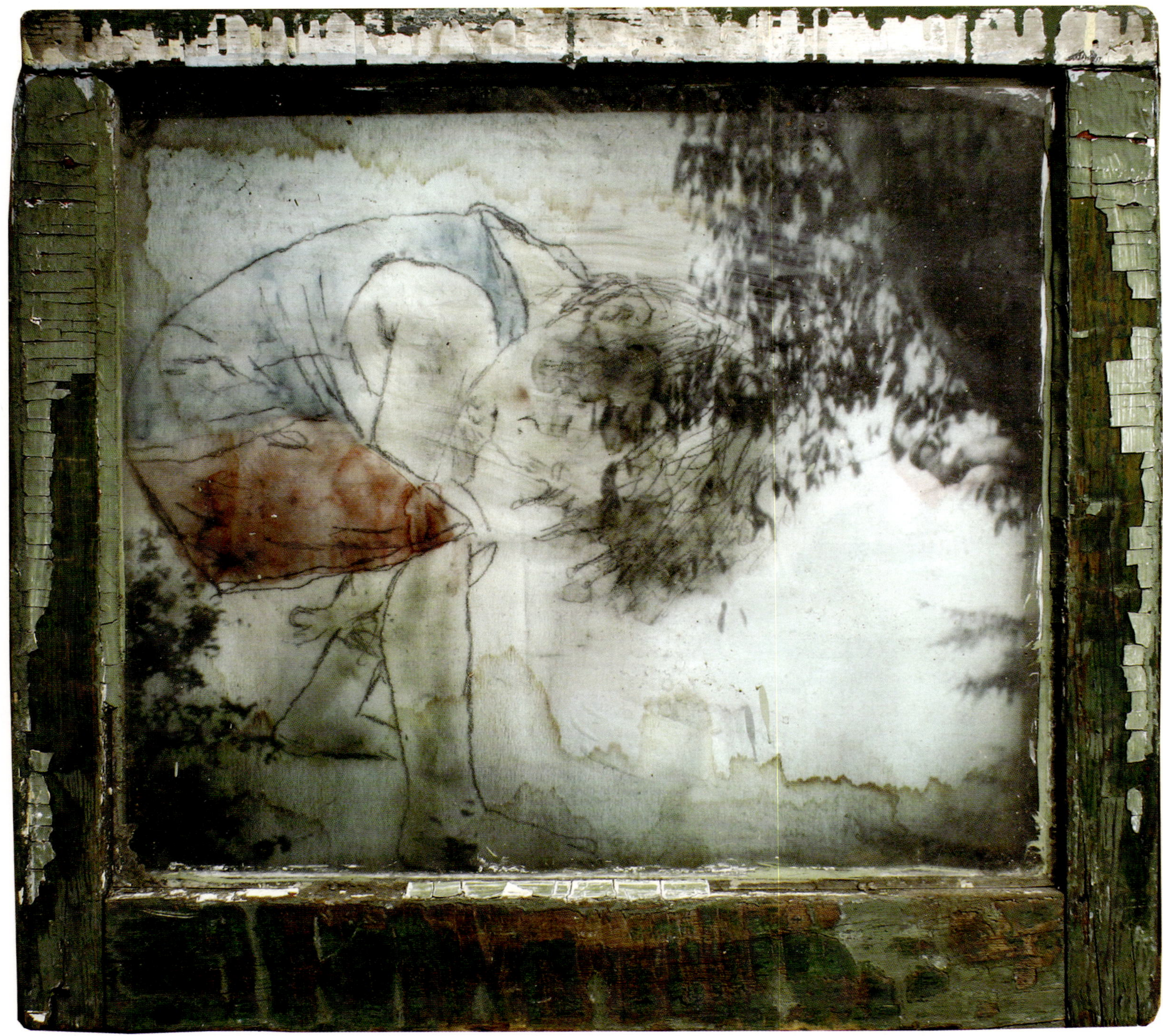

Wind In My Ear
2007
Mixed Media
62.3 x 55.9 cm
Courtesy of the Artists,
Gallery Turpentine, Iceland and
The Agency Gallery, UK

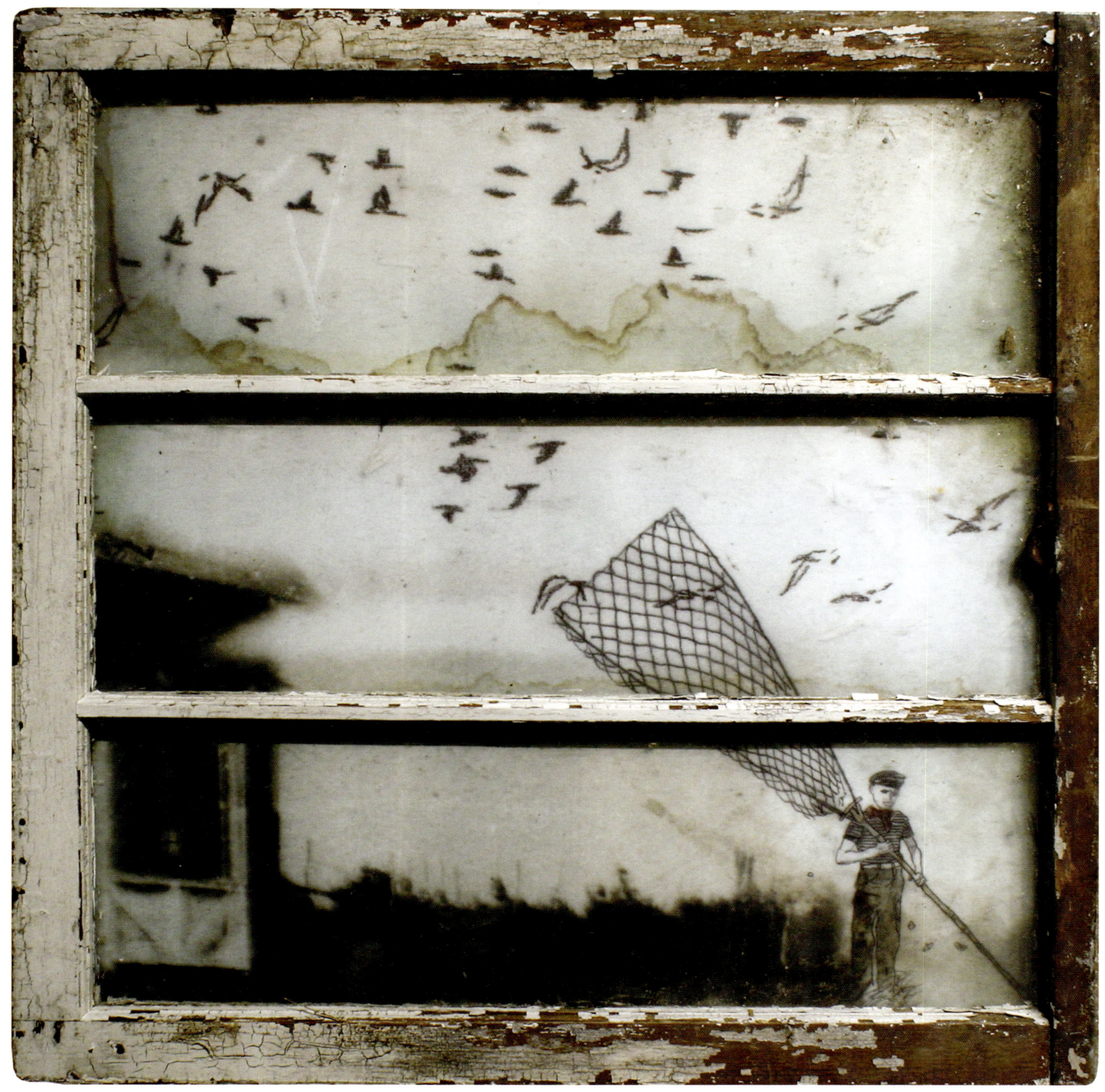

Rain Down My Favorite Songs
2007
Mixed Media
78.8 x 81.3 cm
Courtesy of the Artists,
Gallery Turpentine, Iceland and
The Agency Gallery, UK

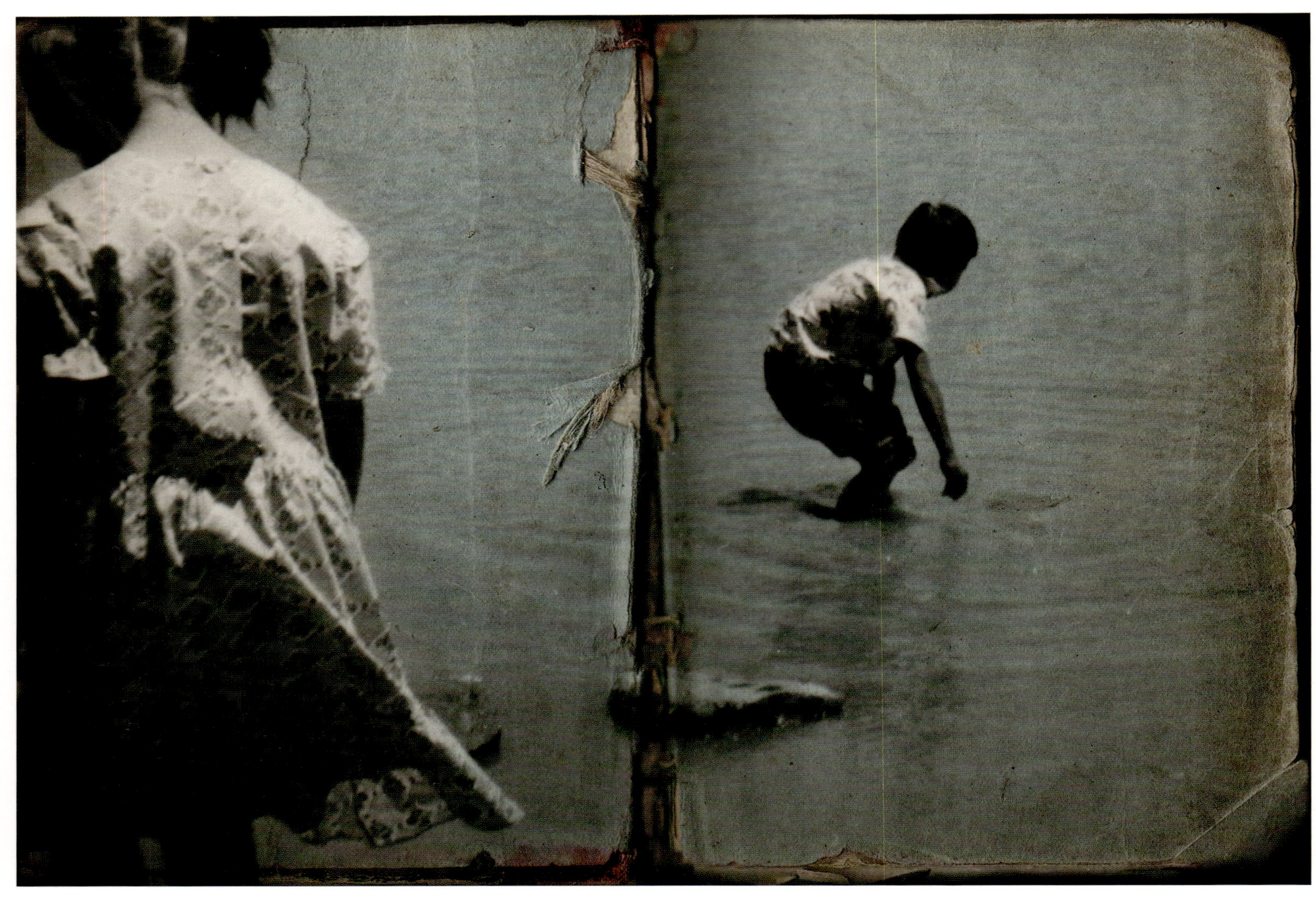

In The Sea
2007
Lithographie
56 x 76 cm
Courtesy of the Artists,
Gallery Turpentine, Iceland and
The Agency Gallery, UK

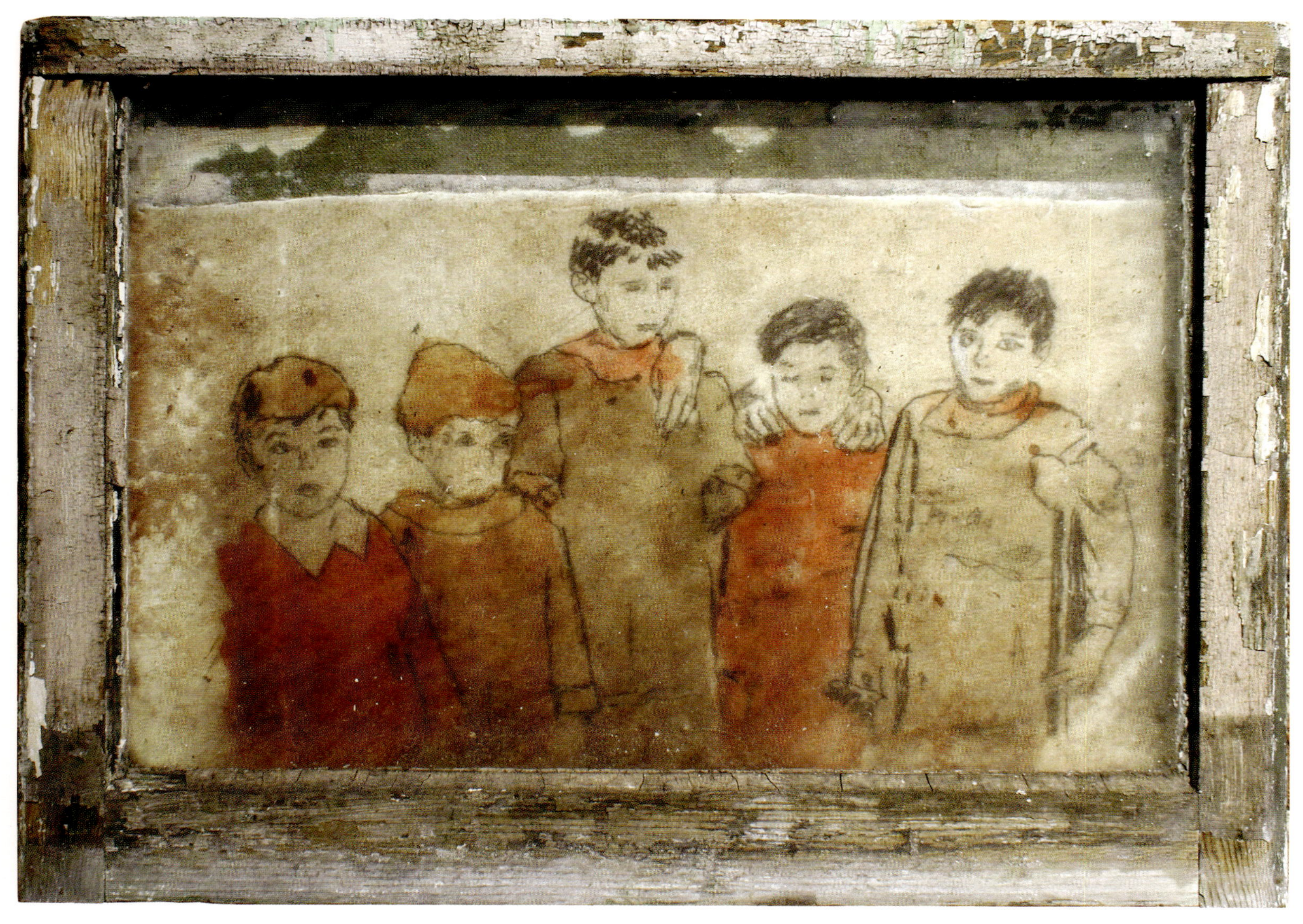

Dog Saviors
2007
Mixed Media
71.1 x 49.5 cm
Courtesy of the Artists,
Gallery Turpentine, Iceland and
The Agency Gallery, UK

PATTI
SM

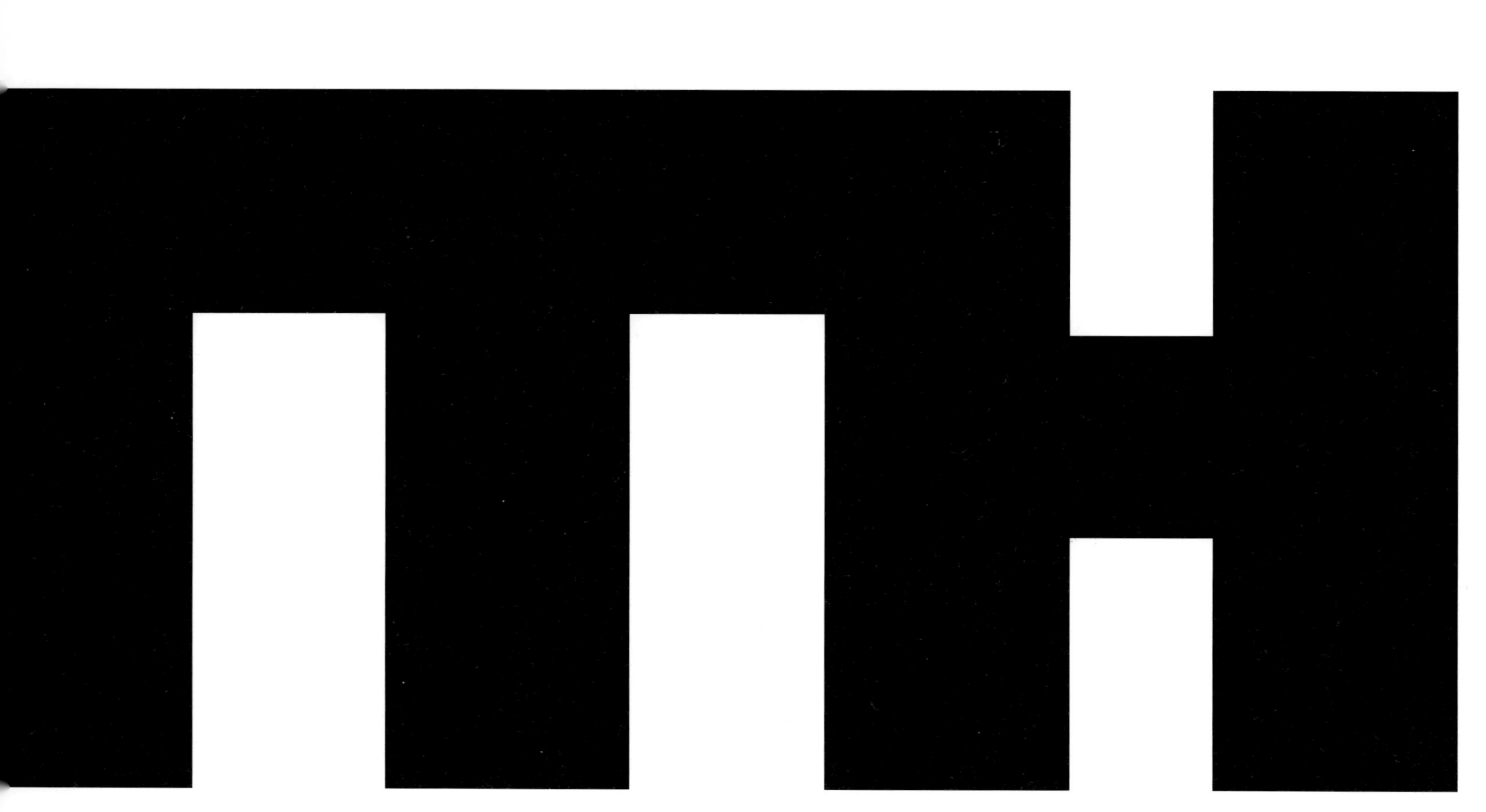

Through her writings, poetry readings, and songs, Patti Smith has imbued words with a distinctive resonance and eloquence, and turned poetry into a radical, incantatory, spiritual, and healing form of music. An influential force in the music scene of the '70s, Smith combined stripped-down music with powerful lyrics, and through albums like Horses, Radio Ethiopia, and Easter, earned the title of "punk's poet laureate". But Patti Smith is also an artist who for 40 years has forged her own path, broken down walls, and defined a visual world of her own. Her work runs from drawings to photography, film to manuscripts, and can be read as visual odes – instants dedicated to the inspiration she finds in life. Just as her poetry is full of imagery, her photographs are almost whispering voices. Whether she seizes similar spirited objects on her journey, and whether she seizes upon objects that are meaningful to her, or pays tribute to people and places that have inspired her, Patti Smith's artworks are windows on the world, inviting us to imagine and explore the stories behind the visible layers.
— Patti Smith was born in Chicago in 1946, and lives in New York City.

PATTI SMITH INTERVIEWED BY AUDREY MASCINA

BEFORE BECOMING AN ARTIST, A POET, A PERFORMER, A MUSICIAN, YOU DID STUDIES TO BECOME AN ART TEACHER. WHY?

I chose to be an art teacher because I did not have the money to go to art school. I like sharing information and speaking in front of people, so I thought it could be a way to have some art education. But I didn't complete the course and decided instead to go to New York and pursue art itself instead of teaching it.

WERE YOU ALREADY PRODUCING ARTWORKS AT THAT TIME?

I've been drawing since I was a child. I've drawn all my life, and I started to take photographs in the '60s.

YOUR FIRST EXHIBITION WAS AT GOTHAM BOOK MART IN 1973. WHAT DID YOU SHOW?

I was exhibiting drawings.

WHAT PROMPTED YOU TO PERFORM YOUR POETRY LIVE AND TURN IT INTO MUSIC?

One aspect of poetry is to be oral. Some of my work is more in the oral tradition of Vachel Lindsay or Allen Ginsberg – it's best vocalized. I added electric guitar during my poetry readings to give them more depth and more energy. I wanted to do something new with poetry; I didn't want it to be static. It was in 1971 and no one was working with electric guitar. A lot of the beat poets performed with piano.

HOW DO YOU RELATE MUSIC WITH YOUR VISUAL ART WORK?

I'm not a rock 'n' roll singer who does art. I don't consider myself essentially as a singer or a rock star. I consider myself primarily an artist. To me, rock 'n' roll is a way to convey my ideas or my political concerns or messages directly to the people. When you perform poetry, do work in a museum, or show drawings, it does not reach as many people. So when I feel I need to reach more people, rock 'n' roll is the perfect form for that.

WHAT DEFINES YOUR PHOTOGRAPHIC WRITING?

My photographs are sort of little poems. They are very meditative. Especially when I am on the road – moving very quickly from city to city, with nine people in a bus, surrounded by technology, electric guitars, and a lot of energy – it's nice for me to go off alone with my Polaroid camera, and go down to a poet street, a museum, and find something that speaks for myself, where I don't depend on collaboration, technology, or crew. I take my pictures by myself, in natural light, with a very limited, almost primitive camera.

WHAT WERE YOU PHOTOGRAPHING IN THE '60S?

In the '60s I used to take photographs to put in collages, or photograph my friends. Unfortunately with various moves and being robbed in New York, most of my pictures have been lost. The few that I have left are photographs of Robert Mapplethorpe, and things I did for collage. I started again to use the Polaroid comprehensively in 1995, after the death of my husband. It was very difficult for me to write. It gave me a way to express myself without words.

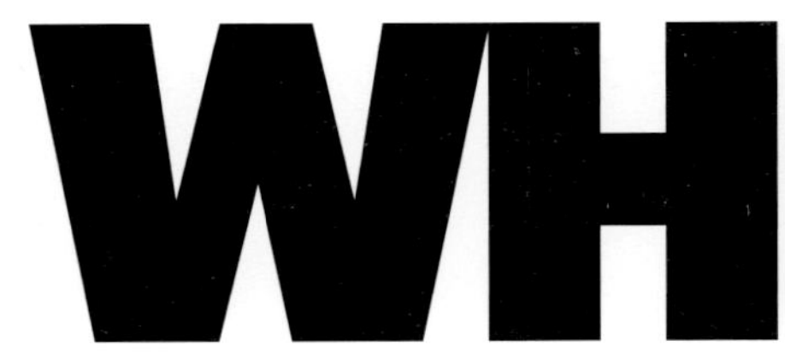

WHY DID YOU CHOOSE THE POLAROID AS YOUR CAMERA OF CHOICE?

It is a technically simple media. A child could use the camera; it's a Land 250. It only has dark-light, near-far. So it teaches you to really understand light because there are no tricks. I don't use any additional lights but an understanding of light and my little camera. The one thing it does have is a very good lens; it has a Zeiss Rangefinder.

YOUR PHOTOGRAPHS EMBODY TRACES, EVIDENCE, SOUVENIRS, OF ADMIRED PAST ARTISTS AND WRITERS, WITH A VERY TENDER LOOK – LIKE A TRIBUTE – TO THEM. COULD WE DEFINE THEM AS A DIARY AND CARTOGRAPHY OF YOUR INTERESTS AND REFERENCES?

The photographs are like little charms. When you visit places of a Saint, you often are given little medals that represent the Lord. I think of my photographs as holy medals, souvenirs. They are souvenirs of Virginia Woolf's bed, Hermann Hesse's typewriter…

YOU'RE MAINLY MAKING BLACK AND WHITE PHOTOGRAPHY. DO YOU THINK ABOUT WORKING IN COLOR OR SHIFTING TO A PHOTOGRAPHIC MEDIUM OTHER THAN POLAROID?

I spent a lot of time understanding light and how to make a good black-and-white picture, not just a snapshot. It's possible I could move to color, but that would be another struggle. Perhaps in the future.

> My photographs are sort of little poems. They are very meditative.

YOUR CURRENT RETROSPECTIVE AT THE FONDATION CARTIER, IN PARIS, INCLUDES ALL THE MEDIUMS YOU USE. IS THIS THE FIRST TIME YOU'RE GATHERING YOUR ENTIRE VOCABULARY IN ONE EXHIBITION? HOW ARE YOU APPROACHING THIS NEW CHAPTER?

The exhibition merges photographs, films, drawings, manuscripts. There are a lot of new artworks mingled with earlier ones, retracing 40 years of my artistic career, since 1967. I cre-

SPERING VOICES

ated part of the exhibit the week it opened, with installations and films. I did a short film honoring the remembrance of René Dumas, and exhibited some photographs I just took in Berlin of beautiful statues of angels. I want it to be an exhibition that has many levels that will be perhaps fun to look at. This exhibition has certain belongings, things of mine that are very rare, like the edition of 'A Season in Hell' that Arthur Rimbaud printed by himself, or my husband's electric guitar. There are other types of symbolic objects. I've been to the river where Virginia Woolf committed suicide. I found a very heavy, round stone in the river. This was the stone she was looking for when she took her life.

YOUR APPROACH TO EXHIBITING IS REALLY ABOUT THE IDEA OF SHARING YOUR EXPERIENCES – YOUR WORLD – WITH THE AUDIENCE; IS THAT RIGHT?

I travel so much with my band, I have an opportunity to see more cities and more places than anyone, and capture things people may have never seen. Especially Americans, who don't travel so much, or certainly aren't going to go to 45 cities in 60 days. I try to work out ways to share my experience. In the exhibition, people will learn more of the work I've done in 40 years, about other poets, and might be inspired to create artwork themselves.

YOU HAVE DONE INSTALLATIONS IN THE PAST. IS THIS AN AREA YOU PLAN TO EXPLORE MORE?

I did installations in the past but I didn't exhibit them. I've restaged, for example, the loft where Robert Mapplethorpe and I lived together. I've made those installations for myself till now. It's nice to be able to show them today. I hope they'll be inspiring to people.

YOU'VE MADE SOME SHORT FILMS, ALONE AND IN COLLABORATION WITH OTHER PEOPLE, LIKE JIM COHEN, ROBERT FRANK. IS FILM A MEDIUM YOU WOULD LIKE TO WORK MORE IN?

I've always loved film, but I'm not very good technically. I'll just wait and see. My dream now is to write an opera.

It's nice for me to go off alone with my Polaroid camera, and go down to a poet street, a museum, and find something that speaks for myself, where I don't depend on collaboration, technology, or crew.

AN OPERA WHERE YOU COULD INTEGRATE THE DIFFERENT FACETS OF YOUR VISUAL WORK?

An opera that would mix some, but that would be as traditional as I would know how to make an opera. Not a rock opera. I love Puccini, Verdi, Wagner. It would be very nice to create something classic and beautiful with the abilities that I have.

ARE THERE SOME CONTEMPORARY VISUAL ARTISTS WITH WHOM YOU WOULD LIKE TO COLLABORATE?

I like collaborating with my friends, like Jim Cohen, a contemporary filmmaker; or Flea, a contemporary composer and musician. But one of the things I like about art is that I don't have to collaborate. Rock 'n' roll is completely collaborative; it is a union of crew, band, and the people. I like the possibility of the solitude of the artist but I also like to work with my friends. Some of them are musicians, and some, like Ann Demeulemeester, who is known mostly for fashion, are artists. I have done many projects with her; I very much like her. We've collaborated with pieces of clothing but I've also done music for her. She worked with me on an installation for a big show I had in Munich. She will also be in my films. We have many plans for the future but they are between us.

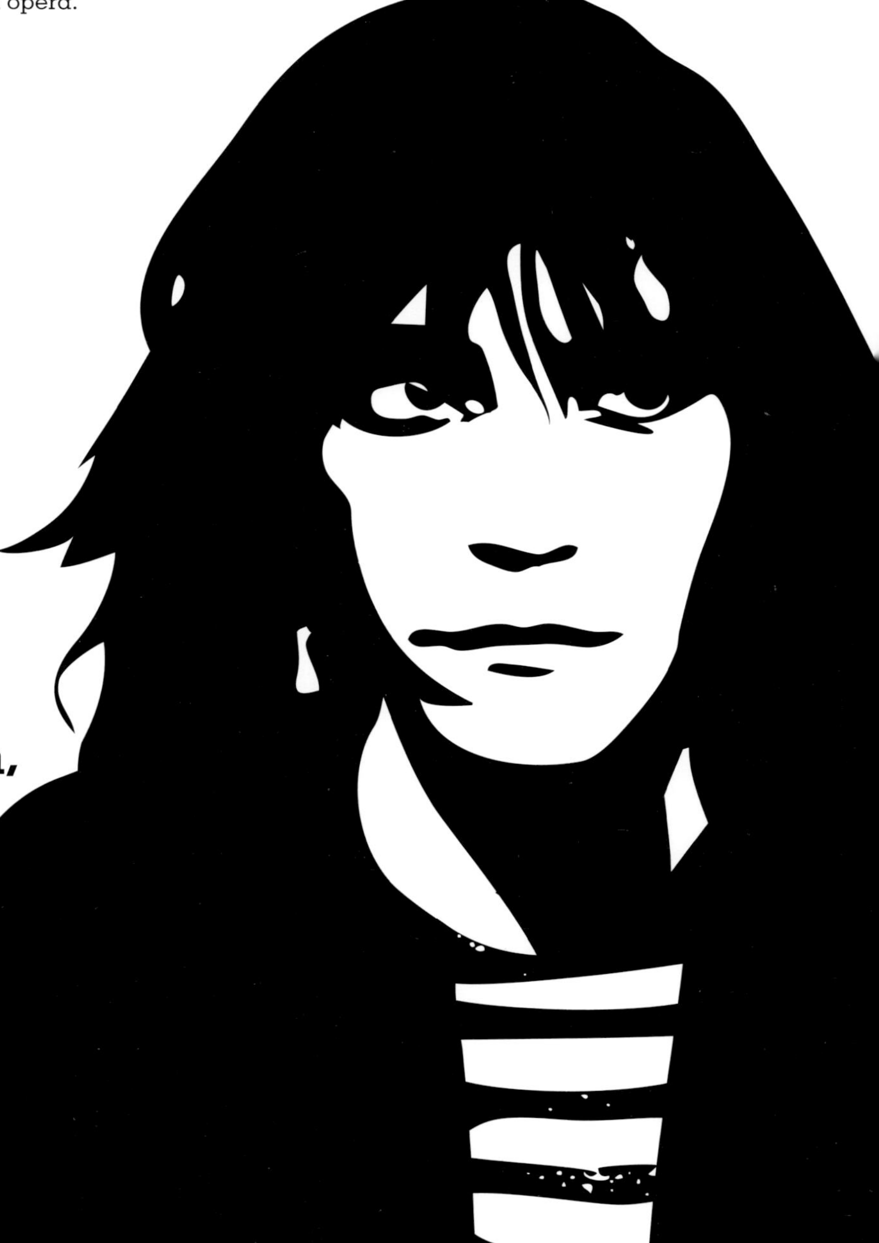

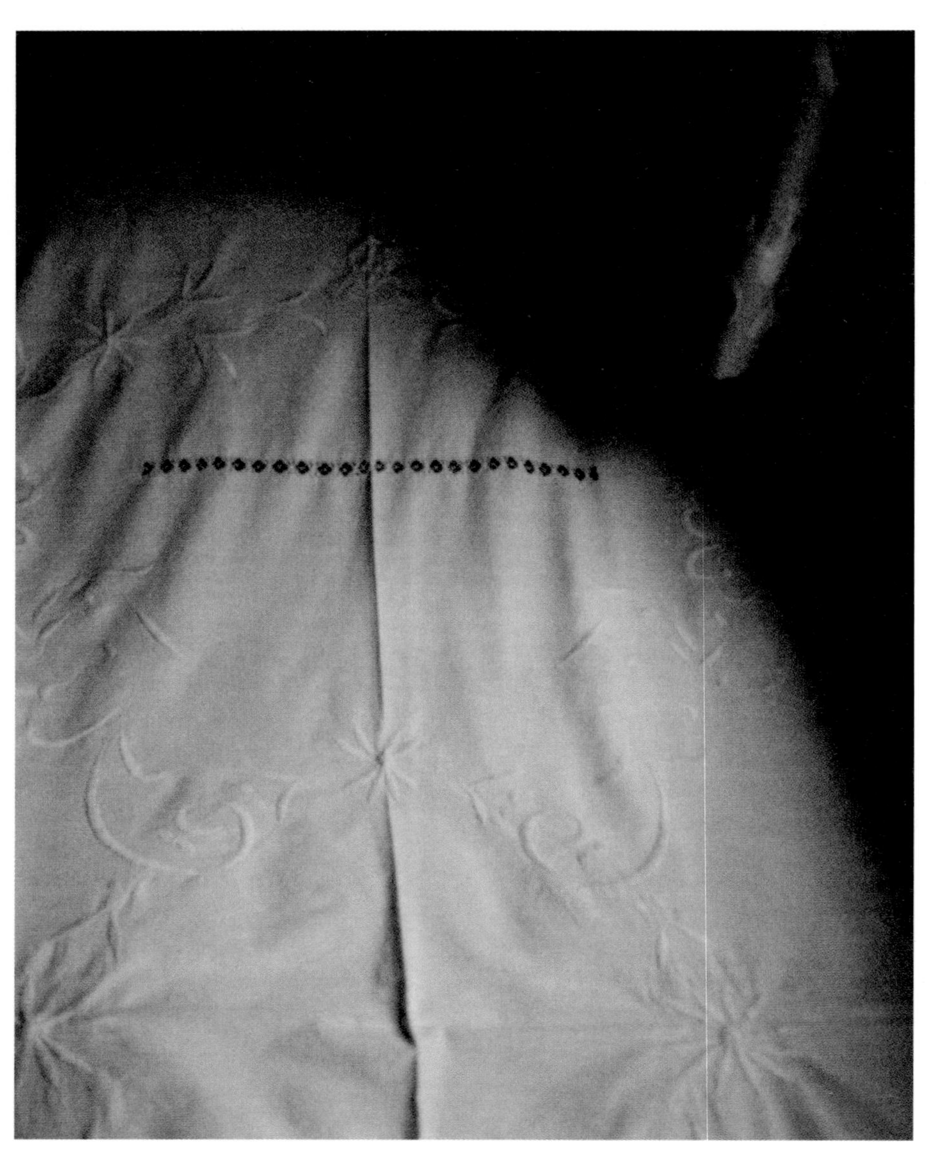

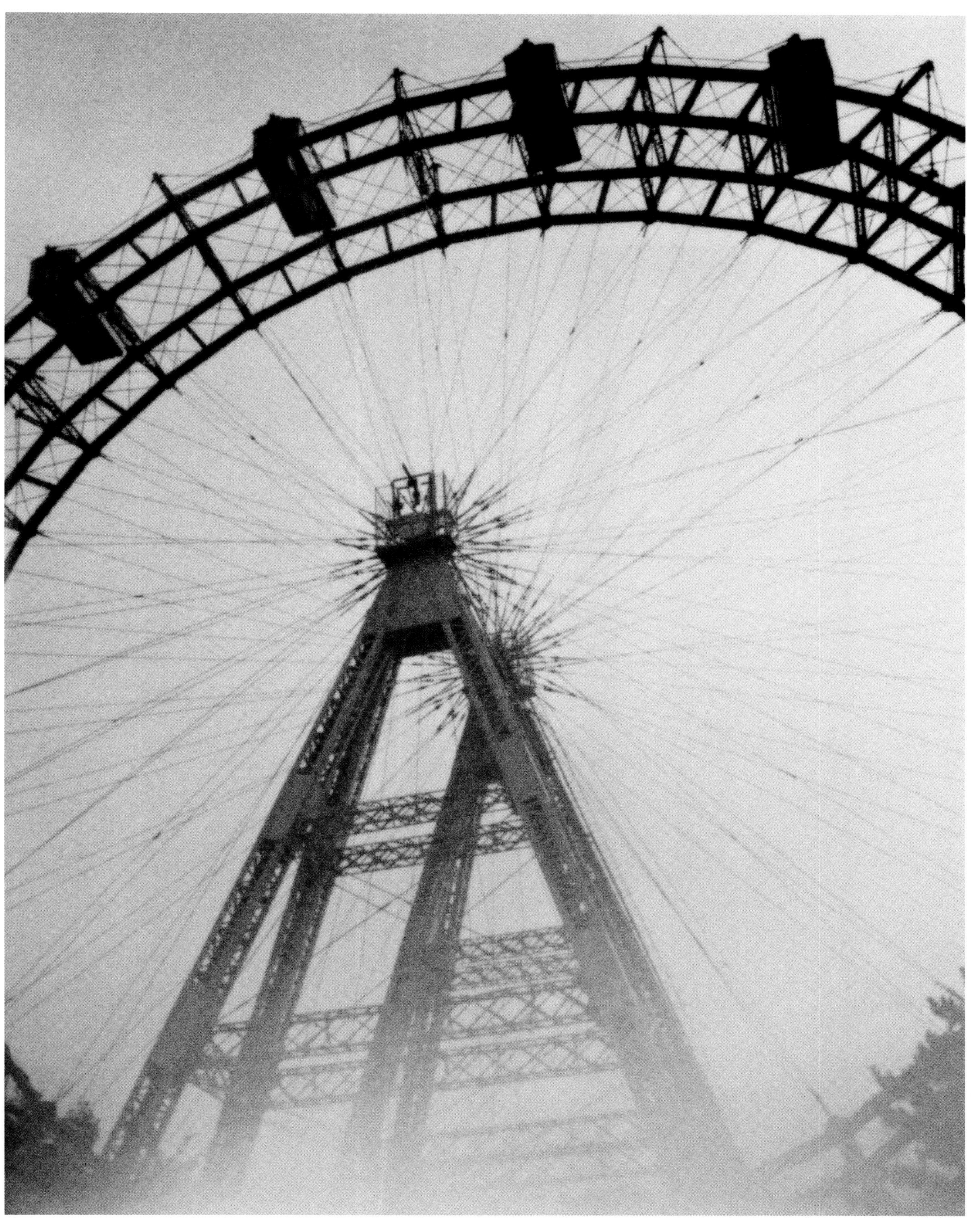

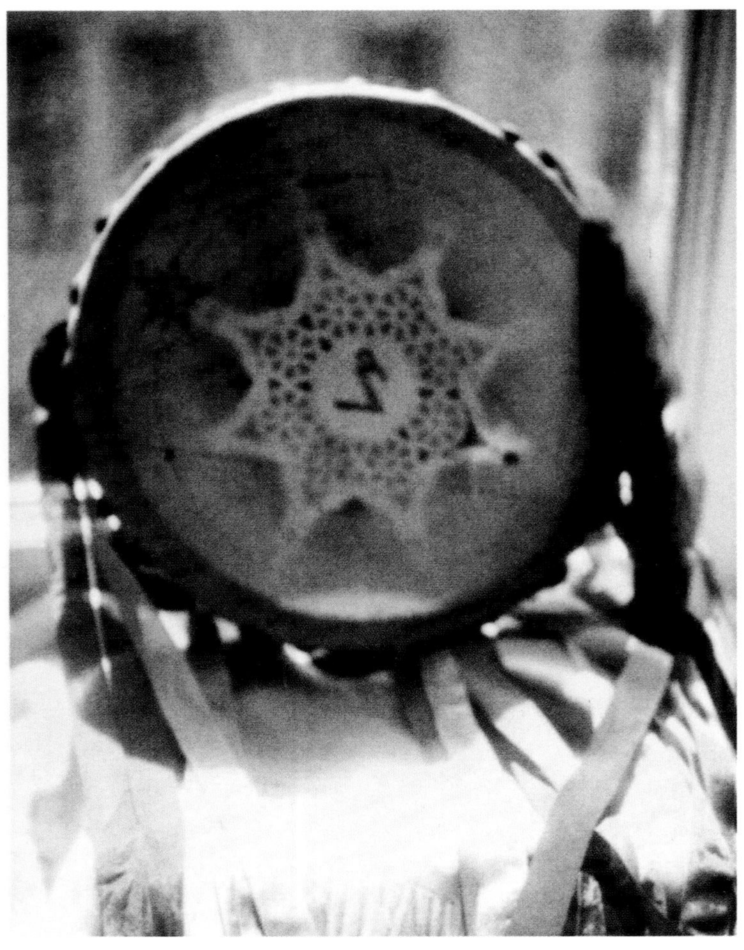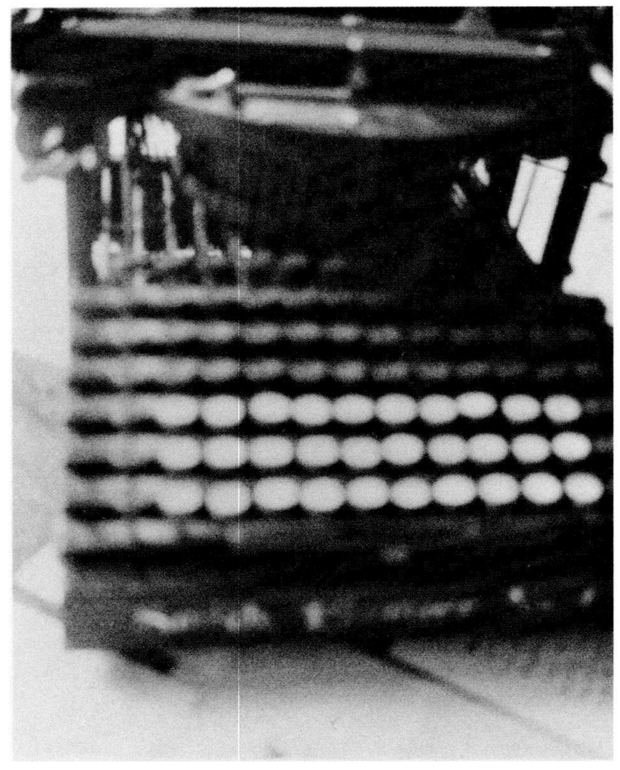

Page 174
Virginia Woolf's Bed 1, Monk's House
2003
Gelatin Silver Print
25.4 x 20.32 cm
Courtesy of Robert Miller Gallery, New York

Page 175
Wiener Riesenrad, Vienna
2003
Gelatin Silver Print
25.4 x 20.32 cm
Courtesy of Robert Miller Gallery, New York

Tambourine made in 1968 by
Robert Mapplethorpe
2006
Gelatin Silver Print
25.4 x 20.32 cm
Courtesy of Robert Miller Gallery, New York

Hermann Hesse's Typewriter
2003
Gelatin silver Print
25.4 x 20.32 cm
Courtesy of Robert Miller Gallery, New York

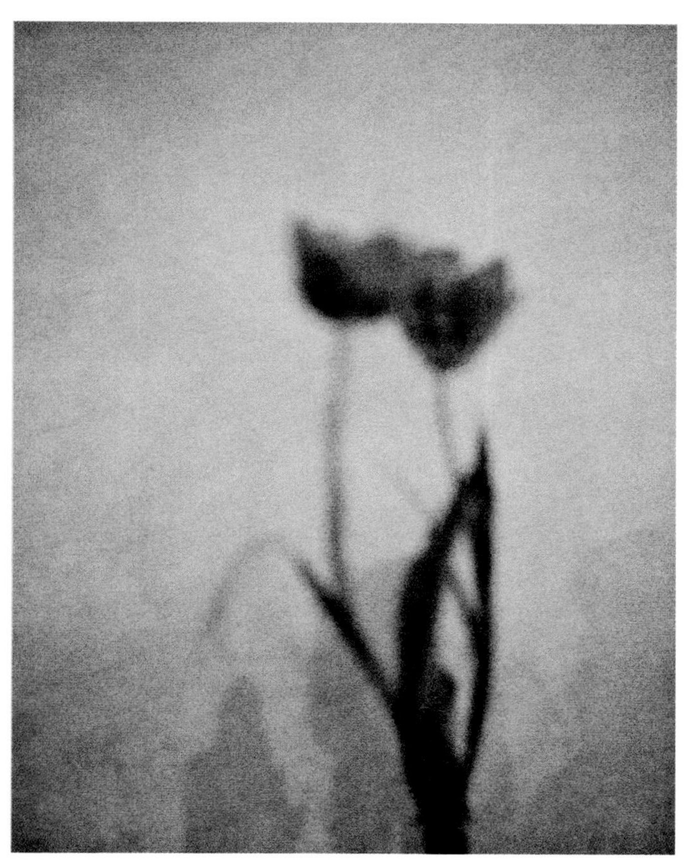

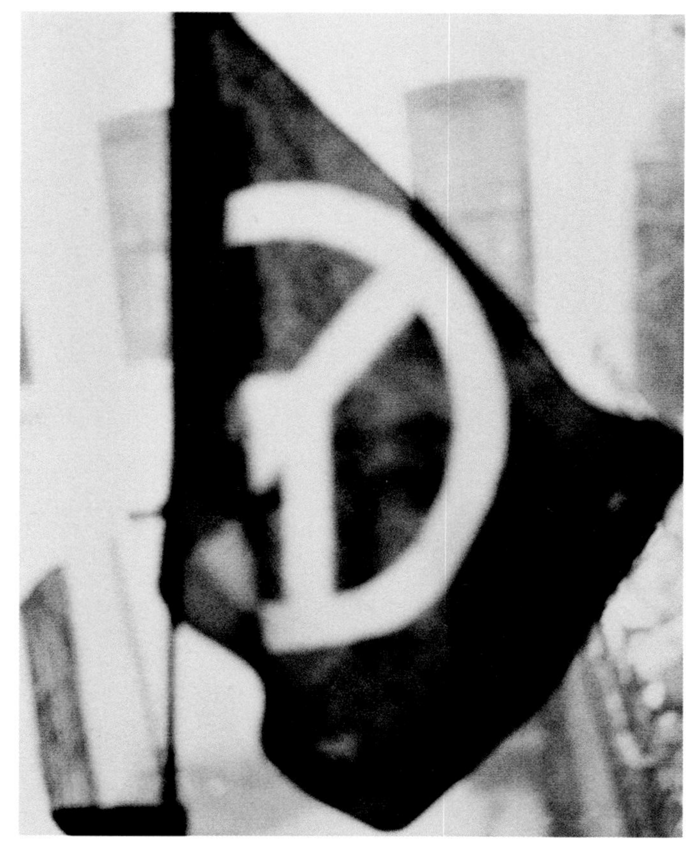

Tulips
2003
Gelatin Silver Print
25.4 x 20.32 cm
Courtesy of Robert Miller Gallery, New York

Peace Flag
2002
Gelatin Silver Print
25.4 x 20.32 cm
Courtesy of Robert Miller Gallery, New York

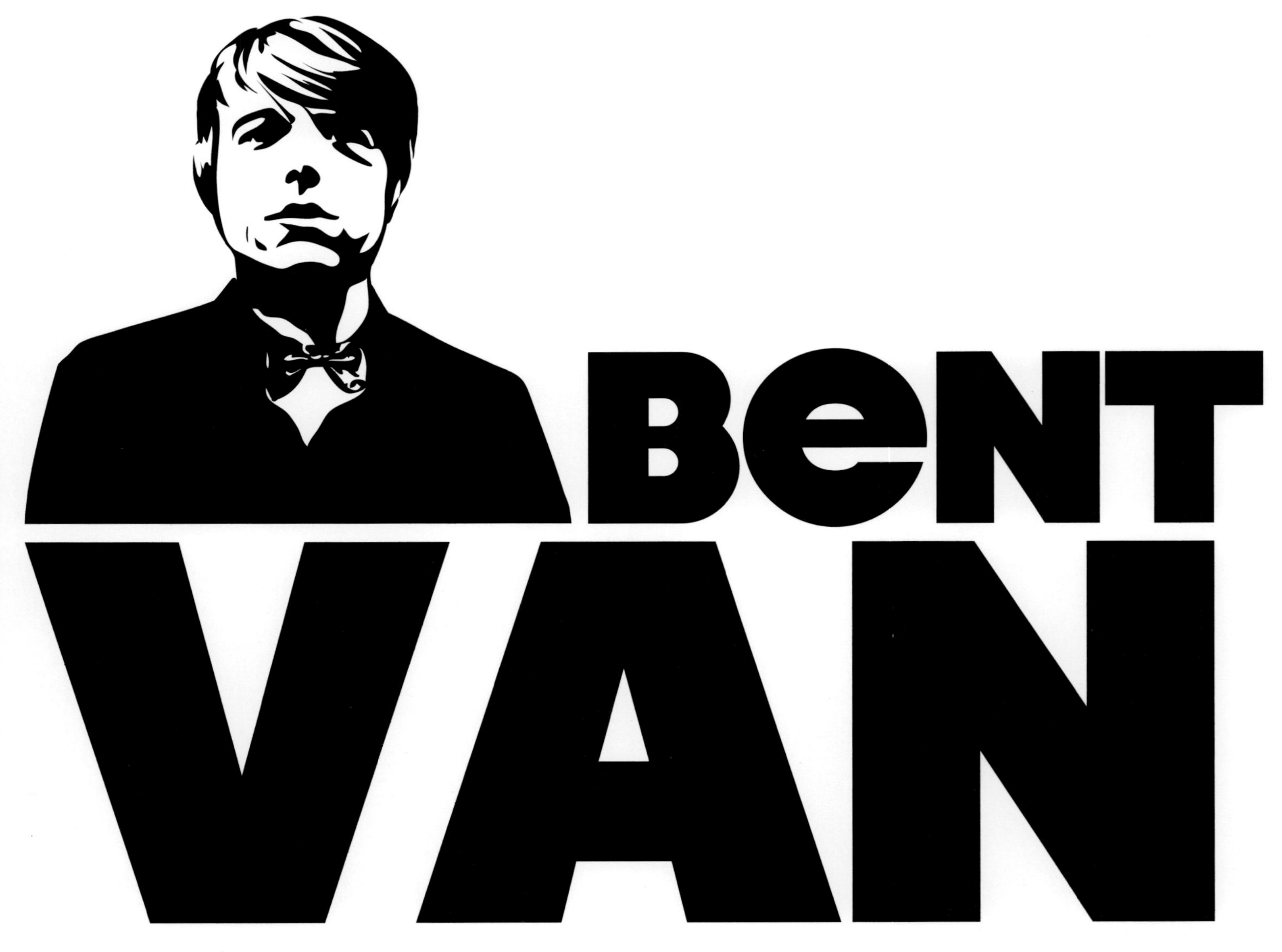
BENT
VAN

LOOY

ROCK'N' ROLL ON PAPER

While in high school in the '90s in Ghent, Belgium, art student Bent Van Looy formed a band with some friends. Within a few years, that band would become the internationally known Das Pop, which, as the name suggests, is devoted to the pursuit of a pure form of pop music. Bent, who divides his time today between Ghent and Paris, has always placed a particular importance on the visual arts, especially graphic design, photography, film, and video. His main focus today is on painting – acrylics, on square canvases that resemble enlarged album covers. These paintings portray scenes from daily life, in vivid colors contrasted with dark backgrounds, and populated with overwhelming figures. The overall effect is often threatening and alienating, within a larger ironic context.
— Bent Van Looy was born in Ghent in 1976, and today lives and works in Ghent and Paris.

BENT VAN LOOY INTERVIEWED BY JÉRÔME SANS

HOW LONG HAS DAS POP EXISTED?

Das Pop met in high school and has managed to stick together. In the '90s we could be seen practicing insane prog-rock in the playground, using only a cello, three bongos, and a five-stringed acoustic guitar. We were called Things To Come at that time. Luckily, someone decided to change it to Das Pop. Our third album will be released this summer.

WHAT IS THE MEANING OF DAS POP? IS IT A REFERENCE TO POP MUSIC OR POP ART?

Exactly! No other word manages to be as brief and as vast at the same time. Very specific, yet as broad as it gets. Covering both Paris Hilton and David Hockney. When we were sitting around the kitchen table once, trying on band names, the word "pop" just had to be in it! Its magic made us dream.

HOW WOULD YOU DEFINE YOUR MUSIC?

As… pop.

BEFORE BEING A MUSICIAN AND SINGER WITH THIS GROUP, YOU WERE ALSO A PAINTER. WHY THIS MEDIUM? WHEN AND HOW DID YOU START AS A VISUAL ARTIST?

Music and painting have always gone hand in hand. As a kid I was either playing the drums, painting, or thinking about painting and playing the drums. Sport was completely out of the question; I am afraid of balls. I got beat up because I wouldn't play. My drawings became a powerful weapon: I used them to pay off bullies. Art-loving bullies, they were.

HOW WOULD YOU DEFINE YOUR ARTISTIC APPROACH?

It all begins with the image; painterly formalities take second priority. My paintings have their origin in a found image. It can be a picture I stumble upon in the TV pages of a newspaper, that moves me to the extent that I just have to paint it. I'll save it and will try to translate its power onto the canvas. The found image is more of a guideline rather than a genuine source. My paintings are what they are because painting comes more natural to me than making a photograph. A painting might even justify the existence of a throwaway image.

ALL YOUR PAINTINGS ARE SQUARE. IS THIS A REFERENCE TO MINIMAL ART OR ALBUM COVERS? WHY THIS OBSESSION WITH A SINGLE FORMAT?

Almost all of my canvases are square. Show me a thirteen year old in the '80s who wasn't spinning records, staring at the amazing covers of Michael Jackson (baby tigers!), Pink Floyd, or Bow Wow Wow (Déjeuner sur l'Herbe, with real naked girls!). Square images are more aggressive than normal rectangular ones.

WHAT IS THE LINK BETWEEN THE MUSIC AND THE ART THAT YOU PRODUCE?

I think I use both songs and painting to seduce the audience, only to knock them off of their feet seconds later. I aim to make wolves. Wolves in sheep's clothes.

WHICH CONTEMPORARY VISUAL ARTISTS DO YOU APPRECIATE?

I really love figurative painters like Gertsch, Fischl, Rauch, or, in Belgium, Michaël Borremans – a musician, too! And I think the graphic work of Parra, Will Sweeney, or So Me is absolutely amazing. Rock 'n' roll on paper.

> I use both songs and painting to seduce the audience, only to knock them off of their feet seconds later.

UNTIL NOW YOU'VE PRODUCED ALL THE ALBUM COVERS FOR DAS POP. WHY FOR YOUR LATEST MAXI-SINGLE DID YOU USE YOUNG FRENCH GRAPHIC DESIGNER LAURENT FÉTIS?

Painting is very satisfying but quite boring and lonely/solitary if you compare it to making music. Music is about working together, feeding off one another's impulses. Laurent, for example, has been a hero to us for some time. It's wonderful to finally collaborate with him on our new album sleeves.

HAVE YOU PRODUCED COVERS FOR GROUPS OTHER THAN YOUR OWN?

A long time ago I painted a sleeve for a Belgian band called Gorki. A funny yet weirdly tense portrait of two children on an inflatable animal. I've heard that singer Luc De Vos still has the painting in his bedroom.

WHAT ARE YOUR FUTURE PROJECTS?

It looks like we'll be on the road with Das Pop for the better part of the year. Twelve months on a bus. That'll be watercolors, at best!

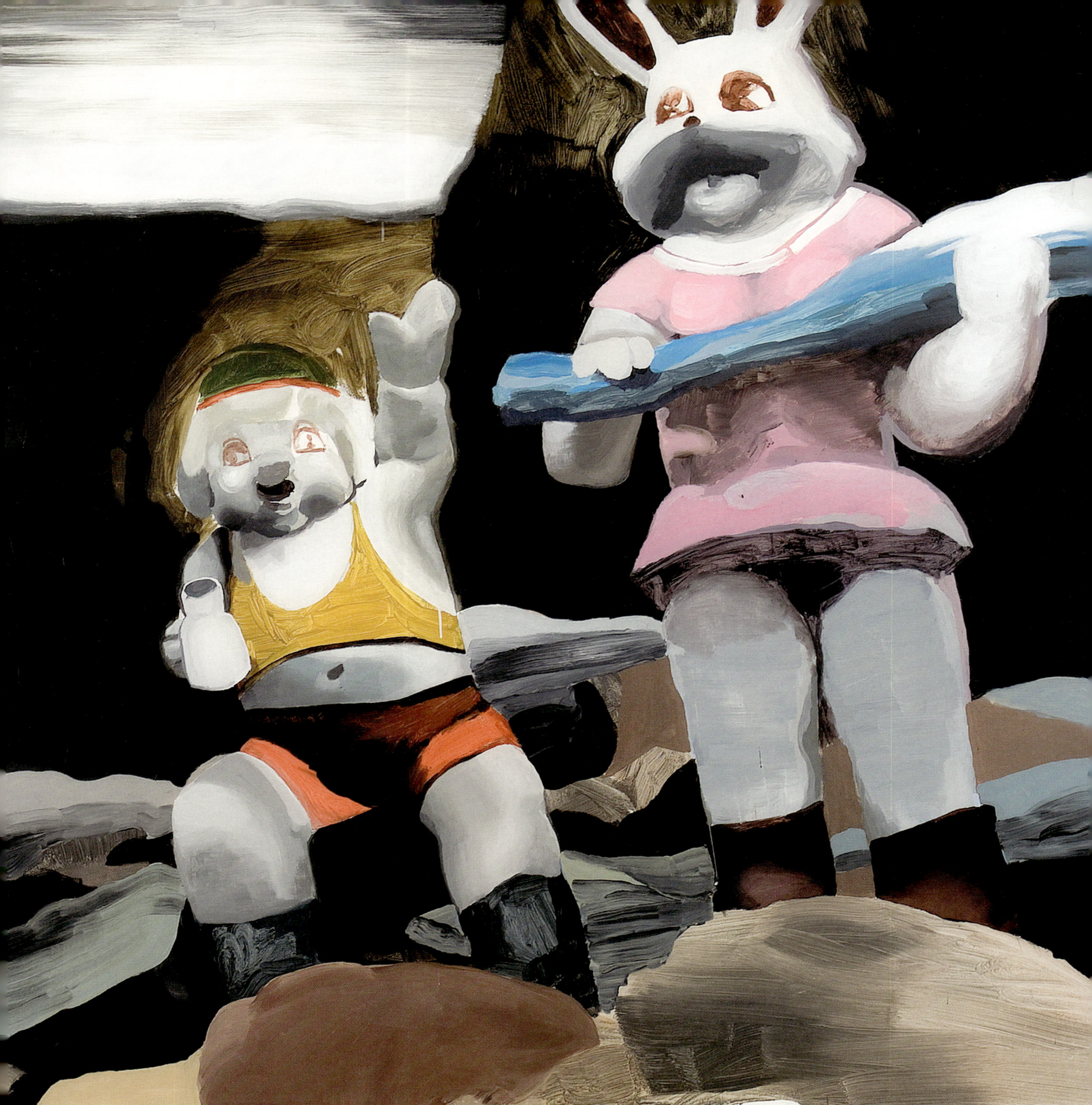

Untitled
2006
Acrylic paint on canvas
160 x 160 cm
Courtesy of the Artist
Photo Credit © Philippe De Gobert

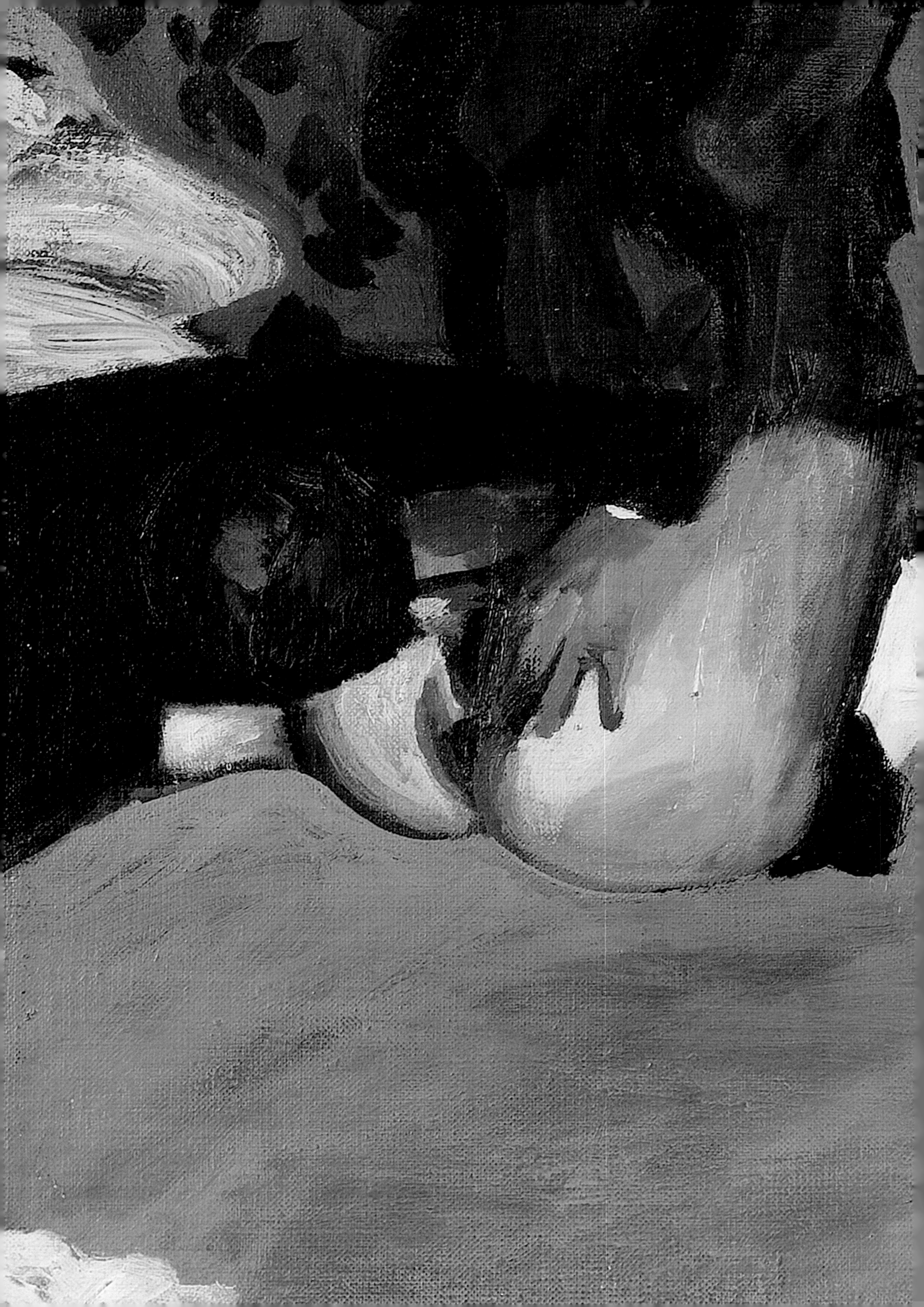

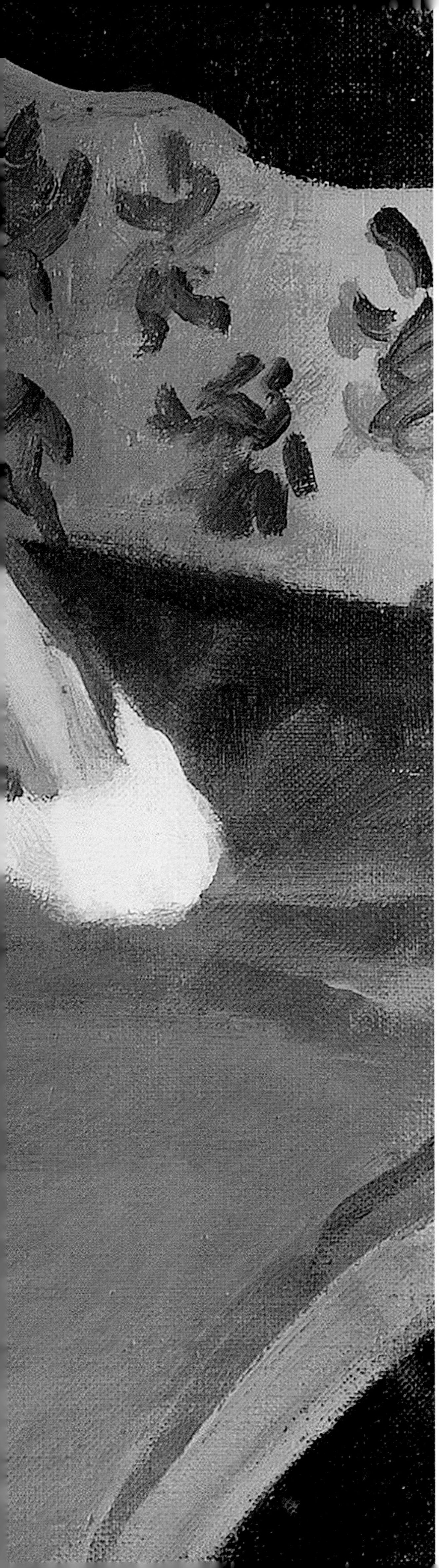

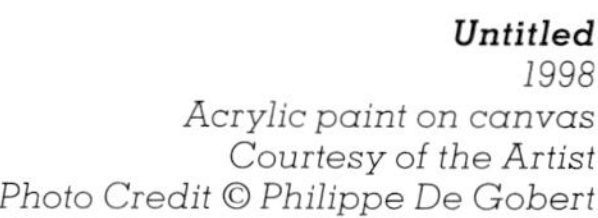

Untitled
1998
Acrylic paint on canvas
Courtesy of the Artist
Photo Credit © Philippe De Gobert

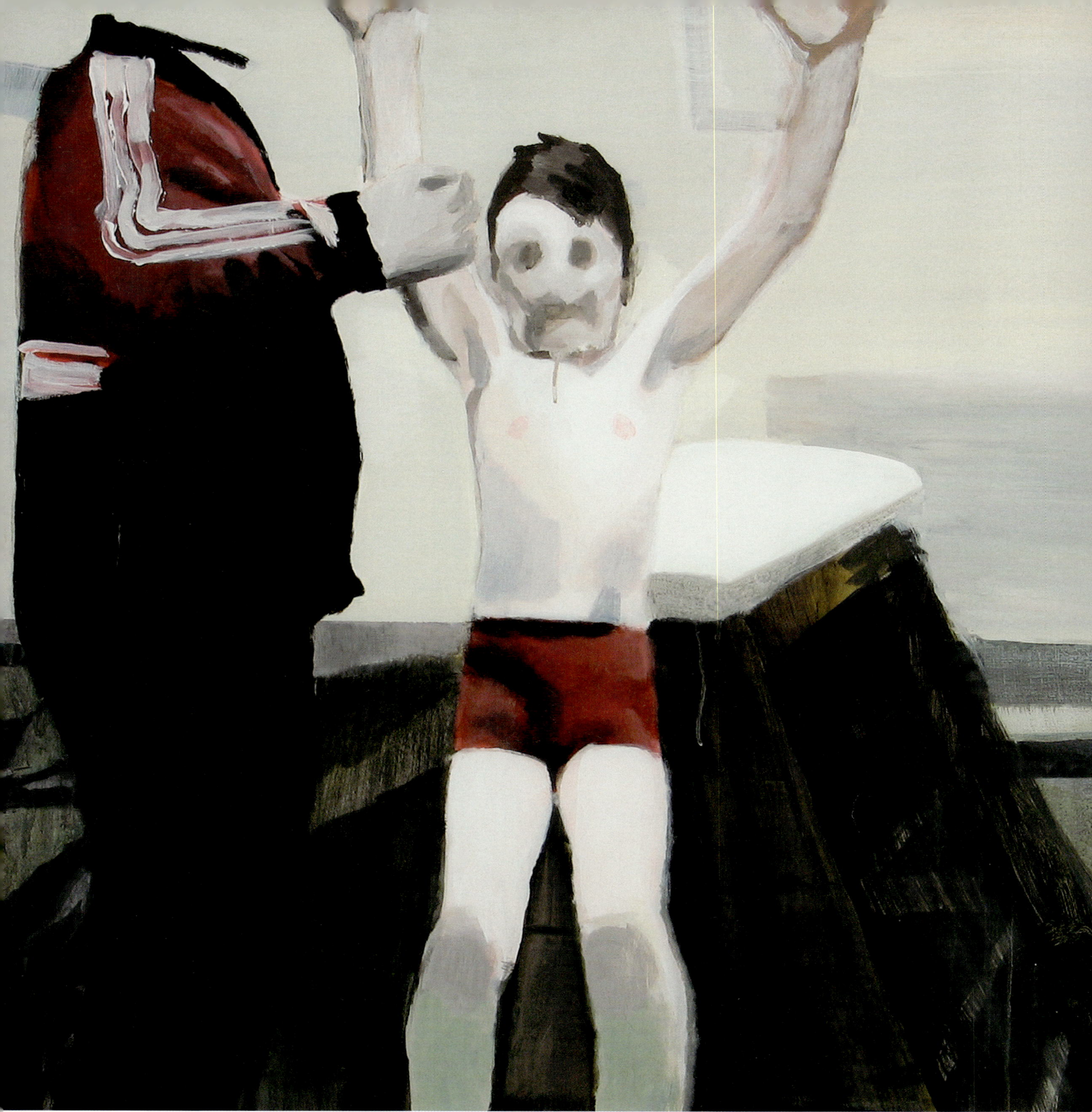

Untitled
2000
Acrylic paint on canvas
100 x 100 cm
Collectie Centrum
Beeldende Kunst, Dordrecht
Courtesy of the Artist
Photo Credit © Fred van Rijen

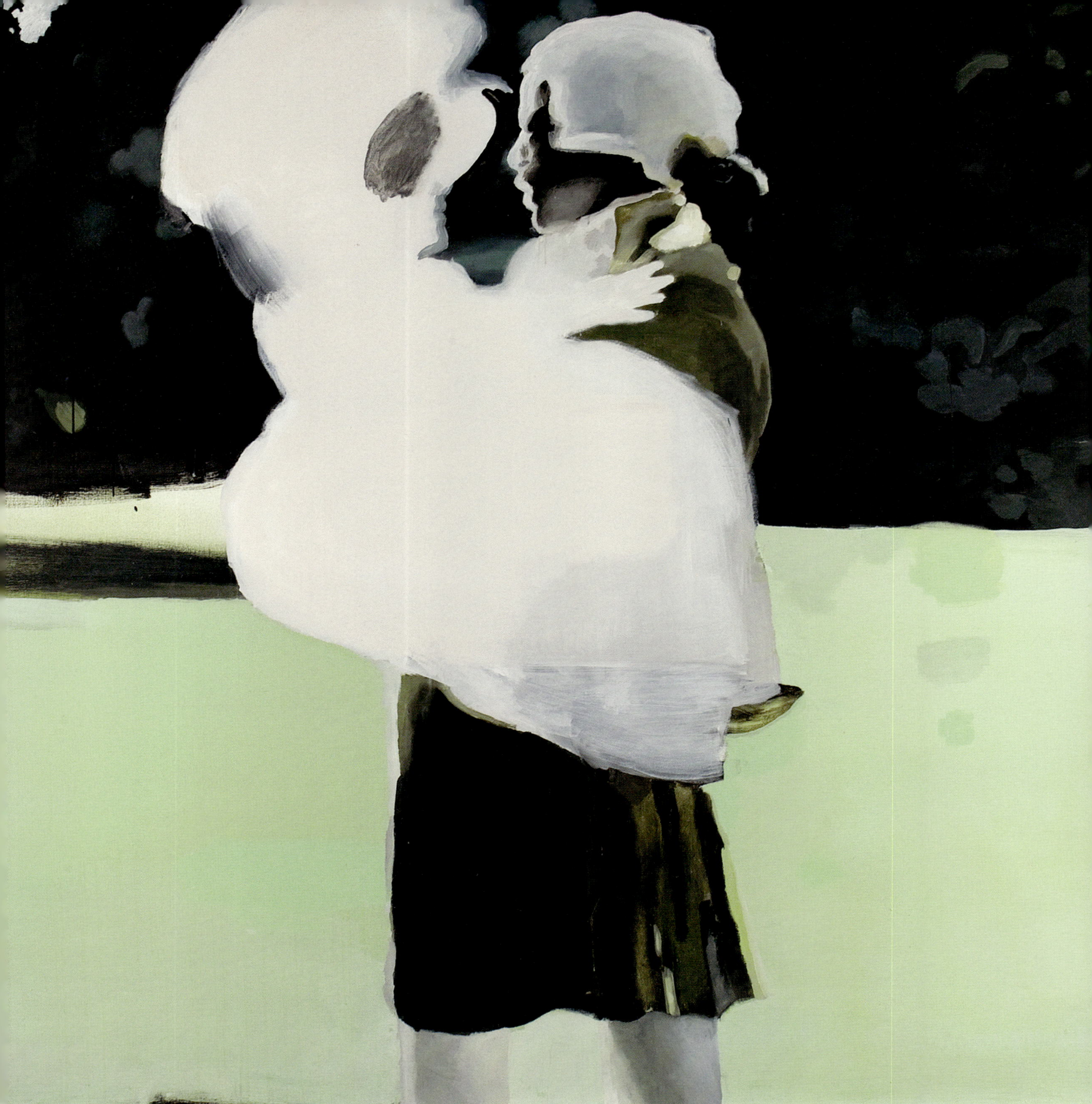

Untitled
2003
Acrylic paint on canvas
200 x 200 cm
Courtesy of the Artist
Photo Credit © Philippe De Gobert

ALAN
Ve

GA

A LIGHT FOR THE LIGHT ITSELF

Since the '70s Alan Vega has been known primarily as half of pioneering minimalist electronic rock duo Suicide. Under this moniker, Vega and musical collaborator Martin Rev were among the earliest rock musicians to incorporate a drum machine into their compositions. The essential elements of their music – repetitive binary rhythms; dark, hypnotic keyboards; and vocals ranging from shouts to spoken word – opened up a world of possibilities for electronic and rock musicians that would follow.

A visual artist before becoming a musician, Alan Vega in 1974 founded Project of Living Artists, a Warhol-esque gallery in Manhattan open 24/24. Dedicated to art, music, and cinema, the gallery went on to become the launching pad for such groups as the New York Dolls, Television, and Blondie. In this buzzing environment Alan Vega simultaneously launched his artistic and musical careers. From an initial focus on painting, his artwork evolved as he explored the influence of light on pictorial perception, and began to integrate light into his canvases. Little by little, light took precedence over painting, ultimately leading to those famous "light sculptures", assemblages of various items, illuminated by lamps and neon lights.

— Alan Vega was born in Brooklyn, New York in 1948, and today lives and works in New York City.

ALAN VEGA INTERVIEWED BY JÉRÔME SANS

IN THE '60S, BEFORE YOU WERE MAKING MUSIC, YOU WERE MAKING PAINTINGS. WHY?

When I was a young man I attended art school, at the City University of New York, Brooklyn (CUNY). So, in school you tend to explore all mediums, but mainly I focused on painting at first. I was into abstract art but I also loved doing portraits of homeless people – called bums in those days. After art school, in order to make some money, I started doing painted portraits of people, on commission. But I never stopped drawing portraits of the unknown men – desperate, homeless people. For some reason I identify with them, being that I am the "king of the bums".

DO YOUR EARLY WORKS STILL EXIST?

I'm not sure. Over the years I have seen a few of the things that I sold. I would imagine that some of the commissioned painted portraits I did are still in some people's homes. This was so long ago, and I have moved to so many different places, and I never really kept very much from move to move. But along the way I gave drawings, paintings, and light sculptures to some of my friends. So those still exist.

WAS ART SCHOOL IMPORTANT FOR YOU?

I was fortunate to have some truly great teachers in art school. They were great artists in their own right and because of that they were truly inspiring. At the same time this became a difficulty. I was influenced by their work to the point where when I left art school it became harder to find my own voice. It took me ten years to find my own style, my own self. While this was happening I was also making electronic music – not thinking that I was ever going to have a career in music – just for fun.

DO YOU REMEMBER THE NAMES OF THESE TEACHERS?

Many I will never forget. Ad Reinhardt was a huge influence on me, with his black-on-black paintings. Kurt Seligman, one of the original surrealists. And some other great artists, like Burgoyne Diller, a pretty damn good painter, and Jimmy Ernst, the son of Max Ernst. As you can see, I was pretty lucky to have had some amazing teachers. At the time, it was overwhelming, so much information. At times I felt really over my head, wondering what I was doing in the midst of such greatness.

AND HOW DID THE IDEA OF THE LIGHT SCULPTURES COME ABOUT?

For several weeks, I was working on a very large canvas that ultimately worked its way into becoming a one-color painting – purple. One day I noticed that as I walked across the room, back and forth in front of the painting, the color would change from brownish purple to bluish purple, etc. The problem was, since there was only one light, coming from the ceiling, I had little control over how the color on the painting was perceived. I didn't like that. I wanted it to be that one color. I wanted to have more control of the color. All of a sudden a light bulb went off in my head; I had an epiphany! Why not take the light down from the ceiling and plaster it right onto the painting to be able to control the color? That's when I became a light artist. That began a new creative life for me. First I put one light on the painting, then several lights. And then one day I took the painting out of the equation and it became just light sculptures. Light for the light itself.

DID YOU EXHIBIT THESE PIECES AT THAT TIME?

No, I didn't show the light sculptures right away. It was a few years later, when I was in a group show at the Project of Living Artists. One day a famous art critic from Canada came to the show. He must have really liked what he saw because he then went to see Ivan Karp at OK Harris, and mentioned my work to him. Ivan discovered Andy Warhol, Roy Lichtenstein, James Rosenquist, and he had a gallery in Soho. Mary Boone was also in Soho then, so there was an art gallery scene forming. Anyway, the next day, Ivan came to the show. He told me he wanted to show my work at his gallery, and asked if I could be ready in three weeks. In those days, when an art dealer discovered you it could take years to actually get a show because they had scheduled shows well in advance for their current artists. Here, I was being invited to have a show in three weeks. It was mind-boggling and I was blown away. I said I'd be ready in three minutes. I had four or five one-man shows with Ivan at the OK Harris Gallery starting in the earlier '70s.

TELL ME ABOUT THE PROJECT OF LIVING ARTISTS, A GALLERY OPEN 24/24 HOURS, WASN'T IT?

About six of us got together and applied for a grant from the New York State government – an art grant. We got the grant and used it to open up this space, and called it the Project of Living Artists. It was not a traditional gallery, just an open space for anybody to do art, music, or any creative thing – whatever they felt like. We kept it open 24 hours a day and anyone who wanted to use the space was welcome to it. We took turns watching the place and keeping it clean. Every month we got a little salary, and I basically lived there for a while. I was homeless in those days.

WAS THE PLACE YOU CREATED AT THAT TIME LIKE A FACTORY, A CRAZY PLACE WHERE EVERYTHING COULD HAPPEN?

Yes, it was a kind of Warhol Factory in a way. There were some crazy people around. Sometimes it was rather difficult.

> First I put one light on the painting, then several lights. And then one day I took the painting out of the equation and it became just light sculptures.

Starting in the late '60s I was always making electronic music, with all kinds of stuff, whatever I could get my hands on. And then the Project of Living Artists, it gave me a place to create in. And that's where I met Marty Rev, and together we formed Suicide. One day Marty just showed up. He had been immersed in the jazz world with his band Reverend B, and I think he was feeling that in some ways jazz was coming to an end for him. And I was feeling I needed to expand my art into another dimension, something with a performance element. So we both kind of needed each other, not always for the same reasons. And that was it. Suicide started and the rest became history, I guess.

WHY DID YOU CALL YOUR BAND SUICIDE? WAS IT TO KILL THE OTHER PART OF YOU?

We were brainstorming on band names and came up with Ghost Rider, a comic strip character, which was made into a film recently, with Nicolas Cage. In those days I was into comic books and he was my favorite character. A title of one particular Ghost Rider story was 'Saint Suicide'. We thought about it and said, "Let's call it Suicide because it means a lot of things". It is not only about death; it is also about life, changing your life. It's suicide when your life as you know it is about to end and become something else. You know what I mean? Also, these were very bad years with the Vietnam War, and it was a very bad time for the City of New York. Our beloved city was crumbling around us, but I loved it. I used to say that it was the "best of times and the worst of times", like Dickens. And yet we all had a great time. We had this wonderful space where we made art and music. I was showing with Ivan Karp. I did great shows but I didn't sell much. So, I felt very rich creatively but I was dirt-poor.

YOU WERE ONE OF THE FIRST TO BRING ELECTRONIC MUSIC INTO A ROCK CONTEXT. HOW DID YOU COME UP WITH THIS FORM OF MUSIC?

Yes, in some ways. We were the first "rock" band to use a drum machine; I know that. Marty and I both knew that the '60s style of rock 'n' roll was already dead. We didn't use the drum machine yet, but we knew it was time for a new direction. Actually, for the first show, we had a guitar player, Paul, a painter and sculptor as well. He was not a traditional guitar player, only one who made noise with the guitar. By the second show, Paul quit, so there was only two of us and no guitar, no drums. We thought about getting a drummer, and then we found a drum machine. And that was it. We had found our sound.

WHAT IS YOUR POINT OF VIEW ABOUT TODAY'S MUSIC? DO YOU LIKE IT?

There is always going to be one crazy thing that I will like, and the rest for me is nothing. Most of the sound of the music I hear is not new to me. But then I'll hear something

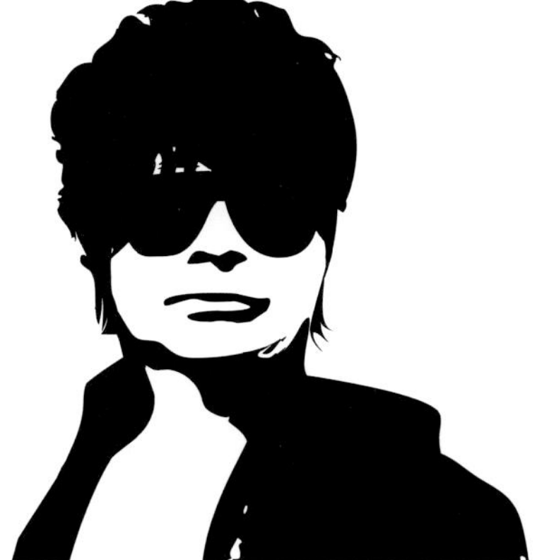

that really catches my attention. I felt it when rap first got out. But I wouldn't say that I listen to a lot of other people's music these days, mostly because I'm busy making my own music and working with a few different musicians. To me, doing music is my life, more than listening to other music. In general for me it doesn't sound as powerful. I like powerful music, you know what I mean?

OF COURSE; WE LOVE SUCH MUSIC. DO YOU STILL COLLABORATE WITH THE SAME PARTNER FOR YOUR NEW MUSIC, YOUR NEW ALBUM?

On my last album, Station, I collaborated with my wife, Liz Lamere, and my longtime engineer, Perkin Barnes. They are both great musicians, so I've chosen to work with them for many years – the last six solo albums. My nine-year-old son, Dante, who did a vocal track on Station has been playing keyboards in the studio, on the new stuff, so it is truly a family affair. Lately I've also begun working with a couple of the guys from A.R.E. Weapons – Brain McPeck and Matt McAuley. They are great guys, with true energy and passion for the music. We've done a few songs and are still going, so we'll see where it takes us. Over the years, I've done many collaborations, with Pan Sonic, Alex Chilton and Ben Vaughan and Ric Ocasek. I've also produced other bands, and contributed vocals to many songs by other artists. I often get stuff sent to me and sometimes I hear something. If I feel a connection I'm usually pretty open to working with other artists.

BUT HAVE YOU KEPT DOING ART DURING ALL THESE YEARS?

Yes. I love making art; it keeps me alive. I always have works-in-process lying around in various states. When I'm approached to do a show, I focus in and bring it to completion. I like to keep a lot of things going at once – the music, the visual art, and writing. I'm starting to get back into photography. I have ideas about what I'd like to do with photographing light, but haven't yet figured out the technology. Usually I just go by trial and error to figure out how to realize my idea. Sometimes, with so much going on between the music, the art, living life, and raising my son, it's difficult to keep it all going. But I love it all.

WOULD YOU SAY THAT THE ONE CONSTANT IN YOUR VISUAL WORK IS YOUR PORTRAITS, WHICH, AS YOU EXPLAINED TO ME A FEW DAYS AGO, YOU WORK ON IN THE EVENING?

Oh yes, the thing that I do most consistently is the portraits. They are therapeutic. I draw them almost nightly. There must be hundreds of them lying around, and more in boxes in storage. I also write daily, just to keep my thoughts warm. I have piles of notebooks, and these random thoughts and doodles end up being where I go to when it comes time to write lyrics. And when I get stuck writing lyrics, when I can't write, I start drawing faces. I love faces. And that gets me into the writing. That just relaxes me, cools me out. Sometimes I never get back to the writing because I get so into the drawing of portraits. That's where it really starts.

THESE DRAWINGS ARE A BIT LIKE A DIARY?

Absolutely. I was just searching for a word. Yes, you are right; it's like a personal journal or diary. When I look at them I say, OK, that's where I see how I was that night. Because they are each different, depending on my state of mind, even though there is a consistent style that has carried on throughout the years that I have been doing this. Yet when I first started, they look a bit stiffer, and then looser and looser as I get older. When I was in art school I studied anatomy and we had to do that. We did figure drawing, studying the human figure. I spent a lot of time on that stuff. So, in some sense I had an academic training where the figures were concerned. Early on, in my student days, I was more a classically trained artist.

COULD WE SAY THAT YOUR DRAWINGS ARE ELECTRICAL? FOR ME THEY ARE NOT CLASSICAL.

It's so hard to get out of that classical training, to find your own style. That takes years. I used to be so classical, like a mathematician who makes everything by equation. It took so long to get free. And the sculptures help me with that because it's something I do abstractly. When you look at the wires on my sculptures, they are like little drawings, like pencil lines, ink lines. They might be abstract-looking, but they freed up my drawing. I need these wires in crazy ways. When I'm making a piece, I don't think about how the wire will affect things. So much of the wire is used in making things stable. So much wire is used to make lines stick to the sculptures. I get into crazy shapes of wires. Afterwards, when I am looking at the finished piece, I realize that the wires create something. And the shadows cast by the piece are a whole other trip. When I did my shows at OK Harris, people would come in and they'd be talking to me about how educated, complicated, the work was. They're looking at the wire things, saying, "Wow, look at this". And then at a certain point I looked at my drawings and said, "If I trace those lines, my drawings could be the wires". That's how the sculptures actually help me free up my drawings. When I was young the drawings were in another place. Now, yes, they have become more electrical – impulses creating the movement of the lines. At some point, when you reach a certain age, you say, "Fuck, I don't care". Although I still never thought of showing these drawings. I did a poetry book with Henry Rollins, Cripple Nation, and that was the first time I published some of the drawings. I hadn't thought of showing them when I was with Barbara Gladstone, a dealer who showed my work in the '80s, after Ivan. And I haven't shown them to Jeffrey Deitch, who represents me now. Just having a look at them is great. I haven't shown them to anybody else. But my wife sees them, my kid sees them; that's about it. I don't have that pressure of somebody who has to show in a museum or a gallery.

HAVE YOU EVER THOUGHT OF DOING SPECIFIC SETTINGS FOR YOUR SHOWS, TO MIX ART AND MUSIC?

I feel that my sculptures have never gotten a full treatment in a show. I always felt that each piece should have its own space and light. Maybe in a room with partitions, to control the light created by each piece. With my music, each song is separate. No matter how connected to the album as a whole, it also gets individual treatment. I'd like to get that more with my sculptures. The whole thing is about light. When you are alone with the piece, you can see all the shadows that come over its surroundings. When I work on a piece, I work alone in the dark room, creating the shadows and their directions. In most gallery or museum situations, there are other pieces around. The light of other pieces affects each piece. Because the room they hang in is different, the environmental qualities of a lot of the pieces are lost. They lose the quality of

the light, the spirituality I feel for the light. My dream is to give each piece a separate room, because environmentally it will create a certain aura. Up until now, the pieces haven't had that – unless somebody bought it for their own – to free themselves.

YES I AGREE. THAT'S WHY YOU WILL HAVE YOUR OWN ROOM IN OUR SHOW.

That would be a dream come true.

HAVE YOU EVER THOUGHT OF CONNECTING YOUR MUSICAL PERFORMANCES ONSTAGE WITH YOUR VISUAL ART?

When performing music, I have always wanted to have visual pieces there. But when you are traveling, it's a lot to carry these things around. The works are fragile, heavy. If I had a big show, I would play with really big pieces. I would love to do that, of course, but to be honest, it becomes a pain in the ass when it just requires too much to execute. It numbs the creativity for me. That's why when I'm doing concerts I never go to the sound check anymore. I want to hit the stage and just go for it. It's 30-plus years that I've been doing this, so loading it in is a pain in the butt. Still, over the years I've done some combinations of the sculptures with the music and performance. The last one was in Haarlem, Holland a few years ago, maybe 2004. I made a light sculpture, hung from the rafters in a church. It looked like the crucifixion of Christ. Hundreds of small strobe lights, set at different speeds, hanging from the ceiling and pooled on the floor. And dueling smoke machines blowing smoke through the light. The performance was at sundown, and the ceiling was all skylights. So, after I put the lights together in the morning, the crew spent the afternoon covering the ceiling with tarps and tape, and draping black curtains around the piece so it was tent-like for the performance. There were several places where the covering fell a bit to let light sneak through and beam across the space – which was cool – and dissipated as the sky darkened. Liz, Dante, and I came out and did some crazy performance of some music we were working on at the time. We played basically through a boom box, with minimal vocal amplification. People came in and surrounded us in a circle; the sculpture became a campfire on Pluto.

DO YOU HAVE A NEW ALBUM OR MUSIC COLLABORATION ON THE WAY?

I'm always working on my new album. My last album, Station, has been out since last spring, and as I was finishing it, musically I broke into another, new place. So I didn't wind down after Station. I'm probably pretty close to having another solo album done, but who knows how long it takes. I hope not five years like the last one. If I have five years left anymore, for Christ sakes.

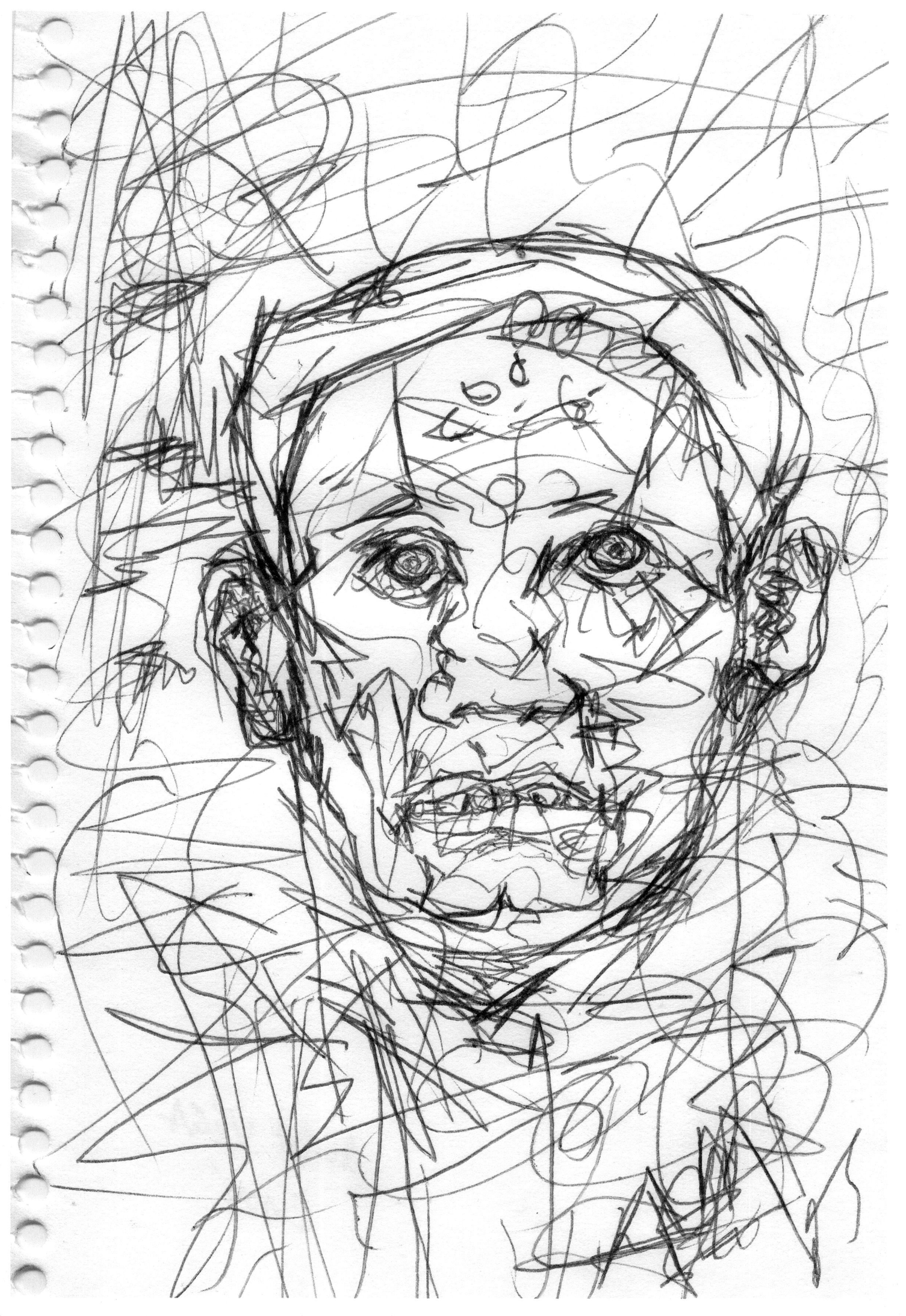

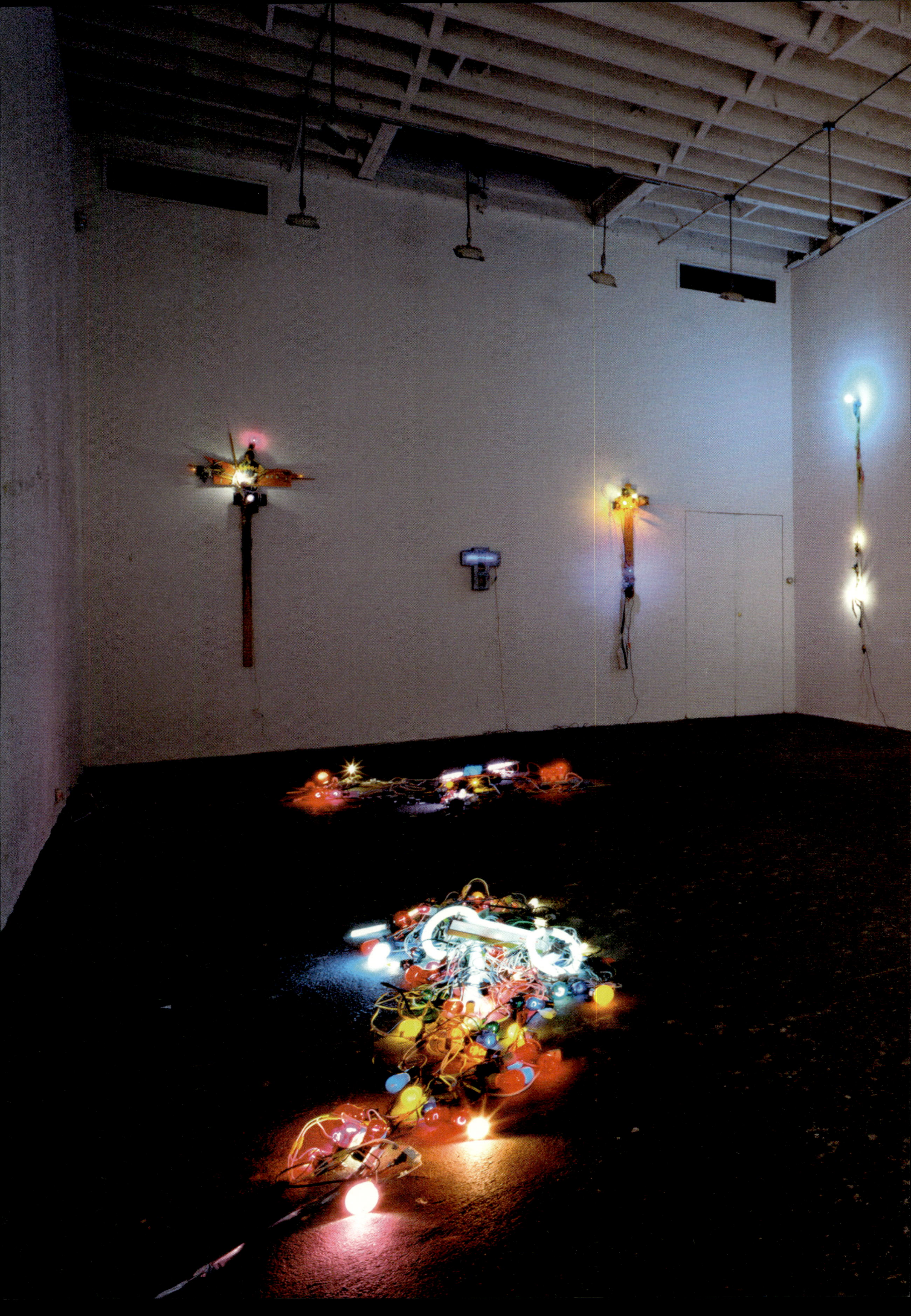

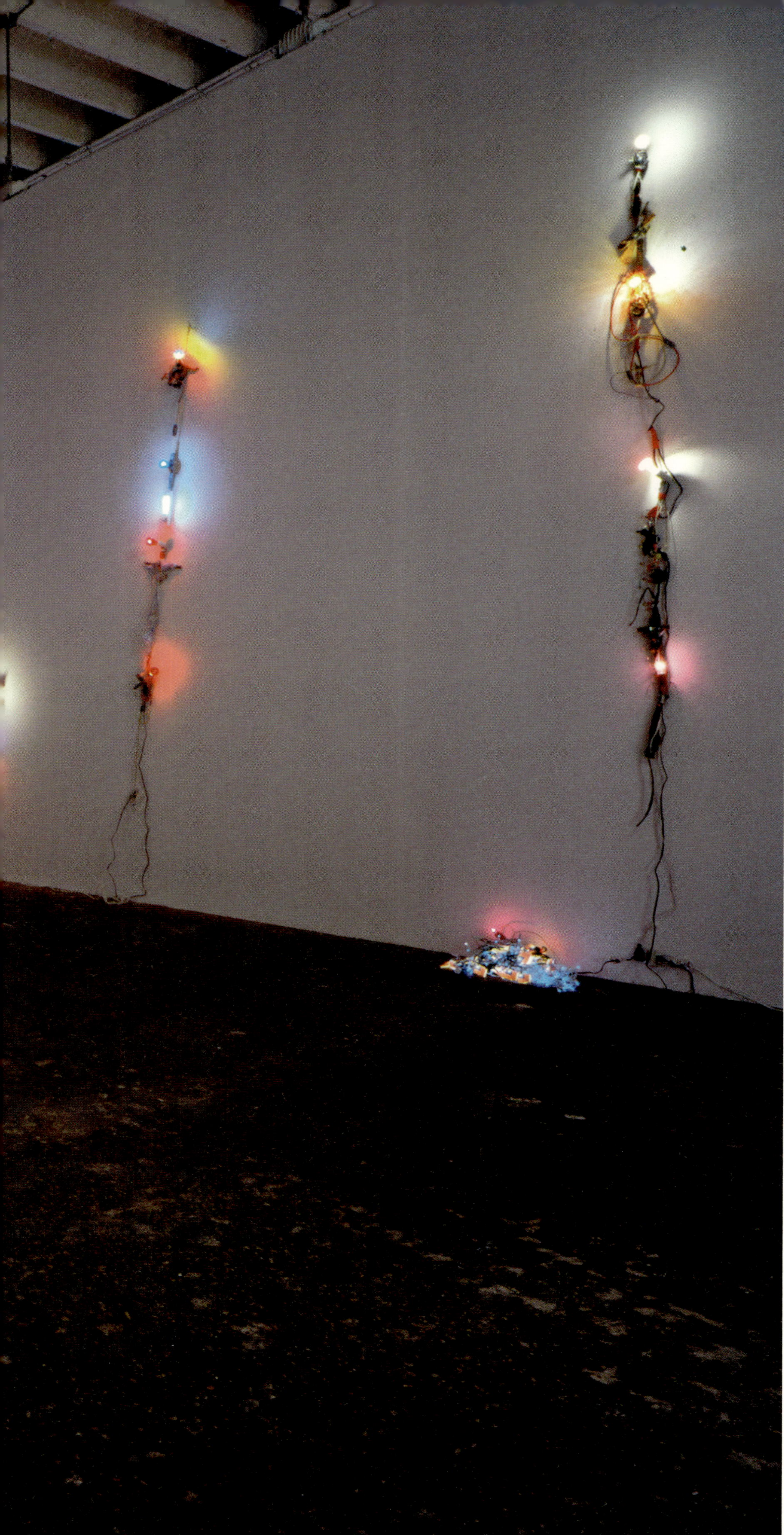

Page 191
Mickey D. Shakes
2007
Drawing
Photo Credit © Alan Vega

Installation view
Alan Suicide
Collision Drive
January 12 – February 23, 2002
Deitch Projects, 76 Grand Street,
New York, NY
Courtesy of Deitch Projects, New York
Photo Credit © Tom Powel Imaging,

Page 194/195
Installation view
Alan Suicide
Collision Drive
January 12 – February 23, 2002
Deitch Projects, 76 Grand Street,
New York, NY
Courtesy of Deitch Projects, New York
Photo Credit © Tom Powel Imaging

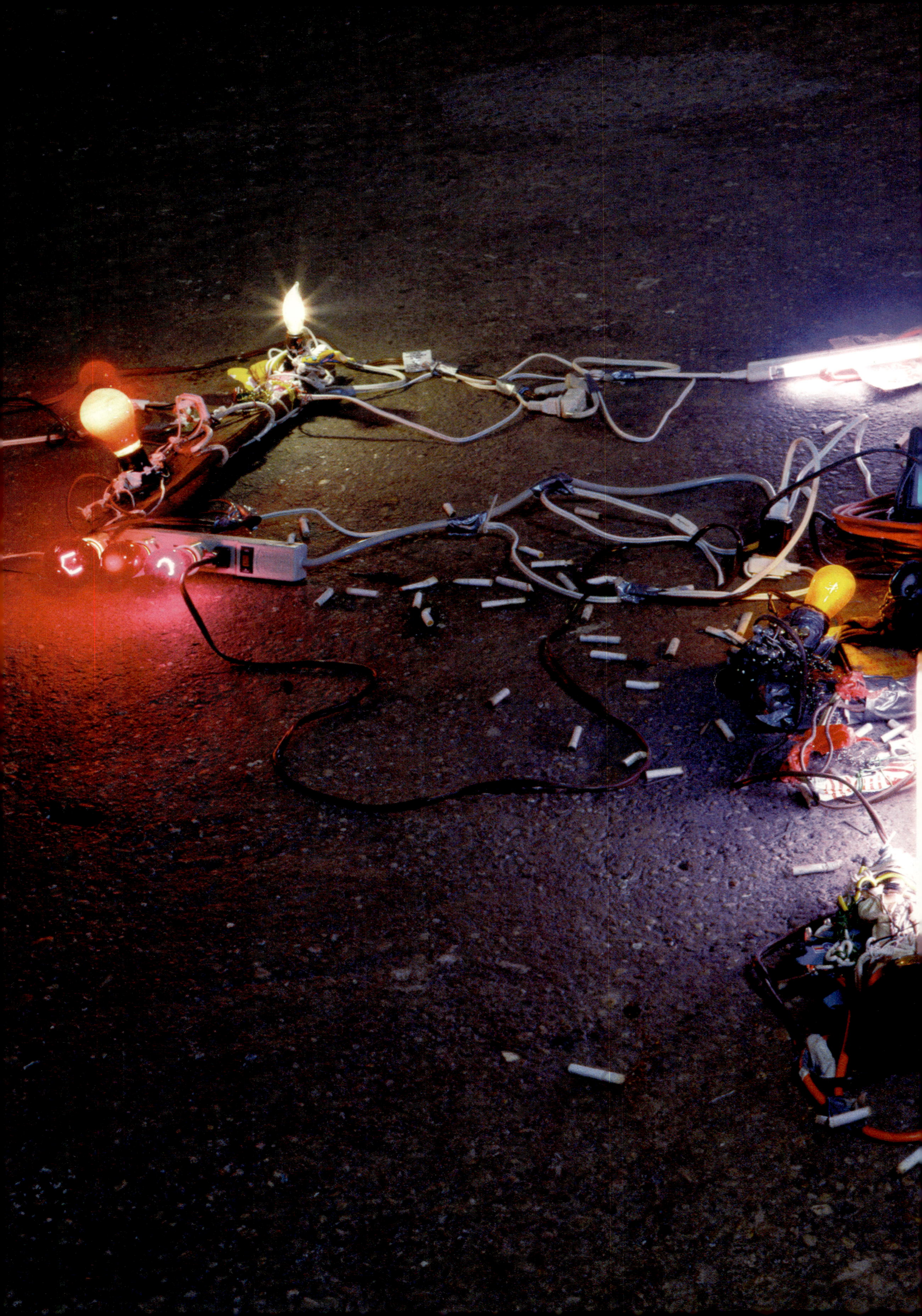

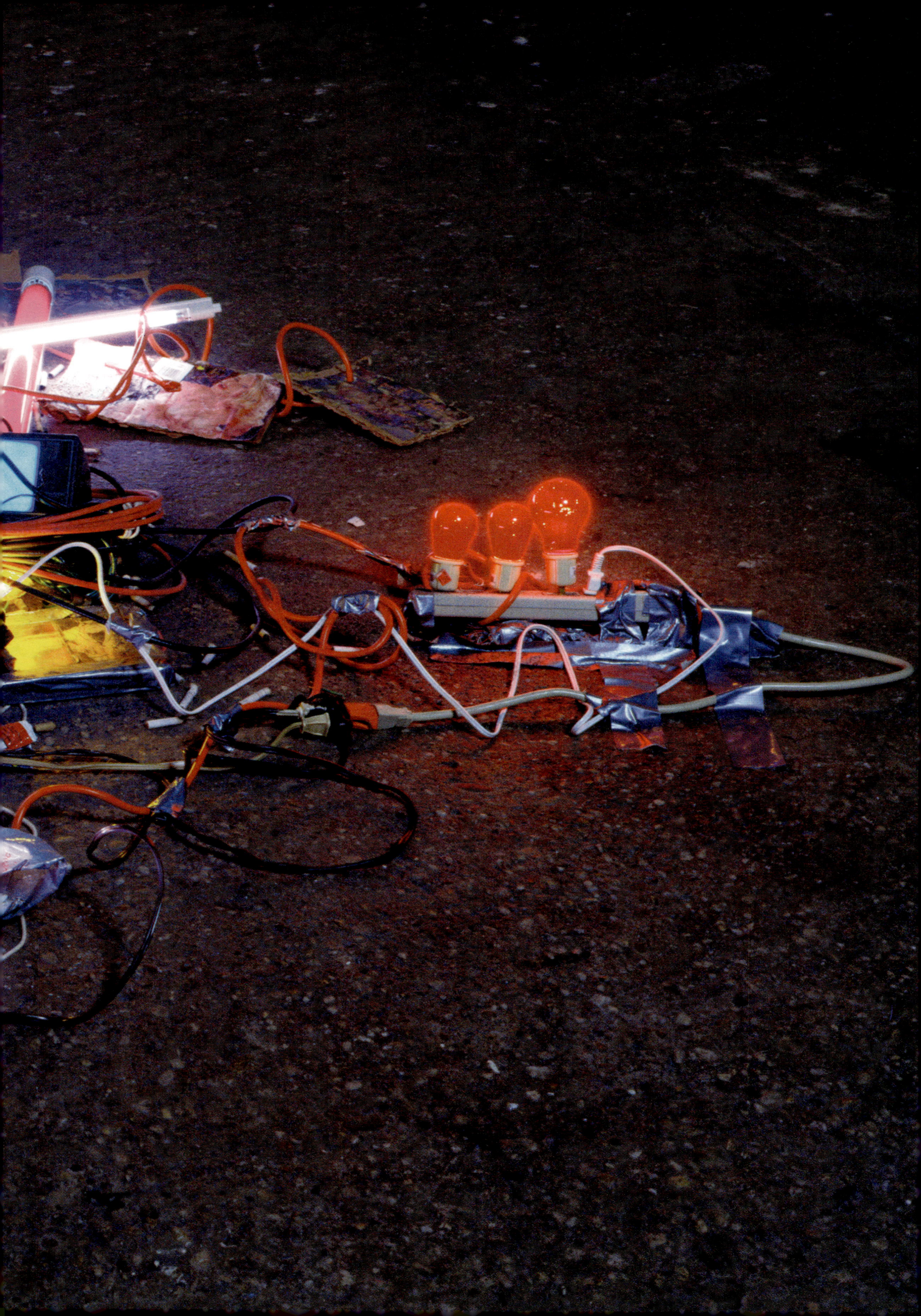

NICK
ZIN

NeR

TIME SHOTS: TO ESCAPE AND REMEMBER

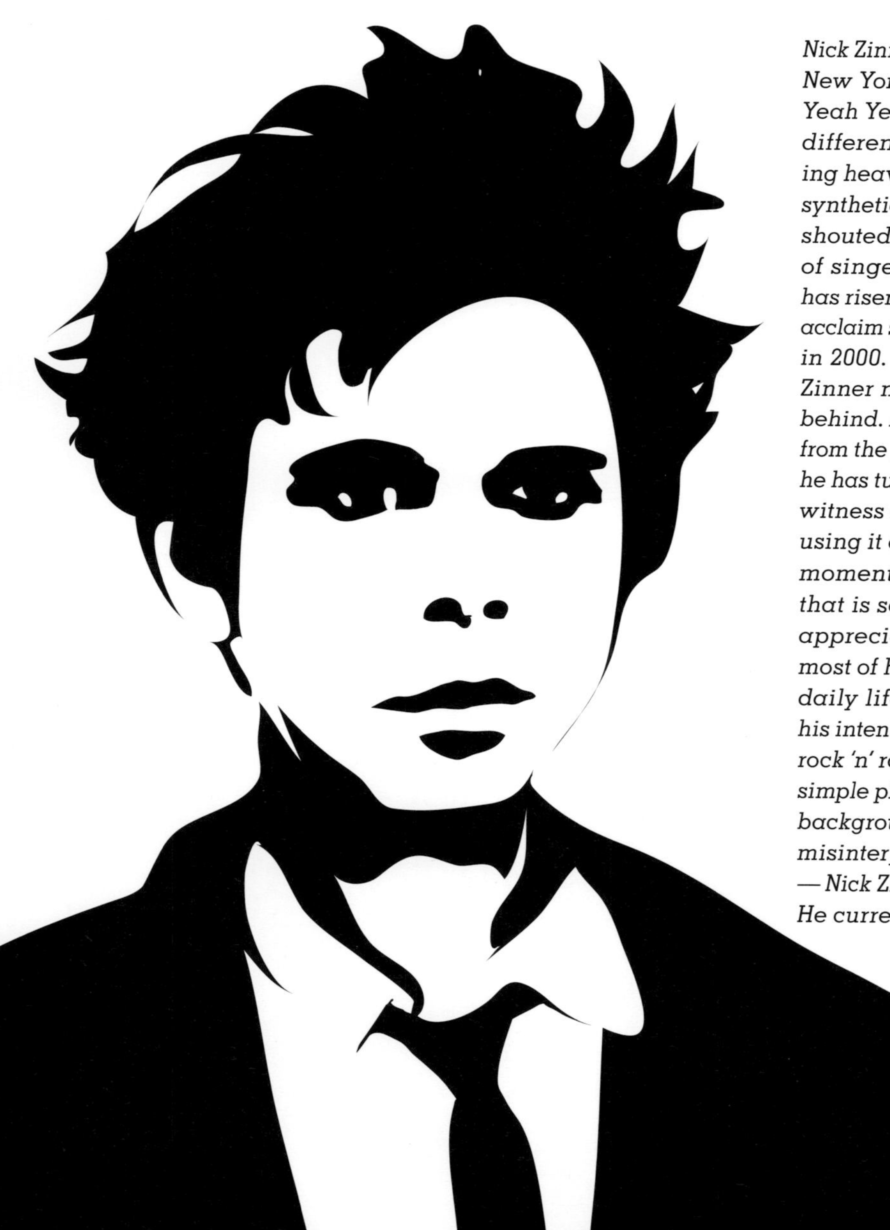

Nick Zinner is guitarist with young New York-based group the Yeah Yeah Yeahs. At the crossroads of different retro styles – combining heavy rock/punk guitars and synthetic sounds – and led by the shouted vocals and blues tones of singer Karen O, their music has risen quickly to international acclaim since the band's formation in 2000. Besides his guitar, Nick Zinner never leaves his camera behind. A photography graduate from the prestigious Bard College, he has turned this tool into his key witness of a life in the fast lane, using it as a third eye to capture moments in a daily adventure that is sometimes impossible to appreciate in real time. While most of his snapshots come from daily life in a successful band, his intent is to avoid the clichés of rock 'n' roll imagery and produce simple photos that are free from a background context and can't be misinterpreted over time.
— Nick Zinner was born in Boston. He currently lives in New York.

NICK ZINNER INTERVIEWED BY JÉRÔME SANS

WHEN DID YOU START PHOTOGRAPHY?
I started taking photos when I was in high school. My girlfriend at the time was into photography, and I remember taking her camera and taking photos of her – in the forest or something – looking goth, like what you do in high school. After that I got a camera and would just go about taking photos of situations I found myself in, or places I would go, never with an intent of making art, but more using the camera to seize and remember what I was seeing and where I was. It seemed once a photograph was taken of a moment or place, I could then move on from it.

WHY THIS MEDIUM AND NOT ANOTHER ONE?

I've always had urges to create and document; I've just never felt I've had any of the strengths that one needs to be a writer or a painter. There's an interesting theory I also have as to why this medium works for me, and that has to do with the way I see: my eyes don't quite work together, so as a result I have very little depth perception. Meaning there is very little difference in how I see, and how a two-dimensional photograph reproduces distance and depth. When you look at a photograph of a landscape with a mountain range behind it, you are looking at something flat but you perceive the distance between the vantage point of the photographer and the mountain. Whereas I think most people have this definitive sense of being able to tell actually in real life how far the mountain may be, I really can't tell the difference. Who knows? I could be wrong. The other major aspect of photography for me is the ability to document and indefinitely hold onto – and to a certain degree, manipulate – a passing moment. The more I travel, and the more concerts my band plays, the easier it is for details to be lost, faces to be forgotten, as weeks blend into hours in the mind. Photos somehow put everything into both a historic and sentimental order for me.

HOW WOULD YOU DEFINE YOUR PHOTOGRAPHS?

At first I was much more interested in the sense of capturing a time and a place, and perhaps a person in that time and place only. But in the last few years I have become more fascinated with the ambiguity of an image. If you remove the facts and the dates and are just left with the image, that image to me is strongest, when each viewer can attach their own meaning to it. I'm trying to apply this way of shooting to everything, from composed portraits to drunken snapshots. Having said that, a lot of my work is documentary, of being in a rock band and being able to travel to a new place every day. But at the same time, the work is also about escaping that and not getting lost in the clichés that come with rock 'n' roll.

YOU STUDIED PHOTOGRAPHY AT BARD COLLEGE AND ALSO IN PARIS. WERE YOU ALREADY MAKING MUSIC AT THAT TIME?

I've been playing music since I was a kid, studying violin, living actually outside Brussels for a few years, so that's one thing that's always been constant. I learned violin through the Suzuki method, which trains your ear more than it teaches you how to read music. When I went to college I wasn't even planning on studying photography. I wanted to study music but I didn't know how to read music, so that option basically got thrown out the window. I had a band in college; we played parties, and some shows outside of school. But that basically disintegrated when I moved to New York City.

YOUR BOOK 'I HOPE YOU ARE ALL HAPPY NOW' (2005) IS A RECOLLECTION OF YOUR LIFE ON TOUR – EVERY CROWD YOU'VE PLAYED FOR, EVERY HOTEL ROOM YOU STAYED IN. IS PHOTOGRAPHY A WAY FOR YOU TO SHARE WITH YOUR AUDIENCE THE BACKSTAGE LIFE OF THE BAND?

Although about 90% of the images that I made into that book are from being on tour or with the band, I tried very hard to not make it a "behind the scenes of the Yeah Yeah Yeahs" book. The subject matter and the context is obviously taken from rock 'n' roll or whatever, but I didn't want any of the exploitation or typical characteristics of so-called rock photography to be present. Basically I was trying to make a punk-rock art book about music, or about some things I saw that were interesting to me. But I certainly was not trying to show the outside world "what it's really like". Most of my favorite shots from that time haven't been published because they are too personal for me or for the people I was with, and it's never been my intention to exploit my friends. I love taking photos of the crowd, though. I think it's so interesting to document a group of people together only for a certain time, and a certain place.

> ## Photos somehow put everything into both a historic and sentimental order for me.

MOST OF YOUR PICTURES ARE SNAPSHOTS; ARE YOU ALSO TAKING OTHER TYPES OF PHOTOGRAPHS?

No, not really. I've tried some fashion-esque photography recently, which is fun, but for the most part I don't like setting anything up.

ARE YOUR PHOTOGRAPHS LIKE A PERSONAL DIARY – AN EXPRESSION, A TESTIMONIAL OF YOUR LIFE?

They are absolutely that. But what I shoot and what I choose to show is still far and few between.

JIM JARMUSCH WROTE THE INTRODUCTION TO 'I HOPE YOU ARE ALL HAPPY NOW'. WHAT IS YOUR RELATIONSHIP WITH HIM?

He is one of my favorite directors in both the content and pacing of his films, and his choices of D.P.'s. He also represents a period and style of New York City that I feel is really diminishing, and I thought that he would really understand what I was trying to portray with this particular book.

WHAT ARE YOUR OTHER BOOKS ABOUT – 'NO SEATS ON THE PARTY CAR' (2001) AND 'SLEPT IN BEDS' (2003)?

Those were books that came about as collaborations between Zach Lipez and Stacy Wakefield. Zach is a writer and Stacy is a designer, and like most good – and bad – ideas, these books were birthed in late-night bars out of creative frustration.

HOW DID THE YEAH YEAH YEAHS START?

We started because we were bored, and there was nothing really happening in the scene we were involved with at the time, that was making us excited.

HOW DID YOU COME UP WITH THAT BAND NAME?

It's a common nervous expression in New York.

FROM THIS MOMENT ON, MUSIC BECOMES MORE IMPORTANT THAN YOUR VISUAL ART?

Neither one is more important than the other. I consider them both passions, and for me they go hand in hand.

HOW DO YOU RELATE YOUR VISUAL ART WITH YOUR MUSIC?

Contextually, both are born out of the same place, but I have the advantage of being able to document what happens in the process of making and performing music. Usually in the editing process I look for images that can evoke the same sort of strong, instant, emotional reaction as music can.

WHO ARE YOUR REFERENCES IN CONTEMPORARY ART, PHOTOGRAPHY, OR OTHER ART FIELDS?

I look at a lot of cinematographers, like Robbie Muller, who has shot movies for Jarmusch and Wim Wenders; and also a mix of the classics, like Robert Frank and Cartier-Bresson, and some contemporaries like Nan Goldin, Ryan McGinley, Terry Richardson, and Wolfgang Tillmans.

DO YOU HAVE ANY ART PROJECTS IN THE FUTURE?

I've been working on a new book for the past year or so that I'm hoping will be more abstract-based and evocative.

199

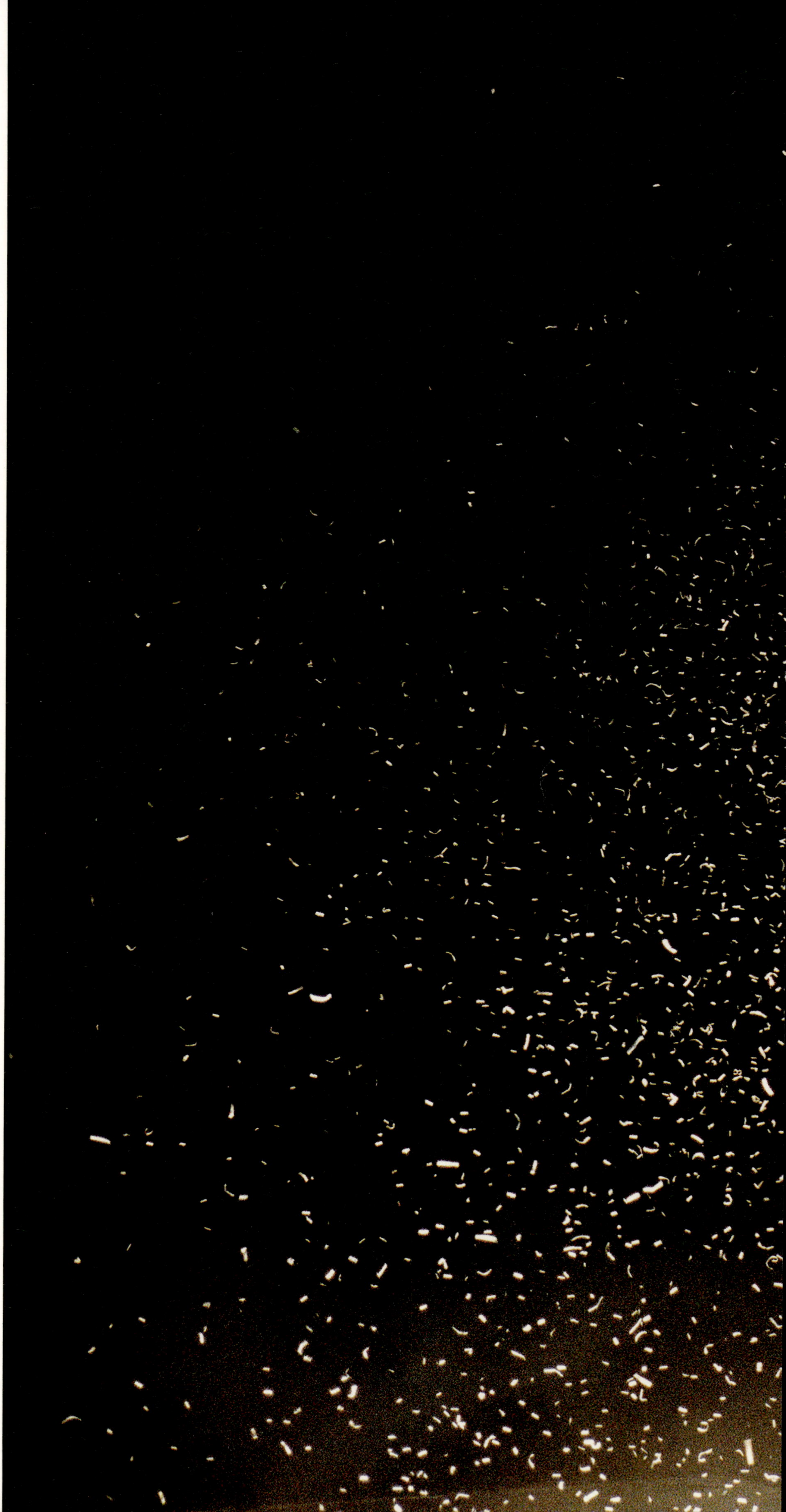

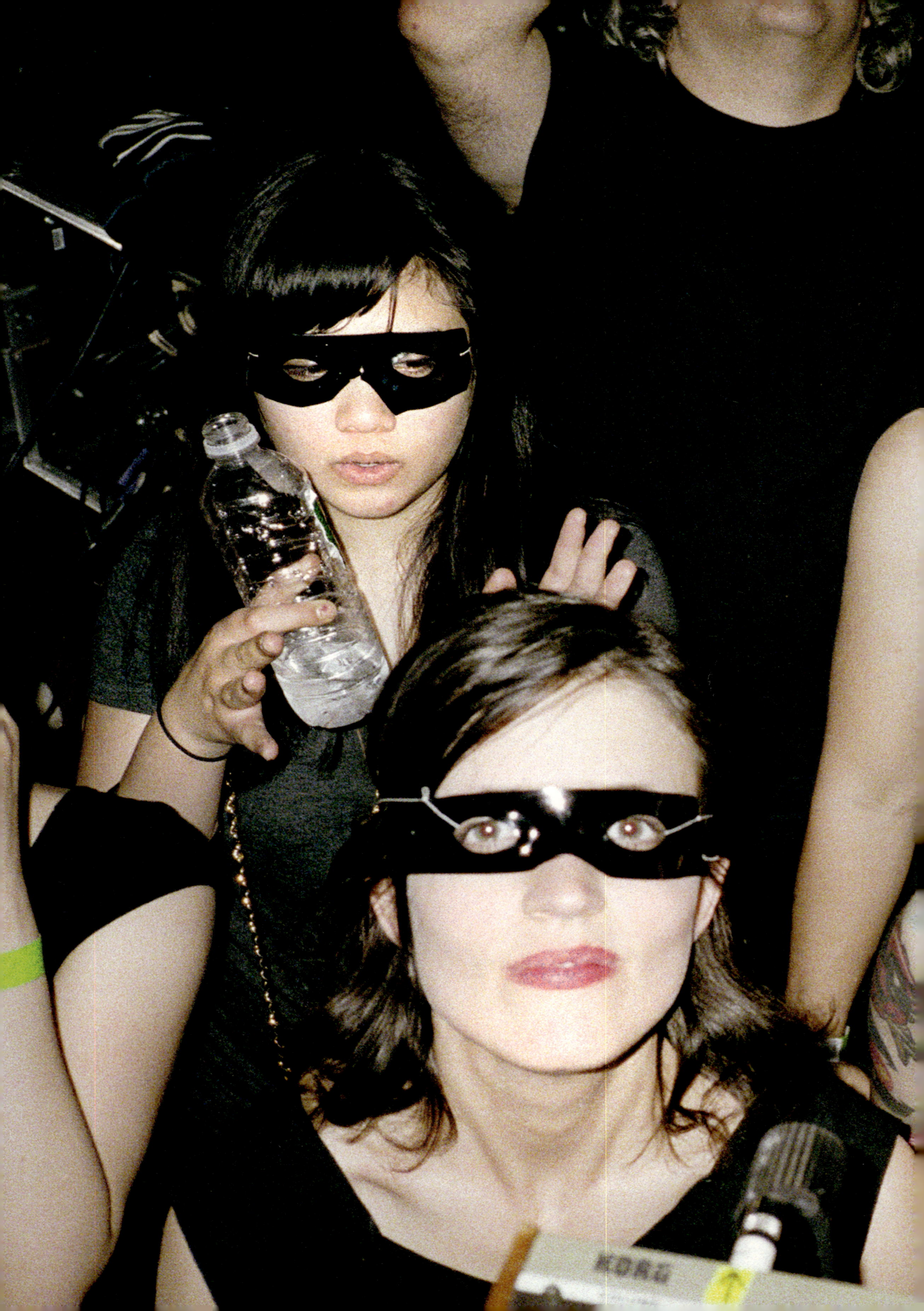

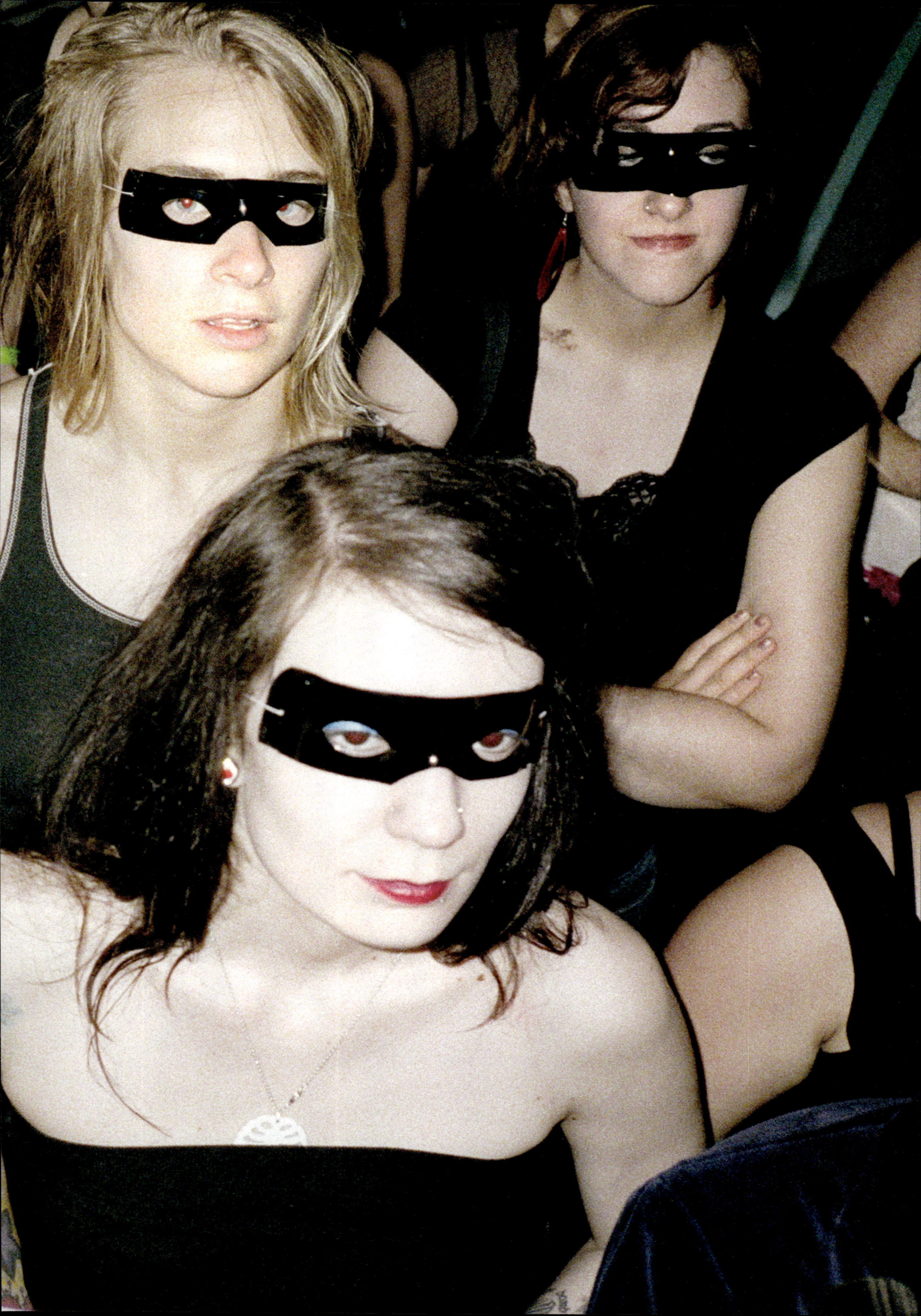

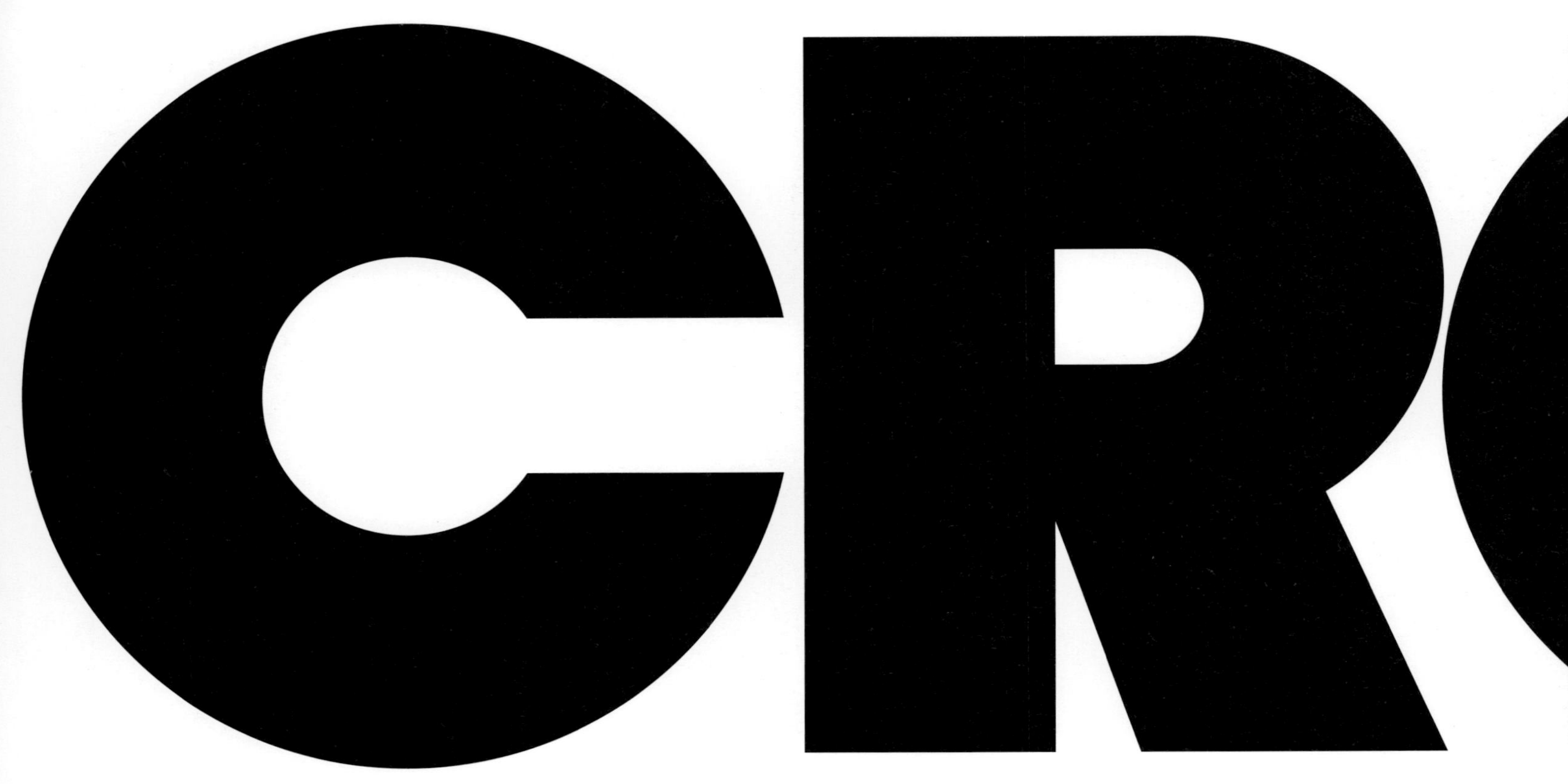

BOZAR

**CHIEF EXECUTIVE OFFICER
ARTISTIC DIRECTOR**
Paul Dujardin

DEPUTY ARTISTIC DIRECTOR
Pablo Fernandez

BOZAR EXPO

DIRECTOR EXHIBITIONS
Johan Vansteenkiste

SENIOR DIRECTOR EXHIBITIONS
Anne Mommens

COLLABORATORS
Axelle Ancion
Ann Flas
Sophie Lauwers
Laurence Leunen
Alberta Sessa
Maïté Smeyers
Lore Vandebeek
Elizabeth Vandeweghe
Frederik Vandewiele
Frank Vanhaecke

ARTISTIC CONSULTANTS
Hélène Bussers
Claude Lorent
Vincent Delvaux

TECHNICAL COORDINATION
Stéphane Vanreppelen
Jo Heyvaert
Rudi Anneessens
Roger Vander Meulen
Joris Erven

BOZAR PLANNING

**DIRECTOR TECHNICS, PRODUCTION,
INVESTMENTS,
SAFETY & SECURITY**
Stéphane Vanreppelen

MANAGER PRODUCTION
Willem De Coster

COLLABORATORS
Claire Bossaert
Julien Tilkens
Frédéric Vandervelde
Kim Vloebergs

BOZARTICKETS

COORDINATOR BOX OFFICE
Fabienne Van Buggenhout

BOZAR FUNDING

HEAD OF FUNDING
Elke Kristoffersen

MEMBERSHIP
Catherine Carniaux
Félicie Martin

CORPORATE DEVELOPMENT
Annik Halmes
Lydia Vandam
Marion Van der Horst

BOZAR STUDIOS

COORDINATOR
Tine Van Goethem

COLLABORATORS
Vera Claessens
Cathy Cruyt
Sarah Deloenen
Laurence Ejzyn

BOZAR COM

**DIRECTOR MARKETING,
COMMUNICATION & SALES**
Leen Gysen
Lian Verhoeven

AUDIENCE DEVELOPMENT EXPO
Séverine Degée
Aude Jacomet
Catherine Mussely
Geraldine Jonville

PRESS
Leen Daems

WEBMASTER
Wendy Schuppen

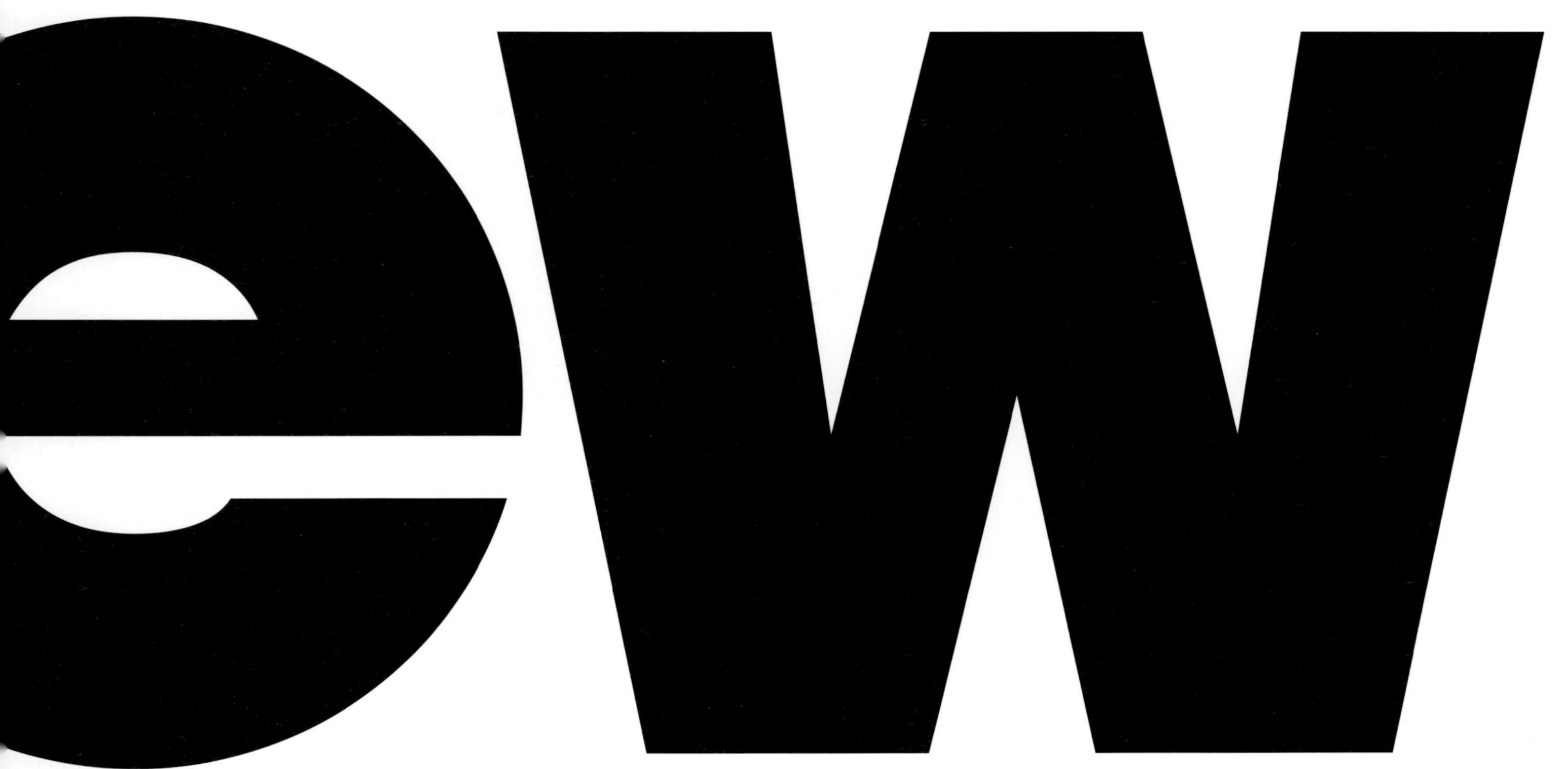

EXHIBITION

GENERAL DIRECTION
Paul Dujardin, Johan Vansteenkiste

CURATOR
Jérôme Sans

SENIOR DIRECTOR EXHIBITIONS
Anne Mommens

COORDINATION EXHIBITION
Laurence Leunen
with the collaboration of
Daria de Beauvais
Nicole Vuilleumier

TECHNICS, PRODUCTION, INVESTMENTS, SAFETY & SECURITY
Stéphane Vanreppelen

TECHNICAL COORDINATION
Roger Vander Meulen
Jo Heyvaert
Joris Erven

ART HANDLING & INSTALLATION
CMVD
Aorta

SURVEYANCE
Dimitri De Beukelaer
Karina Van Driel

PUBLICATION

PUBLISHER
Bom Publishers, www.bompublishers.com

EDITOR
Jérôme Sans

COLLABORATORS
Daria de Beauvais
Audrey Mascina
Nicole Vuilleumier
Murielle Lenglez

TRANSLATIONS
Steve Blackah
Katie Mayne

FINAL EDITING
BaseWord

ILLUSTRATIONS
Moulay Guisse

PRODUCTION
BaseDesign, www.basedesign.com

COORDINATION
BaseDesign, www.basedesign.com
Elizabeth Vandeweghe, Centre for Fine
Arts, Brussels

GRAPHIC DESIGN AND TYPESETTING
BaseDesign, www.basedesign.com

PHOTOGRAVURE
KZG

PRINTING
Ingoprint, Barcelona

DISTRIBUTION
Actar-D, www.actar-d.com

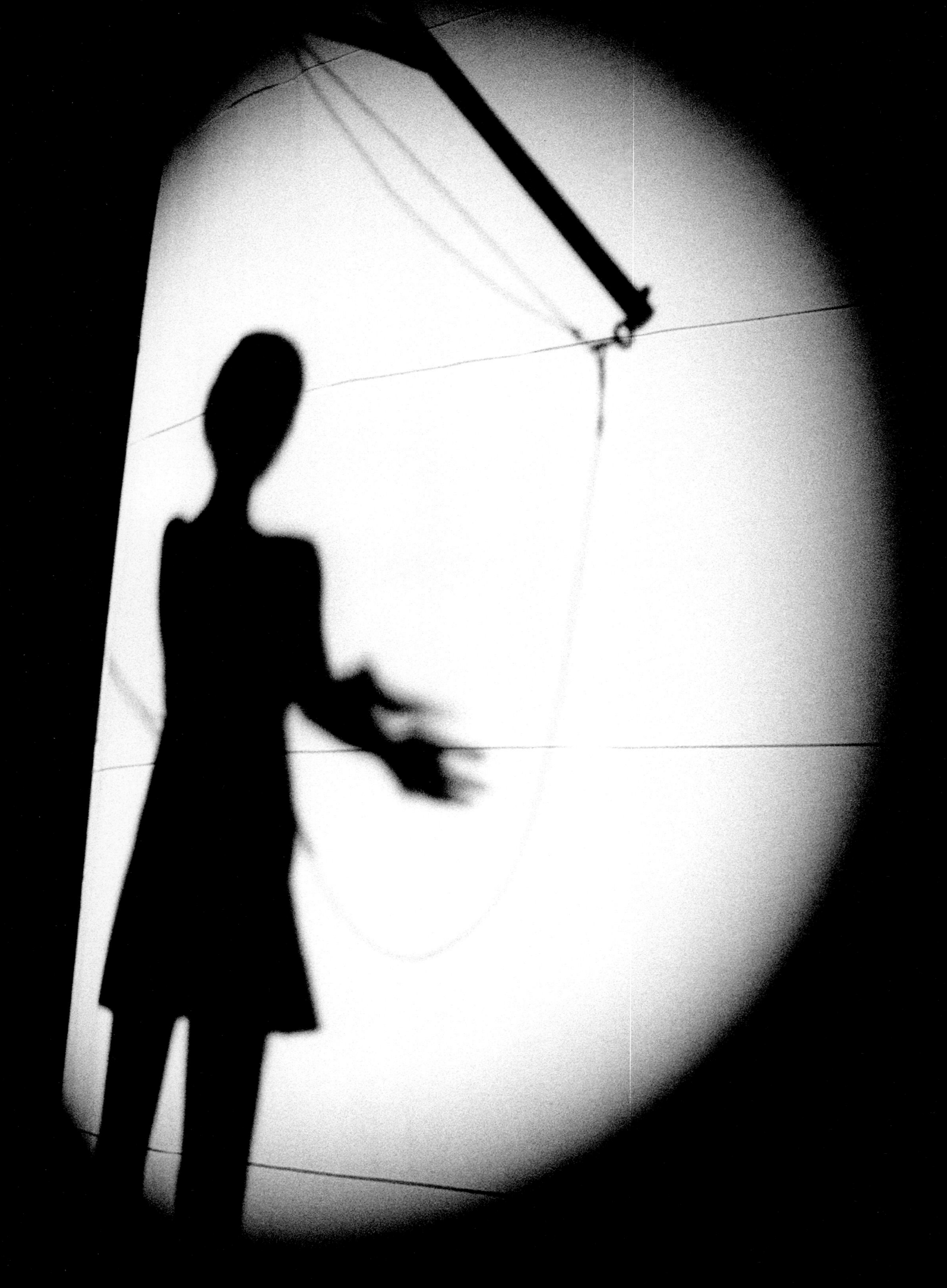

THANKS TO

Emma Banks, Samantha Barroero, Robin Barton, Will Becton, Sibyl Bender, Nele Bigaré, Michael Bracewell, Jennifer Brennan, Rebecca Bronfein, Thierry Brunfaut, Carlos Cardenas, Juliette Cavenaile, Michael Chambati-Woodhead, Hervé Chandès, Linda Hervé, Frédéric Collier, Rebecca Cuglietta, Steve De la Borie, Olivia De la Borie, Miranda de Wijs, Jeffrey Deitch, Homer Flynn, Suzanne Geiss, Aram Goldberg, Suzana Gostimirovic, Michiel Groeneveld, Frédéric Grossi, Simon Guzylack, Laura Haber, Brad Hampton, Britt Helbig, Jon Hendricks, Teddy Hillaert, Karl Hinojosa, Royce Howes, Rainer Hugsam, Adrian Hunter, Joie Iacono, Amaryllis Jacobs, Rodolphe Janssen, Dimitri Jeurissen, Amanda Keeley, Elizabeth Lamere, Emma Lavigne, Aurore Lechien, Simon Lee, Shaun MacDonald, Angela McMahon, Karla Merrifield, Andi Midge, Jean-Luc Moerman, Alison Mosshart, Adi Nachman, Dominic Norman-Taylor, Annie Ohayon, Lauren Panzo, Grazia Quaroni, Nick Robertson, Leslie Rosa, Tom Sarig, Herman Schueremans, Davina Silver, Paul Smith, Phoene Somsavath, Danielle Spencer, Jenny Steadman, Roel Vergauwen, Iain Watt, Katharine Welsh, Clare Wright

BO
ZAR
EX
PO

FORTIS

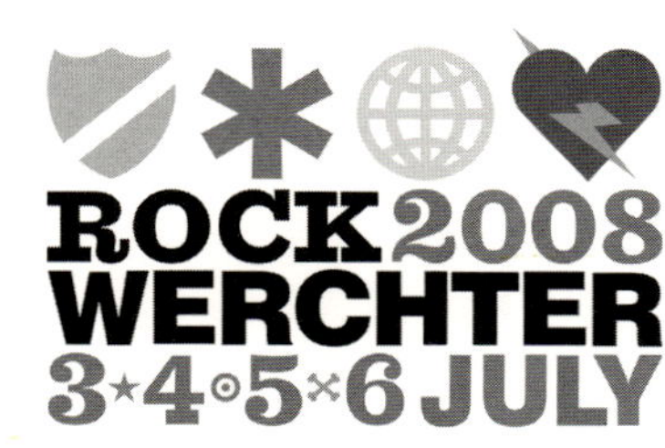

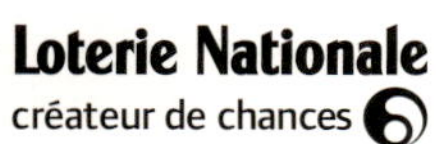

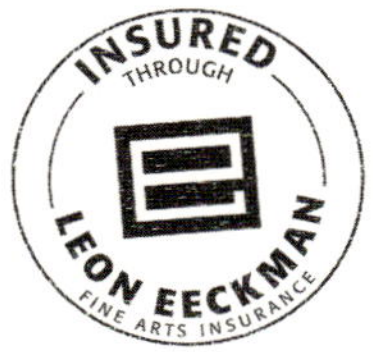

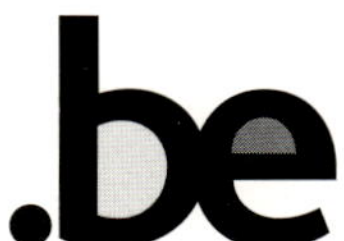

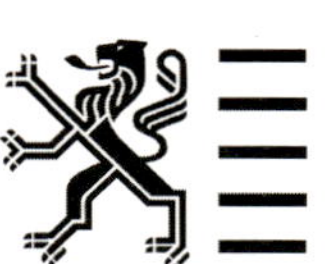

ISBN 978-84-935844-6-7
DL: B-27073-2008